Reader's Digest
Healthy
One-Dish
Cooking

Published by the Reader's Digest Association Limited
London • New York • Sydney • Montreal

Contents

Healthy one-dish cooking is all about creating all-in-one balanced meals with the minimum of fuss. In this section you'll find tips, ideas and simple guidelines for useful reference. There's guidance on how to prepare less familiar fruit and vegetables, how to joint a chicken, how to use herbs, spices and other aromatics to add flavour, as well as recipes

one-dish cooking

for making homemade stocks. If you want to know when to add different ingredients or how to ring the changes in your recipes with easy swaps and variations, it's all here, along with ideas for boosting your meals with simple accompaniments and ways to achieve your five-a-day intake of fruit and vegetables.

How to use this book

Healthy one-dish cooking includes a **wide variety** of recipes; some cooked in just one pot, others involving a little preparation before coming together in one dish. From hearty soups and stews, tempting roasts and oven-bakes, creamy risottos and satisfying pasta dishes to speedy stir-fries, main-meal salads, sandwiches and pizzas, there are delicious dishes for **all tastes and occasions.**

About the recipes

All the recipes in this book are designed to provide a healthy balance of energy and nutrients, while restricting saturated fats, salt and refined sugar. The recommended 'five-a-day' fruit and vegetable intake has also been included and every recipe contains at least one portion (80g) towards your target. In general, the recipes emphasise:

- **fresh ingredients** over packaged or processed foods
- **liberal usage** of fruit and vegetables
- **wholegrains** over refined grains.

The analyses

Every recipe has a **nutritional analysis** per serving based on the following standards unless otherwise stated on individual recipes.

- **Fruit and vegetables** are medium-sized.
- **Eggs** are free-range and medium-sized.
- **Milk** is semi-skimmed (switch to skimmed or soya 'milk' if you prefer).
- **Extra salt** has not been included, but we suggest seasoning to taste where appropriate. Boiled potatoes, pasta and rice are also analysed without salt.
- **Potatoes and pulses** are not included in the vegetable count; they are counted as carbohydrates.
- **No optional ingredients** have been included.
- **Simple, no-cook serving ideas** (ie bread or salad) are sometimes suggested in the recipe introductions, but these are not included in the nutritional analyses. Bread may be recommended to boost the carbohydrate or fibre value of a meal, and a salad may be suggested to provide extra fruit or vegetables.
- **Certain foods**, such as sausages, bacon, cheese, olives, bread and some sauces are relatively high in sodium, so sodium figures for recipes including

The balloons

Both **kcals** and the number of **portions of fruit and vegetables** provided by each recipe are highlighted in balloons, for quick and easy reference.

Recipes that are particularly well suited to being **prepared ahead** are also highlighted by balloons. These are suitable for either cooking completely and then chilling or freezing, or cooking elements of the dish in advance. When reheating a cooked dish that has been chilled or frozen, make sure it is piping hot all the way through.

Look out too, for recommendations such as 'great for kids' or 'quick & easy'.

339 kcals

3 portions fruit & veg

quick & easy

them may be slightly higher than the ideal targets set. But it's fine to enjoy these dishes occasionally.

- **Stocks have been counted** as being salt-free, based on the recipes for homemade stock on pages 28–29. If you use a commercial stock cube or powder, the figures for sodium will be slightly higher than stated in our analysis.
- **Where appropriate**, readily available, reduced-fat dairy products have been used – such as half-fat crème fraîche, Quark and low-fat yoghurt.
- **You can also now buy** an increasing range of reduced-salt products, such as reduced-salt soy sauce, bacon and canned beans. Using them will help to reduce sodium values further.
- **Meat products**, such as minced meat, sausages and bacon, have been analysed based on good quality, lean meat, trimmed of excess fat. Poultry is generally skinned, unless otherwise stated.

The symbols

✱ **Great for freezing** Many dishes, such as soups, stews, curries and casseroles, usually freeze well so why not make double quantity of these recipes and freeze one for a later date? Or simply prepare the dish ahead when you have time to cook, then pop it in the freezer for eating another day.

V **Suitable for vegetarians** For strict vegetarians, check the packaging on cheeses to make sure they are suitable. Most are, or you can buy vegetarian varieties. Some cheeses, made by traditional methods, use animal rennet. Parmesan is one example, but you can choose Italian-style premium hard cheese instead.

Healthy eating

It is neither difficult nor time-consuming to eat healthily. You just need a good variety of foods in the right proportions. So include plenty of complex carbohydrates, a wide variety of fruit and vegetables, a little good quality protein, low-fat milk and dairy foods for essential fatty acids, vitamins and minerals. And restrict foods that are high in saturated fats, salt and sugar.

How much of each food should you eat?

Daily guidelines for nutrients are based on average energy (calorie) requirements, depending on age, sex and activity levels. The following figures are based on the recommended intakes for an average man or woman aged 19–49 years.

Food group	Women	Men
kcalories	2000	2500
carbohydrate	259g	340g
fruit & vegetables	400g	400g
protein	45g	55g
total fat (maximum)	71g	93.5g
of which saturates (maximum)	21.5g	28.5g
fibre	18g	19g
sodium (maximum)	2400mg (or 6g salt)	

Carbohydrates

At least half of your daily calories should come from carbohydrates (and mainly the starchy type) such as bread, pasta, rice, cereals, pulses and potatoes or other starchy vegetables. They provide half the calories of the same weight of fat. Ideally, go for wholegrain, unrefined varieties, which offer three main health benefits:

- they are rich in fibre, which can help to prevent constipation, bowel disease, heart disease and many other health problems
- they contain higher levels of nutrients, such as B group vitamins
- they are a good source of complex carbohydrate, which provides the body with slow-release energy that will keep you satisfied for longer.

Glycaemic index

All carbohydrate foods have a ranking of 1–100, known as the Glycaemic Index (GI). This indicates how quickly the food is broken down by the body and released as glucose into the blood stream.

The lower a food's GI, the more slowly it is digested and the lower the rise in blood glucose. For a steady release of energy that will keep you satisfied for longer and help to avoid fluctuating energy levels and the desire to snack between meals, choose low or medium GI carbohydrate foods. Good choices include pasta, noodles, long grain and basmati rice, oats and pulses.

> All the recipes in this book include a good selection of starchy carbohydrates with an emphasis on the low to medium GI types.

What counts as a portion of fruit & vegetables?

You can get your 'five-a-day' in a variety of ways. Add extra vegetables to a soup, casserole or pizza topping, add seasonal salads on the side and choose more vegetarian-style dishes. The following is a general guide to portions:

- **1 medium glass** of fruit or vegetable juice (Remember that this only counts as one portion per day, no matter how much you drink)
- **1 medium-sized piece of fruit**, such as an apple, orange, nectarine or banana
- **2 small fruits**, such as plums or satsumas
- **A handful of very small fruits** such as cherries, grapes or berries
- **3 dried fruits** such as apricots or figs (This only counts as one portion per day)
- **6 tbsp canned fruit or vegetables**
- **3 tbsp cooked vegetables**
- **a small bowl of salad.**

Fruit & vegetables

Everyone should aim to eat at least five portions (400g) of fruit and vegetables each day. Fresh and frozen are ideal, but canned and dried are good too. Vegetables and fruit are packed with vitamins, minerals and other antioxidant nutrients that help to protect us against illness, and they offer vital dietary fibre, needed for a healthy digestion. Try to include a wide variety in your diet, as different types contain different combinations of nutrients, including vitamins and antioxidants.

- **orange, yellow and red fruit and vegetables** such as carrots, peppers, sweet potatoes, mangoes and strawberries are rich in vitamin C and beta-carotene, a powerful antioxidant that is thought to help fight against cancer, heart disease, cataracts, arthritis and general ageing.
- **tomatoes** are an excellent source of vitamin C and also lycopene, another powerful antioxidant.
- **brassicas,** including cabbage, cauliflower, broccoli, Brussels sprouts, kale and swede contain antioxidants and are a good source of vitamin C, folates and minerals.
- **onions, garlic** and others of the onion family contain allicin, a phytochemical believed to help to lower blood cholesterol and stimulate the immune system.

Protein

Meat, poultry, fish, dairy, eggs and vegetarian alternatives, such as tofu, pulses and nuts, contain protein which is essential for growth and cell repair, as well as providing minerals such as iron, zinc and magnesium and B vitamins (B_{12} is found only in sources of animal protein.) The body doesn't require a huge amount of protein, and for optimum health, women should eat about 45g and men about 55g a day.

Protein foods can be high in fat so choose lean meat and meat products, trim visible fat and skin poultry. Eat fish at least once a week: white fish is low in fat and oily fish (such as herring, mackerel, sardines, trout and salmon) are rich in omega-3 fatty acids, which are believed to help to reduce the risk of heart disease. Pulses are naturally low in fat, as is tofu, made from soya beans. Nuts, although high in fat and calories, contain mainly the 'healthier' unsaturated type.

> **Ways of restricting fat are always applied to the protein foods in this book.**

Dairy

Milk, yoghurt, cheese and fromage frais are all excellent sources of calcium, needed for strong bones and teeth, blood clotting, muscle contraction and a healthy nervous system. Dairy foods are particularly important for young children, for adolescent girls – to prevent osteoporosis later in life – and for women in general. As dairy products can be high in saturated fat, try to go for low or lower-fat varieties. (Young children under the age of 2 years need full-fat versions to provide sufficient energy.)

- Aim to include 2–3 portions of dairy foods per day.
- A portion could include: a glass of milk; a small pot of yoghurt; 125g cottage cheese, or a matchbox-sized piece of Cheddar cheese (about 40g). (For a dairy-free diet, include dark green, leafy vegetables and canned fish, eaten with the bones.)

Fats

A small amount of the right kind of fat is essential for a healthy diet, providing valuable fat-soluble vitamins and essential fatty acids. Some fat also makes food taste good. However, no more than one-third of your daily calorie intake should come from fat. Fats can be divided into three main groups:

- **Saturated fats** (found mainly in meat and dairy foods). A high intake of these fats increases the level of cholesterol in the blood, which raises the risk of heart disease and some cancers. Current guidelines recommend cutting down on these fats as much as possible.
- **Monounsaturated fats** (found mainly in olive oil, groundnut oil, rapeseed oils and avocados).
- **Polyunsaturated fats** (found mainly in most vegetable oils). Certain polyunsaturated fatty acids (known as essential fatty acids) must be supplied by food. There are two groups, omega-3 fatty acids from oily fish, nuts and vegetable oils, such as soya and rapeseed, and omega-6 fatty acids from vegetable oils, such as olive and sunflower. Both groups are essential for good health.

> **All the recipes contain less than 30g total fat and a maximum of 8g saturated fat per serving.**

Salt

A small amount of salt is needed for healthy body function but most people eat far too much, which can lead to high blood pressure and increased risk of heart disease, stroke and kidney failure. The World Health Organisation currently recommends no more than 6g of salt (or 2400mg sodium) a day, although most adults need only about 4g (or 1600mg sodium) a day. Eating processed, fast and ready-made foods, and adding salt to food at the table lead to over-consumption. There is also 'hidden' salt in bread, cheese, cured meats and smoked fish. Other high-salt foods include sauces, condiments and canned foods, so always check the label and look for reduced-sodium alternatives.

> Recipes in this book contain no more than 800mg sodium per serving, apart from a handful, such as pizzas, and bacon and sausage-based recipes where the recipe we provide is far less salty than would normally be the case.

Sugar

Added sugars contain no vitamins, minerals or fibre and simply provide the body with empty calories. Sugar also has the highest GI ranking of 100, so it can cause rapid fluctuations in blood glucose and energy levels, if eaten regularly or in excess. However, a small amount of sugar adds to the enjoyment of food and does no harm, so you can include occasional sweet foods as part of a well-balanced diet. Remember that fruit contains fructose (a natural fruit sugar) and this can frequently be used for sweetening dishes rather than using added sugar.

Drinking enough

Drinking plenty of liquid is essential for healthy body function, and you should aim to drink at least 2 litres of non-alcoholic liquid each day. Water is the best choice, but fruit or herbal teas, fruit juices and semi-skimmed milk are good alternatives.

A moderate amount of tea and coffee can count towards your fluid intake, but they are natural diuretics that cause the body to lose fluids, taking useful nutrients with them, so don't drink too much of them.

Consuming moderate amounts of alcohol has been linked to a reduced risk of heart disease and stroke. If you do drink, enjoy small amounts of alcohol with food, and make sure you have a few alcohol-free days each week.

Preparation techniques

Don't be put off using unfamiliar vegetables when they're available because you don't know how to use them. Preparation is usually very simple; it's just a case of following the right routine.

Asparagus Young spears need no preparation but if the stems seem coarse, snap off or trim away the woody ends. (The ends are great for adding flavour to homemade stock so don't throw them away.) Asparagus is best steamed, microwaved with a splash of water or char-grilled. For stir-frying, slice the stems and cook them for a little longer than the delicate tips.

Aubergine It was once recommended to degorge aubergines (sprinkling them liberally with salt and leaving them to stand for about 20 minutes) to draw out the bitter indigestible juices. New varieties are rarely bitter although salting is still a good idea as it helps the fibrous flesh to absorb less oil when cooked. Rinse off the salt and pat the aubergine dry before cooking. Slices can be lightly brushed with oil and grilled rather than fried in oil.

Avocado A ripe avocado should yield slightly when gently pressed in the palm of your hand. If bought hard, place in a paper bag and ripen at room temperature. Store ripe avocados in the fridge for up to two days. To halve, cut lengthways through to the stone, using a stainless steel knife, then twist the two halves in opposite directions to separate them. Remove the stone, then peel. To prevent avocados from turning brown after cutting, sprinkle with a little lemon juice.

Fennel Reserve the feathery fronds for garnishing, then thinly slice the bulb as you would for celery. It can be eaten raw in salads or cooked – but should be put in acidulated water once sliced to prevent cut surfaces turning brown.

Okra Trim away the stalks but don't tear the pods and expose the seeds, which can give a slightly gloopy texture to dishes. However, if this is what you want – for a gumbo, for example, slice thickly or thinly according to the recipe.

Pak choi (or bok choy) Roughly chop the leaves into wide strips and the stalks into slightly smaller pieces or simply separate the stems and leave whole. The smaller the plant, the more tender the vegetable will be. Ideal for stir-fries or steaming and should be quickly cooked.

Grilling peppers Grill halved or quartered peppers skin-side up, for about 10 minutes under a hot grill, until the skins are charred. Put the hot peppers in a plastic bag and leave for about 10 minutes until cool enough to handle. The steam created in the bag will help to loosen the skins so that they slip off easily. The peppers will also have a wonderfully sweet and slightly smoky flavour.

Broad beans

Broad beans are best when young and should be eaten as fresh as possible. Remove beans from the pods, then boil or steam for 5–10 minutes, depending on size and age. Very young broad beans (up to 7cm long), can be cooked whole in their pods for 5–7 minutes. Mature (late-season) beans are best skinned after cooking.

Butternut squash

Butternut squash Peel off the tough skin using a vegetable peeler, then cut in half lengthways and scoop out the seeds and fibrous pulp using a teaspoon. Cut the flesh into chunks or as required for the recipe. It's good boiled, then mashed, roasted or cooked in soups or casseroles. The squash can also be pricked with a fork and baked whole. These cooking methods apply to all varieties of summer and winter squash, including pumpkin.

Celeriac

Celeriac Remove the tough nobbly skin using a vegetable peeler, then slice or dice using a large sharp knife. Immerse the cut flesh in a bowl of acidulated water (water with lemon juice or vinegar added) to prevent discolouration. It can be added to soups and stews or boiled for 15–20 minutes until tender, then mashed or briefly blanched for salads.

Corn cobs

Corn cobs Trim the ends with a sharp knife, then remove the husks (leaves) and silks (fine threads). Cook whole cobs in boiling water for 8–10 minutes, without salt as this may toughen the kernels. They can then be grilled, roasted or barbecued, or just eaten as they are. Baby corn can be used whole or sliced lengthways and is ideal for cooking in stir-fries and other Oriental dishes. Take care not to overcook them as they can become tough and lose their sweetness.

Spinach

Spinach (and kale) These can have tough stalks that should be removed before cooking. Always wash spinach thoroughly, then cook very briefly in just the water clinging to the leaves. A large quantity wilts down to a small heap, so always prepare plenty. Baby spinach leaves need no preparation and are ideal for salads.

Sweet potato

Sweet potato There are two main types – red-skinned with white flesh and brown-skinned with orange flesh. Peel and cook in chunks, or boil or bake in their jackets, peeling off the skins after cooking. Deliciously sweet and wonderfully versatile, use them as you would normal potatoes for soups and casseroles. You can roast or mash them or boil then char-grill.

Skinning tomatoes

Skinning tomatoes Cut a cross in the base of each tomato and place in a bowl. Pour boiling water over them and leave them to stand for about 30 seconds. Drain, refresh in cold water to cool quickly, then drain again and peel. The skins will slip off easily. (This blanching technique is also useful for peeling shallots quickly and easily. Allow to stand in the boiling water for 10 minutes.)

Preparing a chicken

It is much cheaper to buy a whole chicken and cut it up than to buy large numbers of chicken pieces. Here are six easy steps to jointing a chicken.

1 Place the chicken, breast side up, on a board. Gently pull one leg away from the body and use a heavy cook's knife to cut through the skin between the body and leg. Bend the leg outwards until the ball pops out of the socket joint, then carefully cut through the flesh under the joint. Repeat with the second leg.

2 To separate the drumstick from the thigh, stand one leg on the board so that it forms a natural V-shape. Firmly hold the end of the drumstick in one hand and cut through the joint where the two bones meet at the centre of the V. Repeat with the second leg.

3 To separate the wings from the body of the chicken, make a deep cut into the breast meat near to the inside of each wing. As you do this, angle the knife diagonally across the neck end of the bird so that the uncut breast forms a diamond shape. Cut down into the meat far enough to expose the bones.

4 To free the wings from the carcass, use a pair of poultry shears or strong kitchen scissors to cut between the ball and socket joints and through the remaining flesh and bone. Make sure there are no sharp splinters of bone embedded in the cut portions.

5 To remove the breast meat, lay the carcass on its side then use shears or scissors to cut through the thin rib cage on either side of the backbone.

6 Divide the breast into two, cutting crossways or lengthways through the bird's flesh using a knife and then through the bones and cartilage with the shears or scissors. Use the carcass to make stock (see page 28).

Prep terms

Have you ever wondered what exactly is meant by 'dice' or 'cube'? Here are some chopped vegetables showing relative sizes.

Dice cut into small squares.

Cube cut into bite-sized chunks.

Julienne cut into fine sticks, about 4cm long.

Ribbons peel lengthways into wide strips using a vegetable peeler.

Zest (pare) thinly remove outer rind and not the bitter white pith, from citrus fruits using a vegetable peeler, or use a grater or citrus zester tool to take off fine shreds.

Healthy flavourings

There is a wealth of wonderful and exciting flavours to be found in herbs, spices and other seasonings. Getting to know them better and using them freely will add a whole new flavour dimension to your cooking.

Herbs

Fresh herbs are now widely available in greengrocers, supermarkets and Continental and Asian food stores. It's also easy to grow your own, in a herb bed in the garden, in pots on a patio or in a window box. They are great for imparting flavour to all kinds of dishes. Herbs can be divided into two groups:

Robust herbs (such as rosemary, thyme, sage, oregano and bay leaves) are particularly good used in stews and casseroles, as well as marinades and stuffings. They are usually added at the start, because long, slow cooking mellows their powerful taste, and should be used sparingly. They're best removed before serving as woody twigs, stalks and leaves are not palatable.

Tender herbs (such as basil, mint, tarragon, coriander, chives, dill and parsley) have a much fresher flavour and are usually added to dishes at the last minute. Prolonged cooking will generally spoil their delicate flavour and appearance. Use liberally in soups, salads and stir-fries, and for pretty garnishes.

Chopping herbs

Herbs can be chopped with a sharp knife on a chopping board, but it's generally quicker to put them in a mug or jug then snip down into them with a pair of kitchen scissors. Fresh basil should be simply torn into rough pieces or can be rolled up tightly, then shredded with a sharp knife. For fresh chives, simply snip into short lengths using scissors.

Herb	Especially complements	Ideal for
Basil	tomatoes, green vegetables, soft cheeses, lamb, eggs	salads, soups, pasta sauces, Mediterranean dishes
Bay	meat, poultry, fish and vegetables	soups, stews, casseroles, pot-roasts
Chives	eggs, cheese, potatoes, fish, chicken	soups, salads, omelettes
Coriander	chicken, fish & seafood, rice, tomatoes	Thai, Indonesian, Indian, Chinese and Middle Eastern stir-fries and curries
Dill	chicken, fish, eggs, cheese, potatoes	soups, salads, sauces, marinades
Mint	lamb, potatoes, peas, tomatoes	salads and vegetable dishes
Oregano	pork, poultry, game, fish, vegetables (especially tomatoes)	pasta sauces, stuffings and Italian dishes
Parsley	lamb, chicken, ham, fish, vegetables, eggs and cheese	soups, salads, sauces, casseroles
Rosemary	lamb, pork, game	stuffings, casseroles and for spiking joints
Sage	pork, duck, offal, tomatoes	stuffings and casseroles
Tarragon	eggs, fish, chicken and vegetables	salads and sauces
Thyme	fish, chicken, beef, game	stuffings, casseroles, marinades, pasta sauces

Spices

A good selection of spices will add warm, fragrant scents and exotic flavours to a wide range of dishes. They are best bought in small quantities and whole if possible, to be ground when required, to retain their freshness. A pestle and mortar or an electric coffee grinder is ideal for grinding your own. Spices should be stored in airtight containers, in a cupboard, away from direct heat and sunlight and used within 6 months.

For general seasoning Pepper complements all savoury dishes. It has a warm, pungent taste of its own and brings out the flavour of other ingredients. Use black peppercorns, freshly ground in a pepper mill, or white pepper when a more delicate flavour is required.

Hot spices For a spicy kick, use crushed dried chillies or chilli powder (sold in both mild and hot varieties). Pure chilli powder (and cayenne pepper) is extremely hot, so just a pinch, or ½ tsp, is plenty. Chilli seasoning blends, which usually include chillies, cumin, oregano and garlic, can be used much more freely – up to 1–2 tbsp to flavour a typical dish. Paprika is far milder with a sweet, earthy aroma and it's ideal for stews and sauces.

Warm spices include coriander, cumin, star anise and turmeric and impart an aromatic flavour to dishes. They are usually included early in the cooking process to allow their flavours to mellow. Turmeric is ideal for many Indian and vegetarian dishes, but choose saffron for a subtle and distinctive honey-like colour and flavour in risottos, paellas and seafood dishes. It can be bought either as powder or strands, and is best infused in a little boiling water or stock before adding it to a dish.

Sweet spices Cinnamon, ginger, cardamom and nutmeg, and other sweet spices, add depth of flavour and fragrant, spicy undertones to stews and simmered dishes. A cinnamon stick (or piece of bark) is better than ground for savoury dishes. Nutmeg is always best freshly grated. Cardamom pods can be added whole for a subtle flavour (the pod is not edible) or crushed before using and just the seeds added to the dish.

Spice	Especially complements	Ideal for
Cardamom	fish, meat, rice, vegetables and yoghurt	curries, stews and pilafs
Chilli	meat, poultry, fish, tomatoes and peppers	Indian, Mexican and South East Asian dishes
Cinnamon	meat, rice and spinach	curries, stews and spicy casseroles
Coriander	meat and vegetables	spicy meat and vegetable stews
Cumin	meat, poultry, rice, pulses and vegetables	curries, Mexican and Moroccan dishes and tomato sauces
Fennel seed	fish, pork, potatoes and rice	oily fish dishes, salads and risottos
Ginger	fish, poultry and root vegetables	curries, stir-fries and marinades
Nutmeg	beef, milk, cheese and vegetables, especially spinach, carrots and mushrooms	Italian pasta dishes and sauces
Paprika	pork, chicken and vegetables, especially potatoes	soups and stews
Saffron	chicken, fish and seafood, rice and potatoes	paella, risotto, couscous and fish soup
Star anise and five-spice powder	fish, chicken or meat, especially pork	Chinese braised dishes and stir-fries
Turmeric	fish, vegetables, rice and eggs	curries, pilafs and vegetarian dishes

Fresh aromatics

The health benefits of garlic are now widely recognised and it has become a favourite and essential flavouring for everyday cooking. However, how familiar are you with other aromatics, such as fresh ginger, lemongrass and chillies? These too are readily available from supermarkets and greengrocers and can add an exotic and distinctive note to a variety of dishes.

Lemongrass (above) is widely used in Southeast Asian dishes to provide a heady, citrus accent. To prepare, remove any wrinkled outer leaves and discard the root end of the stalk, then finely chop the bulbous base and about the first 10cm of the stem.

Fresh root ginger (left) has a hot, yet refreshing flavour and is essential for Chinese stir-fries and Thai-style dishes. To prepare, pare off the brown knobbly skin using a vegetable peeler, then grate or finely chop. The unpeeled root will keep well for about one month, wrapped in cling film in the fridge.

Fresh chillies There are many different varieties of chilli, ranging from the fiery habanero and bird eye chillies to the milder fresno (be advised by the heat guide on the packs). Care must be taken when preparing chillies because the oily compound, capsaicin, found in the ribs near the seeds, can irritate the eyes and skin. Cut the chilli in half lengthways, scrape out the seeds and ribs using a sharp-pointed knife, then slice widthways. For the full chilli heat, leave in the seeds, or for a milder flavour, add the whole uncut chilli, then remove before serving. Always wash your hands well after handling chillies, or prepare them wearing rubber gloves.

More flavourings

- **Citrus juices and zests** can pep up spicy soups, fish, stews and stir-fries. Add just before serving to get the full, fresh flavour impact.
- **Flavoured oils and vinegars** can be used in cooking in place of regular ones or drizzled over cooked dishes, salads and vegetable accompaniments.
- **Red or white wine**, used to replace part of the stock or cooking liquid, will boost the flavour of stews, casseroles, sauces and stocks. Wine is usually added at the start of the cooking process and may be reduced to concentrate the flavour.
- **Condiments** such as mustard, pesto, anchovy essence, tomato purée and Worcestershire sauce are all great flavour enhancers, but they are also generally high in salt, so taste before adding extra salt.

The question of salt

Dishes that are well flavoured with herbs and spices are likely to not need any, or at least very little salt. Generally, it's best to season a dish towards the end of cooking when all the other flavouring ingredients have had a chance to impart their flavour and to add salt only if necessary. The rule is simply to taste and to trust your own judgement.

Marinades & rubs

These are a great way to add flavour to meat, fish, poultry, tofu and vegetable dishes before cooking.

- **A marinade** is a seasoned liquid used to flavour and tenderise as well as add moisture, especially to foods that are to be grilled or barbecued. It can also be used for basting while cooking. Marinades generally include an acidic ingredient (such as lemon juice, vinegar, wine or yoghurt) to tenderise, oil to add succulence and herbs or spices to add flavour. Fish needs only brief marinating (about 30 minutes), whereas red meat is best marinated for several hours or overnight.
- **Rubs** are the dry equivalent of marinades and are a means of adding flavour by rubbing a mixture of dried herbs and spices into raw food before cooking. They can add instant flavour or be applied ahead for a longer, more intense flavouring time. On cooking, the flavour is absorbed into the food, leaving a coating of the rub mixture on the outside.

Getting the timing right

All ingredients have **different cooking times,** so you need to add them at the right stage to make sure they are all **cooked to perfection** when the dish is complete. This basic guide groups ingredients according to whether they need **longer, medium or quick cooking.** Size also affects cooking time, so small pieces will cook much faster than larger pieces of the same ingredient.

Longer-cooking

- **Joints of meat, braising and stewing cuts** (casserole meat) and **whole birds.** It is important that pork and poultry are cooked right through.

- **Dried pulses** require overnight soaking, then simmering in liquid for about 1 hour, until tender. All dried pulses (with the exception of chickpeas and lentils) should be boiled for 10–15 minutes at the start of cooking to destroy possible toxins.

- **Brown rice or wholegrain rice** take longer to cook than white rice, so allow about 30 minutes in boiling liquid.

- **Onions, garlic and fresh root ginger** are pungent flavourings and are usually added at the beginning of cooking to help to flavour the whole dish.

- **Root vegetables,** including potatoes, carrots, turnips, parsnips, swede, celeriac and fresh beetroot need to be boiled, baked, roasted or slowly cooked in a soup or casserole with liquid.

- **Winter squash,** such as pumpkins and butternut squash, have cooking properties similar to root vegetables and need to be boiled, baked or roasted until tender.

- **Tomatoes,** when used as the base of a sauce, usually require long, slow cooking to bring out their flavour.

- **Dried fruits** are usually added to stews and casseroles at the beginning of cooking to allow them to plump up and sweetly flavour the dish.

- **Robust herbs** (such as sage, rosemary, bay, oregano and thyme) and warm and hot spices, including chilli, to provide a subtle, balanced flavour.

Medium-cooking

- **Minced meats, chicken portions, chops** and **sausages.**
- **Whole fish, fish steaks** and **fillets.**
- **Rice** (white, basmati, risotto, wild), **pasta** and **dried lentils.** Times vary depending on the type of rice and size and shape of pasta so follow pack instructions. Cook in boiling or simmering water or stock.
- **Crisp vegetables** such as fennel and celery, and brassicas such as broccoli, cauliflower, Brussels sprouts, cabbage and kale. Cook until just tender and take care not to overcook. (A flat skewer is useful for testing.)
- **Peppers, aubergine** and **courgettes** are especially delicious stuffed, grilled or char-grilled and roasted. (They can also be quickly cooked by stir-frying.)
- **Corn on the cob** and **baby corn cobs** need to be cooked in boiling water, then grilled, barbecued or roasted. Baby (dwarf) corn cobs need a shorter boiling or steaming time and can also be sliced and stir-fried.
- **Beans,** such as broad beans, runner beans and green beans, need to be cooked until just tender.
- **Leeks** are more subtle in flavour than onions and simply need to be cooked until they are soft, but still retain some shape and colour.
- **Dried mushrooms** should be soaked first, then cooked for 15–20 minutes. They give a great flavour boost.

Quick-cooking

- **Steaks, escalopes, pork tenderloin** (fillet), **lean cubes of meat or poultry** for kebabs and **thin slices/strips** for stir-fries.
- **Cured meats,** such as bacon, ham and chorizo.
- **Shellfish,** such as cooked prawns, just require a quick heat through or they'll toughen.
- **Tofu** (soya bean curd).
- **Chinese noodles, couscous, bulghur wheat** and **instant polenta.**
- **Canned pulses** should simply be drained and rinsed, before adding to the pot. Heat through for a hot dish.
- **Tender fresh pods, shoots and sprouts,** such as peas, mange-tout, asparagus and bean sprouts.
- **Fresh mushrooms** are best cooked briefly to retain appearance.
- **Tender leafy vegetables,** such as spinach and pak choi, should be only very briefly cooked until just wilted.
- **Frozen and canned vegetables.**
- **Salad vegetables,** such as spring onions, avocado, cucumber, celery and watercress, do not require cooking but may be briefly cooked for hot dishes such as soups.
- **Fresh fruits** generally don't need cooking but are added for flavour, colour and appeal. Warm through gently to retain their shape.
- **Tender, delicate herbs** should be tossed in at the last minute to retain their fresh, aromatic flavour.
- **Nuts** should be added at the end to retain their crunch.

Creating your own dishes

One-dish meals are highly adaptable. You can vary ingredients and flavourings according to personal taste and dietary requirements, what you have available and what's in season.

Good swaps

Most ingredients can be replaced by other foods that fall into the same 'family group', or those with a similar taste, texture and cooking properties. For example, different white fish, such as cod and haddock, or sweet root vegetables, such as carrots and parsnips, are mostly interchangeable. You can also swap lean meat for poultry or even tofu to make a vegetarian dish. Here are some simple suggestions.

- **leeks** in place of **onions** or **shallots**
- **Swiss chard** or **spring greens** in place of **spinach**
- **Chinese leaves** in place of **pak choi**
- **peas** in place of **broad beans**
- **fennel** in place of **celery**
- **butternut squash** in place of **pumpkin**
- **mange-tout** in place of **asparagus**
- **pears** in place of **apples**
- **peaches** in place of **mango** or **papaya**
- **dried apricots** in place of **prunes** or **figs**
- **swordfish** in place of **fresh tuna**
- **haddock** in place of **cod** or **halibut**
- **trout** in place of **salmon**
- **chicken** or **turkey** in place of **pork**
- **tangy goat's cheese** in place of **blue cheese**
- **couscous** in place of **bulghur wheat**
- **almonds** in place of **pine nuts**

Making more

You can also boost dishes with extra ingredients, either to make a dish more substantial or to feed more people. Most recipes can be easily doubled, or you can just stretch a dish with an extra handful of vegetables, beans, pasta or rice, or an extra portion of meat or fish.

Stock up

Keep your storecupboard and freezer well stocked with staple foods and you'll always able to rustle up delicious meals. The following list is not meant to be exhaustive, but includes the essentials you need for healthy cooking.

- Condiments: soy sauce, redcurrant jelly, honey, cranberry sauce, pesto, mustard, tomato purée, mayonnaise and horseradish sauce
- Canned vegetables: whole plum and chopped tomatoes, sweetcorn
- Canned fish: tuna, sardines, salmon
- Pasta: various varieties (particularly wholewheat)
- Pulses: canned (or dried) beans, lentils and chickpeas
- Rice (different types), couscous, polenta and bulghur wheat
- Rolled oats
- Dried fruits, nuts and seeds
- Dried herbs, spices, sea salt and black pepper mills
- Oils and vinegars
- Flour, cornflour and sugar

Healthy options

Here is how to vary ingredients according to when they are available or in season. Peppers stuffed with beef and tomatoes (see page 287) could be made with any number of different ingredients. It makes a great main meal for two, or can be served as a light meal for four with crusty bread and a simple side salad. The recipe can easily be doubled.

Use large green or red peppers instead of yellow ones or replace the peppers with large courgettes, thick rings of marrow or large tomatoes.

Any kind of minced meat could be used, such as lamb, pork, turkey or Quorn.

Replace the breadcrumbs with some cooked rice, bulghur wheat or couscous to bind the stuffing together and add carbohydrate.

Fennel is braised in the dish with the peppers, but sliced celery would work equally well.

Canned tomatoes in the stuffing mixture could be replaced with three large skinned and chopped fresh tomatoes.

Omit the cheesy topping and sprinkle the stuffing mixture with a few roughly chopped nuts instead.

Good alternative cheeses to Cheddar are any well-flavoured hard or semi-hard cheese, such as Lancashire, Gruyère or Parmesan.

Boosting your meals

The recipes in this book have been designed to give a healthy balance of nutrients and to be complete lunch or dinner dishes, served with good bread or a simple salad. But allowing for variation in appetites and the fact that some recipes are naturally lighter than others, you may sometimes want to boost the recipe to provide a more substantial meal or to feed unexpected guests.

Boosting carbs

Adding lots of filling starchy carbohydrates is one of the best ways to stretch a meal for lots of hungry people.

Bulghur wheat (cracked wheat) is a delicious alternative to rice, with a wholesome, nutty flavour. Pour boiling water over it, leave to soak for about 20 minutes, then drain. Enjoy it plain, or toss with a little olive oil and lemon juice to moisten and add plenty of chopped fresh herbs. It is especially good with grilled meats and fish, roasts and casseroles.

Couscous goes particularly well with saucy stews and casseroles (called tagines in North Africa, where couscous is a staple).

Pasta and noodles come in all kinds of shapes, sizes and flavours and are a perfect low-fat accompaniment. For those following a wheat-free diet, choose rice and buckwheat (soba) noodles and corn varieties.

Rice is great with stews, casseroles, curries and stir-fries. Wholegrain varieties, including brown, red (Camargue) and wild rice are especially healthy.

Beans and lentils are a tasty, high-fibre carbohydrate option to serve with roasts or braised and grilled dishes. Mashed or crushed, they make a healthy alternative to creamed potatoes.

Bread

Bread is the simplest accompaniment, as it requires no cooking and there are so many different varieties. Choose from:

- wholemeal, multigrain (or seeded) or rye bread
- French baguettes, ciabatta or focaccia (plain or flavoured)
- crumpets, bagels, English muffins, pitta, breadsticks (grissini), potato scones or oat cakes
- naan, chappatis or parathas
- Irish soda bead
- Greek daktyla (sesame seed), oatmeal or walnut bread.

Bread is best freshly baked or served warm. Part-baked breads, that you can keep in the freezer and bake just before serving, are ideal.

Potatoes

Try these quick ideas:

- toss steamed or boiled baby new potatoes with a little olive oil, lemon zest and chopped fresh mint.
- make a warm new potato salad by tossing sliced, boiled new potatoes with a little vinaigrette dressing, snipped chives and /or chopped fresh parsley.
- for healthy oven chips, cut scrubbed potatoes (with the skin) into thick wedges, then brush lightly with olive oil on a baking sheet and bake for 30–40 minutes in a hot oven. If liked, sprinkle with dried herbs or fennel seeds, or for a spicy flavour, sprinkle with paprika or Cajun seasoning.
- add a little pesto, mustard or horseradish sauce to mash.
- for a mixed root mash, boil 2–3 different root vegetables together (choose from carrots, swede, parsnips, celeriac, potatoes or sweet potatoes), then mash with Greek yoghurt or crème fraîche and some chopped chives or spring onions.

Potatoes make a popular accompaniment to stews, casseroles, roasts and grills. Here they have been roasted in a little olive oil and rosemary.

Beans & lentils can be a little bland served plain, so jazz them up by tossing them with a little extra virgin olive oil and crushed garlic, lemon juice or crème fraîche with chopped fresh herbs, or a little pesto or tomato sauce.

Mediterranean roast lamb
(See page 214)

Extra carbs

Couscous

To prepare, put the couscous in a bowl, pour over boiling water or stock, leave to soak for about 5 minutes until the couscous has absorbed the liquid, then drizzle with olive oil and fluff up with a fork. To add flavour, stir in a handful of chopped dried fruit, nuts, sun-dried tomatoes or olives and plenty of chopped fresh herbs.

Pasta & noodles couldn't be simpler to cook in a pan of boiling water, following pack instructions for timings, then served plain or tossed with a little olive or sesame oil, plus garlic, fresh herbs, lemon zest, Parmesan or freshly ground black pepper. Noodles are especially good with Asian-style stir-fries, but you can really choose any type you fancy.

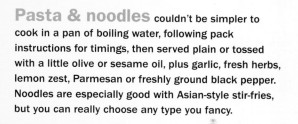

Peas & beans (fresh or frozen) combined look more interesting than a single vegetable. Steam or gently boil, then toss with some chopped parsley or snipped chives.

Spinach & oranges Fresh baby spinach leaves or watercress, tossed with orange or ruby grapefruit segments, make a zingy salad. Sprinkle with a little olive oil, citrus juice and black pepper.

Extra fruit & vegetables

Courgettes & pine nuts Stir-fry some diagonally sliced courgettes with a handful of pine nuts, almonds or unsalted cashews, until they are lightly golden.

Peppers & squash Chunks of sweet red pepper and butternut squash can be roasted in the oven at the same time as the main dish.

Boosting your five-a-day

A side salad adds refreshing flavour to a meal and boosts your intake of essential vitamins and minerals. Here are some tempting, quick ideas – but be adventurous and experiment with your own combinations.

- **lamb's lettuce** with sliced tomatoes and kiwi fruit.
- **mixed leaves** tossed with sliced raw mushrooms and toasted hazelnuts.
- **thinly sliced fennel and oranges** with black olives.
- **chickpeas** tossed with rocket and halved cherry tomatoes.
- **grated carrot** with thinly sliced apple and celery.
- **sliced avocado** sprinkled with lemon juice and chopped walnuts.
- **courgette ribbons** tossed with sun-dried tomatoes, a little olive oil and lemon juice and snipped chives.
- **carrot and cucumber julienne** combined with mange-tout, bean sprouts and toasted peanuts, sprinkled with a spicy chilli dressing.
- **finely shredded carrots** and white cabbage mixed with sliced radishes, chopped spring onions and sultanas, with a little reduced-fat mayonnaise stirred into natural low-fat yoghurt.
- **red kidney beans,** diced onions and tomatoes combined with red or green pepper and sweetcorn, and a little finely chopped red chilli if liked.

Hot vegetable ideas

If you prefer a hot vegetable side dish to a salad, here are some simple ideas. The healthiest ways to cook vegetables are to steam, stir-fry or microwave them.

- **dress up** steamed cauliflower florets with a sprinkling of garlicky breadcrumbs or chopped hard-boiled egg.
- **serve steamed French beans** topped with a fresh tomato salsa and torn basil leaves.
- **cook carrot sticks in orange juice** with a little chopped stem ginger.
- **sprinkle steamed broccoli** with a pinch of crushed dried chillies.
- **stir-fry spinach briefly with garlic,** then toss in a handful of pine nuts.
- **toss steamed courgettes** with a little crème fraîche and plenty of chopped fresh dill or tarragon.
- **toss cooked baby broad beans** with rocket, chopped fresh mint and lemon zest.
- **stir-fry** any selection of mixed vegetables (whatever you happen to have) with ginger and garlic.

Three easy extras

Here are some dips and dressings to boost a one-dish meal. Guacamole and raita make great quick-and-easy side dishes, and a homemade dressing perks up any salad.

Zesty guacamole

SERVES 4

1 large ripe avocado, stoned and mashed
2 tomatoes, chopped
grated zest and juice of 1 lime
2 spring onions, chopped
1 garlic clove, crushed
1 tbsp chopped fresh coriander

Combine all the ingredients together shortly before serving. (Add ½ fresh green chilli, deseeded and finely chopped or a dash of Tabasco for a spicy kick.)

Vinaigrette dressing

MAKES about 150ml

120ml extra virgin olive oil
2 tbsp red wine vinegar or lemon juice
1 tsp Dijon or wholegrain mustard
½ tsp runny honey or pinch of sugar
freshly ground black pepper

Put all the ingredients in a screw-topped jar, put on the lid and shake. This will keep well in the fridge to be used when required. Add crushed garlic, finely chopped stem ginger or chopped fresh herbs, if liked. Shake well before using.

Banana mint raita

SERVES 4

1 large banana, sliced
150g natural low-fat yoghurt
1 tbsp chopped fresh mint
1 tsp runny honey
pinch of paprika

Stir the sliced banana into the yoghurt and add the mint and honey. Sprinkle with ground paprika. (For a cucumber raita, use ⅓ cucumber, diced, in place of the banana and add 1 crushed garlic clove.)

Make your own stock

Homemade stock is a far cry from salty, over-seasoned ready-made cubes, and cheaper than fresh chilled stock. After chilling and removing the fat, you can boil the stock until it is reduced and **concentrated in flavour,** then cool and freeze it in ice-cube trays. The frozen stock cubes can then be packed in a freezer bag and used individually – **add them frozen** to hot liquids in soups, stews and casseroles and they will melt almost instantly.

Beef, veal or lamb stock

You can use fresh, raw, or cooked bones to make a meat stock, plus any lean meat scraps. Trim any fat or fatty skin from meat or bones before using for the stock.

MAKES about 1.5 litres *
PREPARATION TIME 20 minutes
COOKING TIME 2–3 hours

900g meat bones (beef, veal or lamb)
2 sprigs of fresh thyme
2 sprigs of fresh parsley
1 large bay leaf
2 onions, roughly chopped
2 celery sticks, roughly chopped
2 carrots, roughly chopped
6 peppercorns

1 Place the bones in a large saucepan and add about 2 litres of water, enough to cover the bones. Bring to the boil, skimming off the scum as it rises to the surface.

2 Tie together the thyme, parsley and bay leaf and add to the pan with the onions, celery, carrots and peppercorns. Cover and simmer gently for 2–3 hours.

3 Strain the stock through a sieve into a bowl, discarding the bones and vegetables. Leave to cool, then chill. Skim any fat from the surface and discard before using the stock.

cook's tip

● If you prefer a richer, brown stock, first roast the bones at 230°C/ gas mark 8 for 40 minutes.

Chicken stock

This stock, made with the leftovers from a roast chicken, can be used as a base for soups, casseroles, sauces and gravies.

MAKES about 1.5 litres *
PREPARATION TIME 10 minutes
COOKING TIME 2 hours

1 chicken carcass or the bones from
   4 chicken pieces (or fresh chicken wings,
   browned first)
1 onion, roughly chopped
1 large carrot, roughly chopped
1 celery stick, roughly chopped
1 large bay leaf
6 black peppercorns

1 Break up the chicken carcass or bones and put into a large pan. Add the vegetables, bay leaf and peppercorns. Pour over 2 litres of water.

2 Bring to the boil over a high heat, then turn the heat down so the liquid is simmering gently. Cover the pan and leave to bubble for 2 hours.

3 Strain the stock through a sieve into a bowl, discarding the bones and vegetables. Skim any fat from the surface with a spoon, if using the stock straightaway. Alternatively, chill the stock first, which will make it easier to remove the fat.

Vegetable stock

Use this light stock as a base for delicate soups and sauces, and in risottos and similar dishes.

MAKES about 1.7 litres [V] *
PREPARATION TIME 15 minutes
COOKING TIME 1 hour

15g butter
225g leeks, roughly chopped
225g onions, roughly chopped
1 large bay leaf
several sprigs of fresh thyme
several sprigs of fresh parsley
225g carrots, roughly chopped
150g celery, roughly chopped
5 black peppercorns

1 Melt the butter in a large saucepan or stockpot over a moderate heat. Stir in the leeks and onions, then reduce the heat to low. Cover with a tight-fitting lid and leave the vegetables to cook gently for 20 minutes without lifting the lid.

2 Tie the herbs together into a bouquet garni. Add it to the pan with the carrots, celery, peppercorns and 2 litres of water. Increase the heat and bring slowly to the boil, skimming the surface if necessary to remove any scum. As soon as the water boils, reduce the heat to low and simmer for 35 minutes.

3 Strain the stock into a large heatproof bowl and set aside to cool. Keep chilled or freeze.

Fish stock

Fish trimmings – the head, skin and bones – from any white fish with a good flavour, such as sole, cod or plaice, can be used. (Oily fish are not suitable for making stock as they give it a strong, fatty flavour.)

MAKES about 1.2 litres *
PREPARATION TIME 10 minutes
COOKING TIME 30 minutes

900g trimmings from white fish, including skin,
   bones, and heads without gills
1 onion, thinly sliced
4 sprigs of fresh parsley
2 bay leaves
2 carrots, thinly sliced
2 celery sticks, thinly sliced
4 black peppercorns

1 Rinse the fish bones and heads well, then place in a large saucepan. Add the onion, parsley, bay leaves, carrots, celery and peppercorns and 1.3 litres of water. Bring to the boil, then reduce the heat and simmer gently for about 30 minutes, skimming the froth from the surface as it appears.

2 Remove from the heat and leave to cool, then strain the stock through a fine sieve into a heatproof bowl. Discard the fish trimmings and vegetables. Use the stock at once or cool and chill or freeze.

variations

● For special-occasion fish dishes, use 300ml white wine and just 1 litre of water.
● Make a shellfish stock using prawn, crab, lobster or mussel shells, instead of the white fish trimmings.

cook's tip

● Fresh stocks will keep in the fridge for 3–4 days or in the freezer for up to 6 months.

Soups

Nourishing, easy to make and incredibly versatile, flavoursome soup is the ultimate one-dish meal. The ingredients – fresh seasonal produce, satisfying carbohydrates and vital protein – are simmered together in a nutritious stock, retaining all of their goodness. For a real fruit and vegetable boost, why not try a Provençal vegetable pistou, or choose Chilled melon soup with prawn and avocado to cool the sultriest of summer evenings? From light, chilled soups to hearty broths packed with chunky fish or spicy meatballs, soups make a great, healthy choice for simple family meals or fuss-free dining with friends.

Onion family soup with Gruyère croûtes

The secret of this rich, warming soup lies in the **slow cooking of the onions and leeks,** in just a little butter and oil, until **lightly caramelised.** Thinly sliced potatoes add extra carbohydrate and help to thicken the stock. Complemented by crunchy cheese and walnut-topped croûtes, it makes a **satisfying lunch or supper dish.**

SERVES 4
PREPARATION TIME 10 minutes
COOKING TIME about 1 hour

15g unsalted butter
1 tbsp olive oil
3 large onions, halved and thinly sliced
2 leeks, halved lengthways and thinly sliced
1 garlic clove, crushed
2 tsp fresh thyme leaves
½ tsp caster sugar
1 tbsp sherry vinegar
3 small potatoes, about 300g in total
1.4 litres beef stock (well-flavoured)
4 fresh chives, snipped

GRUYÈRE CROÛTES
3 thick slices wholemeal bread
1 garlic clove, cut in half
2 tsp French mustard
75g Gruyère cheese, coarsely grated
50g walnuts, roughly chopped

variation

• For a vegetarian soup, use a good vegetable stock instead of beef stock and stir in ½ tsp yeast extract for a richer flavour and colour. For the croûtes, use Emmenthal cheese as Gruyère is not suitable for strict vegetarians.

cook's tip

• Sherry vinegar is matured in wooden barrels by methods similar to those used for sherry itself. It has a rich, mellow flavour but if unavailable you can use red wine vinegar instead.

1 Heat the butter with the oil in a large saucepan. Add the onions and leeks and 1 tsp water. Cook over a medium heat for 7–8 minutes, stirring frequently until they begin to soften. Turn down the heat to very low, cover and cook gently for 20–25 minutes, stirring occasionally. Increase the heat slightly, add the garlic, thyme and sugar and cook, stirring, for 1 minute. Then add the vinegar and continue cooking, stirring frequently, for 3–4 minutes until the onions and leeks are light golden.

2 Peel the potatoes, cut in half lengthways and thinly slice. Add to the onion mixture with the stock. Bring to the boil, then reduce the heat, cover and cook for 15–20 minutes until the potatoes are tender and just beginning to break down and thicken the soup. Season to taste. Preheat the grill to medium.

3 Meanwhile, prepare the croûtes. Trim the crusts off the bread and cut each slice into 4 triangles. Place on the rack of the grill pan and toast very lightly on both sides. Gently rub each croûte with the cut surface of the garlic, then spread very thinly with mustard. Top with the cheese and walnuts, pressing down gently.

4 Pop the cheese-topped croûtes back under the grill and toast for 2–3 minutes until the cheese is just starting to bubble and brown and the walnuts are lightly toasted.

5 Sprinkle the soup with snipped chives, then serve with the croûtes popped on top.

2.5 portions fruit & veg

411 kcals

each serving provides 411kcals • 15g protein 23g fat of which 7g saturates • 39g carbohydrate of which 11g sugars • 6.5g fibre • 416mg sodium • 200g vegetables

Smoked bacon & lentil soup

A satisfying and comforting soup packed with a **good mix of healthy vegetables** which take you well on the way to your five-a-day. Enjoy hunks of warm Granary bread with this **winter warmer.**

SERVES 4 ★
PREPARATION TIME 20 minutes
COOKING TIME 40–45 minutes

1 tbsp olive oil
2 garlic cloves, crushed
2 lean smoked back bacon rashers, chopped
1 large onion, chopped
2 carrots, peeled and diced
½ large swede, peeled and diced
1 litre chicken or vegetable stock
125g green lentils
grated zest of 1 lemon
4 parsnips, peeled and diced
2–3 tbsp chopped fresh parsley

each serving provides

301kcals • 17g protein
7g fat of which 1.5g saturates
45g carbohydrate of which
19g sugars • 13g fibre
434mg sodium • 338g vegetables

1 Heat the oil in a large saucepan. Add the garlic, bacon, onion, carrots and swede and mix well. Cook over a medium heat, stirring frequently, for 5 minutes until the bacon has changed colour and the onion has softened.

2 Stir in the stock, lentils and half the lemon zest. Bring to the boil, then reduce the heat, half cover the pan and cook gently for 10 minutes.

3 Stir in the parsnips, cover and continue to cook gently for 25–30 minutes until the lentils and vegetables are tender.

4 Use a vegetable masher or hand-held blender to crush some of the lentils and vegetables into the soup, leaving the majority chunky. Stir in half of the parsley and season to taste. Serve sprinkled with the remaining parsley and lemon zest.

variations

• For a vegetarian soup, omit the bacon and use vegetable stock. Serve sprinkled with mixed lightly toasted sunflower and pumpkin seeds with the lemon and parsley.
• Celeriac makes a good alternative to parsnips.

301 kcals

prepare ahead

4 portions fruit & veg

SERVES 4 V
PREPARATION TIME 20 minutes
COOKING TIME about 20 minutes

1.2 litres vegetable stock
2 small leeks, thinly sliced
3 carrots, peeled and diced
2 courgettes, diced
400g can chopped tomatoes
200g French beans, cut into
   short lengths
400g can flageolet beans,
   drained and rinsed
100g dried vermicelli, broken
   into short lengths
40g Parmesan, or Italian-style
   hard cheese, shaved

AÏLLADE
3 garlic cloves
25g fresh basil leaves, roughly
   chopped
1 tomato, skinned, deseeded
   and chopped

each serving provides

265kcals • 16g protein
4g fat of which 2g saturates
41g carbohydrate of which 12g sugars
7g fibre • 334mg sodium
422g vegetables

Provençal vegetable pistou

Classic vegetable and pasta soup from the South of France, topped with a **richly flavoured garlic and basil paste, called aïllade,** and a sprinkling of Parmesan, makes a **nourishing main meal.** Serve with crusty bread, such as **chunks of warm olive focaccia.**

1 Bring the stock to the boil in a large pan and add the leeks, carrots, courgettes and canned tomatoes with their juice. Bring back to the boil, then reduce the heat slightly, cover and simmer for 15 minutes.

2 Stir in the French beans, flageolets and vermicelli, bring back to the boil, then reduce the heat slightly and simmer for 5 minutes or until all the vegetables and pasta are tender. Season to taste.

3 Meanwhile, to make the aïllade, use a mortar and pestle to pound the garlic, basil and tomato until smooth. Season to taste. (The aïllade can be prepared ahead and can be added to the soup when ready to serve).

4 Ladle the soup into wide bowls and add a spoonful of aïllade and some thin shavings of cheese to each serving.

variation

• Depending on the season, almost any fresh, diced vegetables can be added to the soup, and if supplies are short you can add a few frozen vegetables such as broad beans or sweetcorn.

5 portions fruit & veg

prepare ahead

265 kcals

Mixed bean chilli soup

This **heart-warming soup** is perfect for a chilly evening. It's packed full of **vegetables and mixed pulses,** making it an excellent **source of fibre.** Enjoy it with some **crusty French bread** to mop up the delicious liquid.

SERVES 4 V ★
PREPARATION TIME 20 minutes
COOKING TIME 25 minutes

cook's tips

• Canned mixed pulses contain soya, pinto, black-eye, red kidney and aduki beans, and chickpeas. If unavailable, use any combination of these beans or just a single type. Rinse thoroughly in a sieve under cold running water to remove as much salt as possible.

• Add chilli powder according to your own preference. True chilli powder is very fiery so you only need a little. Chilli seasonings (see page 18) are blends of spices which usually include cumin and are milder, so you could add up to 1 tbsp and omit the separate cumin.

• A 750g jar of tomato passata could be used instead of the combined canned tomatoes and tomato juice, with a little extra stock as needed.

each serving provides

232kcals • 9g protein
11g fat of which 4g saturates
26g carbohydrate of which
16g sugars • 7.5g fibre
638mg sodium • 248g vegetables

prepare ahead
232 kcals
3 portions fruit & veg

2 tbsp vegetable oil
1 onion, chopped
2 garlic cloves, crushed
1 red pepper, deseeded and chopped
1 green pepper, deseeded and chopped
125g button mushrooms, sliced
½ tsp chilli powder, or to taste
1 tsp ground cumin
400g can mixed pulses, drained and rinsed
400g can chopped tomatoes
600ml tomato juice
300ml vegetable stock
2 tbsp chopped fresh coriander

TO SERVE 4 tbsp half-fat crème fraîche, fresh coriander sprigs

1 Heat the oil in a large saucepan. Add the onion, garlic and peppers and fry them gently, stirring constantly, for 2–3 minutes until softened. Add the mushrooms, chilli powder and ground cumin and cook gently, stirring, for about 30 seconds.

2 Tip the mixed pulses and tomatoes into the saucepan. Add the tomato juice, stock and chopped coriander. Stir well, bring to the boil, then reduce the heat. Partially cover the pan with a lid and simmer gently for 20 minutes until all the vegetables are tender.

3 Ladle the soup into bowls and garnish each portion with 1 tbsp of crème fraîche and some coriander sprigs.

Mushroom & fennel soup

Sweet aniseed-flavoured fennel and mushrooms make a delicious combination in this smooth vegetable soup, topped with a cheesy garnish. Serve with chunks of rustic bread to make a satisfying meal.

SERVES 6 Ⓥ ★
PREPARATION TIME 25 minutes
COOKING TIME 35 minutes

2 fennel bulbs
grated zest and juice of ½ lemon
1 tbsp olive oil
1 large onion, roughly chopped
4 potatoes, about 800g in total,
  peeled and diced
250g closed cap brown
  mushrooms, halved
100ml dry sherry
600ml vegetable stock
300ml semi-skimmed milk
175g Caerphilly, Lancashire
  or Cheshire cheese, finely
  crumbled

variations

• Use Jerusalem artichokes instead of the potatoes or a head of celery instead of the fennel. Leeks would also be delicious with the potatoes and mushrooms as an alternative to fennel.
• For a really hearty meal, spread the cheese and fennel mixture onto thick slices of French bread, then toast until golden and bubbling. Serve with the soup.

1 Trim any feathery tops from the fennel and reserve for garnishing the soup. Cut the bulbs into quarters. Finely chop one quarter and place in a bowl with the lemon juice, stir well and set aside for topping the cooked soup. Roughly chop the rest of the fennel.

2 Place the olive oil in a large saucepan. Add the onion and roughly chopped fennel, cover and cook over a moderate heat for 5 minutes, shaking the pan occasionally. The vegetables should be slightly softened but not well browned.

3 Add the potatoes and mushrooms, stir well, then pour in the sherry and stock. Bring to the boil, reduce the heat, cover and simmer for 30 minutes, stirring once or twice, until the potatoes are tender and falling apart.

4 Purée the soup in a blender or food processor until smooth, or in the pan using a hand-held blender. Stir in the milk and lemon zest, season with freshly ground black pepper, then reheat if necessary. Mix the reserved chopped fennel with the cheese. Ladle the soup into bowls, top with this mixture and garnish with the feathery fronds.

prepare ahead

3 portions fruit & veg

299 kcals

each serving provides 299kcals • 13g protein 13g fat of which 6.5g saturates • 30.5g carbohydrate of which 7g sugars 5g fibre • 186mg sodium • 248g vegetables

Chilli-spiced butternut soup

This golden, velvet-textured soup is very satisfying and perfect for a **warm light lunch on a chilly day.** Bramley apple adds a **sweet-sour tang** to the flavour, with added zip from chillies.

SERVES 4 ✶
PREPARATION TIME 30 minutes
COOKING TIME 1 hour

85g pepperoni sausage, diced
1 large onion, chopped
1 butternut squash, peeled, deseeded and chopped
1 Bramley apple, peeled, cored and chopped
1 garlic clove, crushed
sprig of fresh thyme or ½ tsp dried
½ tsp crushed dried chillies
600ml chicken stock

TO SERVE wholemeal bread croûtons (made from 2 medium-thick slices of bread)

1 Put the pepperoni in a large, heavy-based saucepan and fry gently for 3–4 minutes until the fat runs off and the pieces are lightly browned. Lift out and drain on kitchen paper, leaving the fat in the pan. Reserve the pepperoni for garnish.

2 Add the onion to the pan and fry gently in the pepperoni oil for 4–5 minutes, stirring occasionally, until softened.

3 Stir in the squash, apple, garlic, thyme and chillies, cover and leave to cook on a very low heat for 45 minutes, stirring occasionally, until the squash is tender.

4 Remove the sprig of thyme and tip the contents of the pan into a food processor or blender. Add about half the stock and process to a smooth purée. (You may need to do this in 2 batches.) Return to the pan and add the remaining stock. Reheat gently and season to taste.

5 Serve the soup hot, with a few pieces of pepperoni and the croûtons sprinkled over.

variations

• For a vegetarian version, replace the chicken stock with vegetable stock and use soya bacon bits or toasted pumpkin seeds to sprinkle over the soup in place of the pepperoni. You'll also need 1 tbsp olive oil to fry the onion.

• If you prefer, a generous dash of chilli sauce can be added to the soup instead of the crushed dried chillies.

cook's tip

• To make crispy, low-fat croûtons, toast the bread on both sides, then cut off the crusts and cut into cubes.

4.5 portions fruit & veg

282 kcals

prepare ahead

each serving provides 282kcals • 10g protein • 9.5g fat of which 3.5g saturates 42g carbohydrate of which 23g sugars • 7g fibre • 496mg sodium • 380g fruit and vegetables

SERVES 4 V ✳
PREPARATION TIME 20 minutes
COOKING TIME 35–40 minutes

1 tbsp olive oil
1 onion, roughly chopped
2 celery sticks, roughly chopped
1 carrot, peeled and roughly chopped
1 garlic clove, crushed
1 tsp ground cumin
½ tsp ground coriander
175g split red lentils
1.2 litres vegetable stock
400g can plum tomatoes
2 tsp tomato purée
1 bay leaf

TO GARNISH 4 tbsp Greek yoghurt,
    2 tbsp chopped fresh coriander

variation

• For a spicy lentil and parsnip
soup, stir in ¼ tsp crushed dried
chillies with the spices and add
225g roughly chopped parsnips
instead of the celery.

Tomato & lentil soup
This simple soup is **flavoured with warm spices,** then blended to a **velvety smooth texture.** Serve it as a **fast and sustaining lunch** with warm garlic and coriander naan bread.

1 Heat the oil in a saucepan. Add the onion and cook over a low heat for 7–8 minutes, stirring occasionally, until beginning to soften. Stir in the celery and carrot and cook for 3 minutes, stirring frequently. Add the garlic, cumin and coriander and cook for a further minute, stirring constantly.

2 Add the lentils, stock, tomatoes with their juice, tomato purée and bay leaf. Bring to the boil, reduce the heat, then half-cover the pan with a lid and simmer for 25–30 minutes until the lentils and vegetables are very soft.

3 Meanwhile, stir the coriander into the yoghurt for the garnish.

4 Remove the bay leaf from the soup. Blend the soup in the pan using a hand-held blender, or tip into a blender or food processor, process until smooth, then return the soup to the pan. Check the consistency; it will be fairly thick, so if you prefer it thinner, dilute with a little more stock. Season to taste, then reheat until just bubbling. Serve drizzled with some of the coriander yoghurt and sprinkled with freshly ground black pepper.

2 portions fruit & veg

prepare ahead

243 kcals

each serving provides 243kcals • 14g protein • 7g fat of which 3g saturates
34g carbohydrate of which 10g sugars • 4g fibre • 103mg sodium • 173g vegetables

SERVES 4 V ✱
PREPARATION TIME 15–20 minutes
COOKING TIME 40–45 minutes

1 tbsp olive oil
2 carrots, peeled and sliced
2 celery sticks, roughly chopped
1 onion, chopped
1 fennel bulb, sliced
3 tomatoes, roughly chopped
300g cooked beetroot, peeled
    and sliced
2 oranges, grated zest and juice
1 litre vegetable stock

BEETROOT SALSA
1 tsp olive oil
100g cooked beetroot, peeled
    and finely chopped
1 tomato, finely chopped
2 spring onions, finely chopped

TO SERVE 4 seeded wholewheat
    bagels, halved and toasted,
    200g low-fat soft cheese,
    1 tbsp hot horseradish sauce

each serving provides
476kcals • 22g protein • 10g fat of
which 3g saturates • 81g carbohydrate
of which 33g sugars • 10g fibre
892mg sodium • 430g fruit
and vegetables

hot or cold

5 portions fruit & veg

476 kcals

Beetroot & orange soup
A luscious soup packed with **vibrant vegetables.** The beetroot provides the **vivid fuchsia colour** and the carrots, fennel, celery and orange all contribute to the **superb flavour.** It's also good served chilled.

1 Heat the olive oil in a heavy saucepan over a medium heat. Add the carrots, celery, onion and fennel. Reduce the heat to low and gently cook the vegetables, with the pan covered, for 10–15 minutes until softened but not browned.

2 Add the tomatoes to the pan with the beetroot and cook for about 3 minutes longer. Stir in the orange zest with the vegetable stock. Bring the mixture to the boil, stirring occasionally, then cover the pan, reduce the heat and simmer for about 25 minutes until all the vegetables are tender.

3 Meanwhile prepare the salsa and bagels. For the salsa, simply combine the ingredients together in a bowl. Then, for the bagel topping, blend the soft cheese with the horseradish sauce until well mixed.

4 Remove the soup from the heat, blend in a blender or food processor until completely smooth, then return to the pan. Alternatively blend the soup in the pan using a hand-held blender. Stir in the orange juice, and extra stock if too thick, then reheat gently and season to taste.

5 Spread the cheese mixture over the toasted bagel halves. Serve the soup topped with a little of the beetroot salsa and accompanied by the bagels.

SERVES 4
PREPARATION TIME 15 minutes,
    plus at least 1½ hours chilling
COOKING TIME 2 minutes

2 medium cucumbers
2 Charentais, Cantaloupe
    or Ogen melons
juice of 1 lemon
2 tbsp chopped fresh mint
250g cooked peeled prawns,
    thawed and drained if frozen
1 firm, but ripe, avocado

TO GARNISH fresh mint leaves

variation

• For a vegetarian version of this
soup, omit the prawns and add an
extra avocado.

each serving provides

163kcals • 14g protein
8g fat of which 2g saturates
10g carbohydrate of which
10g sugars • 4g fibre
139mg sodium • 329g fruit
and vegetables

prepare
ahead

163
kcals

4
portions
fruit &
veg

Chilled melon soup with prawn & avocado

Fresh fruit soups can be prepared ahead and are fresh and cooling on a hot summer's day. Serve with grissini (Italian breadsticks) for a light lunch.

1 Peel the cucumbers and cut in half crossways. Divide each half lengthways, then using a teaspoon, scoop out the seeds. Chop the flesh roughly. Drop into a saucepan of lightly salted boiling water and cook gently for 2 minutes. Drain in a sieve, then refresh under cold running water.

2 Halve the melons and remove the seeds. Scoop out the flesh using a tablespoon and put into a blender or food processor. Add the cucumber, lemon juice and chopped mint, then whizz together until blended. Turn out the mixture into a bowl. Pour 200ml of water into the blender or processor and whizz briefly, then stir this liquid into the melon and cucumber mixture.

3 Stir in the prawns and season lightly with freshly ground black pepper. Chill for at least 1½ hours and up to 12 hours.

4 Just before serving, peel, stone and dice the avocado and add to the soup. Snip in some mint leaves to garnish and season to taste with more pepper if needed.

SERVES 4 ✶
PREPARATION TIME 15 minutes,
   plus 5 minutes standing
COOKING TIME 30 minutes

1 tbsp olive oil
25g fresh root ginger, peeled and
   finely chopped
2 lean unsmoked back bacon rashers
1 onion, chopped
1 small carrot, peeled and diced
2 celery sticks, chopped
2 leeks, thickly sliced
750ml boiling water
170g can crab
3 potatoes, about 675g in total,
   peeled and cut into small chunks
225g frozen sweetcorn
2 tbsp chopped fresh dill (optional)

TO GARNISH 4 tbsp half-fat
   crème fraîche or fromage frais,
   1 small red chilli, deseeded
   and finely diced (optional)

variation

• Instead of crab, use 350g peeled
raw tiger prawns, adding them with
the sweetcorn, or add 225g peeled
cooked prawns, thawed and drained
if frozen, at the end of cooking.

Corn chowder with crab

Leeks, sweetcorn and potatoes make this chunky seafood chowder **a satisfying main meal soup.** Serve garnished with a **swirl of crème fraîche or fromage frais** and some crusty **wholegrain bread** to accompany.

1 Heat the oil in a large saucepan. Add the ginger, bacon, onion, carrot and celery and stir over a high heat for 1 minute. Add the leeks, reduce the heat to moderate and cook for a further 4 minutes, stirring occasionally. Pour in the water and bring to the boil. Reduce the heat, cover the pan and simmer for 5 minutes.

2 Drain the crab, reserving the liquid, and set it aside. Stir the potatoes and reserved crab liquid into the soup. Bring back to simmering point, cover again and cook for about 10 minutes until the potatoes are tender.

3 Stir in the sweetcorn. Heat again to simmering point, then cover the pan and simmer for 5 minutes until the potatoes break up slightly and thicken the liquid. Lightly stir in the crab and dill, cover the pan and remove it from the heat. Leave to stand for 5 minutes to allow the flavours to infuse. Season with freshly ground black pepper to taste.

4 Serve the chowder in warmed bowls topped with a spoonful of crème fraîche or fromage frais and a sprinkling of chilli, if liked.

each serving provides

319kcals • 20g protein • 6g fat of which 1g saturates
49g carbohydrate of which 10g sugars • 6g fibre
462mg sodium • 200g vegetables

319 kcals

2.5 portions fruit & veg

great family lunch

variation

• For a special occasion, replace about 100ml of the stock with dry white wine, replace the seafood cocktail with whole mussels in the shell and the cod with monkfish. Cook until the mussel shells open (discarding any which stay closed), and add a handful of cooked whole prawns in the shell for garnish.

SERVES 4
PREPARATION TIME 10 minutes
COOKING TIME about 20 minutes

1 tbsp olive oil
2 shallots, finely chopped
1 garlic clove, crushed
900ml fish or chicken stock
pinch of saffron
1 bay leaf
250g potatoes, peeled and cut into 1cm dice
225g frozen mixed vegetables
3 tomatoes, about 300g in total, skinned, deseeded and diced
200g cod fillet, cut into 2.5cm chunks
340g seafood cocktail (mussels, squid rings and prawns), thawed if frozen

Quick fish soup

Mixed seafood combined with white fish, simmered with chunks of potato, tomatoes and some handy frozen vegetables, make a main course soup that is bursting with flavour and goodness. It is delicious served with Irish soda bread.

1 Heat the oil in a large pan and fry the shallots and garlic gently for 5–6 minutes, to soften but not brown. Add the stock, saffron and bay leaf and bring to the boil.

2 Add the potatoes to the pan, reduce the heat, cover and simmer gently for about 10 minutes until tender.

3 Increase the heat to high and add the frozen mixed vegetables. Bring back to the boil, then stir in the tomatoes, cod and seafood cocktail. Reduce heat and simmer gently, without stirring, for about 3 minutes until the cod is white and firm. Season to taste, then serve immediately.

each serving provides 219kcals • 25g protein • 5g fat of which 1g saturates 19g carbohydrate of which 5g sugars • 4g fibre • 272mg sodium • 148g vegetables

1.5 portions fruit & veg

219 kcals

SERVES 4
PREPARATION TIME 10 minutes
COOKING TIME 25–30 minutes

2 tbsp vegetable oil

2 leeks, halved lengthways and thinly sliced

1 litre semi-skimmed milk

350g potatoes (floury variety), peeled and diced

fresh nutmeg, grated, to taste

350g broccoli florets, roughly chopped

350g undyed, smoked haddock fillet, skinned and cut into bite-sized pieces

TO GARNISH 6 fresh chives, snipped

cook's tip

• The soup can be cooked and blended up to the end of step 3 in advance, then reheated with the smoked haddock added shortly before serving.

Leek & broccoli soup with smoked haddock

Comfort food at its best, this soup is based on the traditional Scottish recipe 'Cullen Skink', but updated so it is just as satisfying but lighter in fat and calories, and with added broccoli for extra goodness. Serve with hunks of crusty wholemeal bread.

1 Heat the oil in a large, heavy-based saucepan over a medium heat. Add the leeks and stir around for about 5 minutes until soft, but not coloured.

2 Stir in the milk, then add the potatoes and broccoli and freshly grated nutmeg to taste. Slowly bring to the boil, then reduce the heat to low and leave to simmer for 15–20 minutes until the vegetables are tender.

3 Purée the soup in the pan using a hand-held blender, or ladle into a blender or food processor and process until smooth. If using the latter, return the soup to the saucepan and reheat gently. Add a little more milk if needed to thin the consistency.

4 Add the haddock and simmer gently for 3–5 minutes until it is cooked through and flakes easily. Season to taste with freshly ground black pepper and more nutmeg if liked, to taste. Salt shouldn't be necessary as the smoked haddock is quite salty. Ladle the soup into serving bowls and sprinkle with chives.

prepare ahead

351 kcals

2 portions fruit & veg

each serving provides 351kcals • 33g protein 12g fat of which 4g saturates • 31g carbohydrate of which 16g sugars 5g fibre • 790mg sodium • 168g vegetables

Creole-style chicken & prawn gumbo

From the Deep South of the USA comes this piquant gumbo with **rice, chicken, prawns and vegetables,** a cross between a soup and a stew – **a filling feast in a bowl.** The sliced okra not only **contributes towards your five-a-day,** but gives the gumbo its traditional thickened texture.

SERVES 4
PREPARATION TIME 30–35 minutes
COOKING TIME 50 minutes

150g chorizo sausage, finely diced
2 tbsp vegetable oil
3½ tbsp plain flour
2 celery sticks, finely chopped
   with leaves reserved for garnish
2 onions, finely chopped
2 green peppers, deseeded
   and chopped
3 garlic cloves, crushed
400g can chopped tomatoes
1 litre chicken or vegetable stock
200g okra, thinly sliced
2 tbsp chopped fresh parsley
1 tsp dried thyme
1 bay leaf
pinch of cayenne pepper
175g basmati and wild rice, rinsed
3 skinless chicken thigh fillets,
   cut into bite-sized pieces
250g peeled large raw prawns

TO SERVE hot pepper sauce

variations
• The combination of peppers, onions and celery is called the 'holy trinity' by Cajun cooks, and is used to flavour many dishes, but red or yellow peppers can be substituted for the green.
• Okra is thought to have originated in Africa. When cut, it releases a sticky substance with thickening properties, which makes it popular in this kind of dish. Okra can now be found in many supermarkets and grocery stores.

1 Put the chorizo sausage in the base of a flameproof casserole or heavy-based saucepan over a medium heat. Fry the sausage, stirring frequently, until it has rendered some fat and is crisp at the edges. Drain on kitchen paper and set aside.

2 Add the oil to the sausage fat remaining in the pan. Reduce the heat to low and sprinkle in the flour, stirring constantly, until well blended. Cook very gently, stirring occasionally, for 5 minutes until the roux turns a rich brown.

3 Increase the heat slightly, stir in the celery, onions, green pepper and garlic and continue frying, stirring frequently, for 5 minutes or until soft. Add the tomatoes with their juice, the stock, okra, parsley, thyme, bay leaf and cayenne pepper. Bring to the boil, then reduce the heat, half cover the pan and simmer for 30 minutes, stirring frequently, until the okra thickens the soup.

4 Increase the heat and bring the liquid to the boil. Stir in the rice, then reduce the heat to low, add the chicken and simmer for 15–20 minutes until the rice is tender and the chicken is cooked through. Pour in a little extra stock if needed. Add the prawns and reserved chorizo and simmer for 1 minute or until the prawns turn pink and the sausage is heated through.

5 Remove the bay leaf. Season to taste, then ladle into bowls and garnish with the reserved celery leaves. Serve with hot pepper sauce.

each serving provides
575kcals • 42g protein
18g fat of which 5g saturates
63g carbohydrate of which
13g sugars • 6g fibre
589mg sodium • 320g vegetables

4 portions fruit & veg

575 kcals

2 tbsp vegetable oil
2 onions, finely chopped
2 large garlic cloves, crushed
1 tsp ground coriander
1 tsp ground cumin
¼ tsp ground cayenne pepper,
   or to taste
¼ tsp ground cloves
¼ tsp ground ginger
¼ tsp ground turmeric
1 litre chicken or vegetable stock
400g can chopped tomatoes
450g skinless chicken breast fillets,
   cut into 5mm strips
225g runner beans, trimmed
   and chopped
400g can chickpeas, drained
   and rinsed
2 tbsp chopped fresh coriander

TO GARNISH 4 tbsp low-fat natural
yoghurt, sprigs of fresh coriander

variations

• Extra vegetables can be added
for a chunkier soup. Sliced carrots,
courgette or sweetcorn are ideal.
• If you don't have a can of
chickpeas, canned cannellini or red
kidney beans, or green lentils would
also work well.

Chicken masala soup

Chicken soup is often credited with being **a panacea for all kinds of ills,** and this version – with its **warming Indian spices and vibrant colour** – should perk up anyone. Serve with **wholemeal chapattis.**

1 Heat the oil in a large, heavy-based saucepan or flameproof casserole over a medium heat. Add the onions and fry for 3 minutes, stirring. Add the garlic and continue stirring for about 2 minutes longer until the onions are softened, but not brown.

2 Reduce the heat slightly and stir in the spices. Continue stirring over a gentle heat for a few minutes so the spices release their aroma. Take care not to let the mixture burn.

3 Stir in the stock and tomatoes, with their juice, increase the heat and bring to the boil. Then reduce the heat to a gentle simmer.

4 Add the chicken, green beans and chickpeas to the pan, bring back to the boil, then reduce the heat, cover and leave the soup to cook gently for 8–10 minutes until the chicken is cooked through and the beans are just tender. Taste a bean to test if it is cooked and cut a piece of chicken in half to make sure it is no longer pink in the centre. Stir in the chopped coriander and season to taste. (If freezing the soup, add the coriander after reheating).

5 Ladle the soup into individual bowls, then add a tablespoon of yoghurt to each serving, sprinkle with a little cayenne pepper and garnish with sprigs of coriander.

each serving provides 317kcals • 36g protein
9g fat of which 2g saturates • 24g carbohydrate of which
12g sugars • 5g fibre • 267mg sodium • 240g vegetables

3 portions fruit & veg

mood food

317 kcals

1.4 litres chicken stock (well-flavoured)
2 stalks lemongrass, finely chopped
2 tsp finely chopped fresh root ginger
1 red chilli, deseeded and finely chopped
2 garlic cloves, finely chopped
3 skinless chicken breast fillets, about 400g in total
150g instant soup noodles
175g baby sweetcorn, sliced diagonally
150g baby button mushrooms, thinly sliced
1 tbsp light soy sauce
400ml can reduced-fat coconut milk
1 lime, grated zest and juice
200g pak choi, sliced

TO GARNISH 3 spring onions, finely sliced diagonally, small handful fresh coriander, roughly chopped

each serving provides
373kcals • 32g protein
13g fat of which 6g saturates
35g carbohydrate of which 4g sugars
5g fibre • 113g sodium
139g vegetables

373 kcals

1.5 portions fruit & veg

Oriental chicken noodle soup

This is one of the simplest soups to make with wonderful exotic flavours provided by lemongrass, coconut, ginger and chilli. The addition of instant soup noodles makes it quick and easy to prepare in one pan.

1 Pour the chicken stock into a large saucepan, add the lemongrass, ginger, chillies and garlic and bring to the boil. Add the chicken, reduce the heat and simmer for about 15 minutes until the chicken is cooked.

2 Lift out the chicken, using a draining spoon, put onto a chopping board and allow to cool. Leave the pan of stock on the heat.

3 Break the noodles into the hot stock, then add the baby sweetcorn, mushrooms, soy sauce and coconut milk. Bring the pan back to simmering temperature, then cook for 3 minutes.

4 Meanwhile cut the chicken into fine shreds. Stir the chicken into the soup with the lime zest and juice and the pak choi and simmer gently for 2 minutes until the pak choi has wilted.

5 Ladle into 4 soup bowls and scatter with spring onions and coriander leaves to garnish.

Vegetable soup with meatballs

Adding little meatballs to a vegetable soup turns it into a **satisfying meal** that will appeal to the whole family. Caraway seeds and ginger add a **delicious flavour** to the meatballs, as well as being **great aids to digestion**. Serve with some tasty rye bread.

SERVES 4
PREPARATION TIME 30 minutes
COOKING TIME 15 minutes

MEATBALLS
400g lean minced pork
15g fresh root ginger, peeled and grated
½ tsp caraway seeds, lightly crushed
1 garlic clove, crushed
½ egg, beaten

SOUP
200g new potatoes, scrubbed
2 carrots, peeled
1 large or 2 small leeks
1.5 litres chicken or vegetable stock, hot
¼ Savoy cabbage, finely shredded

variation

• As a quick alternative to making your own meatballs, use good quality, ready-made Swedish meatballs available chilled from supermarkets. They are already cooked so you can just add them to the soup to heat through.

1 To make the meatballs, place the minced pork, ginger, caraway seeds, garlic and beaten egg into a bowl, season with a little salt and pepper, then mix together until thoroughly combined. Roll the mixture into small walnut-sized balls (about 24 altogether) and set aside.

2 Cut the potatoes and carrots into small cubes. Trim and clean the leeks, removing most of the dark green part. Cut in half lengthways and slice thinly.

3 In a large saucepan, bring the stock back to the boil. Add the potatoes, carrots and leeks and simmer for 5 minutes until almost tender. Add the meatballs and simmer gently for 6–8 minutes until cooked through.

4 Finally add the shredded cabbage and cook for 1 minute until just wilted. Serve immediately.

cook's tip

• The meatballs can be prepared a day ahead and stored, covered in the fridge.

1.5 portions fruit & veg

209 kcals

prepare ahead

each serving provides 209kcals • 26g protein
6g fat of which 2g saturates • 15g carbohydrate of which 7g sugars
4g fibre • 95mg sodium • 138g vegetables

South American beef & pepper soup

This cheering, **main meal soup** is sure to appeal to the heartiest of appetites. **Lean pieces of beef** are simmered slowly in a rich, spicy tomato and red pepper broth that's studded with **golden sweetcorn and creamy butter beans.** Serve with warm tortillas to complete the meal.

SERVES 4 *
PREPARATION TIME 10 minutes
COOKING TIME 45 minutes

50g chorizo sausage, diced
450g lean braising steak,
  cut into 1cm strips
2 x 400g cans chopped tomatoes
125g roasted red peppers,
  drained and thinly sliced
400g can butter beans, drained
350g frozen sweetcorn
1 tsp dried oregano
1 tsp paprika
2 tbsp roughly chopped fresh
  flat-leaf parsley

cook's tips
• The whole soup can be made up to 1 day ahead. Allow to cool completely, then keep in the fridge until needed. Reheat gently, taste for seasoning and sprinkle with chopped parsley.
• To lighten the soup, you could replace the beef with the same weight of lean chicken thigh meat.

1 Fry the chorizo in a heavy saucepan or a flameproof casserole over a medium heat for about 5 minutes until some of the fat is released and the chorizo is slightly crispy. Using a draining spoon, transfer the chorizo to a bowl, leaving the paprika oil in the pan. This will add flavour to the soup with no need to add any extra oil.

2 Return the pan to the heat and add the beef. Cook, stirring occasionally, for about 10 minutes until evenly browned.

3 Return the chorizo to the pan with the tomatoes and their juice, peppers and 500ml water. Bring to the boil, then stir in the butter beans, sweetcorn, oregano and paprika. Reduce the heat, cover and simmer over a low heat for about 30 minutes until the beef is tender. Season to taste and serve scattered with parsley.

each serving provides
365kcals • 36g protein
12g fat of which 4g saturates
31g carbohydrate of which
10g sugars • 6g fibre
471mg sodium • 320g vegetables

prepare ahead

4 portions fruit & veg

365 kcals

Salads

Packed with colourful, vitamin-rich fruit and vegetables, one-dish salads are a great way to hit your five-a-day target and cut down on cooking time. Generally they're served cold but some combinations are good warm, making them suitable for all seasons. What's more, the fruit and vegetables are normally included raw, or just slightly cooked, so maximum vitamins and minerals are retained. Impress your hungry family with a Moroccan lamb salad, or for a light lunch, choose Summer fruity cottage cheese salad. Boosted with good carbohydrates and healthy protein, these sensational salads make tempting, well-balanced main meals that really satisfy.

SERVES 4

PREPARATION TIME about 30 minutes, plus overnight marinating (if time allows)

COOKING TIME 1 hour

2 courgettes, quartered
  and cut into chunks
2 red peppers, deseeded
  and cut into chunks
2 yellow peppers, deseeded
  and cut into chunks
2 red onions, each cut into
  6 wedges
2 tbsp olive oil
500g lamb neck fillets,
  trimmed of fat
250g couscous
2 tbsp chopped fresh coriander
1 tbsp chopped fresh flat-leaf parsley
1 tbsp chopped fresh mint
8 stoned black olives, sliced
6 spring onions, sliced diagonally

MARINADE
3 tbsp lemon juice
1 tbsp olive oil
3 garlic cloves, crushed
1 tsp ground cumin
1 tsp ground coriander
pinch of cayenne pepper

DRESSING
6 tbsp tomato juice
2 tbsp balsamic vinegar
1 tsp chilli sauce, or to taste

TO GARNISH fresh coriander
  or mint leaves

Moroccan lamb salad with couscous

Enjoy the fragrant flavours of coriander and mint in this North African-inspired salad, that can be largely prepared ahead. Lamb is a good source of protein, as well as B vitamins, iron and zinc.

1 Preheat the oven to 200°C/gas 6. Put the courgettes, peppers and red onions in a roasting tin, spoon over 2 tbsp of the olive oil and toss together to coat the vegetables. Put the tin in the oven and roast for 30 minutes, turning the vegetables after about 15 minutes.

2 Meanwhile, combine all the marinade ingredients in a shallow dish. Add the lamb, turn to coat, then cover and set aside. Put all the dressing ingredients in a screw-topped jar, shake together and set aside.

3 Stir the vegetables once they have roasted for 30 minutes, arrange the lamb on top and pour over the marinade. Return to the oven and continue roasting for a further 30 minutes until the lamb is cooked but still juicy. (You can prepare ahead up to this stage if more convenient and chill for up to 24 hours).

4 Put the couscous in a heatproof bowl and pour over enough boiling water to cover. Set aside, covered, for about 5 minutes until the water is absorbed and the grains are tender. Fork in the herbs, olives and spring onions.

5 Transfer the lamb to a plate and allow to rest for 10 minutes. Stir the roasted vegetables into the couscous, then thinly slice the lamb and lay it on top of the couscous. Shake the dressing and pour it over the salad. Toss together, then serve warm, scattered with coriander or mint leaves to garnish.

each serving provides 492kcals • 31g protein 19g fat of which 1.5g saturates • 51g carbohydrate of which 16g sugars • 5g fibre • 251mg sodium • 312g vegetables

492 kcals

prepare ahead

3.5 portions fruit & veg

Warm new potato salad with beetroot & pastrami

SERVES 4
PREPARATION TIME 25–30 minutes
COOKING TIME 15–20 minutes

675g small new potatoes
3 cooked beetroot, about 250g in total, peeled
125g frozen peas
85g pastrami
6 spring onions, thinly sliced

DILL DRESSING
4 tbsp low-fat natural yoghurt
1 tbsp mayonnaise
2 tsp wholegrain mustard
2 tbsp chopped fresh dill
1 tbsp bottled capers, rinsed and chopped

TO GARNISH 6 radishes,
thinly sliced

variations

• For vegetarians, omit the pastrami and add the same weight of Emmenthal cheese or 2–3 hard-boiled eggs, cut into quarters, to the salad.
• For a different flavour, swap the pastrami for a drained 250g jar of Swedish herrings or rollmops, cut into strips.

Beetroot adds vivid colour to this lovely warm salad, and is combined with a light, low-fat yoghurt and dill dressing. For a more substantial meal, serve with thin slices of rye or pumpernickel bread.

1 Cook the potatoes whole in their skins in a saucepan of lightly salted, boiling water for about 15 minutes until tender. Drain well and thickly slice.

2 Meanwhile, mix together all the ingredients for the dressing and cut the beetroot into thin julienne strips about 3cm long. Cook the peas for 2–3 minutes in a dish in the microwave or a pan of boiling water until tender, then drain well.

3 Drain the potatoes and thickly slice, then put them in a large serving bowl with the peas, half the spring onions and the pastrami, loosely folded.

4 Just before serving, very lightly stir the beetroot into the salad and drizzle over the dressing. Scatter the remaining onions and the radishes over the top. Serve warm.

each serving provides 253kcals • 13g protein 5g fat of which 1g saturates • 40g carbohydrate of which 13g sugars • 5g fibre • 369mg sodium • 121g vegetables

253 kcals

1.5 portions fruit & veg

Pasta, ham & broad bean salad

This quick and easy pasta salad is just right for busy people. It is appealing and sustaining and the watercress and walnut pesto dressing adds a great punchy flavour.

SERVES 4
PREPARATION TIME 15 minutes, plus 5 minutes standing
COOKING TIME about 15 minutes

300g fusilli (pasta twists)
400g shelled baby broad beans, (fresh or frozen)
400g cherry tomatoes, halved
200g lean cooked ham, diced
3 tbsp snipped fresh chives
1 tbsp extra virgin olive oil
50g watercress, trimmed and roughly chopped

WATERCRESS & WALNUT PESTO
50g watercress, trimmed
50g walnut pieces
1 garlic clove, peeled
4 tbsp extra virgin olive oil
3 tbsp low-fat natural yoghurt
grated zest and juice of ½ lemon

variations
• For a vegetarian salad, omit the ham and add 4 chopped, hard-boiled eggs to the salad with the watercress.
• Instead of broad beans, use 225g small broccoli florets. Cook them with the pasta in the same way.

1 Cook the pasta in a large saucepan of lightly salted boiling water for 10 minutes. Add the broad beans and bring back to the boil, then reduce the heat slightly and cook for a further 2–3 minutes until the pasta is tender and the beans are lightly cooked.

2 Meanwhile, mix together the tomatoes, ham, chives and 1 tbsp olive oil in a large serving bowl. Set aside. To make the pesto, process the watercress, walnuts and garlic together in a food processor or blender until finely ground. Add half the oil and pulse until combined, then add the remaining oil, lemon zest and juice and the yoghurt and blend again. Season to taste.

3 Drain the pasta and beans and immediately add them to the tomato mixture. Mix well, then cover and leave to stand for 5 minutes. Stir the pesto and chopped watercress into the salad, then serve immediately. (If prepared ahead, add the pesto and watercress just before serving. Until then, keep the rest of the salad and the pesto, covered separately, in the fridge.)

2.5 portions fruit & veg

prepare ahead

each serving provides 633kcals • 30g protein 28g fat of which 4g saturates • 69g carbohydrate of which 10g sugars • 10g fibre • 573mg sodium • 225g vegetables

633 kcals

Spiced chicken & mango salad

Here is a **modern, lighter version** of the traditional Coronation chicken. The familiar curry flavours and vegetables are still present but they have a **Southeast Asian flavour,** with spicy Thai curry paste and juicy fresh mango pieces added. This is the perfect salad for a **refreshing summer lunch,** accompanied by toasted naan or pitta bread.

SERVES 4

PREPARATION TIME
20–25 minutes

50g unsalted cashew nuts
4 tbsp low-fat natural yoghurt
2 tbsp reduced-fat mayonnaise
2 tsp mango chutney
½ tsp tomato purée
½ tsp red Thai curry paste
1 globe preserved stem ginger in syrup, about 15g, finely chopped
grated zest of 1 lime
3 skinless, cooked chicken breast fillets, about 400g in total, cubed
4 celery sticks, sliced
100g ready-to-eat dried apricots, thinly sliced
100g rocket
1 mango, peeled, stoned and sliced

variations

• To turn this salad into a wonderful sandwich filling, dice the chicken, celery, mango and apricots, then add the dressing and mix well. Pile onto multigrain bread with some rocket leaves.

• At Easter, Thanksgiving or Christmas time, in fact whenever you have some leftover roast turkey, use in place of the chicken.

cook's tip

• The dressing can be made up to 2 days ahead and stored in the fridge. The salad can be tossed together up to 4 hours ahead and kept chilled.

1 Preheat a hot grill. Spread the cashew nuts on a baking sheet, then put them under the grill to toast for a few minutes until golden. Allow to cool, then roughly chop. Set aside.

2 In a large bowl, make the dressing by mixing together the yoghurt, mayonnaise, chutney, tomato purée, curry paste, ginger and lime zest.

3 Add the chicken, celery and apricots to the bowl and lightly toss together until coated with the dressing.

4 Spread the rocket leaves and mango slices on a serving dish. Spoon the chicken mixture on top, then serve scattered with the cashew nuts.

each serving provides

303kcals • 30g protein
10g fat of which 2g saturates
24g carbohydrate of which
22g sugars • 4g fibre
259mg sodium • 124g fruit
and vegetables

303 kcals

1.5 portions fruit & veg

prepare ahead

Mediterranean roast chicken salad

Save time and effort on hot days with a **wonderfully easy salad**. It uses ready-roasted chicken, and the pasta and sugarsnap peas can be cooked ahead. Feta cheese, rocket and sweet juicy grapes – **rich in antioxidants** – all add to the **feast of flavours**.

SERVES 4
PREPARATION TIME 15 minutes
COOKING TIME 10 minutes

400g conchiglie (pasta shells)
300g sugarsnap peas, trimmed and halved diagonally
3 tbsp extra-virgin olive oil
400g skinless roast chicken meat, torn into bite-sized pieces
125g rocket
1 tbsp balsamic vinegar
225g black or red seedless grapes, halved
3 tbsp chopped fresh mint
100g feta cheese, drained if necessary

variation

• This is a versatile recipe so you can ring the changes, depending on what's available. Well-drained canned tuna chunks, chopped lean ham or turkey breast could be used in place of the roast chicken, juicy, vine-ripened cherry tomatoes rather than grapes and frozen peas or trimmed mange-tout as an alternative to green vegetables. Other good pasta shapes would be fusilli (spirals) or penne (quills).

each serving provides

715kcals • 46g protein
23g fat of which 7g saturates
87g carbohydrate of which
15g sugars • 5g fibre
449mg sodium • 160g fruit
and vegetables

1 Cook the pasta in a large saucepan of lightly salted boiling water for 10 minutes, or according to the pack instructions. Then, 3 minutes before the pasta is cooked, add the sugarsnap peas to the pan and continue boiling until the pasta is al dente and the peas are tender-crisp. Drain both into a colander, then tip them into a large serving bowl.

2 Drizzle over 1 tbsp of the olive oil and stir. Add the chicken and season to taste with freshly ground black pepper. At this point, the salad can be completed for serving warm, or the ingredients can be left to cool to serve later.

3 Just before serving, stir the rocket leaves into the bowl. Mix together the remaining olive oil and the balsamic vinegar, pour over the salad and toss all the ingredients together.

4 Gently stir in the grapes and chopped mint, then crumble the feta cheese over the top. Taste and adjust the seasoning if necessary, but the feta cheese is quite salty so there should be no need to add extra salt.

715 kcals

2 portions fruit & veg

prepare ahead

Duck salad with mushrooms & oranges

In this attractive salad, full-flavoured shiitake and chestnut mushrooms are combined with slices of **tender griddled duck,** juicy orange segments, crunchy water chestnuts and rice, with a fresh **ginger and honey dressing.** Duck meat is in fact **very lean,** once the thick layer of fat and skin has been removed.

SERVES 4
PREPARATION TIME 30 minutes
COOKING TIME 15 minutes

250g basmati and wild rice, rinsed
400g boneless duck breasts, skinned
2 tbsp vegetable oil
125g chestnut mushrooms, sliced
125g fresh shiitake mushrooms, sliced
3 oranges
1 pomegranate
220g can water chestnuts, drained and thinly sliced
50g lamb's lettuce

GINGER & HONEY DRESSING
25g fresh root ginger, peeled and finely chopped
½ tsp orange zest and 1 tbsp orange juice (from 1 of the oranges)
1 tsp Dijon mustard
2 tsp clear honey
1½ tbsp walnut oil
1 tsp wine vinegar

1 Cook the rice in a saucepan of lightly salted, boiling water for 12–15 minutes, or according to the pack instructions, until tender. Drain thoroughly, then transfer to a large bowl.

2 Meanwhile, heat a cast-iron, ridged griddle. Brush the duck breasts on both sides with 2 tsp of the vegetable oil, then cook them on the griddle over a moderate heat for 3 minutes on each side. The meat will be rare, so cook for longer if you prefer it medium or well-done. (If you don't have a griddle, cook the duck on the rack of a grill pan under a moderate grill.) Transfer the duck to a board and leave to cool. Brush the griddle with half of the remaining oil and add half the mushrooms. Cook for 3–5 minutes until tender, turning them occasionally. Remove and set aside, then repeat with the remaining oil and mushrooms.

3 Grate ½ tsp of zest from 1 of the oranges and set aside for the dressing. Cut away all the peel and pith from the 3 oranges, then cutting between and close to the membranes, remove the segments from each orange, holding the fruit over a bowl to catch the juices. Reserve 1 tbsp of the juice for the dressing.

4 Cut the pomegranate in half and carefully remove the fleshy seeds, leaving all the bitter pith behind. Add half the pomegranate seeds to the rice with the orange segments, mushrooms, water chestnuts and lamb's lettuce.

5 To make the dressing, whisk together the orange zest and juice, ginger, mustard, honey and walnut oil in a small bowl. Season to taste. Add 1 tbsp of dressing to the rice mixture, toss together, then transfer to a serving platter. Cut the duck breasts into thin slices and arrange on top of the rice. Drizzle over the remaining dressing and sprinkle with the remaining pomegranate seeds just before serving.

special supper

3 portions fruit & veg

520 kcals

each serving provides 520kcals • 23g protein • 15g fat of which 3g saturates 73g carbohydrate of which 18g sugars • 3g fibre • 156mg sodium • 262g fruit and vegetables

Roast turkey salad with cranberry dressing

Lean turkey breast and grilled smoked bacon, with the addition of beans, mushrooms, luscious mango and fresh salad leaves, make a delicious, low-fat main course salad. It's all tossed in a fruity cranberry dressing.

SERVES 4
PREPARATION TIME 20 minutes
COOKING TIME 5 minutes

4 lean smoked back bacon rashers
125g mixed salad leaves (such as radicchio, red chard and lamb's lettuce)
400g can borlotti or cannellini beans, drained and rinsed
150g button mushrooms, sliced
1 mango, peeled, stoned and diced
200g sliced cooked turkey breast, cut into strips

CRANBERRY DRESSING
2 tbsp cranberry sauce
1 tbsp balsamic vinegar
4 tbsp olive oil

variations

• Some lightly cooked fine green beans or asparagus spears would also go well in this salad.
• Scatter a few nuts, such as toasted almonds, cashews or walnuts on top of the salad just before serving.

1 Grill the bacon, turning once, for 6–8 minutes or until crisp. Drain on kitchen paper, then cut into thin strips.

2 Arrange the salad leaves on a large serving dish. Scatter over the beans, mushrooms and mango, then add the turkey and bacon.

3 Put the cranberry sauce, vinegar, olive oil and 2 tbsp of water in a screw-topped jar and shake together. Drizzle the dressing over the salad, toss together and serve immediately.

339 kcals

1 portion fruit & veg

super quick

each serving provides

339kcals • 29g protein • 15g fat of which 3g saturates
22g carbohydrate of which 14g sugars • 5g fibre
764mg sodium • 106g fruit and vegetables

SERVES 4
PREPARATION TIME 15 minutes

1 red pepper, deseeded and thinly sliced
1 yellow pepper, deseeded and thinly sliced
1 orange pepper, deseeded and thinly sliced
300g bean sprouts
6 spring onions, thinly sliced
½ cucumber, cut into thin sticks
250g cooked, peeled king prawns
300g cooked long-grain rice
1 tbsp sesame seeds, toasted

SWEET CHILLI DRESSING
2 tbsp dark soy sauce
1 tbsp sesame seed oil
1 tbsp vegetable oil
2 tbsp sherry vinegar or rice vinegar
1 tbsp sweet chilli sauce or 1 red chilli, deseeded and finely chopped
1 tbsp runny honey
15g fresh root ginger, peeled and finely grated

Oriental rice salad with mixed peppers & prawns

A colourful, **crunchy vegetable salad** tossed in a **tastebud-tingling, Oriental-style dressing,** this dish gives a great vitamin boost. Soy sauce is high in salt, so **no extra seasoning** is needed for the dressing.

1 First make the dressing. Put all the ingredients for the dressing into a large salad bowl and whisk together to combine.

2 Just before serving, add all the salad ingredients, apart from the sesame seeds. Toss everything together to coat in the dressing, then sprinkle the sesame seeds on top. Serve at once.

cook's tips
• Rice absorbs roughly 3 times its weight in water when you cook it, so you'll need to cook about 100g of long-grain rice to give you 300g cooked rice. Keep it chilled until ready to add to the salad.
• To save time, you could use a bag of fresh stir-fry vegetables. There are several varieties available, so just choose your favourite.

each serving provides
300kcals • 18g protein
8g fat of which 1g saturates
40.5g carbohydrate of which
15g sugars • 4g fibre
725mg sodium • 248g vegetables

300 kcals

quick & easy

3 portions fruit & veg

Smoked mackerel & beetroot salad

Smoked mackerel and **ruby red beetroot** are a mouth-watering combination, and cannellini beans and **fresh mixed salad leaves** add fibre and vitamin value to this appealing salad dressed with **tangy lime** and horseradish.

SERVES 4
PREPARATION TIME 20 minutes

200g fat-free fromage frais
grated zest and juice of 1 lime
2 tsp horseradish sauce,
**   or to taste**
¼ cucumber, diced
340g smoked mackerel fillets,
**   skinned and flaked**
2 x 400g cans cannellini beans,
**   drained and rinsed**
400g cooked beetroot,
**   peeled and cubed**
100g mixed salad leaves
**   (such as rocket, mizuna, baby**
**   spinach or lamb's lettuce)**
1 red onion, thinly sliced

TO GARNISH lime wedges

variations

• This salad could also be made with diced cooked chicken breast instead of the smoked mackerel.
• For a vegetarian salad, omit the mackerel and add 2 peeled, stoned and diced avocados. Sprinkle with toasted sesame seeds before serving.

1 Mix the fromage frais, lime zest, half the lime juice and horseradish in a bowl, then stir in the cucumber. Check the mackerel for any stray bones, then add it to the bowl with the cannellini beans. Mix lightly to combine the mackerel and beans with the dressing.

2 Toss the salad leaves with the onion and remaining lime juice, then spread on a large shallow serving platter, reserving a few pretty leaves for garnishing. Pile the mackerel and bean mixture on top, then scatter over the beetroot and reserved leaves. Garnish with lime wedges and serve immediately.

each serving provides 512kcals • 31g protein
28g fat of which 6g saturates • 34g carbohydrate of which 12.5g sugars
9g fibre • 736mg sodium • 181g vegetables

2 portions fruit & veg   **512** kcals   **fast food**

variations

• The hot smoked trout can be replaced by smoked mackerel fillets, or fillets from 6 grilled fresh sardines. Canned tuna or salmon, about a 200g drained can, would also be good.
• Quail's eggs make a pretty alternative if they're available – use 4 quail's eggs to replace the 2 hen's eggs and boil for 2–3 minutes. Cut in half.

each serving provides
304kcals • 18.5g protein
14g fat of which 3g saturates
28g carbohydrate of which
5g sugars • 4g fibre
805mg sodium
144g vegetables

1.5 portions fruit & veg   **304** kcals

Smoked trout
Niçoise
A variation on a colourful Provençal favourite, this **hearty salad** is just perfect for an early summer lunch, making the most of **baby new potatoes and asparagus** at the **peak of their season.**

SERVES 4
PREPARATION TIME 10 minutes
COOKING TIME about 30 minutes

600g baby new potatoes, scrubbed
225g asparagus spears, trimmed
   and cut into short lengths
225g cherry tomatoes, halved
40g stoned black olives
2 large eggs
175g Arbroath hot-smoked
   trout fillets, flaked
85g rocket

PARSLEY DRESSING
2 tbsp extra virgin olive oil
1 tbsp lime juice
1 tsp Dijon mustard
1 tbsp chopped fresh parsley

1 First make the dressing by shaking all the ingredients together in a screw-topped jar. Season to taste. Cook the potatoes in a saucepan of lightly salted, boiling water for about 15 minutes until just tender. Lift out the potatoes with a draining spoon, leave whole if they are small or slice thickly, then toss with the dressing and put aside.

2 Bring the pan of water back to the boil and add the asparagus, then reduce the heat and simmer for 4–5 minutes until tender. Remove with a draining spoon, refresh briefly under cold water and drain. (This cools the asparagus quickly and helps to retain the bright green colour.) Stir the asparagus into the potatoes with the tomatoes and olives.

3 Add the eggs to the pan of water and simmer for 7 minutes. Remove, run under cold water until cool enough to handle, then peel away the shells and cut the eggs into quarters.

4 Add the eggs, flaked trout and rocket to the potatoes and toss lightly to coat evenly in the dressing. Serve slightly warm or cold.

Tropical avocado & crab salad

A salad that is ideal for a **special summer occasion.** Crab meat is a good source of low-fat protein and goes beautifully with **juicy papaya and creamy avocado.** Serve with light rye bread.

SERVES 4
PREPARATION TIME 20 minutes

2 Little Gem lettuces, shredded
1 ripe papaya
1 large avocado, firm but ripe
400g can borlotti beans,
    drained and rinsed
200g fresh white crab meat

DRESSING
4 tbsp natural low-fat yoghurt
2 tbsp reduced-fat mayonnaise
grated zest and juice of 1 lime
15g fresh root ginger, peeled
    and finely chopped

1 First make the dressing. Whisk together the yoghurt, mayonnaise, lime zest and juice and ginger in a bowl, then set aside.

2 Spread the lettuce on a large serving platter. Cut the papaya in half lengthways and remove the seeds, then peel off the skin and slice the flesh. Arrange on the lettuce.

3 Cut the avocado in half lengthways, remove the stone, then peel and slice the flesh. Arrange on the platter, alternating the slices with the papaya.

4 Fork the borlotti beans and crab meat together. Spoon the mixture on top of the salad, then drizzle over the dressing and serve immediately.

3

4

cook's tip
• If the avocado is bought hard, place it in a paper bag and ripen at room temperature. Store ripe avocados in the fridge for up to 2 days.

variation
• If fresh crab meat is not available or hard to find, you can replace it with canned crab meat, drained or the same weight of peeled cooked prawns. You could also use the brown and white meat from 2 dressed crabs.

great summer treat

2 portions fruit & veg

297 kcals

each serving provides 297kcals • 16g protein
17g fat of which 3g saturates • 20g carbohydrate of which 10g sugars
7g fibre • 582mg sodium • 195g fruit and vegetables

Seafood tapas salad

A ready-to-use mixed seafood selection provides the base for this tasty and attractive salad, perfect for an **easy summer meal**. Seafood is an **excellent source of zinc,** often lacking in the diet and essential for a **healthy immune system.** Serve with crusty French bread.

SERVES 4
PREPARATION TIME 20 minutes
COOKING TIME 3 minutes

175g fine green beans
250g mixed prepared and cooked
  seafood (such as mussels,
  cockles, squid and prawns),
  thawed and drained if frozen
5 gherkins, finely chopped
12 pimiento-stuffed green olives
2 heads of chicory

TOMATO SALSA DRESSING
2½ tbsp olive oil
juice of 1 small lemon
½ small red onion, finely diced
225g large tomatoes, skinned
  and diced
½ small cucumber, finely diced
1–2 green chillies, deseeded
  and finely chopped
3 tbsp chopped fresh
  flat-leaf parsley

variation

• For a Thai seafood salad, make a mango salsa by mixing 2 thinly sliced shallots, 1 finely diced mango, ½ finely diced cucumber, 2 deseeded and finely chopped red chillies, 1 finely chopped 5cm piece of lemon grass, 1 tbsp Thai fish sauce, 2 tbsp lime juice, 1 tbsp rice vinegar, 2 tbsp chopped fresh coriander and a pinch of caster sugar. Toss with the seafood, 150g bean sprouts and 150g lightly cooked sliced mange-tout.

1 First make the dressing. Whisk together the oil and lemon juice in a bowl with a little freshly ground black pepper to taste. (No salt is needed for seasoning as both the gherkins and olives will add salt to this dish.) Add the red onion and stir to coat, then add the remaining dressing ingredients. Mix together and set aside.

2 Cook the beans in lightly salted boiling water for 3 minutes or until just tender. Drain in a sieve, then refresh under cold running water to prevent further cooking. Cut the beans in half, then put them in a large serving bowl with the seafood, gherkins and olives. Spoon over the salsa dressing and gently mix together.

3 Separate the chicory into individual leaves and tuck them around the edge of the salad. Serve straight away.

light lunch
1.5 portions fruit & veg
150 kcals

each serving provides

150kcals • 11g protein
10g fat of which 2g saturates
5g carbohydrate of which
4g sugars • 3g fibre
680mg sodium
134g vegetables

SERVES 4
PREPARATION TIME
  15–20 minutes
COOKING TIME 3 minutes

12 quail's eggs
2 tbsp bottled capers, rinsed
2 tbsp reduced-fat mayonnaise
1 tbsp low-fat natural yoghurt
100g watercress, tough
  stalks removed
1 small oak leaf lettuce, or
  2 Little Gem lettuces,
  separated into leaves
¼ cucumber, halved lengthways
  and thinly sliced
125g smoked salmon, sliced
2 tsp lime juice

each serving provides

180kcals • 18g protein
11g fat of which 3g saturates
3g carbohydrate of which 2g sugars
1g fibre • 678mg sodium
120g vegetables

1.5 portions fruit & veg
super salad
180 kcals

Egg mayonnaise salad with smoked salmon

This variation on the classic egg mayonnaise uses **little quail's eggs** with a creamy yet light mayonnaise and yoghurt dressing. It is combined with mixed leaves, cucumber and slivers of **succulent smoked salmon.** All you need to accompany the dish is some brown or wholemeal bread.

1 Put the eggs into a saucepan of cold water. Bring to the boil and cook for 3 minutes. Lift out of the pan using a draining spoon and plunge into cold water to cool. Peel off the shells and cut each egg in half.

2 For the dressing, put the capers in a small bowl and mix with the mayonnaise and yoghurt.

3 Arrange the watercress, lettuce leaves and sliced cucumber on a serving plate or in a large shallow salad bowl. Scatter over the eggs, then drizzle with the dressing.

4 Sprinkle the smoked salmon with the lime juice, grind over a little black pepper, then scatter the salmon over the salad.

variations

• If preferred, regular hen's eggs can be used. Cook in a pan of simmering water for 7 minutes so the yolks will be set but still lightly creamy. Plunge into cold water and leave to cool, then crack the shells, peel and roughly chop. Gently stir the chopped eggs into the mayonnaise dressing, then pile on top of the salad leaves.

• Instead of capers, stir 1 very finely chopped shallot and 6 roughly chopped stoned black olives into the egg mayonnaise. Trim the fat off 75g prosciutto, cut the meat into thin strips and arrange these over the salad, instead of the salmon.

variations
• Instead of salmon use mackerel fillets, which are also rich in omega-3 fatty acids, or skinless chicken breast fillets. For chicken, increase the cooking time to 20–25 minutes.
• Canned water chestnuts, drained and sliced, would provide an alternative crunchy texture in place of the bean sprouts.

each serving provides
340kcals • 31g protein
19g fat of which 3g saturates
8.5g carbohydrate of which 7g sugars
2g fibre • 225mg sodium
169g vegetables

heart healthy | **340** kcals | **2** portions fruit & veg

Warm teriyaki salmon salad

The simple technique of cooking salmon in a foil parcel captures all the succulent juices of the fish which, together with the teriyaki baste, makes a superb dressing for a mixed leaf and bean sprout salad. The fat in oily fish such as salmon contains omega-3 fatty acids, which have been shown to boost heart health. Serve with warm, crusty bread.

SERVES 4
PREPARATION TIME 10 minutes
COOKING TIME 15–20 minutes

4 tsp teriyaki marinade
4 tsp vegetable oil
2 tsp Chinese rice wine vinegar
4 skinless, boneless salmon steaks, about 140g each
2 large red peppers, deseeded and thinly sliced
100g baby spinach leaves
85g watercress, thick stalks removed
50g bean sprouts

1 Preheat the oven to 200°C/gas 6. Cut out 4 pieces of foil, each measuring about 30 x 25cm. Mix together the teriyaki marinade, oil and vinegar in a small bowl.

2 Place 1 salmon steak on each piece of foil. Top each steak with one quarter of the pepper slices and spoon over one quarter of the teriyaki mixture. Bring 2 sides of the foil together to make loose parcels, then crimp the edges to seal so that none of the juices can escape.

3 Place the foil parcels on a baking sheet and bake for 15–20 minutes. To test if the salmon is cooked, carefully open 1 of the parcels and cut into the centre of the salmon. The flesh should be pale pink and flake easily.

4 While the salmon is cooking, toss together the spinach, watercress and bean sprouts and divide evenly among 4 plates.

5 Top each salad with a salmon steak and pepper strips, then drizzle over the cooking juices and serve at once.

SERVES 4
PREPARATION TIME 25 minutes
COOKING TIME 6–10 minutes

- 4 large tomatoes
- 1 cucumber, halved, deseeded and diced
- 6 spring onions, chopped
- 2 Little Gem lettuces
- 40g fresh flat-leaf parsley, chopped
- 15g fresh mint, chopped
- 2 tbsp bottled capers, rinsed
- 12 stoned black olives, sliced
- 4 large wholemeal pitta breads
- 4 fresh tuna steaks, about 125g each

DRESSING

- 4 tbsp extra virgin olive oil
- 2 garlic cloves, crushed
- 2 large lemons, finely grated zest and 6 tbsp juice
- ¼ tsp harissa paste

each serving provides

589kcals • 42g protein
20g fat of which 3.5g saturates
64g carbohydrate of which
10g sugars • 9g fibre
722mg sodium
280g vegetables

3.5 portions fruit & veg

589 kcals

Tunisian fattoush with tuna

Versions of this fresh-tasting, crunchy vegetable and bread salad are popular throughout the Middle East, where it is often served as an accompaniment to roast lamb. Here, it is transformed into a filling meal with grilled, fresh tuna steaks, which have a tender, meat-like texture.

1 First prepare the salad dressing. Put the olive oil, garlic, lemon zest and juice and harissa paste in a large serving bowl and whisk together.

2 Cut the tomatoes in half, scoop out and discard the seeds and chop the flesh, then add to the bowl with the dressing. Add the cucumber and spring onions.

3 Cut the lettuces in half lengthways and shred the leaves. Add to the salad bowl with the chopped herbs, capers and olives, toss to mix, then set aside. Preheat the grill to medium.

4 Place the pitta breads under the grill and toast for about 1–2 minutes on each side until crisp and puffed up. Allow to cool slightly, then tear into bite-sized pieces and add to the salad.

5 Sprinkle the tuna steaks with a little freshly ground black pepper. Place on the grill rack and cook for 2–3 minutes. Turn the steaks over and cook for a further 2–3 minutes until just tender.

6 As soon as the tuna is cool enough to handle, flake it into the salad in large pieces. Gently toss everything together and serve immediately.

Red cabbage salad with Edam & walnuts

This crunchy, colourful winter salad provides an excellent nutritional mix. The vegetables and apples are rich in vitamin C and fibre, Edam cheese adds protein and calcium, and walnuts contain essential fatty acids. Serve with oatcakes, if liked.

SERVES 4 Ⓥ
PREPARATION TIME 15–20 minutes
COOKING TIME 7 minutes

1 small celeriac
juice of ½ lemon
1 small red cabbage
1 red onion, thinly sliced
4 tbsp chopped walnuts
125g Edam cheese
1 crisp red dessert apple

DRESSING
2 tbsp walnut oil
2 tbsp vegetable oil
2 tsp balsamic vinegar

1 Peel the celeriac, quarter, then halve each quarter again lengthways. Shred, using the grating disc of a food processor, or finely slice using a sharp knife. Put into a saucepan of boiling water with half the lemon juice, cook for 5 minutes until tender, then drain well and put into a large bowl.

2 Halve the red cabbage, cut out the core, then cut into quarters. Shred as before, then add to the celeriac together with the onion.

3 In a screw-topped jar, shake together the ingredients for the dressing and season to taste. Spoon two thirds of the dressing over the celeriac, cabbage and onion and toss lightly. Set aside. (The salad can be prepared ahead up to this step and kept covered in the fridge for up to 4 hours.)

4 Heat a small non-stick pan over a moderate heat, dry-fry the walnuts for 2 minutes, stirring, then take off the heat and reserve. Cut the Edam into matchsticks. Core the apple, cut it into thin slices, then put on a plate and sprinkle with the rest of the lemon juice to prevent it discolouring.

5 Just before serving, toss the Edam, apple slices and toasted walnuts into the salad. Spoon over the rest of the dressing, toss and serve immediately.

each serving provides 341kcals • 13g protein • 27g fat of which 7g saturates
13g carbohydrate of which 11g sugars • 8g fibre • 414mg sodium • 280g fruit and vegetables

341 kcals   **3.5** portions fruit & veg

250g bulghur wheat
450g ripe but firm tomatoes, diced
1 red onion, finely chopped
50g stoned black olives, halved
   (optional)
1 green or red chilli, deseeded
   and diced (optional)
4 tbsp chopped fresh herbs (such
   as mint, basil and/or coriander)
1 garlic clove, crushed
½ tsp caster sugar
2 tbsp extra virgin olive oil
2 oranges
200g feta cheese, diced
25g toasted flaked almonds

TO SERVE 200g cos lettuce,
   chard and young spinach leaves

each serving provides

508kcals • 18g protein
21g fat of which 8g saturates
64g carbohydrate of which
15g sugars • 4g fibre
740mg sodium • 230g fruit
and vegetables

prepare ahead | 2.5 portions fruit & veg | 508 kcals

Feta tabbouleh with orange

A fabulous main meal salad based on bulghur wheat, generously flavoured with fresh herbs. It is best prepared ahead to give time for all the wonderful flavours to mingle.

1 Put the bulghur wheat in a bowl, pour over enough boiling water to cover and stir well. Leave to soak for 20–30 minutes.

2 Meanwhile, combine the tomatoes, onion, olives, chilli if using, herbs, garlic and sugar in a large serving bowl and stir in the olive oil.

3 Using a zester, remove the zest from 1 orange in fine shreds and add them to the tomato mixture. Slice the top and bottom off both oranges, cut off all the peel and pith, then halve and chop the fruit, removing the pips and any large pieces of membrane from the middle. Add the oranges to the tomato mixture with any juice on the board.

4 Drain the bulghur wheat in a sieve, pressing out excess water, then add it to the tomato mixture. Cool, then cover and chill in the fridge for at least 30 minutes.

5 Just before serving, stir the feta cheese and almonds into the tabbouleh. Season to taste. Serve with salad leaves, crisp enough to use as scoops or large enough to wrap around forkfuls of tabbouleh.

variations

• Omit the feta cheese and add 2 small diced avocados to the salad.
• Instead of almonds, use chopped walnuts or toasted pine nuts.
• Add some chopped dried apricots.

Pear & Roquefort salad with poppy seed dressing

Pears and creamy blue cheese are natural partners in this light and easy salad. Poppy seeds and crunchy toasted pecans add extra interest and mineral value.

SERVES 4 V
PREPARATION TIME 20 minutes

- **1 celery stick**
- **3 ripe dessert pears (preferably red or pink-flushed)**
- **1 head of chicory, separated into leaves**
- **50g lamb's lettuce**
- **25g pecan nuts (or walnuts), lightly toasted**
- **100g Roquefort cheese**
- **4 slices walnut bread, toasted**

POPPY SEED DRESSING
- **2 tbsp walnut oil**
- **1 tbsp sherry or balsamic vinegar**
- **1 tsp Dijon mustard**
- **1 tsp clear honey**
- **2 tsp poppy seeds**

1 First make the dressing by placing all the ingredients in a screw-topped jar and shaking until well combined. As the Roquefort is quite salty, there is no need to add any salt.

2 Cut the celery into 5cm lengths, then slice again lengthways into fine strips.

3 Core and thinly slice the pears lengthways and place in a large bowl with the chicory leaves, lamb's lettuce, pecan nuts and celery. Add the dressing and toss well to coat evenly. Crumble the Roquefort over the salad.

4 Place a slice of the toasted walnut bread on each plate and pile the salad evenly over the top. Serve immediately.

variations

- Other blue cheeses would also work well, such as Stilton or Danish Blue. For a lower-fat alternative, try Feta cheese.
- For a more tropical flavour, you could replace the pears with 2 sliced mangoes.
- For a lighter-flavoured dressing, replace half the walnut oil with a light olive or sunflower oil.

super snack · **1.5** portions fruit & veg · **372** kcals

each serving provides 372kcals • 11g protein 24g fat of which 7g saturates • 31g carbohydrate of which 13g sugars 5g fibre • 655mg sodium • 148g fruit and vegetables

SERVES 4 V
PREPARATION TIME 20 minutes

- **1 orange, finely grated zest and 4 tbsp juice**
- **500g cottage cheese**
- **2 red dessert apples**
- **200g blueberries**
- **16 ready-to-eat dried apricots, finely chopped**
- **2 celery sticks, finely chopped**
- **150g mixed salad leaves**
- **2 kiwi fruit, peeled and sliced**
- **2 nectarines, stoned and sliced**
- **4 tsp sesame seeds, toasted (optional)**

Summer fruity cottage cheese salad

This salad tastes as great as it looks. With its colourful mix of fruit, it is packed with vitamins and fibre and transforms plain cottage cheese into an exciting salad. Serve with sesame-flavoured rice cakes for a low-fat accompaniment.

1 Mix the orange zest into the cottage cheese. Core and dice the apples and mix with the blueberries, apricots and celery in a large bowl.

2 Divide the salad leaves onto 4 serving plates. Top each mound of leaves with equal portions of kiwi fruit and nectarines and sprinkle each one with 1 tbsp orange juice.

3 Share out the cottage cheese and fruit mixture onto the plates and sprinkle with sesame seeds.

variations

• The variations on this are only limited by your imagination – cherries, grapes, mangoes, orange segments, peaches, raspberries, strawberries and dried fruits such as figs, raisins and sultanas, are all suitable.
• If some of the fresh fruits are not in season, use fruits canned in juice, such as pineapple chunks, peach slices or apricots to make up a good variety.

each serving provides

271kcals • 19g protein • 6g fat of which 3g saturates
37g carbohydrate of which 37g sugars • 6g fibre
395mg sodium • 287g fruit and vegetables

271 kcals

sweet treat

3.5 portions fruit & veg

Goat's cheese salad with watermelon

Juicy watermelon makes the perfect partner to tangy goat's cheese in this easy-to-assemble pasta salad. Flavour and texture are provided by crunchy endive, peppery rocket and toasted pine nuts, which combine to give a Mediterranean flair.

SERVES 4
PREPARATION TIME 25 minutes
COOKING TIME 11–13 minutes

200g wholewheat penne
  (pasta quills)
150g medium-fat, firm goat's cheese
½ small watermelon, cubed
  and seeded
100g rocket
50g pine nuts, toasted
2 small heads of chicory
4 slices prosciutto, trimmed of fat
  and cut into strips

DRESSING
2½ tbsp mild olive oil
1 tbsp lime juice
1 tbsp balsamic vinegar
1 tbsp chopped fresh mint

variations

• Feta cheese may be used instead of goat's cheese. Buy in a block rather than ready-cubed and reduce the salt content slightly, by soaking in a bowl of cold water for 2–3 minutes, then draining. Crumble or cut into small cubes.
• Instead of the watermelon, try cubed honeydew or Charentais melon or diced ripe mango. Add the squeezed juice of 2 tbsp freshly grated ginger to the dressing.

1 Cook the pasta in boiling water for 11–13 minutes or according to the pack instructions, until al dente. Drain and rinse under cold running water, then drain thoroughly and set aside to cool.

2 Put all the ingredients for the dressing in a screw-topped jar and shake together well. Season to taste with freshly ground black pepper. Both the cheese and prosciutto are quite salty, so no extra salt should be needed.

3 Crumble the cheese into the cooled pasta and add the watermelon. Pour over the dressing and lightly toss together, then add the rocket and pine nuts.

4 Separate the chicory into individual leaves and arrange on a serving platter or shallow salad bowl. Arrange the salad on top and scatter over the prosciutto.

each serving provides

474kcals • 16g protein
24g fat of which 6g saturates
52g carbohydrate of which
20g sugars • 5.5g fibre
452mg sodium • 268g fruit
and vegetables

3 portions fruit & veg
474 kcals
summer special

variations

• In place of the Brie you could use the same weight of a creamy blue cheese, like Dolcelatte, for the crostini.
• If any of these salad leaves are not available, replace them with other salad leaves, such as frisée, lollo rosso or lamb's lettuce.
• Blueberries also make a great addition to salads. Use in place of the redcurrants.

Mixed leaf salad with peaches & Brie crostini

A delicious way to enjoy the delights of summer, with rust-red salad leaves, redcurrants and peaches all bursting with vitamin C. The addition of crostini with creamy Brie makes this a satisfying salad to serve as a light lunch.

SERVES 4 Ⓥ
PREPARATION TIME 15 minutes
COOKING TIME 6 minutes

1 small white bread baton
150g ripe Brie, thinly sliced
1 large radicchio, separated into leaves
50g rocket
50g watercress
8 radishes, sliced
3 large ripe peaches, stoned and cut into thick slices
125g redcurrants
2 tbsp olive oil
2 tsp balsamic vinegar
25g hazelnuts, toasted and roughly chopped

1 Preheat the grill. Trim the ends from the bread and cut into 12 even slices. Lightly toast on both sides under the grill. Top each toast with a thin slice of the Brie and replace under the grill until the cheese has melted and is just bubbling. Set aside.

2 Combine the salad leaves in a large salad bowl. Add the radishes, peaches and about 100g of the redcurrants.

3 Put the remaining redcurrants in a small bowl, add the oil and using a fork, lightly crush the redcurrants. Stir in the vinegar and season to taste.

4 Pour the dressing over the salad and toss together well to mix. Scatter over the toasted hazelnuts and arrange the Brie crostini on top. Serve immediately.

each serving provides 418kcals • 16g protein 22g fat of which 8g saturates • 42g carbohydrate of which 13g sugars • 5g fibre • 559mg sodium • 216g fruit and vegetables

2.5 portions fruit & veg

418 kcals

Vietnamese tofu & noodle salad

An exciting layered salad combining **crisp vegetables** flavoured with fresh herbs, noodles and **marinated grilled tofu.** The tofu is best prepared several hours in advance as longer marinating will enhance the flavour.

SERVES 4
PREPARATION TIME 45 minutes, plus at least 30 minutes marinating
COOKING TIME 15 minutes

2 x 250g packs firm tofu, drained
250g bean sprouts
200g Chinese mustard greens, Chinese leaves or pak choi, finely shredded
15g fresh coriander, roughly chopped
15g fresh basil, roughly chopped
juice of 2 limes (use zest for the marinade)
2 tsp caster sugar
200g mange-tout
250g medium rice noodles
2 tbsp olive oil
100g unsalted peanuts, chopped
½ cucumber, halved lengthways and cut into sticks

MARINADE
2 green chillies, deseeded and finely diced
2 garlic cloves, thinly sliced
6 spring onions, thinly sliced
4 tbsp light soy sauce
grated zest of 2 limes
1 tsp toasted sesame oil
4 tbsp dry sherry

1 Slice the blocks of tofu in half horizontally and lay flat in a non-metallic, heatproof dish. Mix together all the ingredients for the marinade and sprinkle evenly over the tofu. Turn the slices so that both sides are coated, then cover and leave to marinate for at least 30 minutes.

2 Meanwhile, combine the bean sprouts, shredded greens, coriander and basil in a large, deep serving dish. Sprinkle with the lime juice and half the sugar. Add the mange-tout to a saucepan of boiling water. Bring back to the boil and cook for just 1 minute, then drain in a colander and refresh under cold running water. Scatter over the bean sprout mixture.

3 Refill the saucepan with boiling water and add the noodles. Bring back to the boil, then remove from the heat, cover and leave to stand for 4 minutes or until softened. Drain in a colander and rinse under cold running water, then tip them back into the pan.

4 Preheat a hot grill. Drain the marinade from the tofu onto the noodles, toss and set aside. Leave the tofu lying flat in the dish.

5 Sprinkle half the oil over the tofu, then grill for 4–6 minutes until beginning to brown and form a skin on the surface. Use a large slice to turn the pieces of tofu over. Sprinkle with the remaining sugar and oil and grill for a further 4 minutes. Sprinkle the nuts over the tofu and grill for a final 2 minutes or until the nuts are browned.

6 Tip the noodles on top of the bean sprout mixture to make a separate layer. Slice the tofu into 2cm thick fingers and arrange on top of the salad with the cucumber sticks and toasted nuts. Serve immediately while the tofu is warm.

variation
• Instead of tofu, use thin fillets of turkey breast or lean steak. Boil the marinade for 2–3 minutes in a small bowl in the microwave before adding it to the noodles.

prepare ahead

2.5 portions fruit & veg

608 kcals

each serving provides 608kcals • 26g protein • 24g fat of which 4g saturates 67g carbohydrate of which 11g sugars • 5g fibre • 28mg sodium • 213g vegetables

SERVES 4 Ⓥ

PREPARATION TIME 25 minutes,
plus about 1 hour standing

175g couscous
300ml vegetable stock, hot
2 oranges
400g can chickpeas, drained
   and rinsed
125g stoned dates, roughly
   chopped
50g shelled pistachios,
   roughly chopped
3 tbsp chopped fresh mint

CITRUS DRESSING
½ tsp grated orange zest
2 tbsp extra virgin olive oil
2 tbsp lemon juice
1 tsp paprika

Couscous salad with oranges & dates

Couscous makes **a brilliant base for a quick salad,** as it only needs a brief soaking in hot stock (or water). Here it is combined with **chickpeas, dates, oranges and pistachios** for a **Middle Eastern-style vegetarian dish.**

1 Put the couscous into a large bowl, pour over the hot vegetable stock and set aside for 10 minutes until all the stock is absorbed.

2 Meanwhile, put the grated orange zest into a bowl, add the rest of the dressing ingredients and whisk together. Season to taste.

3 Fluff the couscous with a fork and drizzle over the dressing while still warm.

4 Cut the pith away from the oranges, then cut out the segments between the membranes, placing the fruit on a plate to catch all the juices. Cut each segment in half.

5 Stir the oranges, their juice, the chickpeas, dates, pistachios and 2 tbsp of the mint into the couscous. Season to taste, then leave to stand at room temperature for at least 1 hour to allow the flavours to mingle. Scatter over the remaining mint just before serving.

Hummus salad

Homemade hummus **only takes a few moments** to whizz together and makes a perfect light lunch, served simply with pitta. But for a balanced meal, turn it into this more **substantial salad** with the addition of **crisp salad vegetables.**

SERVES 4 Ⓥ
PREPARATION TIME 25 minutes

HUMMUS
2 x 400g cans chickpeas
3 tbsp tahini (sesame seed paste)
2 tbsp olive oil
2 tbsp lemon juice
2 large garlic cloves, crushed
2 tbsp chopped fresh parsley, coriander or mint

SALAD
½ cucumber, pared into ribbons with a vegetable peeler
2 carrots, peeled and pared into ribbons (or sliced into fine strips)
1 red onion, thinly sliced
85g radishes, sliced
85g mixed salad leaves (such as rocket, mizuna and watercress)
2 tbsp seasoned rice vinegar
50g hazelnuts, toasted and chopped

TO SERVE lemon wedges (optional), 4 sesame pitta breads (or Greek daktyla), warmed

1 Reserve 3 tbsp of the liquid from 1 can of chickpeas, then drain and rinse all the chickpeas and put them into a blender or food processor with the reserved liquid. Add the tahini, olive oil, lemon juice, garlic and herbs. Process for about 30 seconds or until well mixed. Season to taste.

2 Put the cucumber, carrots, red onion, radish and salad leaves into a large salad bowl. Sprinkle with the rice vinegar and hazelnuts and toss together.

3 Heap the salad onto individual plates and spoon the hummus on top. Serve with lemon wedges to squeeze over, if liked, and warmed pitta bread.

cook's tips
• For speed, you can use a ready-made hummus – choose a reduced-fat version if you can.
• Tahini is widely sold in health food stores if you can't find it at the supermarket.

variation
• If you're not keen on chickpeas, replace them with 125g crumbled Cheshire or Wensleydale cheese. Or for a non-vegetarian version, add 225g cooked chicken pieces.

each serving provides
395kcals • 11g protein
14g fat of which 2g saturates
59g carbohydrate of which
27g sugars • 6g fibre
200mg sodium • 114g fruit and vegetables

395 kcals
1 portion fruit & veg
prepare ahead

each serving provides
576kcals • 21g protein • 26g fat
of which 3g saturates • 69g carbohydrate
of which 10g sugars • 11g fibre
613mg sodium • 167g vegetables

576 kcals
2 portions fruit & veg
easily doubled

Pizzas, sandwiches & burgers

Filled, topped, wrapped and sandwiched with scrumptious meat, fish and vegetables, these popular and convenient family favourites contain less fat and salt than most ready-made or take-away versions. Pizzas are topped with extra vegetables, sandwiches are packed out with salad ingredients and spread with tasty relishes, and burgers use lean meat or are made with high-fibre pulses. All make perfect, no-fuss balanced dishes for casual eating, and are the meals children will love best.

SERVES 4

PREPARATION TIME 30 minutes,
 plus about 1 hour rising

COOKING TIME 25–30 minutes

PIZZA DOUGH

350g strong white bread flour

**1 sachet fast-action dried yeast,
 about 6g**

¼ tsp salt

2 tbsp olive oil

about 200ml tepid water

TOPPINGS

150g baby leeks, trimmed and sliced

125g mushrooms, sliced

1 tbsp white wine vinegar

**2 roasted red peppers, drained
 and thickly sliced**

**100g canned artichokes, drained
 and quartered**

150ml passata

1 garlic clove, finely chopped

1 tbsp olive and anchovy tapenade

50g Parma ham, thinly sliced

25g stoned black olives, sliced

50g sun-blush tomatoes, chopped

50g mozzarella cheese, grated

TO GARNISH fresh oregano

Four seasons party pizza

This **tasty pizza** includes a variety of toppings to suit every taste. It is lower in fat and salt than ready-made pizzas, yet has just as much flavour. Don't be put off by the long ingredients list, it is **easy and fun to make.** Serve with a **big green salad.**

1 Mix together the flour, yeast and salt in a large bowl. Make a well in the centre and stir in the olive oil with enough of the tepid water to make a smooth dough. Turn the dough out onto a lightly floured surface and knead for about 5 minutes until smooth and elastic. Place the dough back in the rinsed out and lightly oiled bowl, then cover with a damp tea towel or oiled cling film and leave in a warm place for 1 hour or until it has doubled in size.

2 Meanwhile, preheat the oven to 200°C/gas 6 and prepare the toppings. Put the leeks in a pan with the mushrooms and wine vinegar, cover and cook on a high heat for 3–4 minutes, shaking the pan occasionally, until softened. Mix the peppers with the artichokes. Mix the garlic into the passata.

3 Turn out the risen dough onto the lightly floured surface and knock it back, knead lightly, then roll out or press out with your knuckles to a 30–32cm round on a lightly greased baking sheet.

4 Spread the passata mixture evenly over the pizza base, then pile the leeks and mushrooms over one quarter of the dough, the peppers and artichokes over a second quarter. Over a third quarter, dot the tapenade and scrunch the Parma ham on top. Spread the olives and tomatoes over the last quarter. Sprinkle over the cheese.

5 Bake the pizza for 25–30 minutes until golden around the edges and lightly browned on top. Scatter over oregano leaves and serve warm, cut into slices.

Tray bake
pizza

Everyone loves pizza and, made as a tray bake, it can easily be **cut into squares** and served as party food. This recipe uses a sunflower seed bread mix for a **lovely nutty flavour and texture.**

SERVES 6
PREPARATION TIME 50 minutes
COOKING TIME 25 minutes

**500g sunflower seed bread mix
(or other variety)**
1 tbsp finely chopped fresh rosemary
50g can anchovies in oil, drained
3 tbsp semi-skimmed milk
150ml passata
200g mushrooms, sliced
**2 x 200g cans tuna in spring
water, drained**
200g cherry tomatoes, quartered
2 tbsp bottled capers, rinsed
150g ricotta cheese
1 tbsp olive oil
4 tbsp roughly shredded fresh basil

variations
• If your children do not like the strong flavours of anchovies and capers, you can replace them with diced red peppers, sweetcorn or cubed smoked ham.
• If using a plain bread mix, you could add a handful of sunflower, pumpkin or sesame seeds to the dough.

1 Preheat the oven to 200°C/gas 6. In a large bowl, combine the bread mix with the rosemary, then make up the dough and knead following the pack instructions. Allow the dough to rest for about 5 minutes.

2 Using a rolling pin, roll out the dough to approximately fit a shallow roasting tin that measures about 40 x 27cm. Push the dough into the corners to make a neat fit. Cover lightly with a clean tea towel and set aside in a warm place while preparing the topping.

3 Place the anchovies in a small bowl and cover with the milk. Allow to soak for 5 minutes, then drain and finely chop. (This soaking will remove the excess salt from the anchovies.)

4 Spread the passata all over the pizza base, right up to the edges. Scatter over the sliced mushrooms, then flake over the tuna fish. Dot the tomato pieces, capers and chopped anchovies all over. Using a teaspoon, add little mounds of ricotta over the top, then drizzle evenly with the olive oil.

5 Bake for 25 minutes or until well risen with a golden crust around the edge. Transfer to a wire rack to cool slightly, then cut into 6 pieces. Scatter over the basil and serve warm.

variation
• Strong wholemeal flour or Granary flour can be used for the dough instead of white, but will produce a heavier texture, so they are better mixed half-and-half with white flour. Alternatively you could use a bread mix and make up the dough following the pack instructions.

perfect pizza | **545 kcals** | **2.5 portions fruit & veg**

each serving provides
545kcals • 20g protein
20g fat of which 5g saturates
76g carbohydrate of which
10g sugars • 6g fibre
982mg sodium • 227g vegetables

each serving provides
452kcals • 29g protein
8g fat of which 2g saturates • 64g carbohydrate of which
2.5g sugars • 4g fibre • 763mg sodium • 138g vegetables

1.5 portions fruit & veg

452 kcals

Potato pizza with chicken & rocket

For anyone who enjoys pizza, this **rustic version** with its wafer-thin sliced potato topping, provides a lower-fat alternative. Scattered with **pancetta, ready-cooked chicken and peppery rocket leaves,** these pizzas are satisfying to eat and quick to prepare using ready-made pizza bases. Serve with a **cherry tomato salad.**

SERVES 4 (makes 2)
PREPARATION TIME 30 minutes
COOKING TIME 15 minutes

500g small new potatoes, scrubbed
2 tbsp olive oil
2 red onions, halved and very
  finely sliced
100g pancetta, diced
175g button mushrooms, sliced
1 tbsp fresh rosemary leaves
2 ready-made pizza bases,
  each about 22cm across
6 tbsp semi-skimmed milk

TO SERVE 250g cooked, skinless chicken breast (plain or smoked), shredded, 85g rocket, 25g fresh Parmesan

variations
• For a vegetarian version, omit the chicken and pancetta and top the cooked pizzas with rocket leaves, sliced, hard-boiled egg and thin slices of sun-dried tomato. Drizzle each pizza with ½ tbsp of the oil from the sun-dried tomatoes. Grate Italian-style hard cheese suitable for vegetarians (see page 9) over the tops.
• Flaked drained canned salmon is good with watercress instead of chicken and rocket. Drizzle the can juices from the salmon over the pizzas.

1 Using a mandolin, a fine slicing disc in a food processor, or a very sharp knife, cut the potatoes into wafer-thin slices. Cook in a large saucepan of lightly salted boiling water for 1–2 minutes until just tender, then drain. Preheat the oven to 220°C/gas 7.

2 Heat the oil in the pan and lightly fry the onions with the pancetta for 2–3 minutes until softened, then add the mushrooms and cook for a further 2 minutes. Add the potatoes and rosemary leaves, season with freshly ground black pepper and gently toss, without breaking up the slices.

3 Place the pizza bases on 2 lightly greased baking sheets, then spread the potato mixture evenly over the tops. Trickle the milk over the topping of both pizzas. Bake for 15 minutes until the potatoes are tender and golden.

4 Remove the pizzas from the oven, cut them into quarters and place two quarters on each plate. Equally divide the chicken among the pieces of pizza, then scatter over the rocket. Using a swivel-blade vegetable peeler, peel shavings of Parmesan over each piece. Serve at once.

variation
• For vegetarian calzone, spread each dough round first with a quarter of the ricotta cheese, then with 2 tbsp tomato passata. Top with lightly fried, sliced button mushrooms and sliced, cooked and peeled red peppers. Sprinkle with the Parmesan and fresh thyme leaves. Fold, seal and bake as in the recipe.

1.5 portions fruit & veg   **519** kcals

each serving provides
519kcals • 40g protein
16g fat of which 7.5g saturates
54g carbohydrate of which 4g sugars
5g fibre • 632mg sodium
120g vegetables

1.5 portions fruit & veg   **607** kcals   country fare

each serving provides 607kcals • 37g protein • 21.5g fat of which 5.5g saturates • 71g carbohydrate of which 10g sugars • 5g fibre 572mg sodium • 140g vegetables

Chicken & spinach calzone

Here's an Italian version of a Cornish pasty, using pizza dough instead of pastry. The filling is ready-cooked roast chicken with spinach, red peppers and creamy ricotta cheese. Serve with a side salad.

SERVES 4
PREPARATION TIME 30 minutes, plus 15 minutes rising
COOKING TIME 15 minutes

1 pack pizza base mix, about 280g
350g frozen spinach, thawed in a sieve
200g ricotta cheese
50g Parmesan, freshly grated
2 red peppers in brine, drained and chopped
6 spring onions, finely chopped
2 tbsp shredded fresh basil leaves
freshly grated nutmeg, to taste
200g skinless, boneless roast chicken, finely shredded
1 egg, beaten

1 Make up the pizza dough according to the pack instructions. Knead the dough briefly on a lightly floured work surface until smooth, then put into a lightly oiled bowl and cover with a clean tea towel. Leave to rise for about 15 minutes until doubled in size.

2 Meanwhile, prepare the filling. Use your hands to squeeze all excess water from the spinach. Put the spinach in a bowl and mix in the ricotta, Parmesan, peppers, spring onions and basil. Season to taste with nutmeg, salt and freshly ground black pepper. Preheat the oven to 220°C/gas 7.

3 Knock back the risen dough and cut it into 4 equal pieces. Roll out each piece on a lightly floured surface to a 20cm round. Spread one quarter of the spinach mixture over half of each dough round, taking it to about 2.5cm from the edge. Pile the chicken on top.

4 Brush the edge of each dough round with beaten egg, then fold over the untopped half to make a half-moon shape. Crimp the edges to seal tightly.

5 Place on a lightly oiled large baking sheet. Brush with beaten egg and bake for about 15 minutes until puffed and golden brown. Serve hot.

Ciabatta with feta & roasted vegetables

A feast of colourful vegetables makes a superb topping for a pizza-style ciabatta. The bread soaks up the **aromatic roasting juices** so that it is deliciously moist with a crunchy crust. If you want to boost your vegetable intake even more, serve it with a **leafy herb salad.**

SERVES 4 (makes 8) V
PREPARATION TIME 30 minutes
COOKING TIME 25–30 minutes

1 large part-baked ciabatta
4 tomatoes, diced
3 tbsp tomato purée
2 garlic cloves, crushed
1 tbsp finely chopped fresh rosemary
1 tsp fennel seeds
3 tbsp olive oil
1 aubergine, thinly sliced
1 tbsp cider vinegar
1 tsp sugar
6 spring onions, halved widthways
  and cut into strips
1 red pepper, deseeded and cut
  into fine strips
1 yellow pepper, deseeded and
  cut into fine strips
pinch of dried chilli flakes (optional)
100g feta cheese, finely crumbled

1 Heat the oven to 240°C/gas 9. Slice the ciabatta in half horizontally. Trim a fine sliver off the rounded top so that it sits steadily when turned cut-side up.

2 Mix the tomatoes, tomato purée and half the crushed garlic in a large bowl. Spread this mixture over the cut ciabatta and set aside on a board. In the same bowl, mix the remaining garlic, rosemary, fennel seeds and olive oil.

3 Lay the aubergine slices on a baking sheet and brush sparingly with some of the herb oil. Turn and brush the second sides sparingly – this uses about a third of the oil. Bake for 3 minutes until the slices are just beginning to soften. Turn the aubergines and bake for a further 3 minutes. Remove from the oven and reduce the temperature to 220°C/gas 7.

4 Meanwhile, stir the cider vinegar and sugar into the remaining oil. Add the spring onions, red and yellow pepper strips, chilli flakes, if using, and some pepper to season. Mix well.

5 Top the ciabatta with half the mixed peppers mixture, cover with overlapping aubergine slices, then pile the remaining pepper mixture on top, drizzling over all the herb oil in the bowl.

6 Place the ciabatta on the same baking sheet that was used for roasting the aubergine slices and bake for 15 minutes.

7 Top with the feta, pressing it down lightly with a fork, and bake for a further 10–15 minutes until the feta is golden and the vegetables are well browned. Cut each piece of ciabatta into 4 and serve 2 pieces per portion.

each serving provides 408kcals • 15g protein 17g fat of which 5g saturates • 52g carbohydrate of which 14g sugars • 6g fibre • 790mg sodium • 255g vegetables

408 kcals

3 portions fruit & veg

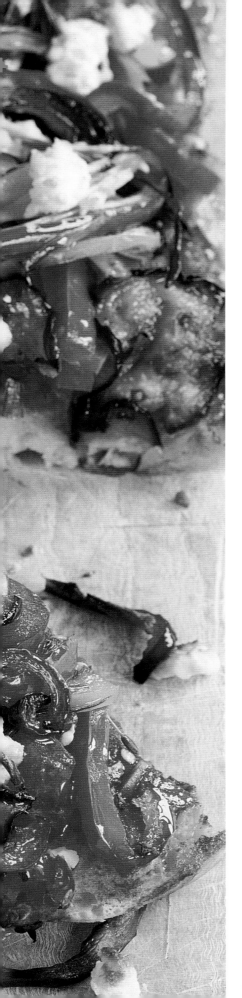

Pitta pizzettes

Made mainly from storecupboard ingredients, these mini pizzas are incredibly quick and easy to prepare. Topped with tasty ham, luscious pineapple and sweet corn kernels, they make a tasty snack and are much lower in salt than most bought pizzas.

SERVES 4
PREPARATION TIME 15 minutes
COOKING TIME 15 minutes

4 wholemeal or sesame pittas
3 tbsp sun-dried tomato purée
1 tsp olive oil
1 tbsp chopped fresh oregano,
   or 1 tsp dried
125g lean sliced ham, cut into
   thin strips
425g can chopped pineapple
   in fruit juice, drained
200g frozen sweetcorn, thawed
125g reduced-fat mozzarella cheese,
   coarsely grated

1 Preheat the oven to 190°C/ gas 5. Place the pittas on a baking tray. Mix together the tomato purée, olive oil and oregano, season with freshly ground black pepper, then thinly spread over the pittas.

2 Arrange half the strips of ham on top, then scatter with a mixture of pineapple pieces (if these are large, chop them into smaller pieces first) and sweetcorn. Top with the remaining ham strips, then sprinkle with mozzarella.

3 Bake the pizzettes for about 15 minutes until the cheese has melted and is beginning to brown. Remove from the oven and allow to cool for a few minutes before serving.

variations

• For tuna pizzettes, spread the pittas with 3 tbsp red or green pesto instead of the tomato purée mixture. Drain a 200g can of tuna in spring water and use instead of the ham. Garnish each pizzette with a few halved, stoned black olives before serving.

• To make onion, blue cheese and walnut pizzettes, gently cook 2 thinly sliced red onions in 1 tbsp olive oil for 7–8 minutes until softened. Mix with 3 tbsp sun-dried tomato purée, a pinch of dried mixed herbs and a pinch of pepper. Spoon over the pittas. Scatter with 150g chopped Gorgonzola cheese. Bake for 8 minutes, then sprinkle with 50g chopped walnuts and bake for a further 3–4 minutes until the nuts are toasted.

each serving provides

360kcals • 22g protein
9g fat of which 4g saturates
51g carbohydrate of which
12g sugars • 4g fibre
808mg sodium • 110g fruit
and vegetables

360 kcals

1 portion fruit & veg

fun food

Asparagus & Parma ham bruschetta

Why are the simplest dishes often the best? Here, a few fine ingredients lift this sandwich from the 'something on toast' category to a **special treat.** It makes a delightful, balanced light lunch when **fresh asparagus** is in season.

SERVES 4 (makes 12)
PREPARATION TIME 5 minutes
COOKING TIME 12 minutes

200g asparagus tips, halved lengthways
3 tbsp olive oil
250g cherry tomatoes
1 ciabatta loaf, diagonally sliced into 12
1 garlic clove, halved
50g wild rocket
75g Parma ham, torn into small pieces
25g fresh Parmesan, peeled into shavings

1 Preheat a cast-iron, ridged griddle. Brush the asparagus spears with 1 tbsp of the olive oil and season with freshly ground black pepper, then place on the griddle with the cherry tomatoes. Cook for about 8 minutes, turning a few times, until tender and lightly charred. Remove and keep warm. (If you don't have a ridged griddle, cook the vegetables on a rack under a preheated moderately hot grill in the grill pan.)

2 Place the ciabatta slices on the griddle and brown lightly on both sides. Rub the cut sides of the garlic over one side of each slice of toast, then arrange on a large serving plate.

3 Divide the rocket among the toasts and top with the asparagus spears and Parma ham. Drizzle with the remaining olive oil, scatter over the Parmesan shavings and top with the cherry tomatoes.

cook's tip

• Trimmed asparagus tips are available in supermarkets, but if you can only find whole spears, use the stem part in soups or risottos.

1.5 portions fruit & veg

tasty treat

338 kcals

each serving provides 338kcals • 16g protein • 15.5g fat of which 4g saturates 36g carbohydrate of which 5g sugars • 3g fibre • 768mg sodium • 125g vegetables

Hot Florentine muffins
Toasted muffins topped with **wilted spinach and poached egg,** then coated with a creamy yoghurt and chive sauce, make a **light yet luxurious lunch** or supper dish.

SERVES 4 V
PREPARATION TIME 15 minutes,
COOKING TIME 5 minutes

1 tbsp vegetable oil
800g baby spinach leaves
4 eggs
1 tsp white wine vinegar
4 wholemeal English muffins, split

YOGHURT & CHIVE SAUCE
2 egg yolks
1 tsp Dijon mustard
150g Greek yoghurt
8 chives

TO GARNISH 8 chives (optional)

cook's tip
• You can buy ready-made Hollandaise sauce from the chilled cabinets of large supermarkets – but remember that it is high in fat and calories so only use 2 tbsp per serving.

1 First make the sauce. Whisk the egg yolks, mustard and yoghurt in a heatproof bowl set over a pan of simmering water for about 10 minutes until thick. Snip in the chives and season to taste. Remove the pan from the heat, but leave the sauce in the bowl over the pan. Cover to keep warm.

2 Heat the oil in a wok or large frying pan, add the spinach and stir-fry over a moderate heat for 2–3 minutes until wilted. Drain in a sieve, pressing down with the back of a spoon to remove excess moisture. Return to the pan and season to taste, then cover to keep warm.

3 To poach the eggs, half fill a large frying pan with water. Add the vinegar and a pinch of salt and heat to simmering. Carefully break in the eggs, one at a time, and cook gently for 2–3 minutes until cooked as you like them, spooning the hot water over the yolks towards the end of the cooking time. Then, while the eggs are poaching, toast the muffins. Using a fish slice or draining spoon, lift the eggs from the water one at a time and drain on kitchen paper.

4 Divide the spinach among the muffin bases, place a poached egg on top and spoon over the warm sauce. Garnish with whole chives, if liked, sprinkle with pepper and rest the remaining toasted muffin halves on the side. Serve at once.

each serving provides 388kcals • 22g protein • 20g fat of which 6g saturates • 34g carbohydrate of which 10g sugars • 9g fibre 755mg sodium • 200g vegetables

2.5 portions fruit & veg

388 kcals

Sardine & pepper toasts

A no-cook recipe is perfect for a **light lunch when time is short.** Remember to include the sardine bones in the mixture, as they are quite soft and mash easily, adding **valuable calcium** to the dish. The **raw vegetables** have maximum food value to keep you going on a busy working day. Follow with some **juicy fresh fruit.**

1 portion fruit & veg

quick & easy

297 kcals

SERVES 4
PREPARATION TIME 10 minutes

2 x 120g cans sardines
   in brine, drained
2 celery sticks, finely chopped
1 red pepper, deseeded and
   finely chopped
1 red onion, thinly sliced
3 tbsp sun-dried tomato paste
3 tbsp lime juice
pinch of celery salt
4 thick slices wholemeal
   or multigrain bread
75g watercress

1 Lightly break up the sardines in a bowl with a fork. Add the chopped celery, red pepper, onion, tomato paste and lime juice to the sardines. Season lightly with celery salt and freshly ground black pepper.

2 Lightly toast the bread slices on both sides until golden. Remove any tough stalks from the watercress, then divide among the slices and spoon the sardine mixture on top. Serve immediately.

variations
• Canned tuna in brine makes an excellent substitute for the sardines.
• If you prefer cooked peppers, char-grill them first. Halve and deseed the peppers, then grill them cut-side down for about 5 minutes until the skins are blackened. Cool, then peel and chop finely.

each serving provides
297kcals • 17g protein
14g fat of which 1g saturates
28g carbohydrate of which 7g sugars
3g fibre • 676mg sodium
111g vegetables

Snappy tuna melt
Boosted with vegetable goodness, this tasty grill is ideal for a quick, mid-week supper dish. Crisp fennel and red pepper bring terrific texture contrast and a really fresh flavour to tuna and sweetcorn toasted on top of focaccia bread with a sprinkling of tangy cheese.

SERVES 4
PREPARATION TIME 20 minutes
COOKING TIME 5–6 minutes

1 plain focaccia
1 small fennel bulb, finely diced
1 red pepper, deseeded
   and finely diced
2 spring onions, thinly sliced
340g can sweetcorn, drained
200g can tuna in spring
   water, drained
4 tbsp reduced-fat mayonnaise
75g Emmenthal or Gruyère
   cheese, finely grated

TO SERVE 85g watercress or mixed salad leaves, 400g cherry tomatoes, halved, ½ cucumber, diced

1 Preheat the grill to high. Slice the focaccia horizontally through the middle into two and place cut-sides down on the grill pan. Grill for 1–2 minutes until browned, then turn the bread over and set aside on the grill pan. Reduce the heat to moderate.

2 Lightly mix the fennel, pepper, spring onions, sweetcorn and tuna into the mayonnaise. Season to taste with freshly ground black pepper. Divide this mixture among the focaccia halves, spread out and press down gently with a fork to cover the bread completely. Sprinkle with the cheese.

3 Place under the moderate grill, well away from the heat, and grill for 3–4 minutes until the cheese is melted and bubbling and just beginning to turn golden brown.

4 Meanwhile, divide the salad leaves among 4 plates. Cut each piece of toasted focaccia into 4 and place 2 pieces on each plate. Arrange the tomatoes and cucumber around the edge and serve at once.

super supper
452 kcals
4 portions fruit & veg

each serving provides
452kcals • 25g protein
14g fat of which 5g saturates • 59g carbohydrate of which 16g sugars
6g fibre • 892mg sodium • 322g vegetables

Chicken, avocado & alfalfa club sandwich

This triple-decker, toasted Granary bread sandwich is packed with **creamy, mashed avocado,** rich in healthy unsaturated fats. **Lean chicken, juicy tomatoes** and **pretty alfalfa sprouts** make up the rest of the tasty filling for this nourishing and satisfying bite.

SERVES 2

PREPARATION TIME 25 minutes

1½ tbsp lime juice
1 tsp olive oil
½ red onion, very thinly sliced
1 small avocado
dash of Tabasco or chilli sauce
2 tbsp reduced-fat mayonnaise
2 tbsp chopped fresh coriander
6 medium slices Granary bread
175g cooked, skinless chicken
   breast fillet, sliced
2 tomatoes, thinly sliced
25g alfalfa sprouts

1 Whisk together 2 tsp of the lime juice, the oil and a little freshly ground black pepper in a small bowl. Add the onion slices and toss to coat. Put aside to allow the onions to mellow in flavour while preparing the remaining ingredients.

2 Roughly mash the avocado with a fork. Add the remaining lime juice and Tabasco or chilli sauce, to taste, and carry on mashing until the mixture is fairly smooth. Mix the mayonnaise with the coriander.

3 Preheat the grill to moderate. Place the bread on the grill pan and toast for 2–3 minutes on each side until lightly browned.

4 Spread 2 slices of toast very thinly with a little of the mayonnaise, then spread with half the mashed avocado, dividing it equally between them. Top with the sliced chicken and onion slices. Spread another 2 slices of toast very thinly with mayonnaise, place on the chicken filling, mayonnaise-side down. Spread half the remaining mayonnaise thinly over the tops of the sandwiches. Spread the remaining avocado, add a layer of sliced tomatoes and the alfalfa sprouts.

5 Finally spread the last of the mayonnaise over the last 2 slices of toast and place on the sandwiches, mayonnaise-side down. Press the sandwiches together, then cut each in half. Serve immediately.

variation

• Mustard and cress or grated carrot can be used instead of the alfalfa sprouts. Bean sprouts are also good in this sandwich – use about 50g.

cook's tip

• Sprouted beans are a good source of vitamin C and B group vitamins, and are easy to grow yourself. Rinse aduki, alfalfa or mung beans and place in a large jar. Half-fill with cold water, then cover with a piece of muslin secured with an elastic band. Leave to soak overnight, then pour off the water through the muslin. Refill the jar with fresh water, then drain and leave the jar on its side in a dark place. Repeat this process twice a day for 2 days until sprouted, then place the jar in a sunny place and continue rinsing for another day or 2 until the sprouts have grown to the desired size. Rinse and discard any unsprouted beans before using.

2 portions fruit & veg • no-cook treat • **574** kcals

each serving provides 574kcals • 40g protein • 22g fat of which 4g saturates
59g carbohydrate of which 9g sugars • 7g fibre • 796mg sodium • 185g vegetables

Toasted turkey & pastrami bagels

With pastrami (cured, smoked beef) and bagels, the inspiration for this thick, filling sandwich can only be New York City. But unlike the Big Apple's favourite snack, this version replaces the mayonnaise with herby, reduced-fat soft cheese and includes lean turkey. It is perfect for a tasty lunchtime bite.

SERVES 4

PREPARATION TIME about 30 minutes

- 4 bagels (plain, poppy seed or onion), split in half
- 6 tbsp reduced-fat soft cheese, about 125g
- 6 cocktail gherkins, rinsed and finely chopped
- 3 tbsp chopped fresh flat-leaf parsley
- 4 iceberg lettuce leaves
- 1 large beef tomato, cut into 4 slices
- 8 thin slices of lean roast turkey breast, about 170g in total
- 8 slices of pastrami, about 110g in total

1 Preheat the grill to high. Put the bagels, cut-sides up, on the grill pan and grill for 3–4 minutes until golden brown and toasted.

2 Meanwhile, beat the soft cheese, gherkins and parsley together in a small bowl.

3 Divide the cheese mixture into 8 portions and spread over the toasted side of each bagel half.

4 Place a lettuce leaf on the bottom half of each bagel, folded to fit, then top with a thick slice of tomato followed by a quarter of the turkey and pastrami, loosely folded. Put the tops back on the bagels and press together. Cut in half to serve.

variations

- Try thinly sliced smoked chicken instead of turkey.
- For a Turkey Bagel Melt, omit the herby soft cheese, pastrami and gherkins. Split open the bagels, without cutting all the way through, and open flat like a book. Toast the cut-side under the grill, then arrange the lettuce, thinly sliced tomatoes and turkey on top. Add 30g thinly sliced mozzarella cheese to each bagel, then pop back under the grill until the cheese melts. Serve at once.

each serving provides

389kcals • 34g protein
6g fat of which 2.5g saturates
54g carbohydrate of which
10g sugars • 3g fibre
894mg sodium • 100g vegetables

New York treat

389 kcals

1 portion fruit & veg

Banana & peanut wedges

The ultimate version of a peanut butter sandwich takes some good hearty bread **packed with sesame and sunflower seeds,** with **sweet mashed banana** as a perfect partner for the peanuts. Serve with crisp apple or fresh, juicy pineapple wedges for extra fruit value.

SERVES 4 Ⓥ
PREPARATION TIME 5 minutes

2 large ripe bananas
8 tbsp crunchy peanut butter
8 thick slices sunflower and
  sesame bread (or other
  good bread)
85g raisins

1 Peel the bananas and slice them into a bowl. Using a fork, lightly mash the bananas to remove most of the lumps.

2 Spread the peanut butter evenly over 4 of the slices of bread. Spoon a quarter of the banana over each slice.

3 Top with the raisins and cover with the remaining bread slices. Cut the sandwiches in half and serve at once.

variations

• In place of the bananas, halve and stone 300g fresh ripe apricots. Finely chop them in a food processor, then stir in 1 tsp runny honey. Spread over the peanut butter.
• Peel 1 ripe mango and cut the flesh away from the stone. Using a fork, mash the mango until almost smooth. Spread over the peanut butter in place of the bananas.
• For a savoury variation, blend 100g reduced-fat soft cheese with 1 tsp Marmite, then spread over the top of the peanut butter.

each serving provides 594kcals • 20.5g protein 30g fat of which 5g saturates • 62g carbohydrate of which 30.5g sugars • 7g fibre • 558mg sodium 86g fruit

594 kcals

great for kids

1 portion fruit & veg

Roast pork & apple baguettes

For a really superb pork sandwich, spread a crusty baguette with **spiced apple and onion sauce** and pack it with **lean roast pork** and **fresh watercress**.

SERVES 2
PREPARATION TIME 20–25 minutes
COOKING TIME 20 minutes

2 tsp olive (or walnut) oil
2 shallots, finely chopped
3 dessert apples (such as Royal Gala), peeled, cored and thinly sliced
juice of 1 lemon
100ml apple juice
25g caster sugar
pinch of ground allspice
1 baton or baguette
125g lean roast pork or smoked pork loin, thickly sliced
50g watercress

variations

• To prepare the apple sauce ahead, cook to the end of step 3, then cover and chill in the fridge for up to 3 days, or freeze and use within 2 months. The sauce is also good made with pears and freshly squeezed orange instead of apple juice and served in a poppy seed baguette.
• For the ultimate impromptu meal, use a good bottled apple sauce or compote.
• Strong-flavoured cheeses go well with apple sauce. Layer 125g thickly sliced mature Cheddar cheese with ½ thinly sliced, small red onion, 1 thinly sliced ripe tomato and 100g thinly sliced cucumber.

1 Heat the oil in a saucepan and gently fry the shallots for 5 minutes or until soft and just beginning to colour. Add the apples, lemon juice and apple juice and heat until bubbling. Cover the pan with a lid, reduce the heat to low and cook very gently for 5 minutes.

2 Stir in the sugar and allspice, increase the heat to medium and cook uncovered, stirring occasionally, for 8–10 minutes until most of the liquid has evaporated and the apple slices are very tender and just beginning to break down.

3 Using a potato masher, partly mash the apples until they are semi-smooth but retain some of the chunky texture. Set aside until cool.

4 Cut the bread open lengthways, keeping it still attached along one side like a hinge. With the baguette opened out flat, thickly spread both sides with the apple sauce. Fill with the sliced pork and watercress, then close up and press together. Slice across the loaf into 2 portions, then cut each portion in half again for serving.

591 kcals

1 portion fruit & veg

prepare ahead

each serving provides 591kcals • 34g protein 9g fat of which 2g saturates • 99g carbohydrate of which 39g sugars • 6g fibre • 760mg sodium 108g fruit and vegetables

variations

• Instead of the red onion relish, use a jar of Swedish-style shredded cabbage (avoid the pickled variety). Warm the cabbage gently with the redcurrant jelly and a dash of balsamic vinegar, then serve in the rolls with the sausages.
• Creamed horseradish sauce would be equally good in place of the mustard, if you prefer.

each serving provides

308kcals • 17g protein
11.5g fat of which 4g saturates
42g carbohydrate of which
11g sugars • 4g fibre
825mg sodium • 131g vegetables

great casual lunch

308 kcals

1.5 portions fruit & veg

Smart sausage hot-dogs

Venison is a **low-fat red meat** which makes delicious sausages for a quick family lunch. Enjoy them in wholemeal rolls with **pan-fried mushrooms** and a **gorgeous red onion relish.**

SERVES 6
PREPARATION TIME 15 minutes
COOKING TIME 25–30 minutes

6 venison sausages
6 finger rolls (preferably wholemeal)
6 tsp Dijon mustard
225g closed cup mushrooms, sliced

RED ONION RELISH
2 tbsp olive oil
3 red onions, thinly sliced
2 tbsp redcurrant jelly
2 tbsp red wine vinegar

1 First, prepare the relish. Heat 1 tbsp of the oil in a frying pan, add the onions and 5 tbsp of water, and gently fry over a moderate heat for 15–20 minutes, stirring from time to time, until the onions are tender. Add the redcurrant jelly and vinegar and simmer for about 10 minutes until almost all the liquid has evaporated.

2 Meanwhile, preheat the grill to medium and cook the sausages for 15–18 minutes until nicely browned all over.

3 When the relish is cooked, transfer it to a bowl. Wash the pan, then add the remaining oil and heat. Add the mushrooms and cook over a moderate heat for 5 minutes or until softened.

4 Split the bread rolls in half lengthways and spread mustard on one side. Spoon in the mushrooms, then place a sausage inside each roll. Finish with a generous spoonful of the onion relish in each, and serve immediately.

Beef & beetroot coleslaw baps

A beetroot and **red cabbage** coleslaw brings a lively flourish of colour and texture to these **hearty baps,** as well as providing a nourishing vegetable accompaniment to the **lean roast beef** filling. Choose wholemeal baps for **extra fibre.**

SERVES 4
PREPARATION TIME 10 minutes

4 tbsp reduced-fat mayonnaise
4 tsp wholegrain mustard
4 large baps (preferably wholemeal)
50g watercress or rocket
300g lean rare roast beef,
    thinly sliced
200g red cabbage, finely shredded
1 small red onion, finely sliced
150g cooked beetroot, peeled
    and coarsely grated
6 tbsp low-fat natural yoghurt

variation

• For a horseradish mayonnaise, combine 2 tsp creamed horseradish, instead of the mustard, with the mayonnaise.

each serving provides

397kcals • 38g protein
12g fat of which 3g saturates
37g carbohydrate of which
14g sugars • 5g fibre
627mg sodium • 120g vegetables

no-fuss lunch

397 kcals

1.5 portions fruit & veg

1 In a large bowl, mix together the mayonnaise and mustard. Split the baps in half and spread the bottom half of each one with this mixture.

2 Top these bases with the watercress or rocket and divide the roast beef among them.

3 In the same bowl as used for the mayonnaise, mix together the red cabbage, red onion and beetroot. Add the yoghurt and stir together to coat. Pile the coleslaw on top of the beef, season with freshly ground black pepper, then put the tops of the baps back on. Serve immediately.

Sloppy Joes

As the name suggests, this has a **messy** appearance – a **bolognese mixture** served between **wholemeal rolls** – but it's a recipe **all the family will love,** and it can be prepared ahead. **Lean minced turkey** is used here as a lower-fat alternative to minced beef, but you could use either.

SERVES 4 ★
PREPARATION TIME 10 minutes
COOKING TIME 40 minutes

2 tbsp vegetable oil
2 celery sticks, finely chopped
1 large onion, finely chopped
1 large carrot, peeled and
    finely chopped
1 aubergine, finely diced
1 garlic clove, crushed
500g lean minced turkey
400g can chopped tomatoes
2 tsp tomato purée
2 tbsp chopped fresh basil

TO SERVE 4 soft wholemeal rolls

variation
• Make this into a more sophisticated dish by spicing it up a little. Add 1 tsp chilli powder (or to taste) with the vegetables as they are softening in step 1 and/or 1 deseeded and finely chopped fresh red chilli with the turkey in step 2.

cook's tip
• You can make the turkey mixture ahead of time. Allow to cool, then transfer to a sealed container and keep in the fridge or freezer until required. Reheat thoroughly.

1 Heat the oil in a large frying pan over a moderate heat. Add the celery, onion, carrot, aubergine and garlic and fry for about 6 minutes, stirring occasionally, until the vegetables are softened.

2 Add the turkey to the pan, stirring well to break up the meat and mix with the vegetables. Cook for 5 minutes, stirring occasionally, until there is no trace of pink left in the turkey.

3 Stir in the canned tomatoes with the tomato purée and basil. Bring the mixture to the boil, then reduce the heat, cover the pan and simmer gently for about 30 minutes, stirring occasionally, until the sauce has reduced and thickened slightly.

4 Just before serving, cut the rolls in half and lightly toast them. Spoon the turkey mixture over the base halves of the rolls, then cover with the top halves and serve immediately.

prepare ahead • **412** kcals • **3** portions fruit & veg

each serving provides 412kcals • 50g protein • 10g fat of which 2g saturates • 33g carbohydrate of which 10g sugars 5g fibre • 378mg sodium • 240g vegetables

1

2

Mediterranean beefburgers with red-hot tomato salsa

Sun-dried tomatoes, garlic and herbs create a Mediterranean flavour, and a fresh chilli and tomato salsa adds extra zip. Making your own burgers is so worthwhile, as they're much lower in fat than most ready-made burgers, and you can flavour them as you please.

SERVES 4
PREPARATION TIME 15 minutes
COOKING TIME 6–8 minutes

500g lean minced beef
25g wholemeal breadcrumbs
2 garlic cloves, crushed
40g sun-dried tomatoes in oil, drained and finely chopped
2 tbsp chopped fresh coriander
4 seeded burger buns
50g rocket

TOMATO SALSA
225g ripe vine tomatoes, finely diced
1 red pepper, deseeded and finely diced
½ fresh mild green chilli, deseeded and finely chopped
1 fresh red chilli, deseeded and finely chopped
2 tsp balsamic vinegar
1 tbsp snipped fresh chives
1 tbsp chopped fresh coriander

1 Preheat a grill or barbecue to moderately hot. (Alternatively, you can use a cast-iron, ridged griddle on the hob for cooking the burgers.) Place the minced beef, breadcrumbs, garlic, sun-dried tomatoes and coriander in a large bowl and use your hands to mix the ingredients together thoroughly.

2 Divide the mixture equally into 4 and shape into burgers, about 10cm across and a similar size to the buns.

3 Brush the grill rack or grill pan lightly with oil and cook the burgers for 3–4 minutes on each side, until browned on the outside and cooked through.

4 To make the salsa, mix together all the ingredients in a bowl. Season to taste. You can chop all the salsa ingredients together in the food processor to save time – just use the pulse button to get the right consistency.

5 Split the buns in half and pop under the grill or onto the barbecue rack to toast lightly. Place a few rocket leaves on each base, top with a burger and add a spoonful of salsa, then replace the tops. Serve immediately.

each serving provides
533kcals • 37g protein • 22g fat of which 7g saturates
50g carbohydrate of which 7g sugars • 3g fibre
719mg sodium • 120g vegetables

533 kcals

prepare ahead

1.5 portions fruit & veg

3

4

cook's tip
• Make the burgers in advance. Cover with cling film and refrigerate for up to 2 days, or freeze for up to 1 month. Thaw before cooking. The salsa can be made the day before and stored in the fridge, covered with cling film.

5

Pork & apple burgers with chilli sauce

Hamburgers are always popular for casual meals, but can be high in saturated fat. This lighter version, made with lean minced pork, is just as flavoursome, and fresh apples and spring onions contribute to your five-a-day. They're delicious spread with sweet chilli sauce.

SERVES 4 ✱ (raw burgers only)
PREPARATION TIME 15 minutes
COOKING TIME 15–20 minutes

300g lean minced pork
2 small green dessert apples,
cored and grated
75g fresh wholemeal breadcrumbs
(made from 4 slices wholemeal
bread with the crusts removed)
4 spring onions, very finely chopped
1 garlic clove, crushed
25g fresh root ginger, peeled
and finely chopped
1 tsp dried thyme
pinch of cayenne pepper

TO SERVE cos lettuce leaves,
halved, ½ cucumber, thinly sliced,
4 soft white floured baps, split,
4 tsp sweet chilli sauce

variation

• Using bottled chilli sauce is a quick option, but it doesn't take long to make your own. Put 1 finely sliced red chilli in a small saucepan with ½ tbsp arrowroot. Slowly stir in 4 tbsp fresh lime juice, 2 tbsp rice vinegar, 1 tbsp soft light brown sugar and ½ tbsp nam pla (Thai fish sauce), stirring to blend. Put the pan over a high heat and bring to the boil, stirring until thickened. Remove from the heat and leave to cool.

1 Put the pork, apples, breadcrumbs, spring onions, garlic, ginger, thyme and cayenne pepper in a large bowl. Mix and squeeze together.

2 Shape the mixture into 4 balls, then press into flat patties about 10cm in diameter and 1.5cm thick. Preheat the grill to moderate and set the shelf on the lower runner position.

3 Place the burgers on a sheet of foil in the grill pan. Grill for about 15 minutes, turning once, until golden brown and cooked through.

4 Divide the lettuce leaves and cucumber slices among the bun bases. Place the burgers on top, then spread with 1 tsp of the chilli sauce. Cover with the bun tops and serve immediately.

Red bean & Brazil nut burgers

These protein-packed veggie burgers are made with a **delicious high-fibre combo** of Brazil nuts and red kidney beans, plus carrots for moistness. They are served in buns, topped with a **juicy fruit chutney.**

SERVES 4 Ⓥ
PREPARATION TIME 25 minutes
COOKING TIME 15 minutes

125g Brazil nuts
2 carrots, cut into chunks
25g fresh parsley
2 garlic cloves, peeled
pared zest of 1 lemon
2 tsp ground coriander
400g can red kidney beans,
   drained and rinsed
4 spring onions
2 tbsp vegetable oil

CHUTNEY
2 crisp dessert apples (such as
   Braeburn), quartered and cored
50g ready-to-eat dried apricots,
   chopped if necessary
4 tbsp mango chutney, chopped
   if necessary
juice of 1 lemon

TO SERVE 4 seeded burger buns, split, 85g wild rocket, ½ cucumber, thinly sliced, 1 red onion, thinly sliced

1 Preheat the grill to hot and set the shelf on the lower runner position. Cover a baking sheet with foil and grease it lightly with oil. Combine the nuts, carrots, parsley, garlic, lemon zest and ground coriander in a food processor and process until finely ground. Add the beans and spring onions and briefly pulse the mixture, to chop the onions and crush the beans. Season to taste.

2 Divide the mixture into 4 and shape each portion into a neat burger about 10cm in width and 2cm thick. Place on the baking sheet. (The burgers can be prepared ahead, cooked or uncooked, and kept chilled, if more convenient.)

3 Brush the burgers with half the oil, then grill for about 5 minutes until well browned and sizzling around the bottom. Turn the burgers and brush with the remaining oil, then grill for a further 5 minutes. Reduce the heat to moderate and turn the burgers over once again. (They tend to crack and may spread slightly as they cook, so pat them gently to keep them neat.) Grill for a final 5 minutes or until well browned. Pat the burgers into shape, if necessary, and leave to stand for 2–3 minutes to firm up.

4 While the burgers are cooking, coarsely grate the apples into a bowl. Stir in the apricots, chutney and lemon juice. Toast the cut sides of the burger buns.

5 Put a little rocket and cucumber on the bottom of each bun, add a burger and top with a spoonful of the chutney and a couple of onion rings. Replace the tops of the buns and serve, adding the remaining chutney and salad.

each serving provides 720kcals • 20g protein • 32g fat of which 7g saturates • 92g carbohydrate of which 38g sugars • 11g fibre 1213mg sodium • 215g fruit and vegetables

Honeyed five-spice chicken pockets

Five-spice powder – a fragrant mix of **cinnamon, cloves, fennel seeds, star anise and Sichuan peppercorns** – is used a great deal in Chinese cooking, and here it adds an oriental flavour to **appetising, pitta pocket** sandwiches.

SERVES 4

PREPARATION TIME 10 minutes, plus at least 30 minutes marinating

COOKING TIME 20 minutes

- **3 tbsp lemon juice**
- **2 tbsp clear honey**
- **½ tsp Chinese five-spice powder**
- **3 skinless chicken breast fillets, about 140g each**
- **4 large wholemeal pitta breads**
- **3 cos lettuce leaves, shredded**
- **16 cherry tomatoes, halved**
- **1 large carrot, coarsely grated**

LEMON & HERB YOGHURT DRESSING
- **150g low-fat natural yoghurt**
- **grated zest of ½ lemon and ½ tbsp juice**
- **2 tbsp chopped fresh parsley**

1 Put the lemon juice, honey and five-spice powder in a shallow dish large enough to hold the chicken breasts in a single layer, and mix together until well blended. Make 3 deep slashes in each chicken breast, then put into the dish. Rub the marinade all over the chicken, and well into the slashes. Cover the dish with cling film and place in the fridge to marinate for at least 30 minutes.

2 To make the dressing, blend together the yoghurt, lemon zest and juice and the parsley and season to taste. Cover and chill until required.

3 When you are ready to cook, remove the chicken breasts from the fridge to bring them back to room temperature. Preheat the grill to medium and line the grill pan with foil. Set the shelf on the lower runner position. Put the chicken breasts on the rack in the grill pan. Grill for 15–20 minutes, basting occasionally with the marinade left in the dish and turning half-way through the cooking time. When thoroughly cooked, thinly slice the chicken breasts on the diagonal and set aside to cool.

4 Sprinkle the pitta breads with a little water and warm under the grill for 2–3 minutes. Meanwhile, toss the lettuce, tomatoes and carrots with the dressing.

5 Slice open one side of each pitta bread to make a pocket. Divide the chicken and salad among the pittas and serve immediately.

variation

- Grilled chicken breasts also make a filling, more conventional sandwich. Lightly toast 2 slices of multigrain bread for each sandwich. Cover 1 slice of toast with mixed leaves and sliced cucumber tossed with the lemon and herb dressing. Add the chicken slices, then top with second slice of toast.

finger food

349 kcals

1 portion fruit & veg

each serving provides

349kcals • 33g protein

3g fat of which 1g saturates

51g carbohydrate of which

18g sugars • 5g fibre

380mg sodium • 89g vegetables

SERVES 4
PREPARATION TIME 15–20
minutes, plus 30 minutes chilling
COOKING TIME about 6 minutes

**2 x 400g cans chickpeas, drained
and rinsed**
2 garlic cloves, crushed
1 tsp ground cumin
1 tsp ground coriander
**1 green chilli, deseeded and
finely chopped**
2 tbsp chopped fresh coriander
1 small egg, beaten
2 tbsp plain flour
2 tbsp vegetable oil

SALAD
100g red cabbage, finely shredded
1 carrot, coarsely grated
**⅓ cucumber, cut into fine
matchsticks**
1 small red onion, thinly sliced

TO SERVE 4 wholemeal pitta breads,
4 tbsp reduced-fat hummus, juice
of ½ lemon

cook's tip
If you'd like to make your own
hummus, follow the recipe on
page 81.

Falafel pittas

These spicy chickpea cakes are a popular street food all over the Middle East. Served in pitta pockets with a colourful crunchy salad, they are deliciously healthy as well as fun to eat.

1 Put the chickpeas in a blender or food processor and process until smooth. Add the garlic, cumin and ground coriander and process again until well mixed. Add the chilli, fresh coriander, egg and 1 tbsp of the flour and process again briefly. Season to taste. Transfer to a bowl and chill for about 30 minutes to firm the mixture.

2 Meanwhile, prepare the salad: put the cabbage, carrot, cucumber and onion in a bowl and mix together.

3 Flour your hands with the remaining flour and shape the chickpea mixture into 8 patties. Heat the oil in a frying pan and fry the patties, in batches if necessary, for about 3 minutes on each side until crisp and golden. Drain on kitchen paper.

4 Meanwhile, warm the pitta breads in a toaster or under the grill and stir the lemon juice into the hummus to thin it slightly. Cut a slit lengthways in the side of each bread to form a pocket. Spread 1 tbsp of hummus inside each pocket, then stuff in 2 falafel with some salad. Serve immediately.

each serving provides 538kcals • 22g protein
17g fat of which 2g saturates • 79g carbohydrate of which
7g sugars • 12.5g fibre • 809mg sodium • 103g vegetables

538 kcals

1 portion fruit & veg

Greek lamb koftas

Pan-fried lamb meatballs make a delicious filling for warm pitta bread pouches, packed out with a **crisp cucumber and leafy salad.** Serve with cherry tomatoes.

SERVES 6
PREPARATION TIME 35–40 minutes
COOKING TIME about 15 minutes

350g extra lean minced lamb
1 egg
2 large garlic cloves, crushed
1 tbsp chopped fresh oregano,
   or 1 tsp dried
1 tbsp chopped fresh thyme,
   or ½ tsp dried
1 large onion, finely chopped
100g fresh wholemeal breadcrumbs
1 tbsp olive oil
25g fresh herbs (such as basil, flat-
   leaf parsley and mint), chopped
6 spring onions, thinly sliced
50g rocket

TO SERVE 6 large pitta breads,
   1 lemon, cut into 6 wedges,
   ½ cucumber, thinly sliced,
   6 tbsp low-fat natural yoghurt

1 Put the lamb in a large mixing bowl and break it up with a wooden spoon. Add the egg, garlic, oregano, thyme and onion and mix well. Then add the breadcrumbs and mix until thoroughly combined, using your hands.

2 Have a large board or plate ready, then roll the lamb mixture into 24 even walnut-sized balls. Flatten the balls slightly on the palm of your hand to make small patties, about 5cm across and about 1cm thick.

3 Heat the oil in a large frying pan. Add the patties, nudging them up to each other – they should just about fit, and they shrink as they begin to cook. Cook over a high heat for 2 minutes until browned underneath, then turn them over and cook for a further 2 minutes. Reduce the heat to medium, turn the patties again and cook for about 8 minutes, shaking the pan occasionally, and turning the patties once more, until cooked through.

4 Meanwhile, mix the chopped fresh herbs with the spring onions and rocket. Warm the pitta breads in a toaster or under the grill, turning them once.

5 Slit the pitta breads open and place 4 kofta in each. Add some cucumber slices and herb salad and squeeze over a little lemon juice. Drizzle with yoghurt and eat at once.

variations

• Ring the changes – use pork with sage, and chicken or turkey with tarragon.
• Instead of filling pitta breads, roll up the kofta and salad in wraps. Spread the yoghurt over the wraps first.
• The cooked kofta could also be tossed with 2 x 400g cans of chickpeas, 200g halved cherry tomatoes and the herb salad, then topped with cucumber raita.

each serving provides

347kcals • 23g protein
9g fat of which 1g saturates
46g carbohydrate of which
8g sugars • 3g fibre
381mg sodium
130g vegetables

347 kcals

1.5 portions fruit & veg

Soft cheese & smoked trout wraps

A delicious, moist filling of **herby soft cheese and flaked, smoked fish** is rolled up inside tortillas with crisp bean sprouts and salad leaves.

SERVES 4 (makes 8)
PREPARATION TIME 25 minutes

½ cucumber, cut into matchsticks
8 soft flour tortillas
200g reduced-fat soft cheese
4 tbsp low-fat natural yoghurt
2 tbsp snipped fresh chives
2 tbsp chopped fresh dill
150g skinless smoked trout fillets, flaked
150g bean sprouts
125g mixed baby leaf and herb salad

variations

• Smoked salmon, smoked mackerel or shredded smoked chicken breast would make equally delicious alternatives to the smoked trout used here.
• Wraps are also delicious filled with taramasalata. Spread the warm tortillas with 200g reduced-fat taramasalata. Grind over a little black pepper, then scatter with ½ finely diced cucumber and ½ deseeded and finely sliced yellow pepper. Sprinkle with the leaves of 2 shredded Little Gem lettuces before rolling up.

1 Preheat the oven to 200°C/gas 6. Put the cucumber sticks in a bowl and sprinkle with a little salt. Mix well, then leave for about 10 minutes. (This draws out some of the moisture so that the filling in the wraps will remain crisp.)

2 Wrap the tortillas in foil and warm in the oven for 5 minutes, or according to the pack instructions. Put the soft cheese, yoghurt, chives and dill into a small bowl and mix together. Stir in the flaked trout and season to taste with a little pepper.

3 Separate the tortillas and spread out on 2 large boards (alternatively, you can prepare 4 at a time). Spread each tortilla with an eighth of the trout mixture.

4 Rinse the cucumber in a sieve, then tip onto kitchen paper and pat dry. Divide among the tortillas, arranging them lengthways so the tortillas will be easier to roll up. Scatter over the bean sprouts and salad leaves.

5 Roll up the tortillas tightly to enclose the filling. Cut each rolled tortilla in half diagonally and serve immediately.

1.5 portions fruit & veg

tortilla treat

378 kcals

each serving provides

378kcals • 25g protein • 8g fat of which 4g saturates
55g carbohydrate of which 8g sugars • 3g fibre • 919mg sodium
120g vegetables

**3 large skinless chicken
  breast fillets**
2 tbsp Cajun spice mixture
few drops of Tabasco, to taste
8 soft flour tortillas
1 papaya
3 tbsp olive oil
juice of 1 lime
**125g pack mixed baby leaf
  salad (or other delicate
  mixed salad leaves)**

variations

• Slices of fresh mango would also
be good as an alternative to papaya.
• Cajun seasoning is a New Orleans-
style blend of herbs and spices
including chilli powder, but you could
use any similar spicy seasoning.

Spicy chicken fajitas

Satisfyingly spicy and **quick to prepare,** chicken and papaya fajitas make an easy, healthy meal. **Sweetly fragrant papaya** is rich in beta-carotene and its gorgeous colour enhances any dish.

1 Cut each chicken breast lengthways into about 8 long strips. Sprinkle the spice mixture over a plate, add the chicken strips and toss to coat. Sprinkle lightly with a little Tabasco, then set aside for 5 minutes.

2 Meanwhile, warm the tortillas, following the pack instructions. Cut the papaya in half lengthways and scoop out the seeds, then cut each half into 8 slices and peel.

3 Heat 2 tbsp of the oil in a large frying pan. Add the coated chicken strips and stir-fry for 6 minutes over a moderate heat. Remove from the heat, sprinkle with half the lime juice and toss, scraping the residue from the pan.

4 Divide the salad leaves among the warm tortillas. Sprinkle over the rest of the oil and lime juice, then top with the chicken strips and slices of papaya. Season to taste, then roll up loosely and serve at once.

each serving provides 509kcals • 35.5g protein • 11g fat of which 2g saturates
72g carbohydrate of which 7g sugars • 4g fibre • 380mg sodium • 114g fruit and vegetables

1
portion
fruit &
veg

509
kcals

SERVES 4 (makes 8) V
PREPARATION TIME 10–15 minutes
COOKING TIME 8 minutes

8 soft flour tortillas
1 tbsp vegetable oil
1 onion, chopped
2 garlic cloves, crushed
1 small green pepper, deseeded
  and chopped
1 small red pepper, deseeded
  and chopped
1 red chilli, deseeded and
  finely chopped (optional)
½ tsp ground cumin
400g can red kidney beans,
  drained and rinsed
175g frozen sweetcorn
1 large tomato, chopped
3 tbsp tomato and chilli ketchup
2 tbsp chopped fresh coriander

TO SERVE ½ iceberg lettuce,
shredded, 50g Monterey Jack or
mature Cheddar cheese, grated,
150g reduced-fat Greek yoghurt

variation
• For a spicier version, include the
seeds of the fresh chilli or add some
chopped jalapeño chillies that you
can buy in a jar from supermarkets.

Mexican bean burritos

A fabulous vegetarian bite that's deliciously healthy as well as **fun to eat.** The bean and vegetable mixture has a **great spicy kick,** and is combined with crunchy salad, grated cheese and **creamy yoghurt** in tortilla wraps.

1 Warm the tortillas following the pack instructions. Meanwhile, make the filling. Heat the oil in a large frying pan, add the onion, garlic and peppers and cook over a moderate heat, stirring, for 3 minutes until they begin to soften. Add the red chilli, if using, and the ground cumin and stir for 1 minute.

2 Put the red kidney beans onto a plate and lightly crush with a fork, then add to the pan together with the sweetcorn and chopped tomato. Stir in the ketchup and 2 tbsp water and continue to cook gently for 3–4 minutes. Add the fresh coriander.

3 Serve the hot bean mixture, lettuce, cheese and yoghurt in separate bowls for everyone to help themselves. To assemble a burrito, place some lettuce in the middle of a tortilla, spoon some of the bean mixture on top, add some grated cheese and top with a dollop of Greek yoghurt. Roll up and eat immediately.

super snack **543** kcals

2.5 portions fruit & veg

each serving provides 543kcals • 21g protein • 10g fat of which 3g saturates • 95g carbohydrate of which 13g sugars 9g fibre • 798mg sodium • 200g vegetables

Risottos, paellas & pilafs

Healthy and versatile, grain-based dishes make great comfort food and are great for both easy family meals and entertaining. Rice and other grains like barley and buckwheat help to boost your intake of healthy complex carbohydrates, and they are wonderfully useful storecupboard ingredients. For a Spanish-style feast, treat your friends to Seafood paella, or make the most of fresh seasonal produce with Spring vegetable risotto.

Pumpkin & corn risotto

A vibrant, golden-yellow **vegetarian risotto** that looks good, tastes wonderful and is packed with healthy beta-carotene and fibre. The mozzarella added right at the end melts into a creamy deliciousness. Serve with a **crisp green leaf salad.**

SERVES 4 Ⓥ
PREPARATION TIME 15 minutes, plus 5 minutes standing before serving
COOKING TIME about 20 minutes

2 tbsp olive oil
1 onion, finely chopped
1 garlic clove, crushed
225g risotto rice
500g pumpkin or 1 small butternut squash, peeled, deseeded and cut into 1cm pieces
2 large fresh sage leaves, finely chopped
pinch of saffron
850ml vegetable stock, hot
150g frozen sweetcorn
125g mozzarella cheese, diced
50g pumpkin seeds

cook's tip

• The secret of a good risotto lies in using the right rice – arborio, carnaroli or vialone nano – and a well-flavoured stock that should be added gradually.

474 kcals

2.5 portions fruit & veg

Italian style

each serving provides 474kcals • 16g protein
19.5g fat of which 6g saturates • 57g carbohydrate of which 6g sugars
3g fibre • 129mg sodium • 213g vegetables

1 Heat the oil in a large, heavy-based pan over a moderate heat. Stir in the onion and garlic and cook gently for 4–5 minutes until softened but not browned, stirring occasionally.

2 Stir in the rice, pumpkin or butternut squash and sage leaves and cook for 2 minutes longer. Stir the saffron into the hot stock, then pour about a quarter of the stock into the pan and stir well until it has almost all been absorbed, stirring frequently.

3 Continue adding the stock, only a ladleful at a time, making sure each is almost completely absorbed before adding the next, and stirring frequently to produce a creamy texture.

4 With the last addition of stock add the sweetcorn and stir well. Once all the stock has been absorbed and the rice is tender (this will take about 20 minutes), stir in the mozzarella cheese.

5 Season to taste, then cover the pan and allow to stand for about 5 minutes. Sprinkle the risotto with the pumpkin seeds and serve at once.

variations

- In summer you can replace the pumpkin with courgettes. Cut these into small pieces and add to the risotto with the sweetcorn in step 4 as they do not need a long cooking time.
- For a greener version of this risotto, omit the saffron, sage and pumpkin and add 150g chopped fresh spinach leaves and 2 tbsp chopped fresh basil leaves with the sweetcorn in step 4.

1 litre vegetable stock
100g asparagus tips
100g baby carrots,
   halved lengthways
200g fresh young peas, shelled
500g baby broad beans, shelled
2 tbsp olive oil
2 baby leeks, thinly sliced
300g risotto rice
1 tbsp pesto sauce
25g pine nuts, toasted

variation

• When fresh peas and broad beans are not in season, or to save time, use frozen peas and beans.

cook's tip

• There are many varieties of pesto sauce on the market and it is a matter of taste which one you use in this recipe. Those that contain Parmesan are not suitable for strict vegetarians. Pesto is salted so you may only need to season the risotto with some freshly ground black pepper. You could of course, also use a home-made pesto.

Spring vegetable risotto
Risotto is comfort food at its best, and you can ring the changes by adding almost any fresh ingredients you have to hand. Here are three ideas.

1 Bring the stock to the boil in a large saucepan, then reduce the heat, add the asparagus tips, carrots, peas and broad beans and simmer for 4–5 minutes until tender. Remove the vegetables with a draining spoon and set aside. Keep the stock simmering over a gentle heat.

2 Meanwhile, heat the oil in a large, heavy-based frying pan and add the leeks. Stir-fry for 2 minutes until they are bright green, then stir in the rice.

3 Add 2–3 tbsp of the hot stock and cook gently, stirring until the liquid is absorbed. Continue adding the stock, a little at a time, until the mixture is soupy and the grains of rice are tender but still have a slight bite. This will take about 20 minutes.

4 Stir in the pesto and season to taste. Gently stir in the asparagus, carrots, peas and beans and cook for a few more minutes until the vegetables are heated through. Serve in heated soup plates and scatter over the pine nuts.

each serving provides 524kcals • 20g protein
16g fat of which 2g saturates • 75g carbohydrate of which 6g sugars
12g fibre • 36mg sodium • 275g vegetables

3 portions fruit & veg

524 kcals

green feast

Mighty mushroom risotto

SERVES 4 ☑
PREPARATION TIME 10 minutes
COOKING TIME 25–30 minutes

30g dried porcini mushrooms,
   soaked in 500ml boiling water
3 tbsp olive oil
1 large onion, finely chopped
2 large garlic cloves, crushed
400g risotto rice
4 tbsp dry white wine or vermouth
250g large, open cup mushrooms,
   stalks trimmed and caps sliced
1 litre vegetable stock, hot
25g butter

TO SERVE 25g freshly grated
   Parmesan or Italian-style hard
   cheese, chopped fresh parsley

1 Heat the oil in a deep frying pan over a medium heat. Add the onion and cook for 3 minutes, then add the garlic and stir for a further 2 minutes until the onion is softened.

2 Add the rice to the pan, stir for about 1 minute, then add the wine or vermouth and cook briskly, stirring, until almost all of it has evaporated.

3 Strain the dried mushrooms, reserving the soaking liquid. Stir the fresh mushrooms into the rice, then start to add the hot stock, a ladleful at a time. When all the stock has been absorbed, gradually add the mushroom soaking liquid and continue cooking until the rice is tender.

4 Stir in the soaked porcini mushrooms and the butter, cover and remove from the heat. Stand for 5 minutes, season to taste, then serve sprinkled with Parmesan and parsley.

each serving provides 559kcals • 14g protein • 18g fat of which 6g saturates
81g carbohydrate of which 4g sugars • 3g fibre • 98mg sodium • 130g vegetables

1.5 portions fruit & veg

559 kcals

Chicken & courgette risotto

SERVES 4
PREPARATION TIME 15 minutes
COOKING TIME 25 minutes

2 tbsp olive oil
50g diced pancetta or lardons
4 skinless chicken breast fillets,
   cut into small cubes
2 leeks, sliced
2 garlic cloves, crushed
2 courgettes, halved lengthways,
   then cut into half-moon shapes
300g risotto rice
125ml dry white wine
900ml chicken stock, hot
200g frozen petits pois

TO GARNISH   shredded fresh basil

each serving provides
575kcals • 44g protein
13g fat of which 3g saturates
64.5g carbohydrate of which
4g sugars • 5g fibre
210mg sodium • 182g vegetables

1 Heat the oil in a large, heavy-based frying pan over a medium heat. Add the pancetta and stir for 2 minutes until it is sizzling and starting to colour.

2 Add the chicken pieces and stir around for 2 minutes. Stir in the leeks, garlic and courgettes and fry, stirring frequently, for 3–5 minutes until they soften.

3 Stir in the rice, then pour in the wine. Increase the heat and simmer, stirring until almost all the wine has evaporated.

4 Reduce the heat to moderate and start adding the stock, a ladleful at a time, stirring frequently.

5 When there are just 2 ladles of stock left, stir in the peas. Continue adding the stock, stirring until the risotto is moist and creamy. Season to taste, then serve sprinkled with fresh basil.

variation
• Sliced green beans or mange-tout would also be good as alternatives to peas.

2 portions fruit & veg

575 kcals

Seafood paella

An ideal dish for entertaining, this colourful and exotic dish is made with a **mixture of white fish and seafood**, plus **red pepper, asparagus, tomatoes and artichokes.** Serve with a green salad.

SERVES 4
PREPARATION TIME 25 minutes
COOKING TIME 35 minutes

1.5 litres fish or chicken stock
1 small onion, halved
large pinch of saffron
3 tbsp olive oil
2 large garlic cloves, crushed
1 red pepper, deseeded
    and chopped
450g paella or risotto rice
150ml dry white wine
350g firm white fish (such as
    cod, hake or haddock),
    skinned and cut into chunks
225g peeled, raw tiger prawns
125g squid, cleaned and sliced
150g asparagus, trimmed
    and sliced
2 large tomatoes, skinned,
    deseeded and chopped
12 stoned olives, sliced
2 tbsp chopped fresh parsley
1 tbsp lemon juice
390g can artichoke hearts,
    drained, rinsed and halved

TO GARNISH lemon wedges,
    chopped fresh parsley

1 Pour the stock into a very large saucepan with the onion and saffron. Bring to the boil, then cover and reduce the heat. Simmer gently for 10 minutes, then strain into a large jug.

2 Heat the oil in the saucepan or a paella pan and add the garlic and red pepper. Cook gently for 2–3 minutes, then add the rice. Cook for 5 minutes, stirring often, until the rice looks transparent.

3 Add the wine, stir, then allow it to bubble up and evaporate. Ladle about one third of the reserved stock into the rice. When it has all been absorbed, add a further third, then cook gently until it has been absorbed.

4 Add all the remaining ingredients to the pan, along with the rest of the stock. Cook gently, stirring occasionally, for about 10 minutes until all the seafood is cooked and the rice and vegetables are tender, adding extra stock or hot water, if needed.

5 Season to taste and tip into a serving dish if not cooked in a paella pan. Garnish with lemon wedges and extra chopped parsley.

706 kcals

2.5 portions fruit & veg

fiesta food

each serving provides 706kcals • 44g protein
13g fat of which 2g saturates • 94g carbohydrate of which 6g sugars
3g fibre • 410mg sodium • 213g vegetables

Chicken & chorizo paella

A little spicy chorizo goes a long way and adds a **fabulous flavour** to this colourful rice and vegetable dish. Camargue red rice is **especially nutritious,** with a **higher fibre** content even than brown rice, and **a wonderful nutty texture.**

SERVES 4
PREPARATION TIME 25 minutes
COOKING TIME 45 minutes

85g chorizo sausage, diced
1 tbsp olive oil
350g skinless chicken breast fillets,
cut into 2.5cm chunks
1 large onion, chopped
2 celery sticks, diced
2 garlic cloves, crushed
1 red pepper, deseeded and diced
1 green pepper, deseeded and diced
1 yellow pepper, deseeded and diced
250g Camargue red rice
4 tomatoes, finely diced
2 bay leaves
2 sprigs of fresh thyme
750ml boiling water
200g frozen peas
200g frozen sweetcorn
15g fresh parsley, chopped

variations

• This rice and vegetable mixture makes a good base for a vegetarian dish. Omit the chorizo and chicken and use 2 tbsp olive oil to cook the vegetables. Season the vegetables with a generous sprinkling of paprika and a little nutmeg when adding the rice. Add 2 x 400g cans of chickpeas with the frozen vegetables. Serve topped with a little half-fat crème fraîche.

• Turkey breast or lean diced pork fillet could be used instead of chicken.

SERVES 4 Ⓥ
PREPARATION TIME 30 minutes
COOKING TIME 45–60 minutes

2 tbsp olive oil
2 shallots, chopped
2 garlic cloves, crushed
1 aubergine, diced
1 red pepper, deseeded
and diced
200g long-grain brown rice
1 litre vegetable stock, hot
2 courgettes, diced
175g closed-cup chestnut
mushrooms, quartered
220g pack smoked tofu, diced
3 tbsp chopped fresh
tarragon (optional)

1 Dry-fry the chorizo in a large, heavy-based saucepan or flameproof casserole over a medium heat for about 2 minutes, stirring continuously. Add the oil and chicken and increase the heat slightly, then cook for about 5 minutes until coloured all over, stirring occasionally. Remove the chicken and chorizo from the pan using a draining spoon and set aside.

2 Add the onion, celery, garlic and peppers to the oil remaining in the pan. Cook, stirring frequently, for 5 minutes until the vegetables are softened slightly. Stir in the rice, tomatoes, bay leaves and thyme, then replace the chicken and chorizo and pour in the water. Bring back to the boil, stirring occasionally. Reduce the heat to low, cover and cook gently for 25 minutes.

3 Add the peas and sweetcorn, forking them lightly into the rice mixture. Re-cover and continue to simmer for a further 5 minutes until the rice is tender and all the liquid is absorbed. Discard the bay leaves and thyme stalks and season to taste, then fork through the parsley and serve.

each serving provides 550kcals
37g protein • 12g fat of which 3g saturates
75g carbohydrate of which 15g sugars
7g fibre • 202mg sodium • 386g vegetables

550 kcals

4.5 portions fruit & veg

great comfort food

Vegetarian paella

A wonderfully rich and satisfying dish, this **vegetarian version of a classic** is a great way to introduce your family to tofu, which is a good source of **low-fat protein, vitamins and minerals.** Serve hot with a tomato salad.

1 Heat the oil in a paella pan or other large, heavy-based pan and fry the shallots and garlic gently for 4–5 minutes, to soften. Add the aubergine and fry over a moderate heat, stirring occasionally, until beginning to brown.

2 Add the pepper slices and stir for a further 2–3 minutes, then stir the rice into the pan, turning to coat evenly. Add about half the stock and bring to the boil, stirring.

3 Partially cover the pan and cook on a low heat, stirring occasionally, for 25–30 minutes, until the rice is beginning to swell. Add a little more stock to moisten, then stir in the courgettes and mushrooms. Continue to cook uncovered for 20–30 minutes, adding more stock as necessary, until the rice is tender and the stock is absorbed. (You might not need all the stock as there will be some variation in absorption depending on the diameter of the pan used and the degree of heat.)

4 Stir lightly and test the rice by tasting a grain – the grains should be tender with just a slight firmness in the centre. Stir in the tofu and tarragon, if using, then warm through and season to taste. Serve hot.

each serving provides
312kcals • 11g protein
10g fat of which 2g saturates
47g carbohydrate of which 6g sugars
4g fibre • 11mg sodium • 214g vegetables

2.5 portions fruit & veg

312 kcals

SERVES 4 V
PREPARATION TIME 12 minutes,
  plus 5 minutes standing
COOKING TIME about 20 minutes

- 2 tbsp vegetable oil
- 2 onions, finely chopped
- ¼ tsp crushed dried chillies,
  or to taste
- 400g toasted buckwheat
- 400g can chopped tomatoes
- 600ml vegetable stock
- 12 mi-cuit (semi-dried)
  tomatoes, chopped
- pinch of sugar
- 30g fresh mint
- 75g feta cheese, drained
- 40g stoned black olives, sliced

cook's tips

- If you can't find buckwheat at the supermarket, it is readily available from health-food shops.
- Mi-cuit tomatoes, sold on the deli counter, are semi-dried tomatoes with a very sweet flavour. Alternatively, use sun-dried tomatoes that have been packed in oil and use the oil from the jar in step 1.

variation

- The feta can be replaced with another semi-soft cheese, such as diced Brie.

Buckwheat pilaf with tomatoes & feta

Also called 'kasha', whole buckwheat grains give a pleasing chewy texture to this hearty vegetarian pilaf. Buckwheat is higher in protein than most grains, as well as providing B vitamins, minerals and fibre.

1 Put the oil in a flameproof casserole or large, heavy-based saucepan with a tight-fitting lid, over a medium heat. Add the onions and chilli flakes and fry, stirring occasionally, for about 5 minutes until the onions are softened, but not coloured.

2 Stir in the buckwheat and continue stirring for about 2 minutes until it smells 'toasty'. Stir in the canned tomatoes with their juice, the stock, mi-cuit tomatoes and sugar. Tie together 5 sprigs of the mint and add these too, with a little seasoning. Bring to the boil, stirring occasionally.

3 Reduce the heat to low, cover the pan tightly and leave to simmer for 10 minutes, without lifting the lid, until the liquid is absorbed and the grains are tender.

4 Discard the bunch of mint sprigs. Crumble over the feta cheese and lightly stir in with the olives. Put a folded tea towel over the top of the saucepan to absorb excess moisture, then replace the lid and leave to stand for 5 minutes.

5 Roughly tear the remaining mint leaves from the sprigs and scatter over the top. Serve at once.

each serving provides 596kcals • 14g protein 20g fat of which 4g saturates • 96g carbohydrate of which 9g sugars • 4g fibre • 689mg sodium • 210g vegetables

2.5 portions fruit & veg

596 kcals

SERVES 4
PREPARATION TIME 15 minutes
COOKING TIME 35 minutes

1 tbsp olive oil
1 onion, finely chopped
2 carrots, peeled and diced
2 celery sticks, diced
1 garlic clove, crushed
225g pearl barley
600ml chicken stock, hot
1 tbsp chopped fresh thyme
  or 1 tsp dried
grated zest and juice of 1 lemon
150g frozen peas
400g skinned roasted chicken
  breast, shredded into small pieces
50g rocket

each serving provides

426kcals • 34g protein
7.5g fat of which 1g saturates
59g carbohydrate of which 8g sugars
4g fibre • 79mg sodium
172g vegetables

special supper   **2** portions fruit & veg   **426** kcals

Lemon barley pilaf with chicken

Barley is a much under-rated and seldom used grain, which is a great shame since it has a pleasing flavour and texture as well as being a good source of fibre. Here is it cooked with a medley of vegetables in a lemon and thyme stock. The addition of cooked chicken turns the dish into a great main course.

1 Heat the oil in a large, heavy-based saucepan over a moderate heat. Stir in the onion, carrots, celery and garlic, then cook gently for about 10 minutes, stirring occasionally, until softened but not browned.

2 Stir in the barley and cook for 1 minute longer. Pour in the stock and bring to the boil. Add the thyme and lemon zest. Reduce the heat to very low, cover and simmer, stirring occasionally, for 20 minutes or until the barley is almost soft.

3 Add the peas, re-cover and simmer for a further 4–5 minutes until the barley is soft but not mushy and all the stock is absorbed. Stir in the lemon juice and season to taste.

4 Add the chicken pieces and rocket leaves and lightly toss together. Serve at once.

variation

• This pilaf is also delicious eaten at room temperature as a salad. Allow the pilaf to cool before adding the chicken and rocket leaves.

Smoked haddock kedgeree

A subtly spiced rice dish, this is based on a classic kedgeree recipe but with extra vegetables to add vitamins. Serve with a side salad.

SERVES 4
PREPARATION TIME 10 minutes
COOKING TIME 25–30 minutes

300g undyed smoked haddock fillet
1 bay leaf
450ml vegetable stock, hot
1 tbsp vegetable oil
2 shallots, finely chopped
½ tsp ground cumin
½ tsp ground coriander
1 tsp mild curry powder
300g basmati rice, rinsed
small strip of lemon zest and
   1 tbsp lemon juice
150g shelled fresh or frozen peas
4 tomatoes, skinned and chopped
2 tbsp snipped fresh chives

TO GARNISH 2 eggs, hard-boiled and quartered

1 Put the smoked haddock in a deep frying pan. Add the bay leaf, then pour over the stock. Heat to simmering point, then reduce the heat, half-cover the pan with a lid and poach for 6–8 minutes until the flesh flakes easily when tested with the tip of a knife. (If preferred, the fish can be cooked in a microwave.) Lift the fish out of the cooking liquid and set aside. Make up the volume of the cooking liquid/stock to 600ml with water and reserve with the bay leaf.

2 Rinse out the pan, then add the oil and heat over a moderate heat for a few seconds. Add the shallots and cook for 4–5 minutes until softened, then stir in the spices, followed by the rice. Stir for a few seconds to coat with the oil and spices, then add the reserved cooking liquid and bay leaf and the strip of lemon zest. Bring to the boil.

3 Reduce the heat to a gentle simmer, cover and cook for 10 minutes. Add the peas, cover again and cook for a further 5 minutes or until the rice is tender and nearly all the stock is absorbed.

4 Meanwhile, flake the fish, removing any skin and bones. Reduce the heat under the pan to very low, then gently stir the fish into the rice together with the tomatoes, lemon juice and chives.

5 Season to taste, bearing in mind that smoked haddock is quite salty, then transfer the kedgeree to a warm serving dish and garnish with the egg quarters.

variations

• For a salmon kedgeree, use salmon fillets and replace the chives with chopped fresh dill.
• For vegetarians, omit the fish and pan-fry 200g sliced, assorted wild and cultivated mushrooms with the shallots and spices. Add 1 ripe but firm avocado, cut into 1cm pieces, to the cooked rice just before serving.

445 kcals

1.5 portions fruit & veg

ideal brunch dish

each serving provides 445kcals • 27g protein
7.5g fat of which 1g saturates • 67g carbohydrate of which 4g sugars
3g fibre • 620mg sodium • 138g vegetables

Salmon & pea pilaf

Canned salmon is very **versatile** and super healthy, being **rich in omega-3 fatty acids.** Combined with rice, subtly flavoured with cardamom, and peas from the freezer, this is a terrific **easy-to-make** main dish.

SERVES 4
PREPARATION TIME 15 minutes
COOKING TIME 40 minutes

140g wild rice, rinsed
1 bay leaf
6 green cardamoms, seeds only
1 litre vegetable stock, hot
418g can pink salmon
200g brown basmati rice, rinsed
2 tsp cumin seeds
280g frozen peas, thawed
4 spring onions, finely sliced
grated zest of 1 lemon
2 tbsp chopped fresh coriander

TO GARNISH lemon wedges

variation

• For a vegetarian pilaf, omit the salmon. Add a cinnamon stick with the stock. Add a 400g can mixed beans or chickpeas, drained and rinsed, with the peas and fork 225g shredded fresh spinach through the rice, 5 minutes before the end of cooking. Add chopped fresh mint instead of the coriander.

each serving provides

514kcals • 35g protein
9.5g fat of which 2g saturates
78g carbohydrate of which 3g sugars
5g fibre • 468mg sodium
80g vegetables

514 kcals

1 portion fruit & veg

1 Place the wild rice in a large saucepan with the bay leaf, cardamom seeds and stock. Bring to the boil, reduce the heat and cover the pan, then simmer for 15 minutes.

2 Meanwhile, drain the salmon and reserve the liquid from the can. Remove and discard the skin and bones and flake the fish, then set it aside. Add the basmati rice and reserved salmon liquid to the wild rice with a pinch of salt. Bring back to the boil and stir once, then reduce the heat and cover the pan. Cook gently for 15 minutes.

3 Roast the cumin seeds in a small, heavy-based pan for 2–3 minutes over a medium heat, shaking the pan until they give off their aroma. Tip the seeds out of the pan onto a small plate as soon as they smell aromatic.

4 Add the peas and cumin seeds to the rice, fork them lightly into the grains, re-cover the pan and cook for a further 5 minutes. Add the salmon, leaving it on top of the rice without forking it in, cover and leave to cook gently for 5 minutes until the rice is tender and all the cooking liquid is absorbed.

5 Finally, add the spring onions, lemon zest and coriander and fork through. Check the seasoning and discard the bay leaf before serving, garnished with lemon wedges.

Prawn & spinach biryani

SERVES 4
PREPARATION TIME 15 minutes
COOKING TIME 15 minutes

400g can chopped tomatoes
2 tbsp vegetable oil
1 large onion, halved and
  thinly sliced
1 red chilli, deseeded and
  thinly sliced
15g fresh root ginger, peeled
  and finely chopped
1 tbsp ground cumin
1 tbsp ground coriander
1 tsp ground turmeric
½ tsp ground nutmeg
225g basmati rice, rinsed
pinch of sugar
300g baby leaf spinach,
  washed and roughly torn
225g peeled, raw tiger prawns,
  thawed if frozen

variations

• Replace some or all of the spinach with thinly sliced mushrooms, adding them to the casserole with the rice.
• Sliced red or green peppers would also work well in this dish. Add them with the onions.
• Serve any leftovers cold the next day as a rice salad.

A **fragrantly spiced** pilaf-style dish that doesn't take much more effort than ringing for a take-away yet is **much healthier** as it is low in fat. Serve with a **refreshing raita** to complete the meal (see page 27).

1 Drain the tomatoes in a sieve over a heatproof measuring jug, then set aside. Bring a kettle of water to the boil.

2 Heat the oil in a large flameproof casserole over a medium heat. Add the onion, chilli and ginger and stir for 3 minutes. Stir in the cumin, coriander, turmeric and nutmeg and continue stirring until the onion is softened.

3 Add the rice and drained tomatoes to the casserole and stir to mix with the spices. Add enough boiling water to the reserved tomato juice to make up to 450ml. Stir this liquid into the rice with the sugar and add a pinch of salt, then bring to the boil.

4 Reduce the heat to low, cover tightly and leave the rice to cook without lifting the lid for 10–12 minutes until all the liquid has been absorbed, the rice grains are tender and tiny holes appear on the surface.

5 Stir in the spinach, as much as you can at a time, adding more as each addition wilts. When all the spinach has been added, lay the prawns on top, re-cover the casserole and turn down the heat to very low. Cook for 2 minutes, then turn off the heat and leave to stand for 1 minute, without lifting the lid, by which time the spinach will have wilted further and the prawns will have cooked through. Gently fork together to combine the rice, spinach and prawns. Serve immediately.

each serving provides 348kcals • 17g protein
8g fat of which 1g saturates • 54g carbohydrate of which 7.5g sugars
3g fibre • 245mg sodium • 240g vegetables

348 kcals

3 portions fruit & veg

3 tbsp olive oil
1 large Spanish onion, finely chopped
2 garlic cloves, finely chopped
½ head of celery, finely diced and
  leaves reserved for garnish
1 red pepper, deseeded and chopped
½ tsp chilli powder, or to taste
1 tsp ground cumin
225g long-grain rice
2 x 400g cans chopped tomatoes
1 tbsp chopped fresh thyme
  or 1 tsp dried
300g skinned monkfish fillet,
  cut into 4 pieces
8 peeled, raw tiger prawns,
  about 75g in total
2 tbsp chopped fresh parsley

TO SERVE 1 lemon, cut lengthways
  into 4 wedges

each serving provides

400kcals • 22g protein
9g fat of which 1g saturates
62g carbohydrate of which 12g sugars
4g fibre • 189mg sodium
360g vegetables

400 kcals

4.5 portions fruit & veg

Deep south jambalaya

The spicy tomato flavour and aroma of this **easy-going rice dish** make it really appealing. Tender monkfish, juicy prawns and **plenty of vegetables** all combine to make a well-balanced, complete meal.

1 Put the oil in a large, deep frying pan and heat gently. Add the onion, garlic, celery, red pepper, chilli and cumin. Cook, stirring often, for 10–12 minutes until softened. Add the rice and cook, stirring, for 2 minutes.

2 Drain the tomatoes in a sieve over a measuring jug or bowl. Reserve the juice, then add the tomatoes to the rice. Sprinkle over the thyme, stir well and reduce the heat a little.

3 Make up the tomato juice to 1 litre with boiling water, pour into the pan and stir well. Bring to the boil, then reduce the heat, cover the pan with the lid slightly ajar, and simmer gently for 10 minutes.

4 Season the rice to taste, then place the pieces of monkfish on top. Continue cooking, partly covered as before, for 5 minutes. Stir the rice carefully and turn the monkfish over, then add the prawns. Partly cover the pan again and cook for a further 5 minutes or until the prawns have turned pink, the monkfish pieces are cooked, and the rice is tender. The dish should be moist, not dry.

5 Remove from the heat, cover tightly and leave for 5 minutes. Scatter the celery leaves and parsley over the top and serve with lemon wedges to squeeze over.

cook's tip

• If you can't find raw tiger prawns, you can use cooked peeled prawns. Add them at the very end of cooking just to warm through, before you leave the dish to stand before serving.

Spicy rice with chickpeas

This lightly curried rice dish makes a simple yet satisfying vegetarian meal, with the chickpeas providing valuable protein. Serve with a yoghurt raita (see page 27) and mango chutney. A fresh, green, baby spinach leaf salad would also make a good accompaniment.

SERVES 4 Ⓥ
PREPARATION TIME 15 minutes
COOKING TIME 20–25 minutes

1 tbsp vegetable oil
1 onion, sliced
3 tbsp medium curry paste
175g basmati rice, rinsed
500ml vegetable stock, hot
1 sweet potato, peeled and
    chopped into small chunks
4 medium tomatoes, chopped
25g sultanas
400g can chickpeas,
    drained and rinsed
3 tbsp chopped fresh coriander
50g unsalted cashews,
    roughly chopped

cook's tip
• The rice needs to be rinsed thoroughly, in a sieve under cold running water, before cooking. This removes excess starch so the rice is light and fluffy when cooked.

variation
• If liked, you could add a small amount of diced firm tofu at the end of cooking, or for a non-vegetarian version, some diced, cooked chicken.

each serving provides
434kcals • 12g protein
14g fat of which 2g saturates
67g carbohydrate of which
14g sugars • 5g fibre
391mg sodium • 175g vegetables

2 portions fruit & veg
434 kcals
sweet & savoury

1 Heat the oil in a large pan and fry the onion on a medium heat for 7–8 minutes, stirring until pale golden. Add the curry paste and stir-fry for about 1 minute.

2 Stir in the rice, then add the stock, sweet potato, tomatoes and sultanas. Bring to the boil, then reduce the heat to a simmer. Cover the pan and leave on a low heat for 20–25 minutes, stirring occasionally, until the rice is just tender and the stock is absorbed. Add a little more stock if the mixture becomes too dry before the rice is cooked.

3 Stir in the chickpeas and gently heat through. Stir in the coriander, season to taste and scatter with the cashew nuts to serve.

Mexican arroz rojo

Flavoured with a small amount of spicy chorizo sausage and crushed dried chillies, this is a traditional taste of Mexico. A quick-to-prepare guacamole (see page 27) and soft flour tortillas complete the meal.

SERVES 4
PREPARATION TIME 10 minutes
COOKING TIME 45 minutes

2 tbsp vegetable oil
75g chorizo sausage, chopped
1 onion, finely chopped
2 garlic cloves, crushed
200g long-grain brown rice, rinsed
2 x 400g cans chopped tomatoes
½ tbsp tomato purée
140g frozen sweetcorn
140g frozen peas
1 bay leaf
200ml vegetable stock or water
½ tsp crushed dried chillies,
    or to taste (optional)
½ tsp sugar

TO GARNISH sprigs of fresh
coriander, lime wedges

TO SERVE 4 flour tortillas

1 Heat the oil in a large flameproof casserole or saucepan with a tight-fitting lid over a moderately high heat. Add the chorizo sausage and stir for 2 minutes. Add the onion and garlic and continue cooking for 3–5 minutes, stirring, until they are soft.

2 Add the rice to the pan and stir for 1 minute, then stir in the tomatoes with their juice, the tomato purée, sweetcorn, peas, bay leaf, vegetable stock, crushed chillies, if using, and sugar.

3 Slowly bring to the boil, stirring occasionally, then reduce the heat to low, cover the pan tightly and leave to simmer for 30–40 minutes until the rice is tender and all the liquid is absorbed. Season to taste.

4 When the rice has finished cooking, remove from the heat and leave to stand for 5 minutes, with the pan covered. Heat the flour tortillas under a hot grill. Garnish the rice with coriander and lime wedges and serve with the warm tortillas.

variation

• In Mexico, this popular 'red rice' dish is made with fresh, bright red, juicy tomatoes. When you have well-flavoured fresh tomatoes, use 600g, deseeded and chopped, in place of the canned tomatoes and increase the amount of stock or water to 600ml.

cook's tip

• Several factors, such as the width of your pan, will affect the cooking time for the rice. It is ready when the grains are tender and all the liquid has been absorbed. Add a little extra stock or water if needed.

each serving provides

538kcals • 17g protein
13g fat of which 3g saturates
94g carbohydrate of which
13g sugars • 7g fibre
349mg sodium • 320g vegetables

4 portions fruit & veg

538 kcals

veg boost

Caribbean coconut rice & peas

This recipe is based on a traditional Caribbean favourite. It's made with **black-eyed beans** or red kidney beans, which are called peas in Jamaica – hence the name of the dish. Red pepper has been added for **extra vegetable content** and a small amount of **lean, smoked bacon** lifts the flavour.

SERVES 4
PREPARATION TIME 15 minutes
COOKING TIME 25 minutes

1 tbsp vegetable oil
3 lean, smoked, thick-cut back bacon rashers, trimmed and diced
1 large onion, finely chopped
1 large red pepper, deseeded and thinly sliced
2 garlic cloves, finely chopped
1 red or green chilli, deseeded and finely chopped
225g long-grain rice, rinsed
450ml boiling water
400ml can reduced-fat coconut milk
400g can red kidney or black-eyed beans, drained
2 sprigs of fresh thyme
2 tomatoes, diced

TO SERVE Tabasco sauce

variations

• Instead of using bacon, just cook the onion in the oil, then add some cooked meat, such as shredded chicken or pork, to the finished dish before serving.
• For a vegetarian meal, simply leave out the bacon.

1 Heat the oil in a large saucepan or deep frying pan, add the bacon and cook over a gentle heat for 2 minutes until lightly browned. Add the onion and cook, stirring, for 3 minutes or until softened. Reduce the heat and stir in the pepper, garlic and chilli and cook for 1 minute.

2 Stir in the rice, then pour in the boiling water and the coconut milk and add a pinch of salt. Bring to the boil, then reduce the heat. Add the drained beans and thyme, then cover and simmer for 10 minutes.

3 Add the tomatoes to the pan and continue to cook gently for a further 10 minutes until the rice is just tender. (The mixture should still be a little sloppy.) Remove the sprigs of thyme and serve with Tabasco sauce to sprinkle over.

1.5 portions fruit & veg

459 kcals

each serving provides

459kcals • 15g protein
14g fat of which 7g saturates
72g carbohydrate of which 10g sugars
8g fibre • 602mg sodium
143g vegetables

Stir-fries & pan-fries

Delicious and healthy, stir-fries and pan-fries are the ideal fast food. The ingredients are prepared in advance and cooked quickly over a high heat, in a wok or a deep-sided frying pan. Quick cooking retains many of the nutritional benefits of the ingredients, and only a little oil is needed. From tasty family suppers such as Cantonese beef with peppers and pasta, to impressive dinner-party dishes like Spaghetti with scallops, asparagus and chard, you can enjoy great tastes from around the world.

Lamb with courgettes & ginger

The addition of chunky potato sticks and **a generous amount of green vegetables** turns a lean lamb stir-fry into a simple but delicious meal, *served straight from the wok.*

SERVES 4

PREPARATION TIME 25 minutes, plus 2–3 hours marinating (if time allows)

COOKING TIME 10 minutes

2 tsp toasted sesame oil
1 tbsp lemon juice
25g fresh root ginger, peeled and finely chopped
3 tbsp chopped fresh mint
350g lean lamb leg or neck fillet, cut into thin slices
700g large waxy new potatoes, scrubbed
3 tbsp vegetable oil
2 courgettes, sliced diagonally
6 spring onions, sliced diagonally
150g shelled fresh or thawed frozen peas
1 tbsp soy sauce
4 tbsp lamb or vegetable stock
2 tsp runny honey

variations

• For a pork and pear stir-fry, use 350g lean pork fillet. Instead of courgettes, quarter and slice 2 firm but ripe pears, preferably red-skinned; add them after the potatoes, at the same time as the spring onions.

• For a vegetarian dish, replace the lamb with a packet of tofu, about 350g, cut into bite-sized cubes. Marinate in a mixture of 2 tsp toasted sesame oil, 1 tbsp soy sauce, 1 tbsp mirin (Japanese rice wine) or sherry, 1 crushed garlic clove and 1 tbsp finely chopped fresh root ginger.

1 Whisk together the sesame oil, lemon juice, half the ginger and 1 tbsp of the chopped mint in a shallow dish. Add the lamb and stir well, then cover and leave to marinate while preparing the remaining ingredients (or, if time allows, marinate for 2–3 hours in the fridge).

2 Put the potatoes in a large pan and pour over enough boiling water to cover them. Bring back to the boil, half-cover the pan with a lid and simmer for 12 minutes or until almost tender when pierced with the tip of a sharp knife. Drain and leave until they are cool enough to handle. Cut across into slices slightly thicker than 5mm, then cut the slices into sticks. Put them in a bowl, drizzle over 1 tbsp of the vegetable oil and gently toss to coat. (This will stop the potatoes from sticking together when stir-fried.)

3 Heat 1 tbsp of the remaining oil in a wok or large frying pan. When the oil is hot, add the lamb and stir-fry over a high heat for 1 minute or until just browned, but still fairly rare. Quickly remove and set aside.

4 Add the remaining oil to the pan and, when hot, add the sliced courgettes. Stir-fry for 1 minute, then add the potatoes. Cook for 3–4 minutes, stirring all the time, until lightly browned, taking care not to break up the potatoes. Add the spring onions and cook for 1 more minute, stirring.

5 Reduce the heat to moderate and add the peas, soy sauce, stock, honey and remaining ginger. Return the lamb with any juices. Stir-fry for 2–3 minutes or until the liquid is bubbling and everything is tender and hot. Season to taste and scatter over the remaining chopped mint, then serve.

410 kcals

1.5 portions fruit & veg

super stir-fry

each serving provides

410kcals • 25g protein
17g fat of which 2g saturates
39g carbohydrate of which
9g sugars • 4.5g fibre
237mg sodium • 144g vegetables

Stir-fried greens with bacon & chestnuts

Stir-frying is a quick method of cooking that retains many of the vitamins and minerals that may be lost during boiling. This is a great way to cook Brussels sprouts and cabbage, sure to tempt even the most reluctant eaters of greens. If liked, serve with wholemeal or seeded rolls.

SERVES 4
PREPARATION TIME 20 minutes
COOKING TIME 10 minutes

1½ tbsp vegetable oil
4 lean thick-cut smoked back bacon rashers, cut into thin strips
2 tsp toasted sesame oil
2 leeks, trimmed and thinly sliced
225g Brussels sprouts, sliced
½ Savoy cabbage, shredded
240g can or vacuum-pack chestnuts
1 tbsp soy sauce
3 tbsp orange juice

variations

• For a vegetarian dish, replace the bacon with 250g cubed smoked tofu, adding it with the chestnuts and without frying first.
• Use fresh chestnuts if available. To prepare, score a cross in the base of each chestnut with a small, sharp knife. Cook in a pan of boiling water for 7 minutes, remove using a draining spoon, then when cool enough to handle, peel off the shell and inner skin. Return to the pan of boiling water and simmer for 10–12 minutes until tender.

1 Heat the oil in a wok or large, deep frying pan, then fry the bacon for about 2 minutes until lightly browned. Remove from the pan with a draining spoon and set aside, leaving the fat and juices behind in the pan.

2 Pour the sesame oil into the pan and heat for a few seconds, then add the leeks and fry gently for 30 seconds until just softened. Add the Brussels sprouts and cabbage and stir-fry for 4–5 minutes until almost tender.

3 Return the bacon to the pan together with the chestnuts, then stir in the soy sauce and orange juice. Cook for 2 minutes to heat through and to allow the greens to finish cooking. Season to taste with freshly ground black pepper. (There is no need to add salt as plenty is in the dish already from the bacon and soy sauce.) Serve straight away.

2.5 portions fruit & veg

268 kcals

each serving provides 268kcals • 13g protein
11g fat of which 2g saturates • 31g carbohydrate of which 12g sugars
9g fibre • 684mg sodium • 200g vegetables

Stir-fried chicken livers with mushrooms

The delicate flavour and creamy texture of chicken livers work well with **chestnut mushrooms and sherry,** while colourful shoots of purple-sprouting broccoli add further **vitamins and minerals.** The stir-fry is served on toasted ciabatta to soak up the juices.

SERVES 4
PREPARATION TIME   15 minutes
COOKING TIME   10 minutes

400g chicken livers,
   thawed if frozen
200g small chestnut
   mushrooms, sliced
200g purple sprouting
   broccoli spears
2 tbsp olive oil
1 red onion, finely chopped
2 garlic cloves, finely chopped
75ml dry sherry
1 tbsp redcurrant jelly

TO SERVE   1 ciabatta, cut into
   8 thick slices

1 Tip the chicken livers into a colander and rinse gently under cold running water. Drain thoroughly, then pat them dry with kitchen paper.

2 Using kitchen scissors, trim off any stringy white pieces and any discoloured edges. Season and put aside.

3 Wipe the mushrooms with a damp cloth to remove any grit but do not wash. Trim the broccoli to remove any coarse or woody stems, leaving the upper leaves and stems as well as the heads.

4 Gently heat the oil in a large, non-stick frying pan. Add the onion and cook, stirring frequently, until it is soft and translucent. Add the livers and gently stir-fry over a medium heat for 2 minutes until they are lightly coloured. Preheat the grill to medium.

5 Add the mushrooms and broccoli and stir-fry for 2 minutes. Add the garlic, sherry and redcurrant jelly. Stir well, then cover the pan and leave to simmer gently for 3 minutes until the broccoli is just tender when pierced with the tip of a sharp knife and the livers are slightly pink inside.

6 Meanwhile toast the ciabatta. Check the stir-fry for seasoning, then arrange the ciabatta on individual plates, 2 slices per serving, and spoon over the livers and vegetables. Serve immediately.

each serving provides

432kcals • 29g protein
12g fat of which 2g saturates
50g carbohydrate of which
10g sugars • 5g fibre
517mg sodium • 129g vegetables

1.5 portions fruit & veg **432** kcals

variations

• Replace the broccoli with coloured peppers – one each green, red and yellow, deseeded and thinly sliced.
• At Christmas time, cranberry jelly or sauce makes an excellent seasonal change to the redcurrant jelly, and you could use port in place of the sherry.

Cantonese beef with peppers & pasta

A popular Chinese-style stir-fry that mixes **distinctively flavoured,** fermented black beans with prime lean beef and pasta to make an **easy wok meal.**

SERVES 4
PREPARATION TIME 20 minutes,
  plus 30 minutes marinating
COOKING TIME 10–12 minutes

2 tbsp dry sherry
2 tbsp dark soy sauce
1 tsp toasted sesame oil
2 large garlic cloves, crushed
15g fresh root ginger, peeled
  and finely chopped
2 tbsp fermented black beans, rinsed
1 tsp sugar
500g lean rump steak, trimmed
  of fat and cut across the grain
  into thin slices
300g penne (pasta quills)
2 tbsp vegetable oil
1 large onion, roughly chopped
2 green peppers, deseeded and
  roughly chopped
220g can water chestnuts, drained

1 Combine the sherry, soy sauce, sesame oil, garlic, ginger, black beans and sugar in a shallow dish. Add the steak, stir to coat with the marinade, then cover and put in the fridge for 30 minutes or so. This will tenderise the steak and allow time for the flavours to soak into the meat.

2 When you are ready to cook, bring a large pan of lightly salted water to the boil. Add the pasta and cook for 10–12 minutes until just tender.

3 Meanwhile, heat the oil in a wok or large, heavy-based frying pan. Toss in the onion and peppers and stir-fry over a high heat for 2–3 minutes until just softened and beginning to brown. Remove the vegetables using a draining spoon so most of the oil is left behind.

4 Put the wok or pan back on the heat and again using a draining spoon, lift out the steak from the marinade and add to the pan. Stir-fry over a high heat for 2–3 minutes until the steak is just tender. Return the vegetables to the pan with the water chestnuts and remaining marinade. Toss everything together over a high heat.

5 Drain the pasta thoroughly and tip into the pan with the stir-fried steak and vegetables. Toss together and serve immediately.

Spicy pork & baby corn stir-fry

A spicy stir-fry with subtle curry flavours. It's quick to cook, includes a range of colourful vegetables and uses straight-to-wok noodles for ease of cooking.

SERVES 4
PREPARATION TIME 20 minutes
COOKING TIME 20 minutes

2 tbsp vegetable oil
350g lean boneless pork, cut into thin strips
1 tsp ground turmeric
1 tbsp ground coriander
50g fresh root ginger, peeled and cut into thin strips
2 garlic cloves, crushed
2 green peppers, deseeded and cut into thin strips
300g baby corn, halved lengthways
6 spring onions, sliced diagonally
4 tbsp dry or medium sherry
4 tbsp chicken or vegetable stock
2 tbsp light soy sauce
300g bean sprouts
300g straight-to-wok noodles
4 tbsp roughly chopped fresh coriander

variations

• Good-quality curry powder or a curry paste can be used instead of turmeric and coriander. Add 2–3 tsp powder or paste to the meat in step 1.

• Chicken, turkey or lamb fillet may be used instead of the pork. Ready-cut, stir-fry pork saves time if you're in a hurry.

• For a vegetarian curry, instead of the meat, stir-fry 200g unsalted, unroasted cashew nuts over a medium heat for 2 minutes until golden. Remove to a plate, continue with the recipe, then toss them into the pan with the vegetables and noodles at the end of cooking.

• A 170g can of bamboo shoots, drained, would make a handy alternative to baby corn.

1 Heat 1 tbsp of the oil in a large frying pan or wok. Add the pork and stir-fry for 5 minutes over a high heat. Reduce the heat, sprinkle in the turmeric and ground coriander and continue to stir-fry for 2 minutes. Transfer the meat to a plate and set aside.

2 Pour the remaining oil into the pan and add the ginger, garlic, peppers, corn and spring onions. Stir-fry for 5 minutes, then return the meat to the pan with any juices on the plate. Stir-fry the meat and vegetables together so they are well mixed.

3 Pour in the sherry, stock and soy sauce, then reduce the heat and simmer for 5 minutes. Add the bean sprouts and noodles, cook for 2 more minutes, then sprinkle over the fresh coriander. Stir and serve immediately, straight from the pan.

each serving provides 367kcals • 30g protein 11g fat of which 1g saturates • 33g carbohydrate of which 7g sugars • 6g fibre • 207mg sodium • 245g vegetables

Turkey mange-tout & corn stir-fry

This crunchy, refreshing stir-fry is just what you need for a **mid-week meal** – it can be on the table in **under 30 minutes** from when you walk through the door. The sweetcorn provides carbohydrate, so you don't even need to cook rice or noodles. Accompany with a **simple tomato salad.**

SERVES 4
PREPARATION TIME 10 minutes
COOKING TIME 10 minutes

1 tbsp oyster sauce
3 tbsp chicken or vegetable stock
3 tbsp vegetable oil
1 tbsp black mustard seeds
8 spring onions, trimmed and thinly sliced
3 large garlic cloves, crushed
400g turkey breast fillets, cut into thin strips
200g mange-tout
340g can sweetcorn, drained and rinsed
1 tbsp sesame seeds

TO GARNISH fresh coriander leaves

each serving provides

312kcals • 30g protein • 12.5g fat of which 2g saturates • 24g carbohydrate of which 10g sugars • 3g fibre 403mg sodium • 141g vegetables

1.5 portions fruit & veg

312 kcals

super quick

1 Mix the oyster sauce and stock together in a small bowl, then set aside.

2 Heat a wok or large frying pan over a high heat, add 1 tbsp of the vegetable oil and heat until it is very hot. Add the mustard seeds and stir-fry them for 10–15 seconds until they crackle and 'jump'.

3 Immediately add the remaining oil, spring onions and garlic and stir-fry for 1 minute. Add the turkey and continue stir-frying for a further 2 minutes.

4 Add the mange-tout to the wok and stir in the reserved oyster sauce mixture. Continue stir-frying over a high heat for about 3 minutes until the turkey is cooked through and the mange-tout are just tender to the bite.

5 Add the sweetcorn and stir around for 2 minutes or until warmed through. Sprinkle with sesame seeds and snip fresh coriander leaves over the top just before serving.

variations

• The turkey can be replaced by thinly sliced, skinless chicken thighs or breast fillets. Other suitable vegetables include small broccoli florets, thickly sliced open-cap mushrooms or sliced red or green peppers.

• If you want a more filling meal, omit the sweetcorn and serve the stir-fry with quick-cooking Chinese egg noodles, available from all supermarkets. Simply put the dried noodles in a heatproof bowl, pour over boiling water and leave to soak as directed on the packet. Drain well, then toss them with the other ingredients in the wok.

• Supermarkets also sell a variety of bottled, ready-to-use, stir-fry sauces, which are useful to have in the cupboard. If you use one, omit the oyster sauce and stock.

cook's tip

• Oyster sauce, made from oysters, brine and soy sauce, is popular in Chinese cooking. It adds a rich flavour to this dish, although it is only used in moderation because of its high salt content. No further salt should be needed.

Lemon chicken with broccoli

A family favourite that mixes succulent strips of chicken with a zesty, hot and sour sauce. The whole cashew nuts add a satisfying crunch.

SERVES 4
PREPARATION TIME about 15 minutes
COOKING TIME about 15 minutes

200g spinach noodles, such as fettuccine or tagliatelle
grated zest and juice of 2 large lemons
1½ tbsp cornflour
125ml chicken or vegetable stock
1 tbsp dark soy sauce
2 tsp caster sugar
½ tsp dried crushed chillies, or to taste
85g whole cashew nuts
2½ tbsp vegetable oil
2 small onions, finely chopped
2 garlic cloves, crushed
500g skinless chicken breast fillets, cut into thin strips
250g broccoli, cut into small florets
25g fresh root ginger, peeled and finely chopped

TO GARNISH 4 tbsp chopped fresh coriander or parsley

cook's tip

• You could use any noodles you have in the storecupboard for this dish, such as Chinese egg noodles or rice noodles. Prepare following the pack instructions, then toss with the rest of the stir-fry just before serving.

each serving provides

609kcals • 44g protein
22g fat of which 3g saturates
61g carbohydrate of which
11g sugars • 5g fibre
307mg sodium
183g vegetables

609 kcals

2 portions fruit & veg

1 Bring a large saucepan of lightly salted water to the boil. Add the noodles and boil for 10–12 minutes, or according to the pack instructions, until tender.

2 Meanwhile, make up the lemon juice to 125ml with water, if necessary, then blend with the cornflour in a bowl or jug until smooth. Stir in the stock, soy sauce and sugar, then add the lemon zest and chillies. Set aside.

3 Heat a wok or large frying pan over a high heat. Add the cashew nuts and stir for about 1 minute until browned in places. Immediately tip them out of the pan and set aside.

4 Return the wok to the heat and add the oil, swirling it around to coat the sides. Add the onions and garlic and stir-fry for 3 minutes or until tender. Add the chicken pieces and stir-fry for 2–3 minutes until the chicken is cooked through and beginning to brown.

5 Pour in the reserved lemon-flavoured sauce and add the broccoli florets and ginger. Bring to the boil, then cover and simmer for 4–5 minutes until the broccoli florets are tender-crisp.

6 Drain the noodles well, then add them to the wok. Use 2 large forks to mix them in with the other ingredients. Scatter over the chopped coriander or parsley and cashew nuts, then serve.

Sweet & sour duck with kumquats

Kumquats are a small citrus fruit, like an orange, but the whole fruit is edible, adding a **great tangy flavour** to this easy stir-fry dish. Kumquats are believed to symbolise good fortune in the Far East.

SERVES 4
PREPARATION TIME 25 minutes
COOKING TIME 15 minutes

2 tbsp light soy sauce
2 tbsp rice vinegar
6 tbsp plum sauce
2 tbsp tomato purée
2 tbsp vegetable oil
8 spring onions, sliced
30g fresh root ginger, peeled and cut into strips
4 duck breasts, about 150g each, skinned and thinly sliced
2 red peppers, deseeded and thinly sliced
8 kumquats, thinly sliced
250g pak choi, sliced lengthways
450g pack straight-to-wok, traditional medium noodles

1 Mix together the soy sauce, vinegar, plum sauce and tomato purée in a jug or small bowl and set aside.

2 Heat the oil in a wok or large frying pan and fry the spring onions and ginger over a fairly high heat for about 30 seconds. Add the duck and stir-fry on a high heat for about 2 minutes until lightly cooked.

3 Add the peppers and continue to stir-fry for 4–6 minutes until the peppers and duck are just tender and the juices have evaporated. Add the kumquats and cook for a further 1 minute.

4 Stir the sauce mixture, then pour it into the pan, tossing everything together to coat with the sauce and heat through. Add the pak choi and stir-fry for about 1 minute or until wilted.

5 Finally, add the noodles to the pan, straight from the pack, and stir-fry for 2–3 minutes until thoroughly heated. Serve immediately.

each serving provides 506kcals • 33g protein 15g fat of which 3.5g saturates • 59g carbohydrate of which 18g sugars 7g fibre • 688mg sodium • 187g fruit and vegetables

2 portions fruit & veg

506 kcals

exotic tastes

3

4

variations
• If pak choi is not available, substitute shredded Chinese leaves or young spring greens.
• To make a vegetarian version of this dish, replace the duck with firm smoked tofu. Look out for tofu made with added almonds and sesame seeds, for extra flavour, texture and nutrients.

5

SERVES 4
PREPARATION TIME 20 minutes
COOKING TIME 12 minutes

3 tbsp smooth peanut butter
4 tbsp reduced-fat coconut milk
2 tbsp chicken stock
finely grated zest of 1 lemon
1 tbsp vegetable oil
2 garlic cloves, crushed
1 red chilli, deseeded and
    finely chopped
350g skinless chicken breast
    fillets, cut into thin strips
1 tbsp Chinese five-spice powder
1 red pepper, deseeded and sliced
2 carrots, peeled and cut
    into julienne strips
175g mushrooms, sliced
2 tbsp chopped fresh coriander

Chicken satay stir-fry

An Indonesian-style stir-fry combining **colourful crunchy vegetables** and **tender chicken strips.** Serve with toasted white, wholemeal or sesame pitta bread.

1 In a small bowl, whisk together the peanut butter, coconut milk, stock and lemon zest until blended, then set aside.

2 Heat the oil in a wok or large frying pan over a high heat. Add the garlic and chilli and stir-fry for 30 seconds to release the flavours.

3 Add the chicken and five-spice powder and stir-fry for 3–4 minutes until the chicken has coloured all over. Add the red pepper, carrots and mushrooms and stir-fry for 2–3 minutes until slightly softened.

4 Add the peanut butter mixture to the wok and stir-fry for a further 2–3 minutes until the chicken is cooked through and tender. Remove from the heat, stir in the chopped coriander and serve immediately.

Phat Thai noodles with prawns

Typical Thai flavours, including **chilli, lemongrass, coriander, lime and coconut,** combine in this aromatic stir-fry of prawns, noodles and oriental vegetables.

SERVES 4
PREPARATION TIME 20 minutes
COOKING TIME 5 minutes

1 tbsp lime juice
1 tbsp soy sauce
2 tbsp Thai fish sauce (nam pla)
24 peeled raw tiger prawns, about 225g in total, thawed if frozen
250g medium dried rice noodles
3 tbsp vegetable oil
1 tbsp Thai green curry paste, or more to taste
1 tsp toasted sesame oil
150g baby sweetcorn, halved lengthways
200g bean sprouts
200g pak choi, finely shredded
220g can water chestnuts, drained and sliced
250ml canned coconut milk

TO GARNISH 1 lime, cut into wedges

1 Mix together the lime juice, soy sauce and fish sauce in a bowl. Add the prawns and toss together, then set aside to marinate for a few minutes.

2 Put the noodles in a large heatproof bowl. Pour over boiling water to cover, add 1 tsp of the vegetable oil and stir gently. Leave to soak for 4 minutes, then drain thoroughly.

3 Lift the prawns out of the marinade and pat dry with kitchen paper. Stir the curry paste into the marinade and set aside. Heat a wok or heavy-based frying pan until very hot, then add 1 tsp of the vegetable oil and the sesame oil and swirl to coat the pan. Add the prawns and stir-fry for about 2 minutes until they have turned pink. Remove with a draining spoon, leaving any remaining oil behind.

4 Add the rest of the oil to the pan. Toss in the sweetcorn and stir-fry for 30 seconds. Add the bean sprouts and pak choi and stir-fry for a minute, then add the curry paste mixture. Cook for a few seconds, stirring all the time, then add the water chestnuts and drained noodles. Continue to stir-fry for 1 minute.

5 Return the prawns to the wok and pour in the coconut milk. Toss everything together over a high heat until bubbling. Serve immediately, with lime wedges to squeeze over.

variation

• Turkey breast fillets could be used in place of chicken, 2 small courgettes rather than carrots and a drained 227g can of bamboo shoots as an alternative to mushrooms.

each serving provides

261kcals • 26g protein
13.5g fat of which 3.5g saturates
9.5g carbohydrate of which
7.5g sugars • 3.5g fibre
126mg sodium • 138g vegetables

1.5 portions fruit & veg
261 kcals
Far East feast

variation

• This dish also works well with 2 large chicken breasts, cut into strips, instead of prawns. Or, for a vegetarian version, use 250g firm tofu, cut into cubes. Alternative vegetables could include mange-tout, fine green beans or par-boiled broccoli florets.

each serving provides 458kcals • 18g protein
16g fat of which 8g saturates • 60g carbohydrate of which
4g sugars • 3g fibre • 721mg sodium • 173g vegetables

458 kcals
2 portions fruit & veg

Peppered monkfish with lemon & basil

Colourful mixed peppers and peas tossed with firm-fleshed monkfish, make this fantastically healthy dish a real winner. Serve with ciabatta or focaccia.

SERVES 4
PREPARATION TIME 10 minutes
COOKING TIME 10–15 minutes

2 tbsp vegetable oil
1 onion, finely chopped
2 red peppers, deseeded
   and thinly sliced
2 yellow peppers, deseeded
   and thinly sliced
175g sugarsnap peas
500g monkfish fillet, skinned
   and cut into 4cm chunks
grated zest and juice of 1 lemon
½ tbsp mixed peppercorns,
   coarsely crushed
175g frozen peas, thawed
85g bean sprouts
15g fresh basil, finely shredded

cook's tips

• Monkfish makes a particularly good choice for a stir-fry because its firm flesh holds its shape well. If unavailable, use skinless, boneless cod or haddock fillet instead.

• A pestle and mortar is ideal for crushing the peppercorns, but if you don't have one, put them in the corner of a strong plastic bag and press down with the end of a rolling pin or the back of a wooden spoon.

1 Heat a wok or large frying pan over a high heat and add 1 tbsp of the oil. Add the onion and stir-fry for 1 minute. Stir in the peppers and sugarsnap peas and continue stir-frying for 3–5 minutes. Remove the vegetables to a plate using a draining spoon.

2 Add the remaining oil to the pan and heat, then add the monkfish and stir-fry on a gentle heat for about 4 minutes, carefully turning the chunks so as not to break them up, until the fish is cooked through and flakes easily.

3 Add the lemon zest, lemon juice and crushed peppercorns. Return the stir-fried vegetables to the pan together with the peas and bean sprouts. Heat through, stirring, for 2–3 minutes. Scatter over the basil and serve at once.

4.5 portions fruit & veg

veg boost

266 kcals

each serving provides 266kcals • 28g protein 8g fat of which 1g saturates • 24g carbohydrate of which 17g sugars • 7g fibre • 36mg sodium • 385g vegetables

Tofu noodles

Popular in Northern Japan, soba noodles are made from buckwheat flour, which gives them a **slightly nutty flavour.** In this quick and simple dish, the thin brown noodles are delicious stir-fried with protein-rich tofu and **crunchy water chestnuts.**

2 tbsp dark soy sauce
2 tbsp dry sherry
2 tsp toasted sesame oil
2 garlic cloves, crushed
½ tsp dried crushed chillies
pinch of caster sugar
250g pack firm tofu, drained
   and cubed
250g soba noodles
1 tbsp vegetable oil
250g pak choi, finely shredded
220g can water chestnuts,
   drained and sliced
2 tbsp sesame seeds, toasted

1 Put the soy sauce, sherry, sesame oil, garlic, chillies and sugar in a bowl. Whisk together with a fork, add the tofu cubes and toss to coat in the mixture. Cover and set aside. (Leave to marinate if convenient.)

2 Bring a large pan of water to the boil, add the noodles and boil for 5 minutes until softened. Tip into a colander and drain well.

3 While the noodles are cooking, heat a wok or large, deep frying pan until hot, then add the oil. Drain the tofu, reserving the marinade, and stir-fry in the hot oil for about 30 seconds. Add the pak choi and water chestnuts and cook for a further minute, stirring all the time.

4 Tip in the cooked noodles and reserved marinade. Cook for a further 1–2 minutes or until heated through and the pak choi has wilted. Serve sprinkled with sesame seeds.

each serving provides 395kcals • 14g protein 12g fat of which 2g saturates • 57g carbohydrate of which 3g sugars • 9g fibre • 450mg sodium • 118g vegetables

1 portion fruit & veg

395 kcals

Teriyaki Quorn with vegetables

Quorn fillets make a great, low-fat vegetarian alternative to chicken or meat in a simple stir-fry. Marinate ahead to add flavour, then quickly cook with vitamin-rich vegetables, just before serving. If liked, serve with sesame breadsticks.

SERVES 4 V
PREPARATION TIME 15 minutes, plus at least 1 hour marinating
COOKING TIME 10 minutes

450g Quorn fillets, thawed if
   frozen, cut into thick strips
150g shiitake mushrooms, halved
1 tsp grated fresh root ginger
200g mange-tout
200g bean sprouts
225g can sliced bamboo shoots,
   drained and sliced
150g frozen peas

MARINADE
2 garlic cloves, crushed
2 tbsp dry sherry
1 tbsp soy sauce
1 tbsp toasted sesame oil
2 tsp vegetable oil
1 tsp rice vinegar
½ tsp caster sugar

1 Combine all the marinade ingredients in a large bowl. Add the Quorn strips and gently toss to coat well. Cover and leave to marinate in the fridge for about 1 hour or up to 4 hours.

2 Heat a large, non-stick frying pan over a moderate heat until quite hot. Tip in the Quorn with the marinade. Cook for about 4 minutes, stirring occasionally. Remove from the heat. Transfer the Quorn to a dish using a draining spoon, leaving the liquid in the pan. Cover the Quorn to keep warm.

3 Return the pan to the heat and add the mushrooms with the grated ginger. Cook for about 2 minutes, stirring frequently.

4 Add the mange-tout and stir-fry for 1 minute, then add the bean sprouts and stir-fry for a further 1 minute. Stir in the bamboo shoots and peas, cover the pan and cook gently for 2 minutes. Return the Quorn to the pan and reheat for 1–2 minutes, if necessary, then serve.

232 kcals

each serving provides 232kcals • 23g protein • 8g fat of which 1.5g saturates • 16g carbohydrate of which 6g sugars 10g fibre • 667mg sodium • 210g vegetables

2.5 portions fruit & veg

Indonesian fried rice

Flavoured with garlic, ginger and chilli, this **tempting dish** with thin and **tender strips of lean beef** and **juicy prawns** is a variation on the classic 'Nasi Goreng'. It's perfect for a relaxed lunch as much of the dish can be **prepared ahead.**

SERVES 4

PREPARATION TIME 25 minutes, plus overnight marinating if convenient

COOKING TIME 10 minutes

2 tsp sesame oil
2 tsp sherry vinegar
2 tbsp dark soy sauce
225g lean rump or fillet steak, cut across the grain into thin strips
350g long-grain white rice
2 eggs
3 spring onions, sliced diagonally
2 tbsp chopped fresh coriander
2½ tbsp vegetable oil
150g peeled raw prawns
2 garlic cloves, crushed
1 green chilli, deseeded and finely sliced
15g fresh root ginger, peeled and finely chopped
2 carrots, peeled and coarsely grated
125g frozen peas, thawed

TO SERVE chilli sauce (optional)

1 Whisk together the sesame oil, vinegar and 1 tbsp soy sauce in a bowl, add the beef and toss to coat in the marinade. Cover and chill for at least 30 minutes or overnight if you have time.

2 Meanwhile, cook the rice in lightly salted boiling water for 12 minutes, or according to the pack instructions, until almost tender, then drain and rinse with boiling water. Spread out on a tray and leave to cool.

3 Lightly beat the eggs in a small bowl or jug, then stir in the spring onions and coriander and season with freshly ground black pepper. Heat 2 tsp of the oil in a non-stick omelette pan and pour in the beaten egg mixture. Cook the eggs for a few seconds, then use a fork to stir gently for about a minute until the base begins to set. Stop stirring and cook for a further 2 minutes until lightly set. Roll up the omelette, slide it onto a plate and cover with foil to keep warm.

4 Heat 1 tbsp of the remaining oil in a wok or large, deep frying pan until hot. Add the beef with the marinade and stir-fry on a high heat for about 1 minute until well browned. Remove with a draining spoon leaving all the juices behind. Set aside.

5 Add the remaining oil to the pan. Add the prawns, garlic, chilli and ginger and stir-fry for 2 minutes until the prawns have just turned pink, then add the carrots, peas and rice and toss on the heat for a further minute. Finally add the cooked beef, sprinkle with the remaining soy sauce and stir-fry for a final 1–2 minutes until everything is heated through.

6 Spoon the rice mixture into a warmed serving bowl. Cut the omelette into thin strips and scatter over the rice. For those who like an extra spicy kick, serve with chilli sauce.

cook's tips

• To prepare ahead, marinate the beef and cook the rice up to 8 hours ahead. You could also make the omelette. Cover and keep everything in the fridge until ready to use. Make sure that the rice is reheated thoroughly.

• This is an ideal way to use up leftover rice and many types can be used, including brown rice and basmati. 'Easy-cook' varieties, which are treated to keep the grains separate, work especially well. Avoid short-grain rice such as risotto and pudding rice and Thai fragrant rice, which becomes sticky with prolonged cooking.

each serving provides

583kcals • 32g protein
16g fat of which 3g saturates
84g carbohydrate of which 5g sugars
3.5g fibre • 597mg sodium
89g vegetables

prepare ahead | **583** kcals | **1** portion fruit & veg

Steak with puttanesca sauce

This is a really quick recipe for dressing up **lean rump steak.** A gutsy tomato sauce, boosted with **anchovies and capers,** is made in the same pan, and all that's needed is some crusty French bread and a side salad for a deliciously easy meal.

SERVES 4
PREPARATION TIME 10 minutes
COOKING TIME 15–20 minutes

25g anchovies, drained
2 tbsp semi-skimmed milk
2 tbsp olive oil
1 red onion, roughly chopped
2 garlic cloves, crushed
1 red chilli, deseeded and
   finely chopped
350g cherry tomatoes, halved
2 tbsp bottled capers, rinsed
1 tsp dried oregano
4 lean rump steaks, about
   115g each

variations

• This sauce is equally good served with pan-fried skinless chicken breasts or chunky white fish steaks, such as cod or haddock.
• For a vegetarian option, leave out the anchovies and serve the sauce with pasta or cheesy potato cakes.

1 Lay the anchovies flat in a small dish, spoon over the milk and leave to soak while you begin preparing the sauce. (This soaking will remove a lot of the saltiness from the anchovies to give a mellower flavour.)

2 Heat 1 tbsp of the oil in a large, heavy-based, ridged frying pan, add the onion and cook gently for 3–4 minutes until softened.

3 Stir in the garlic and chilli, then add the tomatoes, capers and oregano. Drain off and discard the milk from the anchovies, roughly chop the anchovies and add to the sauce. Stir around and cook gently for 5 minutes or until the tomatoes are lightly cooked. Tip the sauce out into a bowl and set aside while cooking the steaks.

4 Rinse out the pan and reheat. Brush the steaks lightly on both sides with the remaining oil and season with some freshly ground black pepper. Place the steaks in the hot pan and cook on a moderately high heat for 2–3 minutes on each side for rare (4–6 minutes on each side for medium).

5 Pour the sauce over the steaks in the pan and heat through, then serve immediately.

each serving provides 237kcals • 28g protein • 11g fat of which 3g saturates • 6g carbohydrate of which 5g sugars 3g fibre • 327mg sodium • 125g vegetables

237 kcals

1.5 portions fruit & veg

Venison & mushroom stroganoff

Tasty venison is extremely **low in saturated fat,** with a **slightly gamey flavour,** and combined with mushrooms, a small amount of meat goes a long way. Cooked in a **creamy sauce** made with half-fat crème fraîche, then tossed with tagliatelle, this makes a luxurious dish.

SERVES 4
PREPARATION TIME 20 minutes
COOKING TIME 10–12 minutes

350g dried green and white
   tagliatelle
2 tbsp vegetable oil
350g lean boneless venison fillet
   or loin steaks, cut into thin strips
1 onion, halved and thinly sliced
1 large garlic clove, finely chopped
300g chestnut mushrooms,
   thickly sliced
2 tbsp dry sherry
75ml beef or vegetable stock
1 tsp cornflour
150ml half-fat crème fraîche
2 tsp fresh thyme leaves
pinch of freshly grated nutmeg
1 tsp ground paprika
pinch of cayenne pepper

each serving provides

553kcals • 33g protein
15g fat of which 5.5g saturates
75g carbohydrate of which
8g sugars • 4g fibre
72mg sodium • 135g vegetables

553 kcals

1.5 portions fruit & veg

treat yourself

1 Cook the tagliatelle in a large pan of boiling water for 10–12 minutes or according to the pack instructions until al dente.

2 Meanwhile, heat 1 tbsp of the oil in a large frying pan or wok over a high heat. Add the venison and stir-fry for about 1 minute until browned all over. Remove from the pan and set aside.

3 Add the remaining 1 tbsp oil to the pan, then reduce the heat to medium. Add the onion and fry for about 4 minutes, stirring frequently until beginning to soften, then stir in the garlic and mushrooms and continue cooking for a further 3–4 minutes until tender. Stir in the sherry and cook for a few seconds, then add the stock.

4 Blend the cornflour with 2 tsp cold water in a small bowl or jug. Stir in the crème fraîche, thyme, nutmeg, paprika and cayenne pepper, then stir this mixture into the pan and cook until it starts to bubble. Return the venison to the pan and cook for a few more seconds to heat through. Season to taste.

5 Tip the tagliatelle into a colander over the sink and drain thoroughly. Add to the stroganoff mixture and gently toss together, then serve straight away.

variations

• Rather than venison, use lean fillet or rump steak, pork fillet or skinless boneless chicken or turkey breasts.
• For a vegetarian stroganoff, use 250g smoked or plain firm tofu, cut into cubes, instead of the venison.

cook's tip

• When preparing the venison (or any red meat for stir-frying), slice the meat across the grain, as this breaks the muscle fibres and helps to tenderize the meat. Pat the strips of meat dry on kitchen paper, so they sizzle and brown when added to the pan, rather than steaming.

Lamb steaks with feta & mint

Lamb steaks with feta & mint This Greek-style dish is simple to cook but *wonderfully flavoured.* It combines succulent lamb steaks with *colourful vegetables, feta and fresh mint* – perfect for easy entertaining.

SERVES 4
PREPARATION TIME 15 minutes
COOKING TIME 20–25 minutes

4 lamb leg steaks, trimmed of fat
4 tbsp olive oil
300g new potatoes, scrubbed
  and thinly sliced
1 large courgette, sliced
1 red onion, sliced
2 red peppers, deseeded
  and sliced
8 garlic cloves, peeled
4 tbsp red wine vinegar
100g feta cheese, drained
25g fresh mint leaves,
  finely shredded

variation

• Pork and fennel is a popular flavour combination in Greece. Replace the lamb steaks with 4 well-trimmed pork loin chops and the courgettes with 2 thinly sliced fennel bulbs. Use white onions and add 1 tsp fennel seeds to the vegetables in step 4.

1 Heat a large frying pan with a tight-fitting lid over a medium heat. Brush the lamb steaks on one side with a little of the oil. Add the steaks to the pan, oiled-side down, and fry for 3–4 minutes until nicely browned.

2 Lightly brush the lamb steaks with a little more oil, then flip them over and continue frying for a further 1 minute. Transfer the lamb steaks to a plate and set aside.

3 Add 1 tbsp of the oil to the pan and heat. Add the potatoes and fry, turning them over occasionally, for 5 minutes or until they become golden and start to soften.

4 Add another 1 tbsp of oil to the pan. Add the courgette, onion, peppers and garlic to the pan and continue frying, stirring occasionally, for 5 minutes or until all the vegetables are tender.

5 Meanwhile, mix the remaining oil with the vinegar in a small jug or bowl. Return the lamb steaks to the pan, placing them on top of the vegetables, and pour in the oil and vinegar mixture. Crumble the feta cheese over the top. Reduce the heat to low, cover the pan and cook for about 5 minutes (for medium-rare), or for 7 minutes (medium-cooked).

6 Uncover the pan and scatter over the mint. Season with freshly ground black pepper to taste. Serve at once, straight from the pan, with the pan juices spooned over.

each serving provides 466kcals • 33g protein 26g fat of which 5g saturates • 24g carbohydrate of which 10.5g sugars • 4g fibre • 376mg sodium • 188g vegetables

2 portions fruit & veg

466 kcals

SERVES 4
PREPARATION TIME 10 minutes
COOKING TIME 55 minutes

1 tbsp vegetable oil
2 large onions, sliced
450g lean minced pork
2 garlic cloves, crushed
8 green cardamoms, crushed
  and pods discarded
1 tbsp cumin seeds
600ml chicken stock, hot
750g small new potatoes,
  scrubbed and halved
2 tsp cornflour
300ml low-fat natural yoghurt
75g ground almonds
250g young leaf spinach
25g toasted flaked almonds

variations

• Use 2 x 400g drained cans of
chickpeas instead of the potatoes.
• Minced lamb would work equally
well, rather than pork, if preferred.

cook's tip

• This dish is better still made ahead,
then reheated. Make up to the end of
step 4, then cool and chill. Reheat
gently, then complete the dish with
the spinach.

Pork korma with potatoes & spinach

Thickened with ground almonds and yoghurt, this minced meat dish is **rich and creamy** yet not as indulgent as traditional Indian korma curries that are full of cream and ghee (clarified butter). Serve with warm **chappatis or naan** to mop up the **delicious, aromatic sauce.**

1 Heat the oil in a large, heavy-based saucepan or flameproof casserole. Add the onions and cook over a medium heat for 10 minutes until softened and lightly browned. Transfer to a bowl and set aside.

2 Add the pork, garlic, cardamom and cumin seeds. Cook, stirring often, for 5 minutes until the meat has broken up and changed colour. Return about half the onions to the pan, pour in the stock and bring back to the boil. Reduce the heat, cover the pan and simmer for 15 minutes.

3 Stir in the potatoes and bring back to simmering point, then cover and cook for about 20 minutes until the potatoes are tender.

4 Meanwhile, blend the cornflour with 6 tbsp of the yoghurt and the ground almonds to make a paste. Stir this mixture into the curry and bring just to the boil, stirring. Reduce the heat and simmer for 1 minute until slightly thickened. Season to taste.

5 Fold the spinach leaves through the korma, reserving a few small leaves for garnishing, until they are just wilted and bright green. Mix the toasted flaked almonds with the remaining onions. Serve the curry drizzled with the remaining yoghurt and topped with the almonds, onions and reserved spinach leaves.

each serving provides 552kcals • 40g protein 23g fat of which 2g saturates • 50g carbohydrate of which 16g sugars • 7g fibre • 166mg sodium • 170g vegetables

2 portions fruit & veg

prepare ahead

552 kcals

Quick Thai chicken curry

It is easy to keep the fat content low in a **tangy Thai curry** as there is **no need to pre-fry** the ingredients; instead they are simply simmered in **light coconut milk** and stock with potatoes, peas and tomatoes.

SERVES 4
PREPARATION TIME 10 minutes
COOKING TIME 20–25 minutes

400ml reduced-fat coconut milk
200ml chicken stock
2 tbsp Thai green curry paste
4 skinless chicken breast fillets,
   600g in total, cut into thin strips
350g new potatoes, scrubbed
   and cut into chunks
6 spring onions, sliced diagonally
2 tbsp lime juice
125g shelled fresh or frozen peas
8 baby plum or cherry
   tomatoes, halved
4 tbsp chopped fresh coriander

1 Place the coconut milk, stock and Thai curry paste in a wok or large frying pan and heat until boiling. Stir in the chicken and potatoes, then bring back to the boil.

2 Reduce the heat and simmer, uncovered, for about 15 minutes until the chicken and potatoes are just tender.

3 Stir in the spring onions, lime juice, peas and tomatoes and simmer for a further 3–4 minutes. Stir in the coriander and season to taste.

variation

• For a change of flavour, replace the new potatoes with the same amount of diced aubergine, or, if you can get them, with Thai 'pea' aubergines, which are available in some Asian stores.

each serving provides 372kcals • 41g protein 13g fat of which 1g saturates • 24g carbohydrate of which 4g sugars • 3g fibre • 222mg sodium • 120g vegetables

1.5 portions fruit & veg

372 kcals

super quick & easy

Blackened chicken

The spiced coating on the chicken breasts cooks to a **delicious crunchy crust,** keeping the inside flesh **really juicy.** It's served on a simple avocado, bean and tomato salad, but add some interesting bread, such as seeded Pan Gallego, to complete the meal.

SERVES 4

PREPARATION TIME 15 minutes

COOKING TIME 15–20 minutes

2 tsp coriander seeds
2 tsp cumin seeds
2 tsp black peppercorns
2 garlic cloves, crushed
2 tsp dried oregano
4 tsp paprika
2 tbsp olive oil
4 skinless chicken breast
  fillets, about 150g each

SALAD
1 avocado
4 tomatoes, sliced
400g can borlotti or pinto beans,
  drained and rinsed
1 tbsp lime juice
1 tbsp olive oil
2 tbsp chopped flat-leaf parsley

TO SERVE lime wedges

variation

• The spice mix is also very good with pork – try it rubbed over lean pork steaks or chops, and char-grill in the same way as the chicken.

1 portion fruit & veg

prepare ahead

401 kcals

each serving provides 401kcals • 42g protein 20g fat of which 4g saturates • 13g carbohydrate of which 3g sugars • 5g fibre • 99mg sodium • 113g vegetables

1 Place the coriander and cumin seeds, peppercorns and garlic in a mortar and crush with a pestle until roughly ground. Add the oregano, paprika and oil and crush to a paste.

2 Use a sharp knife to cut 3–4 deep slashes across each chicken breast. Spread the spice mix over the chicken, rubbing deep into the cuts.

3 Heat a heavy-based frying pan until very hot and add the chicken breasts. Reduce the heat to moderate and fry the chicken for 15–20 minutes, turning occasionally, until it is slightly charred on the outside and thoroughly cooked inside. (It can be served warm or cooled and then chilled, to serve later.)

4 Meanwhile, or shortly before serving, peel and slice the avocado. Combine the avocado and tomatoes in a bowl with the beans. Drizzle with the lime juice and olive oil, add the parsley and season lightly.

5 Heap the salad onto a serving plate. Cut the chicken, on the diagonal, into neat slices and arrange on top of the salad. Garnish with lime wedges to squeeze over.

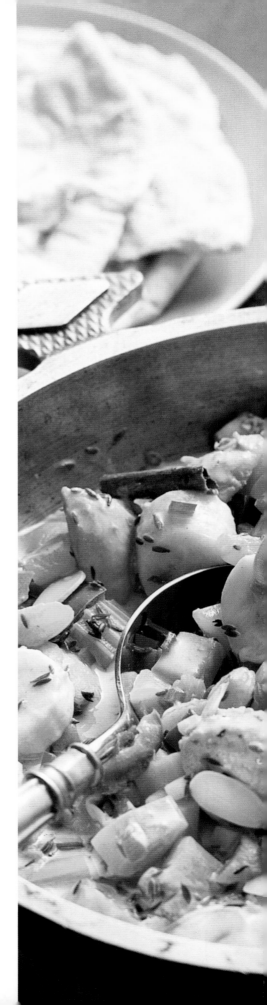

Kashmiri chicken with fruit

Sweet bananas, exotic lychees and creamy Greek yoghurt are combined with chicken and spicy seasonings to make a luscious, yet healthy dish. Serve with warm naan bread.

SERVES 4
PREPARATION TIME 20 minutes
COOKING TIME 20–25 minutes

2 tbsp vegetable oil
1 cinnamon stick
2 tsp fennel seeds
1 tbsp cumin seeds
50g fresh root ginger, peeled and chopped
2 red chillies, deseeded and chopped
1 green pepper, deseeded and chopped
2 carrots, peeled and diced
2 celery sticks, diced
4 skinless chicken breast fillets, about 500g in total, cut into 2.5cm chunks
300ml chicken stock
100g ready-to-eat dried apricots, roughly chopped
200g natural Greek yoghurt
4 small firm bananas, sliced
400g can lychees, drained and halved

TO GARNISH 50g toasted flaked almonds

variations

• Lean boneless pork or turkey fillets can be used instead of the chicken.
• If fresh lychees are available, use 250g fruit. Slit the crisp skins and peel off, then cut in half and remove the stones.
• For a vegetarian fruit and nut curry, add 200g unsalted cashew nuts and 400g canned chickpeas, drained and rinsed, instead of the chicken.

1 Heat the oil in a large, deep frying pan, add the cinnamon, fennel and cumin. Cook over a moderate heat for 1–2 minutes. Add the ginger, three quarters of the chillies, green pepper, carrots and celery. Stir well, then cover and cook gently on a low heat for 5 minutes or until the vegetables begin to soften.

2 Push the vegetables to the side of the pan, then add the chicken and increase the heat slightly. Cook, stirring occasionally, for 4–5 minutes until the chicken begins to brown. Pour in the stock, add the apricots and bring to the boil. Reduce the heat, cover and simmer gently for 10–15 minutes until the chicken and vegetables are cooked.

3 Stir in the yoghurt, bananas and lychees and heat through gently without boiling. Scatter the toasted flaked almonds and remaining chilli over the top to serve.

cook's tip

• To prepare ahead, make up to the end of step 2, then cool and keep chilled in the fridge. Reheat gently before adding the yoghurt and fruit.

prepare ahead

501 kcals

3 portions fruit & veg

each serving provides 501kcals • 39g protein 18g fat of which 4g saturates • 50g carbohydrate of which 46g sugars • 6g fibre • 182mg sodium • 273g fruit and vegetables

West country sausages

Sausages are enjoying a renaissance and now come in a wider range of meats and flavours. Here, **delicious turkey sausages** are simmered in a tomato and vegetable sauce **with fruity cider.** Delicious with crusty French bread.

3 tsp vegetable oil
8 turkey sausages
1 large onion, thickly sliced
1 garlic clove, crushed
4 carrots, peeled and sliced
400g can chopped tomatoes
200ml dry fruity cider
100ml chicken or vegetable stock
1 tbsp chopped fresh
   tarragon (optional)
1 tbsp chopped fresh parsley

1 Heat 1 tsp of the oil in a heavy-based frying pan, preferably non-stick, and cook the sausages over a moderate heat, turning frequently, for about 5 minutes until golden on all sides. Remove from the pan with a draining spoon and place on kitchen paper to blot up any excess fat.

2 Add the rest of the oil to the pan and cook the onion for 6–7 minutes. Add the garlic and carrots and cook for a further 3–4 minutes until the onion is beginning to colour. Stir in the canned tomatoes with their juice, the cider and stock.

3 Bring the mixture to a gentle simmer, then return the sausages to the pan and cook for 15–20 minutes until they are thoroughly cooked and the sauce has slightly reduced. Stir in the herbs and some freshly ground black pepper to taste, then let the sauce bubble for a minute before serving.

each serving provides

295kcals • 19g protein
13g fat of which 4g saturates
22g carbohydrate of which
17g sugars • 7g fibre
971mg sodium
265g vegetables

prepare
ahead

295
kcals

3
portions
fruit &
veg

cook's tips

• This dish can be cooked the day before and reheated thoroughly until piping hot throughout.
• For a deeper tomato flavour, add 1 tbsp tomato purée to the sauce.

variations

• Vegetarian sausages can be used for this dish. Simply pan-fry them for a few minutes until evenly browned, then cook them in the sauce for 5 minutes.
• For a more substantial meal, stir in a drained 400g can of borlotti or mixed beans at the end of step 3.

Turkey with lentils & chorizo

Turkey and spicy **chorizo sausage** combine well with vegetables and lentils, which are naturally low in fat and a good source of fibre, to create this **hearty and flavourful pan-fry.** Serve with a green salad.

SERVES 4
PREPARATION TIME 20 minutes
COOKING TIME 40 minutes

125g chorizo sausage, thinly sliced
1 red onion, finely chopped
1 garlic clove, crushed
1 celery stick, finely chopped
300g skinless turkey breast fillets,
   thinly sliced
1 red pepper, deseeded and sliced
225g Puy lentils
250ml dry white wine
250ml chicken stock, hot

TO GARNISH fresh flat-leaf parsley, chopped

1 Heat a non-stick frying pan, add the chorizo, red onion, garlic and celery and cook over a moderate heat for about 5 minutes until the onion is beginning to soften.

2 Add the turkey pieces and red pepper to the pan and cook for 3–4 minutes until the turkey is coloured all over.

3 Stir in the lentils, wine and stock. Bring to the boil, then reduce the heat, cover and cook gently for about 30 minutes until the lentils are tender, stirring occasionally. Season to taste and serve sprinkled with chopped parsley.

cook's tip

• Puy lentils are tiny, grey-green lentils from the Puy region of France. They have a distinctive flavour and hold their shape and colour when cooked. But if they are not available, you can use any other green or brown lentils.

each serving provides

414kcals • 39g protein
9g fat of which 3g saturates
36g carbohydrate of which
8g sugars • 7g fibre
226mg sodium
108g vegetables

414
kcals

1
portion
fruit &
veg

Halibut with pak choi

Firm, meaty white fish, such as halibut, are perfect for pan-frying as they keep their shape well and don't break up easily. Serve on a bed of tender-crisp vegetables and top with Parma ham, all cooked in the same pan. Some nice crusty bread would complete the meal.

SERVES 4
PREPARATION TIME 15 minutes
COOKING TIME 20 minutes

2 tbsp vegetable oil
4 pieces skinless halibut fillet,
    about 150g each
4 slices Parma ham, about
    60g in total
2 garlic cloves, crushed
2.5cm piece fresh root ginger,
    peeled and finely shredded
1 red chilli, deseeded and
    finely diced
6 spring onions, sliced diagonally
200g mange-tout, halved diagonally
300g shelled young broad beans
200g small pak choi,
    sliced lengthways
1 tbsp dark soy sauce

variations

• Other firm, meaty fish such as hake or monkfish can be used for this recipe. If you prefer, the fish can be cut into 5cm chunks and carefully stir-fried, instead of cooking it in larger pieces.
• A vegetarian version could be made with chunks of firm tofu, or smoked tofu. Lightly fry it in half the oil, then continue from step 3 as in the recipe. Pile the tofu on top of the vegetables and drizzle with soy sauce to serve.
• If pak choi is not available, you can use roughly shredded Chinese leaves.

1 Heat half the oil in a wide, heavy-based frying pan until very hot, then add the fish pieces. Fry for 3–4 minutes until lightly browned underneath. Turn the fish over, reduce the heat to moderate and cook for a further 4–5 minutes until the fish is firm and cooked through. Remove from the pan and keep warm.

2 Add the Parma ham to the pan and fry on a fairly high heat for 1 minute on each side until golden and crisp. Remove and keep warm.

3 Add the remaining oil to the pan and stir-fry the garlic, ginger and chilli for about 30 seconds, without browning. Add the spring onions, mange-tout and beans and stir-fry for 3–4 minutes. Stir in the pak choi and stir-fry for about 2 minutes until the leaves are wilted.

4 Pile the vegetables onto warmed serving plates, place the fish on top and add a crisp piece of ham. Drizzle with the soy sauce and serve immediately.

2.5 portions fruit & veg

316 kcals

each serving provides 316kcals • 44g protein
11g fat of which 2g saturates • 10g carbohydrate of which 4g sugars
7g fibre • 398mg sodium • 200g vegetables

SERVES 4
PREPARATION TIME 20 minutes
COOKING TIME about 15 minutes

2 tbsp olive oil
2 tsp red wine vinegar
4 tuna steaks, about 2cm thick
2 red peppers, halved lengthways
    and deseeded
350g vine-ripened tomatoes,
    skinned and diced
1 small red onion, finely chopped
1 red chilli, deseeded and
    finely chopped
1 large garlic clove,
    finely chopped
pinch of ground cinnamon
pinch of sugar
150g fine green beans, halved
40g stoned black olives, halved
1 tbsp chopped fresh mint
12 large fresh basil leaves,
    roughly torn

Tuna steaks with salsa rossa

Heart-healthy tuna has a unique flavour and a firm texture. Here, it is **briefly pan-fried,** then gently cooked in a **red pepper and tomato sauce.** Delicious with plain or olive ciabatta.

1 Preheat the grill to high. Whisk together 1 tbsp of the oil and 1 tsp of the vinegar. Brush over the tuna steaks and lightly season with pepper. Set aside to marinate while you prepare the vegetables.

2 Put the peppers, skin-side up, in the grill pan and grill for about 5 minutes until the skins are blackened and blistered. Put the peppers in a plastic bag and leave until cool enough to handle, then, working over a bowl to catch the juice, peel the peppers. Cut into 1cm dice and add to the juice in the bowl. Add the tomatoes.

3 Heat a heavy non-stick frying pan, add the tuna steaks and cook over a moderately high heat for 1 minute on each side until lightly browned. The tuna should still be very rare in the middle at this stage. Remove from the pan and set aside.

4 Heat the remaining oil in the pan and gently cook the onion for 5 minutes until soft. Add the chilli, garlic, cinnamon and sugar and stir for a few seconds, then tip in the peppers, tomatoes, green beans, remaining vinegar and 1 tbsp water. Bring to the boil, then cover and simmer for 3 minutes. (The mixture will look slightly dry at first, but will soon become juicy.)

5 Stir in the olives and place the tuna steaks on top of the salsa. Cover and cook for 3–4 minutes until the tuna is cooked to your liking and the beans are just tender.

6 Transfer the tuna to warmed plates. Stir the mint into the salsa and bubble for a few seconds, then stir in half the basil. Spoon the salsa over and around the tuna, scatter over the remaining basil and serve.

cook's tip
• Take care not to overcook the tuna or it will be dry and tough. It should still be very slightly pink in the middle when served.

variation
• Swordfish or other firm fish steaks can be used instead of the tuna.

heart healthy • **2.5** portions fruit & veg • **253** kcals

each serving provides
253kcals • 26g protein
12g fat of which 2g saturates
11g carbohydrate of which 9g sugars
3.5g fibre • 284mg sodium
223g vegetables

Spaghetti with scallops, asparagus & chard

A sophisticated dish, combining pasta with a stir-fry of **creamy white scallops** and **vibrant green vegetables**. The scallops are low in fat and rich in vitamin B$_{12}$ and many minerals. By cooking the vegetables quickly in very little liquid they retain all their nutrients.

SERVES 4
PREPARATION TIME 10 minutes
COOKING TIME 12 minutes

300g spaghetti
1 tbsp olive oil
350g scallops, cut into
  quarters if large
200g asparagus, trimmed and
  cut into 3cm lengths
½ tsp grated fresh root ginger
grated zest and juice of ½ lemon
250g chard leaves,
  coarsely shredded

1 Cook the spaghetti in a large pan of lightly salted boiling water for 10–12 minutes or according to the pack instructions, until al dente. When ready, drain in a colander.

2 While the pasta is cooking, heat the oil in a wok or large frying pan over a high heat. Add the scallops in a single layer and cook, turning occasionally, for about 3 minutes or until lightly golden and almost cooked through. Transfer the scallops to a plate, using a draining spoon, and keep warm.

3 Add the asparagus to the pan with the ginger and lemon zest. Cook, stirring frequently, for about 4 minutes until starting to soften.

4 Add the chard leaves to the pan and lightly toss to mix well. Pour in 75ml water, cover the pan and cook for about 5 minutes until the chard is wilted and the asparagus is tender.

5 Return the scallops to the pan with the lemon juice and season to taste. Add the spaghetti to the pan and gently toss to mix with the scallops and asparagus. Serve at once.

variation

• If chard is not available you can make this using fresh spinach leaves, washed and torn into pieces. Cook as for chard.

divine dinner

409 kcals

1 portion fruit & veg

each serving provides

409kcals • 32g protein
6g fat of which 1g saturates
61g carbohydrate of which
4g sugars • 3g fibre
292mg sodium • 113g vegetables

Prawn & mango balti

A tasty curry with a spicy kick, mellowed with reduced-fat coconut milk. The addition of fresh mango not only adds to the colour and appeal, but boosts the vitamin content of the dish. Serve with warm naan bread and a favourite Indian chutney.

SERVES 4
PREPARATION TIME 20 minutes
COOKING TIME 25 minutes

1 tbsp vegetable oil
1 onion, finely chopped
1 red chilli, deseeded and thinly sliced
3 tbsp balti curry paste
225ml reduced-fat coconut milk
2 vine-ripened tomatoes, skinned and chopped
1 ripe medium mango, peeled, stoned and diced
24 large raw tiger prawns, peeled and deveined (about 225g prepared weight)
2 tbsp chopped fresh coriander

1 Heat the oil in a large frying pan, add the onion and cook on a moderate heat for 5 minutes or until softened. Add the chilli and curry paste and cook for 1–2 minutes, taking care not to allow the paste to burn.

2 Add the coconut milk to the pan and stir well, then add the tomatoes. Cook gently for 10 minutes or until the tomatoes are soft and the sauce has thickened slightly, stirring occasionally.

3 Stir in the mango and cook for 1–2 minutes, then add the prawns and simmer gently for about 5 minutes until the prawns are pink and tender. Stir in the chopped coriander and serve immediately.

variation
• Diced cooked lean pork or chicken would also work well in the fruity sauce in place of the prawns. Heat through gently.

each serving provides
215kcals • 12g protein
11g fat of which 4g saturates
19g carbohydrate of which
16g sugars • 4g fibre
295mg sodium • 200g fruit
and vegetables

2.5 portions fruit & veg

215 kcals

quick & easy

Spicy cod with chickpeas & spinach

Succulent chunks of creamy white cod, gently cooked in an **aromatic, slightly spicy sauce** with a colourful mix of vegetables and chickpeas, makes **a satisfying, yet low-fat meal.** If liked, serve with French bread.

SERVES 4
PREPARATION TIME 20 minutes
COOKING TIME 20 minutes

2 tbsp olive oil
1 onion, finely chopped
1 green chilli, deseeded
   and finely chopped
2 carrots, peeled and diced
2 celery sticks, diced
40g fresh root ginger, peeled
   and finely chopped
2 garlic cloves, crushed
6 green cardamom pods, seeds only
1 tsp ground turmeric
500ml fish, chicken or vegetable
   stock, hot
400g can chickpeas, drained
   and rinsed
500g tomatoes, skinned
   and quartered
150g frozen peas
600g skinless thick cod fillet,
   cut into chunks
250g baby spinach leaves

variations

• Other white fish or salmon fillet can be used instead of the cod. With salmon, try using flageolet or cannellini beans in place of the chickpeas.

• For vegetarians, replace the fish with either 8 halved, hard-boiled eggs (add at the end of cooking and heat through gently), or a 400g can each of red kidney and borlotti beans, drained and rinsed (add with the chickpeas). Use vegetable stock for either option.

1 Heat the oil in a large, deep frying pan. Add the onion, chilli, carrots, celery, ginger, garlic and cardamom seeds. Stir well, then cover the pan and cook over a moderate heat for 5 minutes or until the onions are slightly softened.

2 Stir in the turmeric, then pour in the stock and bring to the boil. Reduce the heat, cover and simmer for 10 minutes or until the vegetables are tender.

3 Add the chickpeas, followed by the tomatoes, peas and cod. Mix in gently, taking care not to break up the fish. Bring back to a simmer. When the stock is bubbling gently, pile the spinach on top – there's no need to stir it in – and cover the pan. Cook for 5 minutes or until the chunks of fish are white and firm, and the spinach has just wilted.

4 Use a fork to combine the spinach gently with the fish and vegetables. Ladle the mixture into shallow bowls and serve at once.

each serving provides 342kcals • 38g protein 10g fat of which 1.5g saturates • 27g carbohydrate of which 13g sugars • 9g fibre • 357mg sodium • 350g vegetables

hi-veg dish

4 portions fruit & veg

342 kcals

Vegetable hash

Traditionally, a hash was the perfect way to use up leftovers from a roast dinner. Here, a glorious mix of colourful vegetables with crumbly Lancashire cheese makes a complete vegetarian dish. Accompany with a good fruity relish or chutney.

SERVES 2 V
PREPARATION TIME 15 minutes
COOKING TIME 15 minutes

1 tbsp olive oil
500g cooked potatoes, cubed
200g Savoy cabbage, shredded
200g carrots, peeled and
    thinly sliced
5 spring onions, trimmed and sliced
50g Lancashire cheese
2 tbsp chopped fresh parsley

1 Heat the oil in a large, non-stick frying pan over a moderate heat. Add the potatoes and fry, stirring occasionally, for about 3 minutes or until lightly browned all over.

2 Add the cabbage and carrots and stir gently to mix with the potatoes. Continue to fry, stirring occasionally, for about 2 minutes until the vegetables start to soften.

3 Pour in 100ml water and cover the pan. Allow the vegetables to steam for about 3 minutes. Stir in the spring onions and cook, covered, for about 6 minutes longer. Season to taste.

4 Crumble the cheese over the vegetable hash and sprinkle with the chopped parsley. Serve immediately.

391 kcals

2.5 portions fruit & veg

variations
• For a non-vegetarian hash, add 175g diced, cooked ham with the spring onions.
• Shredded Brussels sprouts make a good tasty alternative to cabbage.

each serving provides
391kcals • 14g protein
14.5g fat of which 6g saturates
55g carbohydrate of which
14g sugars • 9g fibre
198mg sodium • 225g vegetables

Red Thai curry with tofu

This great-tasting, medium-hot curry is made with tofu – an exceptionally nutritious and low-fat ingredient that soaks up the fragrant flavour of the spice paste.

SERVES 4
PREPARATION TIME 15 minutes
COOKING TIME 15 minutes

1 tbsp vegetable oil
1 large onion, finely chopped
4 tsp Thai red curry paste, or to taste
125g baby corn, halved lengthways
100ml vegetable stock
1 tbsp soy sauce
300ml canned coconut milk
100g broccoli, divided into small florets
100g fine green beans, trimmed
1 red pepper, quartered, deseeded and sliced
350g pack firm tofu, drained and cut into 2cm cubes
300g straight-to-wok medium noodles
2 tbsp roughly chopped fresh coriander

TO GARNISH sprigs of fresh coriander

1 Heat the oil in a wok or large deep frying pan, preferably non-stick. Add the onion and stir over a moderate heat for 7–8 minutes until softened. Stir in the curry paste and cook for a few more seconds.

2 Add the baby corn and stir to coat in the curry paste. Gradually add the stock, soy sauce and coconut milk. Bring to a gentle simmer and cook for 1 minute. Carefully stir in the remaining vegetables and tofu. Bring back to simmering point, then cover and cook for 5–6 minutes until the vegetables are just tender.

3 Add the noodles to the vegetable mixture and stir-fry for a further minute. Stir in the chopped coriander and serve straight away.

variation
• This dish would also work well made with 2 large chicken breast fillets, cut into 2.5cm cubes, instead of tofu. Lightly brown the chicken with the onion in a mixture of toasted sesame and vegetable oils.

cook's tip
• Thai red curry paste often includes shrimp so this dish is not suitable for strict vegetarians.

546 kcals

2 portions fruit & veg

each serving provides
546kcals • 16g protein • 21g fat of which 10g saturates
71g carbohydrate of which 6.5g sugars • 4.5g fibre • 342mg sodium • 160g vegetables

Flamenco eggs This spectacular

Spanish-style egg and vegetable dish looks wonderful and is *incredibly easy to cook* for a light lunch or supper. Serve with crusty bread.

SERVES 4 V
PREPARATION TIME 10 minutes
COOKING TIME 30–35 minutes

**350g potatoes, peeled and
  cut into small dice**
1 tbsp olive oil
1 red onion, thinly sliced
1 garlic clove, crushed
**3 mixed peppers (1 red, 1 green
  and 1 yellow), deseeded and
  thinly sliced**
2 courgettes, sliced
**6 tomatoes, about 400g in total,
  cut into chunks**
2 tbsp chopped fresh oregano
4 large eggs

1 Par-boil the potatoes in a saucepan of lightly salted boiling water for 5 minutes. Drain and set aside.

2 Heat the oil in a large, deep frying pan and fry the onion and garlic over a moderate heat for 2–3 minutes to soften. Add the peppers and courgettes and fry, stirring occasionally, for a further 10 minutes.

3 Add the potatoes and tomatoes and continue cooking, stirring occasionally, for 6–8 minutes or until all the vegetables are tender.

4 Stir in the oregano and season to taste. Make 4 hollows in the vegetable mixture and break an egg into each hollow. Cover the pan, with a lid or a baking sheet, and cook for 8–10 minutes or until the egg whites are set. Serve immediately.

Sweet potato curry with paneer

A light, colourful curry that is very quick and easy to make, this is packed with antioxidant-rich vegetables. Sweet potatoes, in particular, are an excellent source of beta-carotene and vitamin C, and have a higher vitamin E content than any other vegetable. Serve with naan bread.

SERVES 4 [V]
PREPARATION TIME 10 minutes
COOKING TIME 25–30 minutes

1 tbsp vegetable oil
1 onion, chopped
2 garlic cloves, crushed
500g sweet potatoes, peeled and cut into chunks
1 tbsp mild curry powder
1 tbsp finely chopped fresh root ginger
400g can chopped tomatoes
100ml vegetable stock
150g shelled fresh or frozen peas
250g paneer, cut into 1.5cm cubes
2 tbsp chopped fresh mint

1 Heat the vegetable oil in a large frying pan and fry the onion and garlic gently, stirring occasionally, for 4–5 minutes until softened.

2 Add the sweet potatoes and stir-fry for 2 minutes, then stir in the curry powder and ginger and cook for 30 seconds.

3 Stir in the tomatoes with their juice and the stock. Bring to the boil, then reduce the heat, cover and cook gently for 12–15 minutes until the sweet potato is tender.

4 Stir in the peas and simmer for 3 minutes, then add the diced paneer and cook for a further 2 minutes until heated thoroughly. Season to taste, scatter over the chopped mint and serve hot.

variations

• For a non-vegetarian version, fry about 150g chopped lean back bacon with the onion in step 2. Or, for a spicier flavour, add diced chorizo.
• Smoked salmon pieces or flaked smoked mackerel can also be added at the start of step 4.

variations

• Paneer is a lightly pressed Indian cheese available in ethnic grocers and some supermarkets. If you can't find it, halloumi cheese or a firm tofu would make good alternatives.
• For extra texture, scatter a handful of toasted almonds or walnuts over the curry just before serving.
• In the autumn, replace the sweet potato with pumpkin and use sliced mushrooms instead of peas. Step up the spice for a chilly evening with a little more curry powder.

each serving provides

255kcals • 14g protein
11g fat of which 3g saturates
27g carbohydrate of which
11g sugars • 5g fibre
115mg sodium • 313g vegetables

3.5 portions fruit & veg 255 kcals

bright & easy

each serving provides

251kcals • 13g protein
6g fat of which 2g saturates • 38g carbohydrate of which 15g sugars
6g fibre • 279mg sodium • 169g vegetables

2 portions fruit & veg 251 kcals

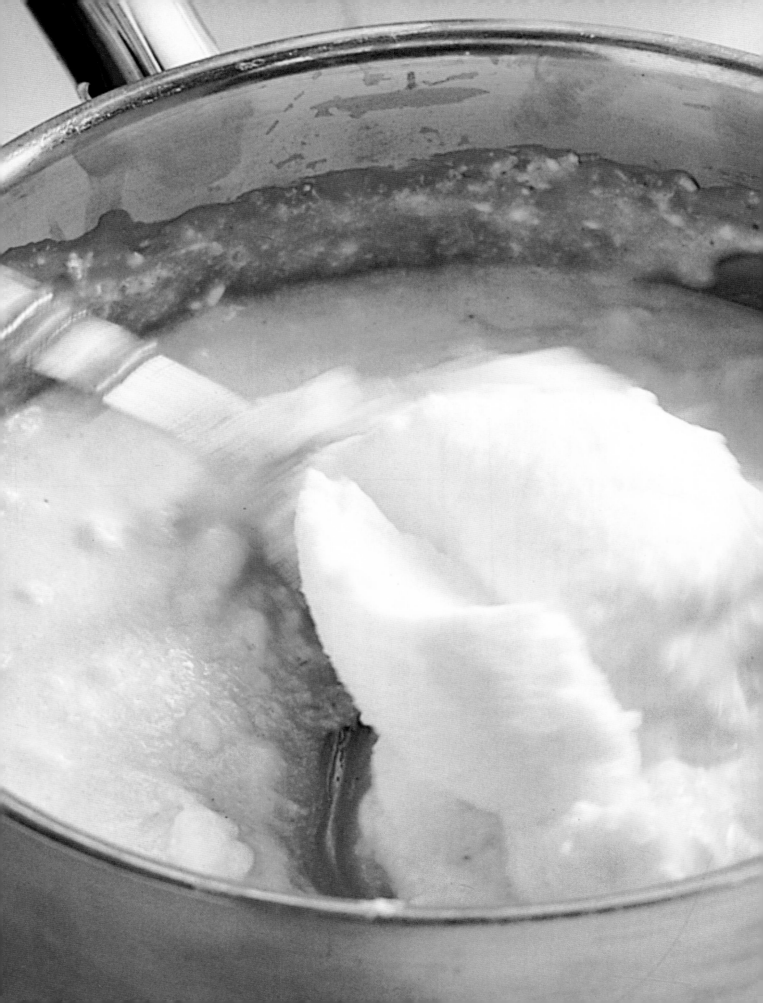

Omelettes, pancakes & soufflés

Eggs are the ultimate convenience food – a good-value source of protein, wonderfully versatile and always handy. Every nationality has its own variation on the basic omelette – why not have a go at an Arabic-style eggah? Pancakes are a guaranteed hit with children and you can prepare them ahead, ideal for a mid-week treat. Or for an impressive rise, try a Goat's cheese soufflé with ratatouille. Eggs are the basis for many easy healthy recipes, ideal for family meals or an informal get-together with friends.

SERVES 4
PREPARATION TIME 15 minutes
COOKING TIME 25 minutes

400g new potatoes, scrubbed
   and cut into 5mm slices
150g frozen peas
4 tbsp vegetable oil
1 large onion, halved and
   thinly sliced
2 large garlic cloves, crushed
6 large eggs
4 tbsp chopped fresh parsley
200g lean cooked ham, about
   5mm thick, chopped
6 cherry tomatoes, quartered

1 Bring a large pan of lightly salted water to the boil. Add the potatoes and peas and return to the boil. Reduce the heat and simmer for 3 minutes or until the potatoes are just beginning to soften. Drain and set aside.

2 Heat 2 tbsp of the oil in a 25cm frying pan with a flameproof handle. When the oil is hot, reduce the heat to medium, add the onion and cook for 2 minutes. Add the garlic and continue cooking for a further 2–3 minutes until the onion is soft, but not brown. Add the potatoes and peas to the pan and continue frying, stirring, for 5 minutes or until the potatoes are tender. Remove the pan from the heat.

3 In a large bowl, lightly beat the eggs with the parsley and a little black pepper, then stir in the ham, the potato, onion and pea mixture and the tomatoes.

4 Place the frying pan back over a medium heat, add the remaining oil and swirl it around. When the oil is hot, pour in the egg mixture, spreading it out evenly. Cook the omelette for 5–7 minutes on a low heat, shaking the pan frequently, until the base is set.

Spanish-style omelette
Colourful and packed with flavours, this thick, flat omelette, called a tortilla in Spanish, tastes good served at any temperature. The **classic recipe** contains only potatoes, onions and eggs, but this version has **extra vegetables** and **lean ham** added. Serve with a green salad.

5 Use a spatula to loosen and lift the edges of the omelette, allowing the uncooked egg mixture to run underneath. Meanwhile preheat the grill to medium.

6 Place the pan under the grill and continue cooking the omelette for 5 minutes until it is golden brown and set. Pierce the top with a knife to make sure it is cooked all the way through. Slide the omelette out of the pan onto a board and leave to cool for 2–3 minutes. Serve cut into wedges.

variation
• Extra or alternative vegetables can be added for variety and to suit your own preference. How about sweetcorn, finely diced red or green peppers or sliced courgettes?

each serving provides
432kcals • 28g protein
25g fat of which 5g saturates
26g carbohydrate of which 7g sugars
4g fibre • 683mg sodium
120g vegetables

1.5 portions fruit & veg

432 kcals

super supper

200g broccoli florets
6 eggs
3 tbsp snipped fresh chives
1 tbsp vegetable oil
15g unsalted butter
418g can red salmon, drained
 and flaked
198g can sweetcorn, drained
25g Parmesan, freshly grated

variation

• For a vegetarian version, replace the salmon with chunks of Quorn tossed with ½ tsp crushed dried chillies. Fry a sliced red onion in the oil before adding the eggs to the pan, then add the broccoli, Quorn and sweetcorn as in step 2.

Broccoli & salmon frittata
A really fantastic midweek dish, this is so easy. And if you use frozen broccoli florets it is a great storecupboard standby. Serve it at the table straight from the pan, with a fresh tomato salad and crusty bread.

1 Blanch the broccoli in a saucepan of lightly salted, boiling water for 4 minutes or until almost tender. Drain well and set aside.

2 Beat the eggs lightly with the chives and season with freshly ground black pepper. Heat the oil and butter in a large, heavy-based frying pan with a flameproof handle, then pour in the egg mixture. Scatter over the broccoli, flaked salmon and sweetcorn, stirring lightly to distribute evenly.

3 Using a palette knife, pull the sides of the egg mixture in slightly to allow the uncooked egg to set, and cook for 3–4 minutes until the underside is golden and the top almost set.

4 Meanwhile, heat the grill to high. Sprinkle the Parmesan over the top of the frittata, then place it under the grill. Cook for 2–3 minutes until the top is bubbling and golden. Serve cut into quarters.

each serving provides 402kcals • 36.5g protein 24g fat of which 8g saturates • 12g carbohydrate of which 5g sugars • 2g fibre • 661mg sodium • 94g vegetables

402 kcals

1 portion fruit & veg

Watercress omelette with Gruyère & tomatoes

Watercress teams well with eggs and is highly nutritious, providing iron and beta-carotene. The Gruyère cheese supplies plenty of taste without too much fat. Serve with crusty French bread for a well-balanced meal.

SERVES 1

PREPARATION & COOKING TIME 15 minutes

2 large eggs
10g unsalted butter
2 ripe plum tomatoes, skinned and chopped
30g Gruyère (or mature Cheddar) cheese, grated
30g watercress, roughly chopped

each serving provides

396kcals • 24g protein
31g fat of which 15g saturates
5g carbohydrate of which 5g sugars
3g fibre • 392mg sodium
200g vegetables

396 kcals

2.5 portions fruit & veg

1 Using a fork, whisk the eggs with 1 tbsp cold water and freshly ground black pepper in a bowl until frothy.

2 Heat the butter in an 18cm omelette pan or non-stick frying pan over a moderate heat until foaming. Tilt the pan to coat the bottom with the butter, then pour in the beaten egg mixture. Cook for about 1 minute, stirring gently with a spatula and pulling the cooked egg in from the edges so that the unset egg runs onto the hot pan and starts cooking.

3 When the egg is lightly set, stop stirring and scatter over the chopped tomatoes. Cook for a further 30 seconds or until the egg is just set and golden underneath. Remove from the heat.

4 Sprinkle over the cheese and watercress, then slide the omelette onto a warmed plate, folding it over in half as it slides from the pan. Serve immediately.

cook's tip

• Plum tomatoes are a good variety to use here as they are firm-fleshed and less watery than regular tomatoes. For strict vegetarians, use the Cheddar cheese option.

Prawn & vegetable foo yung

This Chinese-style dish starts with a stir-fry of colourful vegetables and prawns that is then layered with omelette underneath and omelette ribbons over the top.

SERVES 4
PREPARATION TIME 10–15 minutes
COOKING TIME about 15 minutes

8 eggs
1 tsp toasted sesame oil
3 tbsp chopped fresh coriander (optional)
2 tsp cornflour
1 tbsp light soy sauce
2 tbsp dry or medium sherry
2 tbsp vegetable oil
300g broccoli florets, thinly sliced
1 orange or red pepper, deseeded and thinly sliced
50g fresh root ginger, peeled and cut into thin strips
2 garlic cloves, chopped
4 spring onions, sliced
350g peeled raw prawns, thawed and drained if frozen
200g bean sprouts

1 Beat the eggs with the sesame oil and coriander, if using, then set aside. Mix the cornflour to a smooth paste with the soy sauce and sherry, and set aside.

2 Heat half the vegetable oil in a large frying pan or wok. Add the broccoli, pepper, ginger, garlic and spring onions, and stir-fry for 5 minutes or until the broccoli looks bright green and is just tender. Pour in the cornflour mixture and stir for 1 minute.

3 Add the prawns and cook for 2 minutes, then add the bean sprouts and cook for a further 1 minute or until the prawns are pink. Transfer to a large bowl, including all the juices, and keep warm. Wipe the pan with a piece of kitchen paper.

4 Add the remaining vegetable oil to the pan and heat it for a few seconds. Pour in just over half the egg mixture and swirl the pan to spread it out evenly. Stir once or twice, then let the egg set for about 3 minutes. Loosen the omelette with a slice and transfer it to a serving dish.

5 Quickly add the remaining egg mixture to the pan and cook for 1–2 minutes until just set. Turn out onto a board and cut into ribbons. Spoon the vegetables on top of the whole omelette, scatter the omelette ribbons over the top and serve immediately.

variations
• Frozen stir-fry vegetable mixes are ideal for making a foo-yung in a hurry.
• Omit the prawns for a vegetarian version.

each serving provides
382kcals • 36g protein
21g fat of which 5g saturates
11g carbohydrate of which 5.5g sugars
4g fibre • 514mg sodium
188g vegetables

382 kcals

2 portions fruit & veg

exotic tastes

Courgette & onion eggah

The French have omelettes, the Spanish tortillas, the Italians frittatas and Arabic nations have eggahs. Eggahs are good served **straight from the pan** or left to cool as a light lunch or supper with a colourful salad.

SERVES 4 V
PREPARATION TIME 10 minutes
COOKING TIME 20–25 minutes

4 tbsp olive oil
2 onions, very thinly sliced
2 garlic cloves, finely chopped
4 large eggs
4 tbsp semi-skimmed milk
4 tbsp chopped fresh flat-leaf
parsley or coriander
2 tbsp chopped fresh dill (optional)
1 large courgette, halved
lengthways, then thinly sliced

TO SERVE chilli sauce
or harissa (optional)

cook's tips

• This can be made up to 2 days in advance and stored in the fridge until about 15 minutes before serving. The dill flavour, if used, remains fresh.
• This could serve two for a more substantial meal.

variation

• For a chickpea and spinach eggah, replace the courgettes with 2 x 400g cans chickpeas, drained, omit step 3 and use just 2 tbsp oil.

1 Heat 1 tbsp of the oil in a large, non-stick frying pan with a flameproof handle over a medium heat. Add the onions and stir for 3 minutes, then add the garlic and continue frying for a further 2–3 minutes, stirring occasionally, until the onion is soft and golden brown.

2 Meanwhile, beat the eggs and milk together in a large bowl with the herbs. When the onions are golden, stir them into the egg mixture.

3 Heat another 2 tbsp of the oil in the pan. Add the courgettes and gently fry for about 5 minutes, stirring frequently, until tender and lightly browned. Add the courgettes to the egg mixture.

4 Add the remaining oil to the pan and swirl it around to coat the edge. Pour in the eggs and courgettes, using a spatula to spread them out. Leave the eggah to cook for about 8 minutes, shaking the pan occasionally, until the egg mixture is almost set and only a small amount of unset mixture remains on the surface. Meanwhile, preheat the grill to high and position a shelf about 10cm from the heat.

5 Place the pan under the grill and grill the eggah for 2–3 minutes until the surface is just set. Run the spatula around the edge and invert onto a large platter. Serve immediately or set aside and leave to cool. Serve cut into wedges, sprinkled with chilli sauce or harrisa, if liked.

252 kcals

prepare ahead

2 portions fruit & veg

each serving provides 252kcals • 11g protein
19g fat of which 4g saturates • 10g carbohydrate of which
7.5g sugars • 2g fibre • 105mg sodium • 163g vegetables

Pasta frittata with asparagus & peas

Little soup pasta shapes make a great filling for this Italian-style flat omelette with tender sliced asparagus and frozen peas. It's delicious served hot, warm or cold, with a simple salad for a light meal. Add some garlic bread for a more hearty meal.

SERVES 4 Ⓥ
PREPARATION TIME 25 minutes
COOKING TIME about 10 minutes

250g asparagus, trimmed
200g frozen peas or petits pois
150g soup pasta (such as small
  bows or shells)
8 eggs
6 spring onions, thinly sliced
2 tbsp chopped fresh mint
2 tbsp olive oil
50g Caerphilly or Wensleydale
  cheese, grated or finely crumbled

cook's tip

• The trick for a perfect frittata is to cook over a medium to low heat and allow the mixture to set slowly without stirring. Stirring once the egg has begun to set will break the mixture apart. Too high a heat will burn the base before the egg is set sufficiently to finish under the grill.

402 kcals   **1.5** portions fruit & veg

each serving provides

402kcals • 28g protein • 19g fat of which 6g saturates • 34g carbohydrate of which 4g sugars • 5g fibre 235mg sodium • 127g vegetables

1 Half-fill a large frying pan with water and bring to the boil. Add the asparagus and cook for 4–5 minutes until the spears are just tender. Lift them out with tongs or a draining spoon, transfer to a board and leave until they are cool enough to handle.

2 Bring the water in the pan back to the boil. Add the peas and pasta, bring back to the boil again and cook for 5 minutes or until tender.

3 Meanwhile, beat the eggs in a large bowl. Cut the tips off the asparagus and set them aside. Slice the asparagus stalks and add to the eggs together with the spring onions and mint. Drain the pasta and peas and immediately stir them into the egg mixture.

4 Preheat the grill to high. Dry the frying pan, then heat the oil over a medium heat. Pour in the egg mixture, making sure all the ingredients are evenly distributed. Reduce the heat slightly and cook for about 5 minutes until the omelette is two thirds set, but still moist on top, and browned underneath.

5 Sprinkle the cheese over the frittata and place under the grill. Cook for about 5 minutes to brown the top. Cut into 4 large wedges and serve garnished with the reserved asparagus tips.

Baked spinach & ham pancakes

You can cook the pancakes **well in advance** (see page 180). Assemble the whole dish, then bake just before serving. The pancakes are made with **half wholemeal flour** to be light yet higher in fibre.

SERVES 4 ✱ (pancakes only)
PREPARATION TIME 40 minutes
COOKING TIME 15 minutes

PANCAKES
50g plain flour
50g wholemeal flour
1 egg
250ml semi-skimmed milk
2 tbsp vegetable oil

FILLING
1 tbsp olive oil
6 spring onions, sliced
150g cup mushrooms, sliced
250g fresh spinach leaves
200g cooked smoked ham, diced
½ tsp freshly grated nutmeg
250g ricotta cheese
25g Parmesan cheese, freshly grated

variation
• For a vegetarian version, omit the ham, add 50g chopped walnuts or toasted pine nuts to the filling and use Italian-style hard cheese in place of Parmesan.

cook's tip
• Make sure the spinach is as dry as possible after washing, or it will be too watery.

each serving provides
412kcals • 28g protein
23g fat of which 8g saturates
24g carbohydrate of which
6g sugars • 3.5g fibre
774mg sodium
115g vegetables

prepare ahead

412 kcals

1 portion fruit & veg

1 Preheat the oven to 200°C/gas 6. Then make the pancakes. Sift both flours into a medium bowl, adding the bran left in the sieve to the bowl, add the egg and a pinch of salt, then gradually whisk in the milk to form a smooth batter. (This can be done in a blender or food processor.) Transfer to a jug.

2 Heat a frying pan to very hot and brush lightly with some of the oil. Pour a little pancake batter into the pan and quickly swirl around to coat the base evenly. When the batter is set and the underside is lightly browned, turn the pancake and cook the other side until golden. Remove and place on kitchen paper. Repeat with the remaining batter to make 8 pancakes. Stack them, interleaved with kitchen or greaseproof paper.

3 For the filling, heat the oil in the frying pan and fry the spring onions and mushrooms for 2–3 minutes to soften. On a high heat, add the spinach leaves, stirring until the leaves wilt and all the excess liquid has evaporated. Remove from the heat and stir in the ham. Add the nutmeg and season to taste.

4 Lay the pancakes out flat on a work surface and spoon a little ricotta onto each. Top with a quarter of the mushroom and spinach mixture, then roll up.

5 Place the pancakes, with the seam-sides down, in a lightly oiled, shallow ovenproof dish. Sprinkle with Parmesan and bake for 15 minutes until thoroughly heated and lightly browned. Serve hot.

Spicy Bombay vegetable stack

A colourful vegetable curry makes a perfect filling for a stack of **delicately spiced pancakes** and provides your five-a-day in one meal.

SERVES 2 Ⅴ
PREPARATION TIME 20 minutes
COOKING TIME 20 minutes

PANCAKES
50g plain flour
pinch of chilli powder
pinch of ground turmeric
pinch of ground coriander
1 large egg
100ml semi-skimmed milk
1 tbsp vegetable oil

FILLING
1 tbsp vegetable oil
1 onion, chopped
2 tsp medium curry powder
100g carrots, peeled and diced
1 red pepper, deseeded and diced
200g broccoli, stalks sliced and
head cut into small florets
175g courgettes, diced
75g frozen peas

cook's tip
• The pancake batter can be made up to a day ahead and kept, covered, in the fridge. Cooked pancakes can be made up to 3 days ahead, stacked between sheets of greaseproof paper and wrapped in cling film: store in the fridge or freezer. The vegetable curry can be made up to 2 hours ahead and then gently reheated over a low heat.

1 Sift the flour into a mixing bowl with the spices. Add the egg and stir to combine, then gradually whisk in the milk to form a smooth batter that is about the thickness of double cream. Transfer to a jug and set aside.

2 To make the filling, heat the oil in a large frying pan over a gentle heat. Stir in the onions and curry powder and cook, stirring occasionally, for about 2 minutes until the onions are slightly softened.

3 Stir in the carrots and red pepper and cook for 5–6 minutes, then add the broccoli and courgettes. Cook, stirring occasionally, for a further 5 minutes until softened. Stir in the peas and pour in 75ml water. Cover and cook for about 5 minutes until all the vegetables are tender.

4 Meanwhile heat a frying pan, preferably non-stick, on a moderate heat. Brush lightly with 1 tsp of the oil. Pour in about a third of the pancake batter and quickly tilt the pan around so the batter forms a large even pancake. Cook for about 1 minute on each side, then remove and place on kitchen paper. Repeat with the remaining batter to make 2 more pancakes, greasing the pan with a little more oil each time.

5 Place 1 pancake on a large platter and spoon half the vegetable curry over. Top with the second pancake, add the remaining curry and finish with the third pancake. Cut into wedges using a sharp knife and serve at once.

variation
• For a more substantial main course for meat-eaters, add 200g diced cooked lean turkey to the vegetables.

prepare ahead

5+ portions fruit & veg

403 kcals

each serving provides
403kcals • 19g protein • 18g fat of which 3g saturates • 44g carbohydrate of which 19.5g sugars • 10g fibre • 106mg sodium 430g vegetables

Cheesy chicken & vegetable pancakes

If you have some cooked chicken left over from a roast, why not use it to make this quick filling for savoury pancakes? Perfect for a tempting family meal served with a side salad.

SERVES 4 ✳ (pancakes only)
PREPARATION TIME 1 hour
COOKING TIME 25 minutes

PANCAKES
115g plain flour
1 egg, beaten
300ml semi-skimmed milk
2 tbsp vegetable oil

FILLING
150g frozen peas
150g frozen broccoli florets
25g butter
1 small onion, finely chopped
25g plain flour
300ml semi-skimmed milk
250g skinless roast chicken meat, cut into thin strips
2 tsp chopped fresh tarragon or 1 tsp dried
25g extra mature Cheddar or Parmesan cheese, finely grated

1 Preheat the oven to 190°C/gas 5. First make the batter. Sift the flour into a medium bowl, add the egg and a pinch of salt, and gradually whisk in the milk to form a smooth batter. (This can be done in a blender or food processor.) Transfer to a jug.

473 kcals

1 portion fruit & veg

2 Heat a frying pan, preferably non-stick, and brush lightly with a little oil. Pour one eighth of the batter into the pan and quickly swirl to coat the bottom. Cook for 1–2 minutes until set, then flip over and cook the other side. Remove and place on kitchen paper. Repeat to make 8 pancakes, greasing the pan with oil as necessary. Stack the pancakes, interleaved with kitchen paper.

3 To make the filling, cook the peas and broccoli in a pan of boiling water, or in the microwave, following the pack instructions. Drain, then roughly chop the broccoli. Meanwhile melt the butter in a saucepan, add the onion and cook gently for 3–4 minutes until softened. Add the flour and cook, stirring, for 1 minute, then gradually stir in the milk. Bring to the boil, still stirring, then simmer for 2–3 minutes. Stir in the chicken, peas, broccoli and tarragon and season to taste.

4 Spoon some filling onto the centre of each pancake, spreading it out a little, then roll up to enclose the filling. Arrange the filled pancakes, in a single layer, in a lightly greased, shallow oblong ovenproof dish (such as a lasagne dish), then sprinkle evenly with the cheese. Bake for 25 minutes or until golden.

each serving provides 473kcals • 35g protein • 21g fat of which 8g saturates • 40g carbohydrate of which 10g sugars • 4g fibre 211mg sodium • 90g vegetables

SERVES 4 (makes 12 pancakes) Ⓥ
PREPARATION TIME 20 minutes, plus 5 minutes standing time
COOKING TIME 20 minutes

75g plain flour
25g wholemeal flour
1½ tsp baking powder
25g rolled oats
2 tsp curry paste, or to taste
150ml semi-skimmed milk
2 eggs, lightly beaten
198g can sweetcorn with peppers, drained
175g frozen peas, thawed
2 tbsp vegetable oil

cook's tip
• These pancakes can be made in advance, then gently warmed in a moderate oven before serving.

variation
• To make chilli and coriander pancakes, leave out the curry paste and peas and use 2 x 198g cans of sweetcorn, drained, 1 deseeded and finely chopped red chilli and 3 tbsp chopped fresh coriander.

Spiced pea & corn pancakes

It's always a treat to have pancakes. These high-fibre, oaty mini ones are mildly spicy and packed with **juicy sweetcorn and peas.** Serve with a simple salad for a **nutritious casual meal.**

1 Sift the flours and baking powder into a bowl, adding the bran left in the sieve. Stir in the oats. Blend the curry paste with 2 tbsp of the milk, then stir this into the remaining milk.

2 Make a well in the middle of the dry ingredients and add the eggs and milk. Gradually beat in the flour and oats to make a smooth batter. (Alternatively the batter can be made in a food processor: put the eggs, milk and curry paste in a blender or food processor, add the flours and process to a smooth paste. Add the oats and process for a few more seconds.) Leave the batter to stand for 5 minutes to allow it to thicken slightly.

3 Meanwhile, tip the sweetcorn and peas onto a plate lined with several sheets of kitchen paper, to soak up any excess moisture. Add to the batter, then lightly season and stir well.

4 Heat a large, heavy-based frying pan, preferably non-stick, over a moderate heat, then brush with a little of the oil. Drop 3 or 4 large spoonfuls of the batter into the pan and cook for 2–3 minutes until dark golden. Turn the pancakes over using a fish slice or palette knife, then cook the other side for 2–3 minutes. Remove from the pan and keep warm in a low oven while cooking the remaining batter to make 12 pancakes in total. Serve hot.

each serving provides 305kcals • 12g protein • 12g fat of which 2g saturates • 40g carbohydrate of which 7g sugars • 4g fibre 388mg sodium • 85g vegetables

305 kcals • **1** portion fruit & veg • **prepare ahead**

Goat's cheese soufflé with ratatouille

This dish is a Provençal-style marriage between a light, cheesy soufflé topping and a flavoursome stew of Mediterranean vegetables. Serve for a summer lunch with crusty bread and a green salad.

SERVES 4 V
PREPARATION TIME 20 minutes
COOKING TIME 20–25 minutes

2 tbsp fine dry breadcrumbs
25g unsalted butter
2 tbsp plain flour
250ml semi-skimmed milk, warm
freshly grated nutmeg, to taste
4 eggs, separated
50g soft rindless goat's cheese
25g Parmesan or Italian-style
  hard cheese, freshly grated
1 tsp Dijon mustard
400g can ratatouille

1 Preheat the oven to 200°C/ gas 6 and put a baking sheet in the oven to heat. Lightly oil the inside of a 1.25 litre soufflé dish. Sprinkle with the breadcrumbs, then tilt the dish and tap around the edge to distribute them evenly.

2 Melt the butter in a saucepan over a moderate heat. Sprinkle in the flour, then cook for 1 minute, stirring all the time. Slowly add in the milk, whisking constantly, until the sauce comes to the boil and thickens. Simmer for 2 minutes, stirring occasionally, then season with nutmeg and salt and pepper to taste.

3 Remove the sauce from the heat and cool slightly, then beat in the egg yolks, one at a time. Add the goat's cheese, half the Parmesan and the mustard and beat well to mix. Return the pan to the heat and reheat gently, just until the cheese has melted to make a thick, smooth sauce. Set aside to cool. Meanwhile, gently heat the ratatouille in a separate pan or in a dish in the microwave.

4 Whisk the egg whites in a large, clean bowl until stiff peaks form. Whisk one third of the egg whites into the soufflé mixture to lighten, then use a large metal spoon to fold in the remaining whites.

5 Spoon the hot ratatouille into the bottom of the soufflé dish. Spoon the cheese mixture on top and sprinkle with the remaining Parmesan. Place on the preheated baking sheet and bake for 20–25 minutes until well risen and golden. Serve at once.

each serving provides

333kcals • 17g protein
20g fat of which 8g saturates
22.5g carbohydrate of which
7g sugars • 3g fibre
741mg sodium • 100g vegetables

1 portion fruit & veg

special treat

333 kcals

3

4

variation
• For a spinach and cheese soufflé, omit the ratatouille. Put 450g rinsed young spinach leaves in a saucepan over a moderate heat, with just the water clinging to the leaves, and cook for 2 minutes until they wilt and turn dark green. Squeeze out all excess water and season to taste. Beat into the sauce in step 3, before adding the cheese.

cook's tip
• You will know the egg whites are stiff enough when you can turn the bowl upside-down without them falling out.

5

Cauliflower & Stilton soufflé

A soufflé is always bound to impress. Here's a classic combination that adds vegetable value to a **light and fluffy** soufflé. Serve straight from the oven, with **wholemeal bread** and a tomato salad.

SERVES 4 Ⓥ
PREPARATION TIME 25 minutes
COOKING TIME 35 minutes

1 tsp unsalted butter
15g Parmesan or Italian-style
   hard cheese, freshly grated
15g fine dry breadcrumbs
1 small cauliflower, about 340g
300ml semi-skimmed milk
3 tbsp cornflour
1 bay leaf
4 eggs, separated
85g white Stilton cheese,
   finely crumbled
1 tbsp wholegrain mustard
2 tbsp snipped fresh chives

variation

• Instead of Stilton, any strongly flavoured cheese can be used, such as Gorgonzola or Gruyère. However not all cheeses are suitable for strict vegetarians, so check the information on the packaging.

each serving provides

336kcals • 19.5g protein
18g fat of which 8g saturates
25g carbohydrate of which 6g sugars
2g fibre • 402mg sodium
85g vegetables

336 kcals

1 portion fruit & veg

light delight

1 Preheat the oven to 190°C/gas 5, and put a baking sheet in the oven to heat. Lightly grease a 1.7 litre soufflé dish with the butter. Mix together the Parmesan and breadcrumbs and sprinkle half of this mixture over the bottom and sides of the dish, turning the dish to coat evenly. Set aside.

2 Cut the cauliflower into small florets and cook in a steamer over boiling water for 8–10 minutes until very tender. Tip onto a plate and leave to cool for a few minutes, then purée with 100ml of the milk in a food processor or blender to a smooth consistency.

3 Mix the cornflour with a little of the remaining milk to make a smooth paste. Heat the rest of the milk until almost boiling, then pour onto the cornflour mixture, stirring constantly. Return to the pan, add the bay leaf and stir over a moderate heat until the sauce is thickened and smooth.

4 Pour the sauce into a large mixing bowl and remove the bay leaf. Beat in the egg yolks, one at a time. Add the Stilton and stir until melted, then stir in the cauliflower purée, mustard and chives. Season to taste.

5 Whisk the egg whites in a large, clean bowl, until stiff peaks form. Whisk one third of the whites into the sauce mixture to lighten it, then gently fold in the rest of the whites.

6 Spoon the mixture into the prepared soufflé dish and sprinkle the top with the remaining breadcrumb mixture. Set the dish on the hot baking sheet and bake for 35 minutes or until well risen and golden brown. Serve at once.

Tuna & sweetcorn pots

This is modern-day comfort food, combining an **interesting fusion** of tuna and mixed vegetables in sauce with a crisp topping of bread cubes, **tangy feta and tomatoes.**

SERVES 4
PREPARATION TIME 20–25 minutes
COOKING TIME 15 minutes

225g fine green beans,
  cut into 2.5cm lengths
    (or frozen cut green beans)
2 tbsp cornflour
200g can tuna in spring water
300ml semi-skimmed milk
225g frozen sweetcorn, thawed
4 spring onions, finely sliced
4 tomatoes, diced
100g feta cheese, finely diced
  or crumbled
1 tbsp olive oil
4 thick slices of wholemeal bread
  with crusts on, diced

each serving provides
377kcals • 23g protein
12g fat of which 5g saturates
47.5g carbohydrate of which
10g sugars • 5g fibre
726mg sodium • 208g vegetables

kids love them

2.5 portions fruit & veg

377 kcals

1 Preheat the oven to 220°C/gas 7. Place the beans in a saucepan and cover with boiling water, then bring back to the boil and cook for 3 minutes. Drain and set aside.

2 Mix the cornflour with the water from the tuna in the saucepan. Stir with a whisk until smooth, then stir in the milk. Bring to the boil, whisking vigorously until the sauce is thickened and smooth. Remove from the heat.

3 Use a spoon to stir the sweetcorn into the sauce, then stir in the spring onions, beans and tuna. Season to taste. Divide this mixture among 4 individual ovenproof soufflé or gratin dishes, each about 300ml capacity. Alternatively, turn the mixture into a 1.5 litre capacity ovenproof dish.

4 Mix the tomatoes, feta cheese and olive oil in a bowl. Stir in the diced bread until thoroughly combined. Pile this mixture on top of the tuna sauce, pressing it on gently to stay in place without squashing the topping.

5 Bake for 15 minutes or until the bread is browned and crisp, the cheese has softened and the tomatoes are lightly cooked. Underneath, the tuna mixture should be bubbling. Serve at once.

Grills & kebabs

Grilling is a fast and healthy method of cooking, since only a light basting of oil or a marinade is needed to keep food moist, and it's ideal for tender foods because it seals in their tasty juices. From the spicy, exotic taste of Jerk pork with grilled pineapple and corn, to a vegetarian treat such as Char-grilled halloumi with tomato and olive dressing, you can enjoy the mouthwatering flavours of grilled food all year round. For making kebabs, all kinds of fish, meat, poultry and vegetables are suitable for threading onto skewers, making fun and healthy food the whole family will enjoy.

Jerk pork with grilled pineapple & corn

A **spicy Jamaican paste**, made with **fiery chillies, fragrant allspice and thyme**, flavours and tenderises the pork steaks in this dish. They are served with **wedges of juicy pineapple and corn cobs**, all cooked under the grill. Serve with toasted French bread.

SERVES 4

PREPARATION TIME 20 minutes, plus at least 1 hour marinating

COOKING TIME about 15 minutes

4 pork loin steaks, trimmed of fat
4 fresh corn cobs
15g unsalted butter, softened
1 ripe pineapple
2 tbsp runny honey

JERK SEASONING

2 habanero or Scotch bonnet chillies, deseeded and roughly chopped
10 allspice berries, crushed, or ½ tsp ground allspice
pinch of freshly grated nutmeg
1 tsp chopped fresh thyme
2 garlic cloves, coarsely chopped
2 spring onions, chopped
2 tsp light soft brown sugar
1 tbsp lime juice
2 tbsp vegetable oil

1 Using a pestle and mortar, blender or food processor, blend together the ingredients for the jerk seasoning to make a smooth paste. Thinly brush or spread this mixture over both sides of the pork steaks and place side-by-side in a non-metallic shallow dish. Cover and leave to marinate in the fridge for at least 1 hour and up to 24 hours.

2 When you are ready to cook, preheat the grill to high. Remove the husks from the corn and trim the ends. Cut the corn in half crossways. Add to a pan of boiling water. Bring back to the boil, then reduce the heat and simmer for 5–10 minutes until just tender. Drain well, then lightly brush them with the softened butter.

3 While the corn is cooking, top and tail the pineapple. Cut off the skin, then cut out any remaining hard 'eyes'. Slice the fruit into 8 wedges and cut away the central core from each piece. Brush all over with the honey.

4 Place the pork on the grill pan. Cook for 3–4 minutes until the spicy crust is nicely browned, then turn and cook for another 3–4 minutes. Remove and keep warm.

5 Arrange the pineapple wedges and corn on the grill pan. Cook for 4–5 minutes until the pineapple and corn are lightly singed. Turn the pineapple and corn frequently to prevent them from burning. Serve hot, with the pork, with paper napkins for sticky fingers.

each serving provides 404kcals • 24g protein • 14g fat of which 3g saturates
49g carbohydrate of which 31g sugars • 4g fibre • 9mg sodium • 351g fruit and vegetables

404 kcals

4 portions fruit & veg

hot & spicy

cook's tip
• A compound in the seeds and membranes of chillies will cause burning pain should you inadvertently touch your eyes or lips, so be sure to wash your hands thoroughly after preparing chillies, or wear thin disposable plastic gloves.

variation
• Instead of making your own, you can buy ready-made jerk seasoning (look for it with the spices). Simply mix 2 tbsp with 1 tbsp lime juice and 2 tbsp vegetable oil to make a paste.

Char-grilled devilled steak combo

Onions and mushrooms are natural partners for tender beef steaks, and instead of deep-fried chips, char-grilled new potatoes make a healthier alternative. Serve with relishes and a big green salad.

SERVES 4

PREPARATION TIME 25 minutes, plus at least 20 minutes marinating

COOKING TIME about 20 minutes

1 tsp freshly ground black pepper
½ tsp dried thyme
pinch of paprika, or to taste
4 lean sirloin steaks, about
   150g each
2 tbsp vegetable oil
500g new potatoes, scrubbed
2 red onions, cut into wedges
500g chestnut mushrooms,
   thickly sliced

cook's tip
• If you don't have a pastry brush, use crumpled kitchen paper to oil the pan.

1 Mix together the black pepper, thyme and paprika on a plate. Lightly brush the steaks on both sides using half of the oil, then lay them on the spice mixture and rub the spices onto both sides of the steaks. Set aside to marinate while you prepare the vegetables, or for up to 4 hours in the fridge.

2 Bring a large pan of lightly salted water to the boil over a high heat. Add the potatoes and boil for 12 minutes or until just tender. Drain well. When they are cool enough to handle, thinly slice the potatoes. Set aside.

3 Heat a cast-iron, ridged griddle over a high heat until it is hot enough for a splash of water to 'dance' on the surface. Brush with half of the remaining oil, then add the potatoes and onions. Char-grill for about 7 minutes until the potatoes are browned and crisp and the onions are softened. Transfer the vegetables to a plate, cover with foil and keep warm.

4 Put the steaks on the hot griddle and char-grill for 1 minute on each side for rare, 1½ minutes for medium and 2 minutes for well-done. Remove to another plate, cover with foil and keep warm.

5 Brush the pan with the last of the oil, add the mushrooms and char-grill for 5 minutes or until they are brown and tender. Return the steaks to the pan with any accumulated juices. Add the potatoes and onions, and season to taste. Reheat briefly, then serve.

each serving provides 392kcals • 41g protein • 13g fat of which 4g saturates 29g carbohydrate of which 7.5g sugars • 4g fibre • 128mg sodium • 225g vegetables

392 kcals

2.5 portions fruit & veg

steak treat

SERVES 4
PREPARATION TIME 10 minutes
COOKING TIME about 20 minutes

2 large red peppers, halved
    lengthways and deseeded
2 large yellow peppers, halved
    lengthways and deseeded
6 thick pork sausages, about 400g
2 tbsp tomato ketchup
2 tbsp hoisin sauce
3 heads pak choi, separated
    into leaves
3 tbsp sesame seeds

each serving provides

375kcals • 18g protein
25g fat of which 8g saturates
22g carbohydrate of which
16g sugars • 4g fibre
1061mg sodium • 240g vegetables

375 kcals

3 portions fruit & veg

Sesame sausages with peppers & pak choi

This is **irresistible fusion food,** combining British, Chinese and Mediterranean cuisines. Good quality sausages are finished off with a terrific **sticky glaze and crunchy sesame seeds.** Serve with crusty French bread or Greek sesame seed bread.

1 Preheat a moderate grill. Put the peppers and sausages on the rack of a grill pan and grill for 15–20 minutes, turning them from time to time until the sausages are evenly browned and cooked through and the peppers are tender and lightly charred.

2 Meanwhile, mix together the tomato ketchup and hoisin sauce in a shallow bowl. Tear the pak choi into bite-sized pieces and put into a serving dish.

3 Using tongs, transfer the sausages to the ketchup mixture and roll them over to coat evenly. Cover the grill pan rack with foil. Place the sausages back on the foil and grill for a further 1 minute or until the glaze is bubbling. Turn the sausages and sprinkle with the sesame seeds, then cook for another 1 minute until the seeds are golden.

4 Cut the peppers into wide strips and thickly slice the sausages on the diagonal. Add both the pepper strips and sausage slices to the pak choi, toss together and serve while still warm.

Grilled sardines with lemon & caper couscous

Tasty sardines are **super-healthy** and here they are stuffed with a **refreshing, zesty couscous.** Ask your fishmonger to bone the fish for you, so they're ready to fill.

SERVES 4
PREPARATION TIME 30–35 minutes
COOKING TIME 10–15 minutes

200g couscous
500ml boiling water or fish stock
12 sardines, about 80g each,
   cleaned and heads removed
4 tomatoes, about 200g in total,
   finely chopped
4 tbsp bottled capers, rinsed
4 tbsp finely chopped fresh parsley
finely grated zest of 1 lemon
20 cherry or baby plum tomatoes
   on the vine

LEMON & GARLIC MAYONNAISE
3 garlic cloves
3 tbsp reduced-fat mayonnaise
finely grated zest of ½ lemon
1 tbsp lemon juice

each serving provides
569kcals • 54g protein
26g fat of which 7g saturates
31g carbohydrate of which 4g sugars
4g fibre   661mg sodium
125g vegetables

prepare ahead • **1.5** portions fruit & veg • **569** kcals

1 To make the mayonnaise, grill the garlic cloves, in their skins, for 4–5 minutes until soft. Squeeze out the flesh and stir into the mayonnaise together with the lemon zest and juice. Set aside.

2 Place the couscous in a bowl and pour over the boiling water or stock. Leave to soak for 15–20 minutes until the grains swell and all the liquid is absorbed. Stir with a fork to fluff up the grains.

3 While the couscous is soaking, bone the sardines: place each one belly-down on a board and press down the backbone with your thumbs. Turn over and the bones should lift out easily. Snip the bone off at the tail end with scissors.

4 Stir the chopped tomatoes, capers, parsley and lemon zest into the couscous and season to taste.

5 Lay the sardines skin-side down on a board and spoon about 1 tbsp of the couscous across the centre of each fish. Lift the wide end up over the stuffing, and bring the tail end over it. Secure with a wooden cocktail stick. (You can prepare ahead up to this stage, then cover the stuffed fish and keep them chilled in the fridge until ready to cook, later the same day.)

6 Place the fish under a hot grill and cook, turning once, for 6–8 minutes until golden and cooked through. Add the vine tomatoes about halfway through the cooking time. While the fish is cooking, spread the remaining couscous on a platter. Arrange the grilled fish and tomatoes on top of the couscous and serve with the mayonnaise.

SERVES 4
PREPARATION TIME 20 minutes,
 plus overnight marinating
COOKING TIME 15–20 minutes

4 tbsp olive oil

2 tbsp walnut oil

finely grated zest and juice
 of 1 lemon

3 tbsp medium sherry

4 salmon fillets with skin,
 about 115g each

2 courgettes, peeled into
 thin ribbons

135g pack mixed salad leaves,
 such as rocket, lamb's lettuce,
 baby spinach or green oak leaf

1 ruby grapefruit, peeled and
 cut into segments

50g walnuts, roughly chopped

TO GARNISH sprigs of fresh
 flat-leaf parsley

cook's tips

• To make courgette ribbons, use
a vegetable peeler to peel off thin
ribbons, drawing the peeler along the
length of the courgette until you are
left with a slim centre core, which can
be discarded.

• If you don't have a griddle, cook
both the courgette ribbons and the
salmon under a pre-heated hot grill.

Griddled salmon with sherry & walnut dressing

Fresh salmon is ideal for quick cooking on a griddle. Here it's served on a mixed leaf salad with grapefruit, walnuts and griddled courgette ribbons. Serve with warm, plain or olive ciabatta.

1 Mix together half the olive oil, the walnut oil, lemon zest and juice, and sherry in a shallow dish. Place the salmon fillets in the dish, turn to coat with the dressing, then cover and leave to marinate in the fridge overnight.

2 Place the courgette ribbons in a large bowl, add the remaining oil and toss together. Set aside. Arrange the salad leaves on 4 serving plates, top with the grapefruit segments, then scatter the walnuts over the top. Set aside.

3 Heat a cast-iron, ridged griddle over a high heat and cook the courgette ribbons (in 2 batches, if necessary) on the pan, for 4–5 minutes, turning frequently, to produce charred stripes on the surface. Remove from the pan, set aside and keep warm.

4 Remove the salmon from the marinade and reserve the marinade. Reduce the heat to moderate and put the salmon, skin-side down first, on the pan and cook for 4–5 minutes on each side until cooked through and firm to the touch.

5 Spoon some courgette ribbons onto each portion of salad and top each with a piece of salmon. Pour the marinade onto the griddle and let it bubble on a high heat for 1–2 minutes until reduced slightly. Pour over the salmon and serve immediately, garnished with sprigs of parsley.

494 kcals

2.5 portions fruit & veg

each serving provides 494kcals • 27g protein
38g fat of which 5g saturates • 8g carbohydrate of which 8g sugars
2.5g fibre • 60mg sodium • 200g fruit and vegetables

Seared cod with salsa verde

A punchy herb salsa is the perfect accompaniment for char-grilled white fish, served with **tender asparagus spears and red radicchio,** also cooked on the grill pan. The fish and vegetables are piled on toasted muffins in a style reminiscent of Eggs Benedict.

SERVES 4
PREPARATION TIME 15 minutes, plus 30 minutes marinating
COOKING TIME 10–13 minutes

3 tbsp olive oil
1 garlic clove, crushed
grated zest and juice of 1 lemon
4 thick pieces cod fillet with skin, about 125g each
250g asparagus spears, trimmed and halved lengthways if thick
2 heads radicchio or red chicory, quartered lengthways
4 English muffins, split in half

SALSA VERDE
2 tbsp bottled capers, rinsed
15g fresh mint
50g fresh parsley
25g fresh basil
1 green chilli, deseeded
2 tbsp olive oil
6 spring onions, sliced

variations

• Instead of cod, try salmon or tuna steak or fillet, or small whole mackerel that have been cleaned, boned, split and opened out flat.
• Red pepper strips and spring onions would also be delicious char-grilled to serve with the fish in place of the asparagus and radicchio.
• For a vegetarian alternative, griddle thick slices of halloumi cheese or smoked tofu and serve with the vegetables, salsa and muffins.

1 Put 2 tbsp of the olive oil in a large shallow dish with the garlic and lemon zest. Add the cod and turn each piece in the oil to coat both sides. Cover and set aside for about 30 minutes. Place the asparagus in another dish with the radicchio and pour over the lemon juice.

2 For the salsa, finely chop the capers, mint, parsley, basil and chilli in a food processor. Add the olive oil and spring onions and pulse to mix. Pour in the lemon juice from the vegetables and transfer the salsa to a serving dish. Cover and set aside.

3 Heat a cast-iron, ridged griddle over a high heat. Drain the oil from the cod onto the asparagus and radicchio, then turn the vegetables to coat them. Char-grill the asparagus, turning occasionally, for 4–5 minutes until lightly charred, bright green and tender. Transfer to a serving dish. Char-grill the radicchio, turning once, for 1–2 minutes until attractively charred and just beginning to wilt. Add to the asparagus and cover to keep warm.

4 Put the cod, skin-side up, on the griddle and cook for 2 minutes. Use a fish slice to turn the cod and cook for a further 3–4 minutes until the flesh is opaque and flakes easily. Meanwhile, toast the muffin halves.

5 Brush the toasted muffins with the remaining olive oil. Place the bottom half of each muffin on a plate. Pile the cod and vegetables on top and spoon over the salsa. Lean the other muffin halves against the side and serve.

twist on a classic

1.5 portions fruit & veg

434 kcals

each serving provides 434kcals
34g protein • 17g fat of which 2.5g saturates
38g carbohydrate of which 5g sugars • 4g fibre
544mg sodium • 120g vegetables

cook's tips
• Cook the fish fillets skin-side up first, so that they keep
their shape – the thick skin holds the flakes of flesh together.
Skinless fillets are difficult to turn when cooked on a griddle
as they tend to fall apart; however, you can use skinless fillets
if you are cooking in a frying pan.
• Make the salsa verde in advance and keep it chilled in the
fridge until you need it.
• If you don't have a griddle, cook the vegetables and fish
under a pre-heated hot grill. Cover the grill rack with foil.

Griddled tuna with summer herb crust

Perfect for summer lunches or an **al fresco dinner party,** this informal dish is **simple to make and very healthy.** Serve with extra slices of toasted ciabatta.

SERVES 4

PREPARATION TIME 15 minutes, plus 30 minutes marinating

COOKING TIME about 8 minutes

4 tuna steaks, about 150g each
1 garlic clove, crushed
2 tbsp olive oil
4 tbsp dry white wine
50g ciabatta breadcrumbs
40g pine nuts
2 tbsp chopped fresh basil
2 tbsp chopped fresh parsley
50g sun-dried tomatoes in oil, drained and chopped
juice and grated zest of 1 lemon
4 beef tomatoes
8 large basil leaves

TO SERVE 250g baby spinach leaves

variation

• Swordfish makes a pleasant alternative to tuna. It's another firm, meaty-textured fish, which although lower in fat than tuna, is also rich in omega-3 oils. Take care not to overcook, as it can become dry.

cook's tips

• The tuna can be left in its marinade for several hours or overnight in the fridge, along with the crumb topping and the basil-filled tomatoes. To make the crumbs, whizz day-old bread briefly in a food processor.

• If preferred, the tuna and the tomatoes can be cooked under a preheated moderate grill.

1 Place the tuna steaks in a single layer in a non-metallic dish, sprinkle with the garlic, oil and wine, turning to coat evenly. Cover and leave to marinate in the fridge for about 30 minutes.

2 Meanwhile prepare the crumb topping. Mix the ciabatta crumbs, pine nuts, chopped basil and parsley, sun-dried tomatoes and lemon zest. Season to taste and put to one side.

3 Make a deep, cross-shaped cut into the base of each tomato and tuck a couple of basil leaves deep into the cuts.

4 Preheat a cast-iron, ridged griddle to hot. Lift the tuna steaks from the marinade and place onto the pan. Brush the tomatoes with a little of the marinade and add to the pan.

5 Cook the tuna for about 4 minutes on one side, brushing with the remaining marinade occasionally. Turn carefully, spoon the crumbs on top of the tuna, and sprinkle a few crumbs over the tomatoes. Cook for a further 3–4 minutes until the tuna is just cooked but still slightly pink inside.

6 Spread the spinach leaves on a serving platter, arrange the tuna steaks and tomatoes on top and sprinkle with lemon juice.

each serving provides 471kcals • 41g protein 27g fat of which 4g saturates • 14g carbohydrate of which 7g sugars • 3.5g fibre • 365mg sodium • 225g vegetables

471 kcals

2.5 portions fruit & veg

prepare ahead

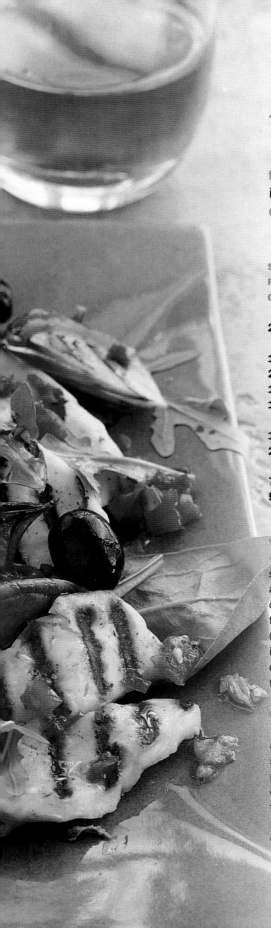

Char-grilled halloumi with tomato & olive dressing

Halloumi is a firm-textured Greek cheese that's delicious char-grilled. Here it's served with red onions on a bed of soft salad leaves, then drizzled with a hot dressing. Serve with seeded bread.

SERVES 4 Ⓥ
PREPARATION TIME 15 minutes
COOKING TIME 8–10 minutes

2½ tbsp olive oil, or oil from the
  jar of sun-dried tomatoes
1 tbsp lemon juice
2 red onions, cut into thin wedges
1 garlic clove, very finely chopped
10 sun-blush or sun-dried tomatoes,
  finely chopped
12 stoned black olives, rinsed
250g halloumi cheese, drained
  and cut into 1cm thick slices
75g baby spinach leaves
50g rocket

variation
• Instead of onion wedges, cut a small aubergine into 1cm slices and brush with 1 tbsp of the dressing. Char-grill or grill the slices for 7–8 minutes on each side (it may be necessary to do this in 2 batches), and keep warm while cooking the cheese. Scatter with a few toasted pine nuts before serving.

cook's tip
• Halloumi cheese will toughen if allowed to cool, so it's important to serve as quickly as possible. If your pan isn't large enough to fit both the onion wedges and cheese slices together, cook the onion first, then pile at the edge of the pan while cooking the cheese.

1 Whisk together 2 tbsp of the oil and the lemon juice in a bowl. Put the onion wedges in another bowl, drizzle over 1 tbsp of this dressing and toss to coat. Set aside. Stir the garlic into the remaining dressing, then add the tomatoes and olives. Mix well and leave to marinate briefly.

2 Heat a cast-iron, ridged griddle over a moderate heat, then brush with the remaining ½ tbsp oil. Add the onion wedges and cook for 3–4 minutes until nicely browned on the underside. Turn the onion wedges over with a palette knife, then put the cheese slices onto the pan. Increase the heat a little and cook the onion wedges for a further 3 minutes and the cheese for 1½ minutes on each side until tinged with brown and just beginning to melt at the edges. (Alternatively, cook the onions and cheese on a sheet of foil under a medium grill.)

3 While the onion and cheese are cooking, mix the spinach leaves and rocket together in a wide salad bowl. Leave in the bowl or serve onto individual salad plates. Arrange the onion wedges and cheese on top.

4 Tip the tomato mixture onto the hot griddle and stir for a just a few seconds until hot and steaming. Spoon over the cheese and salad leaves and serve.

each serving provides 331kcals • 17g protein • 24g fat of which 8.1g saturates • 12g carbohydrate of which 5g sugars 3g fibre • 696mg sodium • 128g vegetables

331 kcals

1.5 portions fruit & veg

cook's tip
• You can grill all the vegetables up to 3 hours ahead and keep, covered, at room temperature. Or, they can be chilled for up to 2 days to serve cold. Add the cooled salsa and Camembert cheese just before serving.

each serving provides
359kcals • 18g protein
21g fat of which 8g saturates
25g carbohydrate of which
16g sugars • 8g fibre
320mg sodium
450g vegetables

5+ portions fruit & veg

359 kcals

prepare ahead

Char-grilled vegetable platter

These colourful grilled vegetables, topped with a **fresh tomato and basil salsa and creamy Camembert cheese**, make a **wonderful vegetarian main course**. The vegetables could also be cooked, all at the same time, on a barbecue. Enjoy with toasted ciabatta slices and a green salad.

SERVES 4 Ⓥ
PREPARATION TIME 15 minutes
COOKING TIME 20 minutes

1 small acorn or butternut
  squash, peeled, deseeded
  and cut into slices
3 tbsp olive oil
2 red onions, thickly sliced
2 courgettes, thickly sliced
1 aubergine, thickly sliced
1 red pepper, deseeded and
  cut into wide strips
1 yellow pepper, deseeded
  and cut into wide strips
200g asparagus, trimmed
2 large flat mushrooms,
  thickly sliced
4 small ripe tomatoes,
  finely chopped
2 garlic cloves, crushed
1 tbsp chopped fresh basil
200g Camembert cheese,
  cut into small pieces

1 Bring a saucepan of lightly salted water to the boil. Add the squash and cook for about 3 minutes until slightly softened. Drain.

2 Preheat a large cast-iron, ridged griddle. Pour the oil into a small pan. Using a pastry brush, very lightly coat the onion slices with oil and char-grill for about 2 minutes on each side. Transfer to a large platter and keep warm. Oil and char-grill the courgette and aubergine slices in the same way, then add to the platter.

3 Char-grill the pepper strips, without oil, for 3–4 minutes on each side until charred and slightly softened. Transfer to the platter. Very lightly oil the asparagus and char-grill, turning occasionally, for about 4 minutes. Add to the platter.

4 Very lightly oil the mushrooms and par-boiled squash and char-grill for about 3 minutes, turning once. Add to the platter.

5 Add the tomatoes, garlic and basil to the oil remaining in the small pan. Heat through gently and season to taste. Pour this mixture over the grilled vegetables and scatter the Camembert over the top.

SERVES 4 V
PREPARATION 10 minutes
COOKING TIME about 30 minutes

1 large aubergine, thinly
   sliced lengthways
3 tbsp olive oil
2 red peppers, halved and deseeded
200g shallots, halved but not peeled
1 red chilli, halved lengthways
   and deseeded
1 garlic clove
500g ready-made polenta,
   thinly sliced
1 tbsp lemon juice
75g stoned black olives
50g Parmesan or Italian-style
   hard cheese

TO GARNISH fresh basil leaves

variations

• Slices of ciabatta bread could
replace the polenta. Brush with oil
and grill until golden, turning once.
• If fresh chillies are not available,
add ¼ tsp crushed dried chillies to
the dressing instead.

each serving provides

634kcals • 16g protein
17g fat of which 4g saturates
105g carbohydrate of which
8g sugars • 4g fibre
526mg sodium • 205g vegetables

634 kcals

2.5 portions fruit & veg

Grilled polenta with vegetables, olives & parmesan

Grilled Mediterranean vegetables, combined with plump olives and a chilli, garlic and lemon dressing, make an exciting topping for ready-made polenta. Arrange on a wide platter for maximum table-top impact.

1 Heat a grill until it is very hot. Brush the aubergine slices on both sides using 1 tbsp of the oil and lay side by side on a baking sheet. Add the peppers, skin-side up, and the shallots, skin-side down. Grill for about 15 minutes, turning the aubergines over halfway through, until the pepper and shallot skins are blackened all over. Set aside on a board or plate until cool enough to handle.

2 Arrange the chilli, cut-side down, unpeeled garlic and polenta slices on the baking sheet. Brush the polenta on both sides with 1 tbsp of the oil. Grill for about 6 minutes, then remove the chilli and garlic and turn the polenta. Grill for a further 6–8 minutes until the polenta is golden brown.

3 Scrape the flesh from the chilli and garlic, mash and mix with the remaining oil and the lemon juice in a small bowl. Peel the skins from the peppers and slice the flesh. Peel the shallots. Arrange the polenta slices around a wide platter. Pile the peppers, shallots, aubergines and olives in the centre and spoon over the chilli dressing.

4 Use a vegetable peeler to shave curls of Parmesan over the vegetables and scatter with basil leaves. Serve immediately.

Middle Eastern kibbeh

Lebanese-style meatballs are great for a relaxed family supper. They're made with **lean minced lamb,** bulghur wheat, herbs and spices, then grilled and served in **pitta bread pouches** with crisp salad.

SERVES 4
PREPARATION TIME 25 minutes
COOKING TIME 8–10 minutes

175g bulghur wheat
400ml vegetable stock, hot
400g lean minced lamb
1 red onion, grated
50g pine nuts, toasted and
   roughly chopped
3 tbsp chopped fresh coriander
¼ tsp ground allspice
½ tsp ground cumin
½ tsp ground cinnamon
½ tsp chilli powder

TO SERVE
4 wholemeal pitta breads
1 Little Gem lettuce, shredded
1 carrot, peeled and grated
¼ cucumber, thinly sliced
8 radishes, thinly sliced and
   tossed in 1 tbsp lemon juice
170g tub tzatziki (cucumber
   yoghurt dip)

1 Put the bulghur wheat in a saucepan and pour over the hot stock. Cover and leave to stand for 15 minutes. Meanwhile, put 8 wooden skewers to soak in cold water; this will prevent them from burning during cooking. Remove the lid from the pan and cook the bulghur wheat over a low heat for 4–5 minutes, stirring frequently, until the excess liquid has evaporated, but the mixture is still moist. Tip onto a tray, spread out and leave to cool.

2 Tip the cooled bulghur wheat into a bowl. Add the lamb, onion, pine nuts, coriander and dry spices and season to taste. Thoroughly mix together with your hands. If you prefer a smoother-textured kibbeh, transfer the mixture to a food processor and blend for a few seconds. (You may need to do this in 2 batches.)

3 Preheat the grill to moderate. Divide the lamb mixture into 16 pieces and shape into oval-shaped balls. Thread the kibbeh onto the soaked wooden skewers, putting 2 on each skewer. Arrange side by side on a foil-lined grill pan and grill for 4–5 minutes on each side until well-browned and cooked through. Remove and wrap loosely in the foil to keep warm.

4 Put the pitta bread on the grill pan and grill for about 30 seconds on each side to warm them; don't let them brown, or they will be too brittle to split open. Run a knife down one long edge of each pitta and gently open out to make a pocket.

5 Half-fill the pitta bread pockets with the shredded lettuce, carrot, cucumber and radishes. Slide the kibbeh off the skewers and divide among the pitta pockets. Add more salad to taste. Drizzle each one with a spoonful of tzatziki and serve immediately.

variation

• Tzatziki is a mixture of yoghurt, grated cucumber, mint and garlic. If you prefer, use reduced-fat hummus mixed with a little low-fat natural yoghurt so that it can be drizzled. Or for a really low-fat dressing, combine 8 tbsp low-fat natural yoghurt with 3 tbsp chopped fresh mint.

1.5 portions fruit & veg

690 kcals

exotic tastes

each serving provides 690kcals • 37g protein • 20g fat of which 2g saturates 94g carbohydrate of which 7g sugars • 6.5g fibre • 611mg sodium • 120g vegetables

2

3

4

5

Chimichurri pork kebabs

Kebabs are always a favourite, particularly for casual entertaining. Here, lean pork is marinated in a **punchy Argentinian-style sauce,** then threaded onto skewers and grilled with **wedges of sweet potato and corn cob slices.**

SERVES 4
PREPARATION TIME 30 minutes
COOKING TIME about 15 minutes

500g pork fillet, fat trimmed
  and cut into 2cm slices
2 orange-fleshed sweet
  potatoes, scrubbed
1 corn cob

CHIMICHURRI MARINADE
5 garlic cloves, finely chopped
6 tbsp chopped fresh
  flat-leaf parsley
4 tbsp red wine vinegar
3 tbsp extra virgin olive oil
1 tsp dried oregano
½ tsp ground cumin
½ tsp paprika
bottled hot-pepper sauce,
  to taste

TO GARNISH lime wedges

cook's tip
• The pork can be left to marinate for up to 1 day in the fridge.

variation
• If preferred, replace the corn with wedges of green or red pepper and the sweet potato with boiled new potatoes.

each serving provides
372kcals • 30g protein
14g fat of which 1g saturates
33g carbohydrate of which
8g sugars • 4g fibre
53mg sodium
175g vegetables

2 portions fruit & veg

372 kcals

BBQ sauce

1 For the marinade, put all the ingredients in a large non-metallic bowl, adding hot pepper sauce to taste. Add the pork and stir around to coat, then set aside to marinate for at least 20 minutes.

2 Meanwhile, bring a large pan of lightly salted water to the boil over a high heat. Add the sweet potatoes and boil in their skins for 12–15 minutes until just beginning to soften. Use a draining spoon to remove the potatoes and set aside to cool. Add the corn cob to the water and boil for 5 minutes until the kernels are tender. Drain well and set aside until cool enough to handle.

3 When the vegetables have cooled, peel off the potato skins, then cut the potatoes first in half lengthways, then widthways into 3cm thick wedges. Cut the sweetcorn cob into 8 x 2cm thick slices. Preheat the grill.

4 Thread slices of pork, sweet potato wedges and corn cob in turn onto 4 long or 8 shorter metal skewers and brush the marinade mixture onto the vegetables. Grill or barbecue the kebabs, turning frequently and basting with any remaining marinade, for about 15 minutes until the pork is cooked through. Serve the kebabs with lime wedges for squeezing over.

cook's tip
• Bacon is high in salt, so if you want to reduce the sodium further in this recipe, use reduced-salt bacon, widely available from supermarkets.

Rosemary-skewered vegetables with bacon

Fresh rosemary stalks make excellent skewers and flavour the ingredients they hold (you can use metal skewers if you prefer). This is a **stylish way of cooking** and serving **simple, healthy ingredients.** Serve with a leafy salad.

SERVES 4
PREPARATION TIME   30 minutes, plus 30 minutes marinating
COOKING TIME   8–10 minutes

24 even-sized baby new potatoes
8 strong, fresh rosemary stalks, each about 20cm long
2 tbsp olive oil
4 tbsp balsamic vinegar
1 tbsp Dijon mustard
4 tbsp apple juice
4 thick leeks, trimmed
8 lean back bacon rashers

1 Cook the potatoes in a saucepan of lightly salted boiling water for about 10 minutes until tender, then lift out with a draining spoon. Put the water back on to boil.

2 Meanwhile, strip the leaves from the rosemary stalks, leaving a tuft at the top. Set the stalks aside. Chop enough of the leaves to make 4 tsp; discard the rest. Mix together the oil, vinegar, mustard, chopped rosemary and apple juice in a large bowl. Add the hot cooked potatoes and stir to coat them. Set aside to marinate for 30 minutes.

3 While the potatoes are marinating, cut each leek into 8 chunks, each about 2.5cm long. Put the leeks in the pan of boiling water, cover and cook gently for about 8 minutes until just tender. Drain well in a colander and set aside.

4 Stretch the bacon rashers with the back of a knife, then cut each rasher across in half. Use a metal skewer to make a hole through the leek pieces. Wrap pieces of bacon around about half of them.

5 Preheat the grill to high. Drain the potatoes, reserving any leftover marinade, and make a hole in each one. Divide the potatoes and leek pieces (unwrapped and bacon-wrapped) among the rosemary stalk skewers, threading them on alternately.

6 Place the kebabs in the grill pan and grill for 8–10 minutes until nicely browned, carefully turning the skewers halfway through cooking and brushing them with the reserved marinade. Serve immediately.

2 portions fruit & veg

418 kcals

each serving provides 418kcals • 17g protein
17g fat of which 5g saturates • 52g carbohydrate of which 9g sugars
7g fibre • 990mg sodium • 175g vegetables

Thai-style chicken skewers

Packed with fresh, **zesty Thai flavours,** these little minced chicken skewers are grilled and served with **baby corn, pepper and spring onion skewers** for a healthy, low-fat meal. Serve with an oriental-style salad for extra vegetables.

SERVES 4
PREPARATION TIME 25 minutes
COOKING TIME 20–30 minutes

24 baby sweetcorn cobs,
** about 250g in total**
1 large yellow pepper,
** halved and deseeded**
8 spring onions
500g minced chicken (or pork)
1 small egg white
2.5cm piece fresh root ginger,
** peeled and chopped**
1 garlic clove, crushed
3 tbsp chopped fresh coriander
2 tsp Thai fish sauce
1 lemongrass stalk, chopped
1 tbsp vegetable oil
2 tsp toasted sesame oil
1 tsp sesame seeds

TO SERVE sweet chilli sauce

cook's tips

• Thai green curry paste from a jar is a useful standby to keep in the fridge and if you're in a hurry it can be used to replace the ginger, garlic, coriander and fish sauce; you'll need about 2 tsp.
• To prepare ahead, make up the mixture for the chicken skewers, then cover with cling film. Keep chilled in the fridge and use within 2 days.

each serving provides

215kcals • 34g protein
7g fat of which 1g saturates
5g carbohydrate of which 4g sugars
2.5g fibre • 108mg sodium
124g vegetables

1 Soak 16 short wooden skewers in a shallow dish of cold water for about 30 minutes. Blanch the baby corn in a pan of lightly salted, boiling water for 2 minutes, then drain. Cut the pepper into 2.5cm chunks. Cut 6 of the spring onions into short 4cm lengths. Thread the vegetables onto 8 of the skewers, alternating the corn cobs with pieces of pepper and onion. Set aside on a plate. Preheat a hot grill.

2 Chop the remaining spring onions and place in a food processor bowl with the chicken, egg white, ginger, garlic, coriander, fish sauce and lemongrass. Process until finely chopped and beginning to bind to a paste, but not completely smooth.

3 Divide the mixture into 8 and use your hands to shape each piece around the remaining skewers. Arrange on a foil-lined grill pan. Mix the vegetable and sesame oils and lightly brush onto the chicken and vegetable skewers. Add the sesame seeds to any remaining oil.

4 Grill the chicken skewers for 15–20 minutes, turning occasionally, until golden. After 10 minutes, add the vegetable skewers to the grill pan and grill for just 8–10 minutes, turning occasionally, until tender and golden. Brush over the remaining oil with the seeds for the last minute of cooking. If you can't fit all the skewers under the grill at once, cook the chicken first, then keep warm while cooking the vegetables. Serve with sweet chilli dipping sauce.

variations

• Other citrus fruits would be good in the marinade, such as 1 small orange with 1 lemon, or 2 limes in place of the lemons.
• If you have some button mushrooms, they could also be threaded onto the skewers or used instead of the baby plum tomatoes.

each serving provides

542kcals • 37g protein
17g fat of which 3g saturates
65g carbohydrate of which
15g sugars • 4g fibre
499mg sodium • 185g fruit
and vegetables

Citrus chicken & pineapple kebabs

Lemon zest and crushed cardamom seeds add a lovely flavour to **marinated, grilled chicken kebabs,** threaded with juicy chunks of fresh pineapple and baby plum tomatoes and served with **crunchy pitta crisps.**

SERVES 4

PREPARATION TIME
35 minutes, plus 1–2 hours marinating

COOKING TIME 15–20 minutes

KEBABS

grated zest of 1 lemon

juice of 2 lemons

3 tbsp olive oil

1 tbsp clear honey

4 green cardamom pods, crushed and pods discarded

2 tbsp chopped fresh coriander

450g skinless chicken breast fillets, cut into 2.5cm cubes

1 pineapple, peeled, cored and cut into chunks

24 baby plum tomatoes or cherry tomatoes

PITTA CRISPS

4 white or wholemeal pitta breads

2 tbsp olive oil

1 large garlic clove, crushed

1 tbsp chopped fresh mixed herbs or 2 tsp dried

1 Mix together the lemon zest and juice, oil, honey, cardamom seeds and chopped coriander in a shallow dish. Season with freshly ground black pepper. Add the chicken and toss to coat well, then cover and leave to marinate in the fridge for 1–2 hours. Soak 12 wooden skewers in cold water for 30 minutes.

2 To make the pitta crisps, preheat the grill to moderate. Cut each pitta bread across in half, then split into 2 layers. Mix together the oil, garlic and herbs and lightly brush each piece of pitta on both sides with the oil mixture. Place the pitta on the rack in a grill pan (you may need to do this in 2 batches). Grill for 4–5 minutes or until lightly browned and crisp, turning once. Place on a plate and keep warm, or transfer to a wire rack to cool.

3 Thread the chicken pieces, pineapple chunks and baby plum tomatoes alternately onto the skewers, dividing the ingredients evenly. Grill for 10–15 minutes, turning occasionally, until the chicken is cooked through and tender. Brush the kebabs regularly with the marinade to prevent them from drying out. Serve with the pitta crisps.

Skewered swordfish with charred courgettes

A real summer dish of cubes of marinated swordfish and lemon wedges, char-grilled (or barbecued) with baby courgettes and eaten with warm focaccia. Swordfish has firm flesh, ideally suited to cooking on kebab skewers.

SERVES 4
PREPARATION TIME 30 minutes, including marinating time
COOKING TIME 10–15 minutes

500g swordfish steaks
3 lemons
3 tbsp olive oil
1 garlic clove, crushed
15g fresh basil
500g small courgettes, trimmed

fish treat

236 kcals

1.5 portions fruit & veg

1 Soak 4 long wooden skewers in cold water for about 30 minutes. Meanwhile, using a sharp knife cut any skin away from the fish steaks, then cut the steaks into 2cm cubes.

2 Grate the zest and squeeze the juice from 1 of the lemons. Combine this zest and juice with the olive oil and garlic. Finely chop the basil leaves and mix into the marinade. Cut each of the remaining lemons into 8 wedges.

3 Halve the courgettes lengthways and score the white flesh with the tip of a sharp knife to make a criss-cross pattern.

4 Lightly brush the cut surfaces of the courgettes with the marinade, then set aside. Mix the swordfish cubes into the rest of the marinade and leave for 5–10 minutes.

5 Thread the swordfish cubes and the lemon wedges onto the soaked skewers. Arrange on a cast-iron, ridged griddle along with the courgettes. Sprinkle with coarsely ground black pepper then cook for 10–15 minutes, turning the skewers occasionally to make sure they are thoroughly cooked. Baste with the remaining marinade. (Alternatively, grill on a rack under a pre-heated hot grill). Serve at once with warm focaccia.

each serving provides 236kcals • 25g protein • 14g fat of which 2g saturates
3g carbohydrate of which 2g sugars • 1g fibre • 164mg sodium • 139g vegetables

3

4

variations

• Change the flavour by altering the marinade: use the zest and juice of 1 lime instead of the lemon, and fresh coriander instead of basil, and add a little chopped red chilli. Use lime wedges on the skewers, and grill quartered red and green peppers alongside the fish.

• Other fish that work well in this recipe include salmon, monkfish, halibut and large raw prawns.

5

Monkfish, prawn & Parma ham brochettes

Sumptuous seafood on skewers with cheerful yellow pepper, baby tomatoes and cubes of bread makes an attractive meal, great for entertaining. A fresh basil and lime mayonnaise completes the dish. Serve with a mixed green or an asparagus salad.

SERVES 4
PREPARATION TIME 30 minutes
COOKING TIME 6–7 minutes

2 limes
2 tbsp olive oil
1 yellow pepper, deseeded and
  cut into 2.5cm squares
24 peeled raw tiger prawns, about
  225g in total, thawed if frozen
350g monkfish fillet, cut
  into 2.5cm cubes
75g Parma ham, cut into
  strips 2.5cm wide
24 baby plum or cherry tomatoes,
  about 300g in total
16 cubes of bread such as
  ciabatta or rustic-type loaf

BASIL MAYONNAISE
4 tbsp reduced-fat mayonnaise
1 tbsp chopped fresh basil

cook's tips
• Don't season the fish with salt before cooking as this will draw out some of the juices which help to keep it moist. Also, both the ham and bread have high salt content, so extra salt shouldn't be necessary.
• To peel the prawns, twist off the head, peel away the legs and shell in one piece, then gently hold the tail and pull out the flesh.
• For speed, you can thaw frozen prawns quickly in a sieve under cold running water, then drain on kitchen paper.

1 Soak 8 long, wooden skewers in cold water for about 30 minutes. Squeeze the juice from 1 of the limes. Put 1 tbsp of the lime juice into a bowl with the oil and whisk together, seasoning with a little freshly ground pepper. Reserve the remaining lime juice and cut the other lime into 4 wedges, then set aside.

2 Add the pieces of pepper to the marinade (there should be about 16 squares) and toss until coated, then remove and set aside, leaving as much marinade as possible behind. Do the same with the prawns and, finally, the monkfish.

3 Wrap each monkfish cube in a strip of Parma ham; the 2 ends should just overlap, leaving the sides of the monkfish showing, so trim if necessary. (Don't use more than a single layer of ham, or the fish will take longer to cook than the other ingredients.)

4 Preheat the grill to high. Thread the wrapped fish onto the skewers, alternating with the prawns, pepper squares and tomatoes (plum tomatoes should be threaded horizontally). Make sure that there is still about 10cm left at the top of each skewer to add the bread.

5 Grill the brochettes for 1½ minutes on each side. Add the cubes of bread to the end of the skewers and grill for a further 3–4 minutes, twisting the bread cubes and turning the skewers as needed, until all the ingredients are golden brown and cooked through.

6 Meanwhile, mix together the mayonnaise with the basil and reserved lime juice. Serve 2 brochettes per person, accompanied with the basil mayonnaise and a wedge of lime to squeeze over the fish.

variations
• Any firm fish could be used as an alternative; swordfish would be ideal.
• Other vegetables which would work well in these brochettes include sliced courgettes, red onions cut into thin wedges, or peeled shallots, blanched in boiling water for 3 minutes.
• If preferred, serve with sweet chilli dipping sauce.

each serving provides 345kcals • 32g protein • 16g fat of which 3g saturates
19g carbohydrate of which 6g sugars • 3g fibre • 843mg sodium • 125g vegetables

345 kcals

smart food

1.5 portions fruit & veg

SERVES 4 Ⓥ
PREPARATION TIME 40 minutes
COOKING TIME 10–12 minutes

5 tbsp crunchy peanut butter
1 tsp dark soy sauce
1 tsp runny honey
1 tsp Chinese rice vinegar
    or cider vinegar
1 large garlic clove
1 spring onion, trimmed and chopped
6 tbsp reduced-fat coconut milk
1 tbsp sweet chilli sauce,
    or to taste
400g firm smoked tofu
1 aubergine
1 red onion
8 baby corn, sliced in half diagonally
½ cucumber
250g bean sprouts
2 tbsp unsalted peanuts

1 Put 12 wooden skewers in cold water and leave to soak for 30 minutes. Meanwhile, combine the peanut butter, soy sauce, honey, vinegar, peeled garlic, spring onion, coconut milk and chilli sauce in a blender or food processor. Blend or process to make a thick, almost smooth mixture.

2 Preheat a moderate grill. Cut the tofu and aubergine into 2.5cm sized cubes. Cut the red onion into chunks about the same size.

3 Blanch the baby corn in a pan of boiling water for 2–3 minutes. Drain in a sieve, then refresh under cold running water. Cut the cucumber into thin sticks about 5cm long. Arrange the bean sprouts, cucumber and corn on a large platter and scatter the peanuts over the top. Set aside.

Tofu satay
Spicy, **peanut-based** satay sauce works well with smoked tofu and diced aubergines in these **delicious vegetarian kebabs,** served on a crisp bean sprout, baby corn and cucumber salad.

4 Thread the tofu, aubergine and onion onto the soaked skewers, spacing the pieces slightly apart. Place on a foil-lined grill pan. Brush with some of the peanut mixture, then grill for 10–12 minutes, turning the skewers frequently and brushing with the peanut mixture. Gently heat the remaining peanut mixture in a small pan or in a dish in the microwave.

5 Set the skewers of tofu satay on top of the salad, spoon over the warm peanut sauce and serve immediately.

variations
• Tofu comes in many forms, from plain to flavoured with sesame or chilli. The best variety to use for this recipe is the organic, naturally smoked tofu, found in chiller cabinets in supermarkets and health food shops.
• In the salad, replace half the bean sprouts with fine green beans, trimmed and steamed or blanched in boiling water for 3 minutes.

each serving provides 331kcals • 19g protein • 22g fat of which 5g saturates 15g carbohydrate of which 9g sugars • 5g fibre • 334mg sodium • 216g vegetables

2.5 portions fruit & veg

331 kcals

Roasts, pot-roasts & braises

Ideal for family get-togethers and cosy winter evenings, roasts and braises make the most of tender cuts of meat and fish, without requiring your constant attention. Succulent and flavoursome, traditional choices such as Roast beef with thyme and fennel crust will always go down a treat. Enjoy fruity combinations such as Pork chops with parsnips and maple pears to boost your fruit and vegetable count, or try Sea bass with chermoula, an impressive centrepiece for any dinner party.

Mediterranean roasted lamb

Just a few **fresh ingredients, simply cooked,** make a warmly satisfying meal. **Aubergines and shallots,** whose flavours intensify with roasting, make perfect partners for tender, succulent lamb. Serve with warm, crusty bread.

SERVES 4
PREPARATION TIME 30 minutes, plus several hours marinating (if time allows)
COOKING TIME 35–40 minutes

3 tbsp olive oil
1 tsp balsamic or red wine vinegar
4 lean lamb leg steaks, trimmed of excess fat
2 tsp black peppercorns
1 tsp cumin seeds
250g shallots
2 large aubergines
2 garlic cloves, crushed
400g cherry tomatoes, pricked

TO GARNISH chopped fresh coriander

variation

• For a vegetarian version, use cheese instead of lamb steaks. First roast the aubergine and onion mixture, sprinkled with cumin seeds, for 25–30 minutes, turning once, then scatter over the tomatoes and roast for a further 5 minutes. Finally top with 225g thinly sliced mozzarella or halloumi cheese and return to the oven for 5 minutes. Scatter with olives or pine nuts.

1 Mix 1 tbsp of the oil with the vinegar and lightly brush this marinade over both sides of the steaks. Crush the peppercorns and add the cumin seeds. Sprinkle the mixture over the steaks, pat it in gently and then place the steaks in a non-metallic dish. Set aside, or cover and refrigerate for several hours.

2 Preheat the oven to 200°C/gas 6. Put the shallots in a large, heatproof bowl and pour over enough boiling water to cover. Leave for 2–3 minutes, then drain. Peel off the skins, then return them to the bowl.

3 Trim the ends from the aubergines and cut them into 2.5cm chunks. Add these to the shallots. Drizzle the remaining oil over the vegetables. Add the crushed garlic, then toss to lightly coat the vegetables with oil.

4 Heat a large, heavy-based roasting tin over a moderately high heat on the hob. Quickly sear the steaks for about 1 minute on each side, then remove and set aside in the original marinade dish.

5 Tip the vegetables into the hot tin and spread them out. Place in the oven and roast for 15–20 minutes until softened. Lay the lamb steaks over the vegetables and drizzle over all the juices left in the dish. Return to the oven to roast for 10 minutes.

6 Scatter the tomatoes into the tin and return to the oven for a further 8–10 minutes until the lamb is cooked to your liking and the vegetables are tender. Season to taste and serve sprinkled with chopped coriander.

comfort food

4 portions fruit & veg

355 kcals

each serving provides 355kcals • 33g protein
21g fat of which 1.5g saturates • 9g carbohydrate of which 9g sugars
5g fibre • 23mg sodium • 338g vegetables

Persian-style lamb shanks with figs

Roasting lamb shanks before **slowly braising** them removes much of the fat and gives **a wonderful flavour,** which perfectly complements the **fragrant vegetable mix** of lentils, tomatoes, courgettes and figs.

SERVES 4
PREPARATION TIME about 30 minutes
COOKING TIME about 2 hours

2 lamb shanks, about 340g each
2 tbsp olive oil
6 shallots, quartered
3 garlic cloves, chopped
2 fresh sprigs of rosemary
1 bay leaf
500g tomatoes, skinned and quartered
300g dried green lentils
850ml lamb or vegetable stock, or as needed
2 tbsp pomegranate molasses
1 tbsp runny honey
8 dried figs, quartered
2 courgettes, thickly sliced

TO GARNISH chopped fresh coriander

cook's tip
• Pomegranate molasses is made with concentrated pomegranate juice. It's stocked in the 'special ingredient' section of larger supermarkets.

each serving provides
603kcals • 46g protein
15g fat of which 4g saturates
75g carbohydrate of which
38g sugars • 12g fibre
115mg sodium • 265g fruit and vegetables

1 Preheat the oven to 220°C/gas 7. When the oven is hot enough, put the lamb shanks in a roasting tin and roast for 25 minutes until they are a rich brown colour on the outside. Drain on kitchen paper. Reduce the oven to 160°C/gas 3.

2 Meanwhile, heat the oil in a large flameproof casserole over a medium heat. Add the shallots and cook for 5 minutes, stirring until lightly browned. Stir in the garlic, rosemary, bay leaf and tomatoes and cook for 1 minute. Stir in the lentils, then add the lamb shanks, pushing them down into the vegetable mixture.

3 Stir the pomegranate molasses and honey into the stock, then pour over the lamb. Slowly bring to the boil, then cover the casserole with a tight-fitting lid and cook in the oven for 45 minutes.

4 Remove the casserole from the oven, add a little more stock if needed and stir in the figs and courgettes (this is easier if you lift out the lamb shanks first, then return them after stirring). Cover and cook in the oven for a further 45 minutes or until the lamb is very tender. Lift out the lamb and carve the meat from the 2 shanks. Discard the bones and return the lean meat to the casserole. Gently stir through, then serve scattered with chopped coriander.

variations
• If liked, add some finely chopped garlic to the crumb mixture. Fresh oregano could be used instead of thyme.
• Spread horseradish sauce over the meat in place of the mustard.
• Use red wine instead of a mixture of water and sherry, Madeira or port to deglaze the roasting tin.

cook's tip
• Calculate the cooking time for the beef at 55 minutes per 1kg, plus 45 minutes for medium, or 65 minutes per 1kg, plus 45 minutes for well-done meat that's still juicy.

SERVES 4
PREPARATION TIME 25 minutes
COOKING TIME 1¾–2 hours

150g fresh wholemeal breadcrumbs
1 tbsp fennel seeds
6 large fresh sprigs of thyme
3 tbsp olive oil
2 tbsp semi-skimmed milk
1.25 kg rolled beef topside, trimmed of excess fat
1 tbsp wholegrain mustard
1 celeriac, peeled
2 sweet potatoes, peeled
4 carrots, peeled
300g shallots, peeled
100ml medium-sweet sherry, Madeira or port

each serving provides
579kcals • 38g protein
15g fat of which 4g saturates
71g carbohydrate of which
25g sugars • 14g fibre
519mg sodium
344g vegetables

4 portions fruit & veg

great sunday lunch

579 kcals

Roast beef with thyme & fennel crust

A crunchy deep crust of herb-flavoured breadcrumbs ensures a succulent roast beef. It's roasted with a selection of root vegetables and served with a rich gravy, made using the pan juices.

1 Preheat the oven to 190°C/gas 5. Mix the breadcrumbs and fennel seeds in a bowl with the leaves from 2 of the thyme sprigs and seasoning to taste. Sprinkle 2 tbsp of the olive oil and the milk over the crumbs and mix thoroughly with a spoon until they are moist and clump together.

2 Place the beef in a large, lightly oiled roasting tin and spread the meat with the mustard. Press the crumb mixture on the top of the meat, pressing it firmly all over with both hands to make a neat, firm crust. Roast for about 1¾ hours for a medium result or about 2 hours for well-cooked but juicy meat. Cover the crust loosely with a piece of foil after 1 hour, to prevent over-browning, then remove the foil for the final 5 minutes of cooking.

3 Meanwhile, cut the celeriac and sweet potatoes into 3.5cm chunks and place in a large bowl. Halve the carrots lengthways, then cut them across into chunky sticks. Add to the bowl with the shallots and the remaining thyme leaves and oil. Mix well.

4 The vegetables require about 1 hour for roasting, so put them in the oven when the beef has been cooking for 45 minutes to 1 hour. Arrange them around the meat, placing any that won't fit in a separate roasting tin or large ovenproof dish, if necessary. Turn the vegetables and baste them once during cooking.

5 Remove the meat and vegetables to a warmed serving dish and cover with foil. Pour 300ml water into the roasting tin and bring to the boil on the hob, stirring and scraping up all the browned cooking residue on the bottom of the tin. Add the sherry, Madeira or port and boil steadily for 5–7 minutes, stirring from time to time, until the liquid is reduced by about half. Season to taste, then strain into a jug.

6 Slice the meat and serve with the roast vegetables and gravy. Any pieces of crust that break off as the meat is sliced can be divided among the plates.

Stuffed roast pork with prunes

Pork and prunes is a classic French combination, and here it is given an extra flavour boost with stem ginger and fresh orange. Cooked with a variety of vegetables it makes an easy roast meal and can be prepared ahead and kept in the fridge ready for cooking.

SERVES 4
PREPARATION TIME 25 minutes
COOKING TIME 1 hour

2 small pork fillets, about 175g each
1 large orange
50g ready-to-eat prunes, sliced
3 globes stem ginger in syrup,
   drained and thinly sliced
6 lean, unsmoked back
   bacon rashers
400g new potatoes, scrubbed
   and cut into 5mm thick slices
2 leeks, thickly sliced
2 carrots, peeled and thickly sliced
2 red-skinned dessert apples
500ml dry cider
2 tbsp chopped fresh parsley

each serving provides

463kcals • 36g protein
11g fat of which 4g saturates
48.5 carbohydrate of which
33g sugars • 8g fibre
937mg sodium
326g fruit and
vegetables

prepare ahead

463 kcals

4 portions fruit & veg

1 Preheat the oven to 200°C/gas 6. Put the pork fillets on a chopping board and cut each in half lengthways, without cutting all the way through. Open the fillets like a book and press down to flatten slightly.

2 Finely grate the zest from the orange and set aside. Using a small, serrated knife, cut away all the white pith from the orange, then slice down between the membranes to remove the orange segments. Arrange the orange segments over the cut surface of 1 fillet. Top with the sliced prunes and ginger, sprinkle over the orange zest, and season to taste.

3 Place the second fillet, cut-side down, on top and gently press the fillets together. Wrap the bacon rashers around the pork and secure in place with kitchen string. Set aside. (Prepare ahead up to this stage and leave in the fridge for a few hours or overnight, if more convenient.)

4 Spread the potatoes over the bottom of a large roasting tin, then scatter over the leeks and carrots. Core and thickly slice the apples, then add to the tin. Place the pork-fillet package on top and pour in the cider. Roast for 1 hour or until the potatoes and carrots are tender and clear juices come out of the pork when it is pierced with the tip of a knife. Lift out the pork and vegetables, cover with foil and leave to rest and keep warm for 10 minutes.

5 Meanwhile, put the roasting tin on the hob and boil the cooking liquid on a high heat until reduced to about 175ml. Add the parsley and season to taste. Slice the pork and serve with the vegetables and the cooking juices spooned over.

3

4

5

SERVES 4
PREPARATION TIME 30 minutes,
plus 20 minutes soaking
COOKING TIME 20–25 minutes

**500g beef topside, cut into
8 very thin slices**
2 tbsp olive oil
**1 tbsp coarsely crushed
black peppercorns**
1 onion, thinly sliced
2 celery sticks, sliced
**400g new potatoes, scrubbed
and cut into 5mm thick slices**
2 carrots, peeled and sliced
600g ripe tomatoes, chopped
300ml beef stock
4 tbsp dry sherry
1 bay leaf

MUSHROOM STUFFING
15g dried porcini mushrooms
2 tbsp olive oil
1 small onion, finely chopped
1 garlic clove, finely chopped
**200g chestnut mushrooms,
finely chopped**
**25g fine fresh breadcrumbs
(made from day-old bread)**
**4 tbsp finely chopped fresh
flat-leaf parsley**
1 tsp dried thyme
finely grated zest of 1 lemon
pinch of cayenne pepper

TO GARNISH
chopped fresh flat-leaf parsley

each serving provides
445kcals • 36g protein • 18g fat of
which 4g saturates • 32g carbohydrate
of which 13g sugars • 6g fibre
163mg sodium • 336g vegetables

prepare ahead • 445 kcals • 4 portions fruit & veg

Beef & mushroom olives

This updated version of a traditional recipe makes an easy and impressive dish to prepare ahead, so is ideal for entertaining. Lean slices of beef are wrapped round a mushroom stuffing to make rolls, which are then braised gently with vegetables.

1 For the stuffing, put the dried porcini mushrooms in a heatproof bowl, cover with boiling water and leave to soak for 20 minutes or until soft. Drain and finely chop the mushrooms, then set aside.

2 Heat the 2 tbsp of oil for the stuffing in a large frying pan over a moderate heat. Add the onion and garlic and cook gently, stirring frequently, for 5–8 minutes, until golden brown. Add the chestnut mushrooms and fry for 5 minutes, stirring occasionally, then stir in the chopped porcini mushrooms and the remaining stuffing ingredients. Season to taste, then set aside to cool slightly.

3 Meanwhile, lay the beef slices between sheets of greaseproof paper or cling film and bash out as thinly as possible using a rolling pin. Place side by side on a board. Divide the stuffing equally among them, then roll up each slice around the stuffing and secure in place with wooden cocktail sticks. Lightly brush the beef olives all over with a little olive oil, then roll them in the crushed peppercorns on a plate. Wipe out the pan.

4 Heat the remaining oil in the frying pan, add the beef olives and fry them on a moderate heat to brown them all over. Remove from the pan using a draining spoon and set aside.

Sausages with Puy lentils

Meaty sausages are simple to cook, **succulent and juicy,** and when combined with **diced vegetables and tender Puy lentils** they make a hearty meal with a healthy balance of nutrients.

SERVES 4
PREPARATION TIME 15 minutes
COOKING TIME 45–50 minutes

2 large onions, chopped
4 garlic cloves, thinly sliced
350g carrots, peeled and diced
1 large fennel bulb, chopped
2 bay leaves
4 sprigs of fresh thyme
grated zest and juice of 1 orange
1 tbsp olive oil
6 good-quality, meaty
   pork sausages
250g Puy lentils, rinsed
300ml red wine
4 tbsp redcurrant jelly
1 tbsp Dijon mustard

TO GARNISH orange wedges

1 Preheat the oven to 190°C/ gas 5. Mix the onions, garlic, carrots, fennel, bay leaves and thyme in a fairly deep roasting tin. Add the orange zest and olive oil and mix thoroughly.

2 Place the sausages on top of the vegetables. Bake for about 25 minutes until the sausages are lightly browned on top.

3 Meanwhile, place the lentils in a large saucepan and cover with boiling water. Bring to the boil, then reduce the heat, part-cover the pan and boil for 15 minutes until just tender. Drain well.

4 Lift the sausages out of the roasting tin and set aside. Stir the wine, redcurrant jelly, mustard and orange juice into the vegetables in the tin, then add the lentils and stir in with a fork. Re-position the sausages on top, turning them browned-sides down.

5 Bake for a further 20–25 minutes, until the sausages are well browned and the vegetables and lentils are cooked. Remove the sausages to a board and thickly slice them on the diagonal. Discard the herbs from the lentil mixture, then lay the sausages back on top and serve garnished with orange wedges.

3.5 portions fruit & veg

624 kcals

each serving provides

624kcals • 30g protein • 21g fat of which 6.5g saturates
71g carbohydrate of which 34g sugars • 11g fibre
729mg sodium • 282g vegetables

---

5 Add the onion and celery to the oil remaining in the pan and gently cook for about 5 minutes until softened. Add the potatoes, carrots and tomatoes and stir around for a couple of minutes, then return the beef olives to the pan. (If your frying pan is not big enough, transfer the vegetables and beef olives to a large flameproof casserole.)

6 Pour in the beef stock and sherry and add the bay leaf. Slowly bring to the boil, then reduce the heat to low, cover and simmer for 20–25 minutes until the meat and vegetables are tender.

7 Lift out the beef olives using a draining spoon and keep warm. Boil the liquid in the pan on a high heat to reduce to the desired consistency. Season to taste. Put the beef olives back into the pan and serve sprinkled with parsley.

cook's tip

• To prepare in advance, follow the recipe to step 5, and chill the casserole for up to a day in the fridge. Then continue from step 6, allowing 5 minutes extra time.

SERVES 4

PREPARATION TIME 20 minutes,
plus 1 hour marinating

COOKING TIME 50–55 minutes

4 lean pork chops,
trimmed of fat
2 tbsp olive oil
2 garlic cloves, finely chopped
2 tbsp chopped fresh sage
½ tsp fennel seeds,
roughly crushed
3 tbsp balsamic vinegar
4 potatoes, about 500g in total,
peeled and quartered
2 large parsnips, peeled and
quartered lengthways
2 red onions, quartered
1 large pear, (such as Comice),
firm but ripe
2 tbsp maple syrup

TO GARNISH fresh sage leaves

Pork chops with parsnips
& maple pears
A superb combination of flavours, conveniently roasted all in one big tin. The pork is best marinated ahead, if time allows. A spicy fruit relish would make a great accompaniment.

1 Place the chops in a wide dish. Sprinkle over the oil, garlic, sage, fennel seeds and 2 tbsp of the balsamic vinegar. Turn to coat evenly, then cover and place in the fridge to marinate for 1 hour.

2 Preheat the oven to 200°C/gas 6. Combine the potatoes, parsnips and onions in a large roasting tin. Add the pork chops with their marinade and turn the vegetables to coat evenly. Spread out the vegetables in a single layer, with the chops on top. Season to taste. Roast for about 40 minutes until the vegetables are tender and golden.

3 Core the pear and cut into 8 slices. Toss in the remaining balsamic vinegar and the maple syrup. Remove the roasting tin from the oven and arrange the pear slices over the chops, spooning over the syrup mixture.

4 Return to the oven and roast for a further 10–12 minutes until the pears are tender. Serve the pork chops topped with the pear slices and juices, with the roasted vegetables alongside and fresh sage leaves scattered over.

each serving provides 448kcals • 33g protein • 13g fat of which 4g saturates 53g carbohydrate of which 23g sugars • 8g fibre • 97mg sodium • 250g fruit and vegetables

3 portions fruit & veg

hassle free roast

448 kcals

1 tbsp vegetable oil
4 thick-cut venison steaks,
   about 125g each
500g red cabbage, thinly shredded
1 red onion, thinly sliced
175g blueberries
25g butter
2.5cm piece fresh root ginger,
   peeled and grated
2 tbsp redcurrant jelly
2 tbsp light soft brown sugar
150ml beef stock
4 tbsp ruby port
finely grated zest and juice
   of 1 small orange

TO GARNISH (optional) 50g walnuts,
roughly chopped, 2 kumquats,
sliced, sprigs of fresh flat-leaf
parsley

cook's tip

• To prepare ahead, cook the
casserole for 2 hours, then cool and
keep chilled in the fridge. Reheat
gently for 45 minutes, adding a little
more stock, if needed.

prepare ahead

2.5 portions fruit & veg

334 kcals

each serving provides

334kcals • 30g protein
11g fat of which 5g saturates
28g carbohydrate of which
26g sugars • 4g fibre
123mg sodium • 213g fruit
and vegetables

Venison with red cabbage & blueberries

Venison steaks slowly braised with red cabbage and blueberries make an ideal special occasion dish for the family or for easy entertaining. Serve with warm crusty rolls or petits pains.

1 Preheat the oven to 170°C/gas 3. Heat the oil in a large, heavy-based, flameproof casserole. Add the venison steaks and sear them quickly.

2 Remove the casserole from the heat. Layer the cabbage, onion and blueberries in the casserole on top of the venison, seasoning each layer with a little freshly ground black pepper. Set aside.

3 Melt the butter in a small saucepan, add the ginger and fry for 2–3 minutes. Stir in the redcurrant jelly until melted, then remove the pan from the heat and stir in the brown sugar, stock, port and orange zest and juice. Pour this sauce into the casserole, cover and cook in the oven for 2–2½ hours until the venison and cabbage are tender.

4 Serve sprinkled with chopped walnuts, if liked, and for a special occasion, garnish with kumquat slices and sprigs of parsley.

Braised pheasant with mushrooms

Pheasant is a succulent meat and although higher in fat than other game birds, most of this fat is monounsaturated. Adding split peas to the casserole provides satisfying carbohydrate and thickens the sauce.

SERVES 4
PREPARATION TIME 20 minutes
COOKING TIME 45 minutes

25g dried porcini mushrooms
100ml boiling water
1½ tbsp olive oil
1 large pheasant, cut into 4 pieces
50g lean smoked back bacon,
 cut into cubes
2 celery sticks, diced
2 carrots, peeled and diced
1 large onion, roughly chopped
100g chestnut mushrooms, halved
150g yellow split peas
250ml red wine
300ml chicken or vegetable stock

TO GARNISH chopped fresh parsley

1 Put the dried mushrooms in a heatproof bowl. Pour over the boiling water and leave to soak for 20 minutes.

2 Meanwhile, heat 1 tbsp of the oil in a large, flameproof casserole over a moderate heat. Add the pheasant pieces and fry for 2–3 minutes on each side to brown well. Transfer to a plate and keep warm.

3 Add the bacon to the pan and cook, stirring frequently, for about 5 minutes until well browned. Add the celery, carrots and onion with the rest of the oil and stir to combine. Reduce the heat, cover and cook gently for 5 minutes until the vegetables are starting to soften.

4 Stir in the chestnut mushrooms and cook, uncovered, for 3 minutes longer, then stir in the split peas.

5 Drain the soaked porcini mushrooms (reserve the soaking liquid) and add to the cassrole. Slowly pour in the soaking liquid, leaving any sediment in the bowl. Add the red wine and stock. Bring to the boil, then reduce the heat to low and simmer for 15 minutes.

6 Return the pheasant joints to the casserole, cover and cook for a further 20–30 minutes until the pheasant is tender. Sprinkle with parsley before serving.

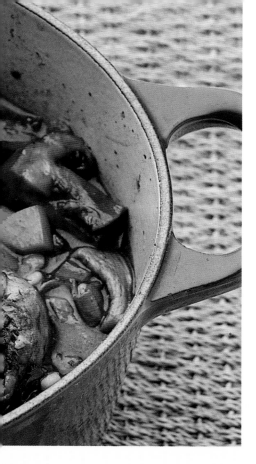

Orange roast chicken dinner

Here's a roast meal, cooked in one pan, that even **makes its own gravy** – the pan juices are so **full of flavour** that nothing else is needed. Use a large roasting pan, so that the vegetables cook in a single layer.

SERVES 4
PREPARATION TIME 15 minutes
COOKING TIME about 2 hours

2 oranges
4 garlic cloves
1 oven-ready chicken, about 1.35kg
3 cinnamon sticks
4 sprigs of fresh rosemary
1 bay leaf
450ml chicken stock or water
2 sweet potatoes
2 corn cobs
2 red onions

variations

• For a dish that cooks in under an hour, replace the chicken with either chicken quarters or whole poussins, and cook all together with the vegetables.
• If sweet potatoes are not available, butternut squash makes a good, equally colourful, alternative.

cook's tip

• The chicken will carve more easily if it is left to 'rest' for 10–15 minutes before serving. Lift it from the tin onto a carving board, cover it loosely with foil and set it aside while you skim the juices and serve the vegetables.

1 Preheat the oven to 180°C/gas 4. Cut each orange into 8 wedges and tuck half of them and an unpeeled garlic clove into the cavity of the chicken.

2 Place the cinnamon sticks, rosemary, bay leaf and remaining garlic in a large roasting pan and set the chicken on top. Pour half the stock or water into the pan. Place in the oven and roast for 1 hour, basting the chicken with the pan juices after 30 minutes.

3 Meanwhile, peel the sweet potatoes and cut into 3–4cm chunks. Cut each corn cob across into 4 pieces. Peel the onions and cut each into 4 wedges. Remove the pan from the oven and add the vegetables and remaining orange wedges, turning them in the pan juices to coat evenly.

4 Add the remaining stock or water to the pan and return to the oven to roast for a further 50–60 minutes until the chicken is cooked and the vegetables are tender. Baste with the pan juices halfway through the roasting time.

5 Remove the chicken from the pan and place on a warmed serving dish. Lift out the vegetables with a draining spoon and arrange around the chicken. Discard the cinnamon, rosemary, bay leaf and garlic cloves. Skim any excess fat from the juices and heat until boiling, then serve with the chicken.

variation

• This dish can also be made with chicken pieces or skinless duck breasts.

cook's tip

• The whole dish can be made up to 2 days ahead and stored, covered, in the fridge. Before serving, allow to come to room temperature, then gently reheat over a very low heat.

each serving provides

422kcals • 31g protein
16g fat of which 4g saturates
30g carbohydrate of which
7g sugars • 5g fibre
279mg sodium • 146g vegetables

1.5 portions fruit & veg

prepare ahead

422 kcals

3 portions fruit & veg

540 kcals

each serving provides
540kcals • 38g protein • 22g fat of which 6g saturates • 50g carbohydrate of which 17g sugars • 6g fibre 161mg sodium • 255g fruit and vegetables

SERVES 4

PREPARATION TIME 35 minutes

COOKING TIME about 1 hour
10 minutes

750g new potatoes, scrubbed
4 large carrots, peeled
4 skinless, boneless chicken breast
    fillets, about 150g each
1 tsp olive oil
1 tbsp lemon juice
3 tbsp chopped fresh tarragon
    or 2 tsp dried
200ml half-fat crème fraîche
150ml chicken stock
1 garlic clove, crushed
4 spring onions, finely chopped

Tarragon chicken
with creamy vegetables

Potatoes and carrots are baked in a luxuriously creamy, crème fraîche sauce, flavoured with garlic and tarragon, with marinated chicken breasts cooked on top. Serve with cherry tomatoes and a green salad.

1 Put the potatoes in a saucepan of lightly salted boiling water. Bring back to the boil, then reduce the heat and simmer for 7 minutes. Add the whole carrots and simmer for a further 5 minutes. Drain and leave until cool enough to handle.

2 Meanwhile, place the chicken breasts in a shallow dish. Mix together the oil, lemon juice and 1 tbsp of the chopped fresh tarragon (or 1 tsp dried) with a little salt and pepper. Drizzle this over the chicken and turn to coat. Cover and set aside to marinate in the fridge while preparing and cooking the vegetables. Preheat the oven to 190°C/gas 5.

3 Peel and thinly slice the par-boiled potatoes. Thinly slice the carrots. Whisk the crème fraîche into the stock, then stir in the garlic, spring onions and half the remaining fresh tarragon or remaining 1 tsp of dried tarragon.

4 Roughly layer the potatoes and carrots alternately in a lightly greased, shallow ovenproof dish, spooning a little of the crème fraîche mixture over each layer. Finish with potato slices covered with the last of the crème fraîche mixture. Cover the dish with foil and bake for 35–40 minutes.

5 Arrange the chicken breasts on top of the potatoes and re-cover with the foil. Bake for a further 25–30 minutes until the chicken is cooked through (the juices will run clear when the chicken is pierced with a thin knife or skewer). Scatter over the remaining fresh tarragon.

2 portions fruit & veg

450 kcals

each serving provides

450kcals • 42g protein • 13g fat of which 6g saturates • 44g carbohydrate of which 15g sugars • 6g fibre • 165mg sodium 160g vegetables

BBQ chicken with beans

This is a great way to cook good-value drumsticks, so that they are moist and tender. A simple barbecue sauce and a mixture of vegetables and beans makes a healthy dish children will love. Serve with a leafy side salad.

SERVES 4
PREPARATION TIME 25 minutes
COOKING TIME about 35 minutes

2 tbsp vegetable oil
4 garlic cloves, crushed
½ tsp dried marjoram
8 chicken drumsticks, skinned
450g leeks, split lengthways
   and sliced
250g carrots, peeled and diced
1 celery stick, diced
300ml chicken stock
350g frozen sweetcorn
400g can cannellini beans,
   drained and rinsed
1 tbsp dark soft brown sugar
2 tbsp cider vinegar
1 tsp chilli sauce, or to taste
3 tbsp tomato ketchup
2 tbsp wholegrain mustard

cook's tip
• The easiest way to skin chicken is to hold the end of the drumstick with a sheet of kitchen paper, then use another sheet of paper to tug off the skin. The paper allows you to get a good grip on the skin.

1 Heat the oil in a large deep frying pan or flameproof casserole. Add the garlic, marjoram and chicken and cook over a moderate heat for 5 minutes, turning the drumsticks to brown them lightly all over. Transfer the drumsticks to a plate.

2 Add the leeks, carrots and celery. Cook for 5 minutes until the leeks are softened. Stir in the stock and replace the drumsticks, shuffling them among the vegetables. Reduce the heat, cover and simmer for 30 minutes until the drumsticks are tender. Use a draining spoon to transfer the drumsticks to a plate.

3 Add the sweetcorn and cannellini beans and heat through for 1 minute. Then, using the draining spoon, transfer the vegetables to a serving dish. Cover and set aside to keep hot.

4 Bring the liquid in the casserole to the boil. Stir in the sugar, vinegar, chilli sauce, ketchup and mustard. Boil hard for about 5 minutes until it has reduced to a slightly syrupy, shiny sauce.

5 Put the drumsticks in the sauce and heat through, turning them to coat evenly. Serve the drumsticks on the vegetables, pouring over all the sauce.

each serving provides 429kcals • 36g protein 14g fat of which 3g saturates • 41g carbohydrate of which 16g sugars • 9g fibre • 754mg sodium • 270g vegetables

429 kcals

3 portions fruit & veg

great family supper

1 large guinea fowl, about 1.5kg
grated zest and juice of 1 lemon
1 tbsp runny honey
2 tbsp olive oil
½ tsp ground ginger
½ tsp ground cinnamon
1 tsp ground cumin
3 small red onions, each cut
into 6 wedges

COUSCOUS STUFFING
300g couscous
¼ tsp saffron
500ml chicken or vegetable
stock, boiling
75g ready-to-eat dried figs,
roughly chopped
50g shelled unsalted pistachios,
roughly chopped

Middle Eastern roast guinea fowl with saffron couscous

Guinea fowl tastes like a cross between chicken and turkey, and is very lean. Here it's roasted with a **fig and pistachio couscous stuffing** and basted with a **spicy lemon marinade** to keep the meat deliciously moist. A leafy salad with fresh oranges makes a great side dish.

1 Remove any trussing strings from the guinea fowl, then rinse the bird inside and out under cold running water and dry with kitchen paper. Put into a large, lightly greased roasting tin. Mix the lemon zest and juice with the honey, olive oil, ginger, cinnamon, cumin and freshly ground black pepper to taste. Brush some of this mixture generously inside the cavity of the bird, then over the outside. Leave to marinate while making the stuffing or for longer, if convenient. Reserve the rest of the marinade.

2 Preheat the oven to 180°C/ gas 4. Put the couscous into a heatproof bowl. Stir the saffron into the stock, then pour over the couscous. Cover and leave to stand for 5 minutes or until all the stock has been absorbed. Stir in the figs and pistachios. Season to taste.

3 Spoon some of the couscous mixture into the neck end of the guinea fowl. Fold the neck skin over and secure with the wing tips or with a wooden cocktail stick. Put the onion wedges into the cavity of the body (or, if you prefer, arrange them in the tin around the bird after it has been roasting for 40 minutes). Spoon the rest of the spiced lemon juice mixture over the guinea fowl and roast for 1 hour.

4 Spoon the remaining couscous around the guinea fowl and roast for a further 25 minutes. To test if the bird is cooked, pierce the thickest part of the thigh: the juices should run clear.

5 Transfer the guinea fowl to a serving platter, loosely cover with foil to keep warm and leave to rest for 10 minutes before carving. Serve with the couscous and onions.

Turkey with red cabbage & apple
For this slow-cooked dish, lightly browned turkey steaks are braised on top of a delicious mixture of red cabbage, baby beetroot, sliced apples and lentils.

SERVES 4
PREPARATION TIME 30 minutes
COOKING TIME 1¾ hours

6 tsp vegetable oil
2 tsp balsamic vinegar
4 turkey breast steaks, about 1cm thick, 500g in total
1 red onion, thinly sliced
1 garlic clove, crushed
500g red cabbage, finely shredded
225g raw baby beetroot, peeled and cut into 6 wedges
2 red-skinned apples, quartered, cored and thinly sliced
finely grated zest and juice of 1 orange
1½ tbsp light muscovado sugar
400g can green lentils, drained and rinsed
4 tbsp chicken or vegetable stock
1 tsp wholegrain mustard

1 Pre-heat the oven to 170°C/ gas 3. Mix together 2 tsp of the oil and 1 tsp of the vinegar. Lightly brush over the turkey steaks and season with freshly ground pepper. Set aside to marinate while you make the braised red cabbage.

2 Heat 3 tsp of the oil in a flameproof casserole with a capacity of at least 3 litres. Add the onion and fry gently for 3 minutes. Add the garlic, cook for a few seconds, then remove from the heat. Add the cabbage, beetroot wedges, apple slices, orange zest and juice, remaining vinegar and sugar to the casserole. Lightly season, then stir the ingredients together.

3 Cover the casserole with a tight-fitting lid and cook in the oven for 1½ hours or until the cabbage is just tender, stirring halfway through the cooking time. Towards the end of the cooking time, pat the marinated turkey steaks dry on kitchen paper.

4 Heat a cast-iron, ridged griddle or heavy frying pan and brush with the remaining oil. Add the turkey steaks and cook on one side only over a moderately high heat for about 1½ minutes until browned. (The steaks will still be undercooked at this stage.)

5 Stir the lentils into the red cabbage, then place the steaks on top, browned-side up. Blend together the stock and mustard and drizzle over the top. Re-cover and return to the oven for 15–20 minutes until the cabbage is tender and the turkey cooked through. Serve at once.

variation
• Pork steaks are also delicious cooked this way. Pan-fry 4 well-trimmed pork (shoulder) steaks for 2 minutes on each side until golden brown. Substitute barely ripe pears for the apples and braise the pork on top of them.

each serving provides
356kcals • 39g protein
8g fat of which 1g saturates
35g carbohydrate of which
23g sugars • 8g fibre
136mg sodium • 297g fruit
and vegetables

3.5 portions fruit & veg

356 kcals

Turkey dinner with apricot & cashew nut stuffing

Turkey breast joints are **lean and easy to carve,** and if you buy two the same size, they can be stuffed and tied together to make a really delicious, **good-sized roast.** A selection of vegetables can be roasted in the same tin to complete a scrumptious festive meal.

SERVES 6
PREPARATION TIME 45 minutes
COOKING TIME 1 hour 35 minutes

- 2 boneless turkey breast joints, about 500g each
- 1 large sweet potato
- 2–3 large baking potatoes
- 2 carrots, peeled
- 6 small parsnips, peeled
- 3 celery sticks
- 2 leeks, trimmed
- 1 red pepper
- 2 tbsp olive oil
- 2 tbsp runny honey
- 4 tbsp vinaigrette dressing

STUFFING

- 3cm piece fresh root ginger, peeled and grated
- 1 small onion, grated
- 1 tbsp olive oil
- 50g ready-to-eat dried apricots, finely chopped
- 40g unsalted cashew nuts, roughly chopped
- 40g fresh wholemeal breadcrumbs
- 1 small egg, beaten
- 1 tsp dried thyme

variations

- If you want to serve this as a less festive meal, then use just 1 turkey joint and roast it unstuffed for about 1 hour in total, surrounded by the vegetables. The stuffing can be rolled into balls and cooked alongside.
- Add 8 chipolata sausages to the vegetables for the last 30 minutes.

1 Make the stuffing first. Cook the ginger and onion in the oil in a small pan for about 5 minutes, until softened. Remove from the heat and allow to cool, then mix in the apricots, chopped nuts, breadcrumbs, egg, thyme and seasoning. Preheat the oven to 190°C/gas 5.

2 Untie the rolled turkey joints or pull off the netting. Spread them out and place them side by side, slightly overlapping. Press the stuffing into the centre, then roll the joints together and shape into a large joint, over-wrapping with the skins if included with the joints. Tie 5–6 times with thin kitchen string to hold in shape. Place the joint in a large, lightly oiled roasting tin. Season and roast for 15 minutes.

3 Meanwhile, prepare the vegetables. Cut the sweet potato and potatoes into equal-sized chunks. Cut the carrots into chunky sticks. Leave the parsnips whole. Thickly slice the celery and leeks. Core the pepper, deseed and cut into chunks.

4 Put all the potatoes into a plastic food bag and drizzle with 1 tbsp of the oil. Rub well together, then tip out around the turkey. Season. Roast the potatoes and turkey for 30 minutes. Toss the remaining vegetables with the rest of the oil in the food bag, then tip out beside the potatoes in the tin. Brush the top of the joint with the honey. Roast for a further 30 minutes, covering the turkey with foil, if necessary, during roasting.

5 Remove the turkey joint to a carving board. Cover with foil and allow the turkey to rest while you continue to roast the vegetables for 15–20 minutes until they are tender and browned.

6 Using a draining spoon, lift the vegetables onto kitchen paper to drain off excess oil, then transfer to a serving dish and keep warm. Carve the turkey into thick slices, saving any juices. Tip the juices back into the roasting pan and add a glass of water, then heat on the hob until bubbling, stirring up any meaty deposits. Mix in the vinaigrette, then strain into a jug and serve as a light sauce with the turkey and vegetables.

special treat

2.5 portions fruit & veg

806 kcals

each serving provides 806kcals • 88g protein 26g fat of which 6.5g saturates • 58g carbohydrate of which 19g sugars 10g fibre • 605mg sodium • 200g vegetables

SERVES 4
PREPARATION TIME 20 minutes,
 plus at least 1 hour marinating
COOKING TIME 35–40 minutes

6 oranges
4 skinless, boneless duck
  breasts, about 175g each
2 tbsp vegetable oil
2 onions, thinly sliced
4 celery sticks, sliced
1 large garlic clove, crushed
500g small new potatoes,
  scrubbed and halved
150ml chicken or vegetable stock
1 red chilli, deseeded and thinly
  sliced (optional)

TO GARNISH chopped fresh parsley

variations
• Pork steaks would also work well
in this dish. Trim excess fat and
cook them for 20 minutes.
• This is a great dish to try in the
spring when ruby-coloured blood
oranges are in season.

each serving provides
488kcals • 40g protein
18g fat of which 4g saturates
45g carbohydrate of which 25g sugars
6g fibre   236mg sodium
417g fruit and vegetables

488 kcals

5 portions fruit & veg

Braised duck breasts with celery & orange

Try this stylish dish for entertaining. With the skin removed, duck breasts are **full of succulent flavour** but **low in fat** and the oranges supply antioxidant vitamin C.

1 Finely grate the zest from 4 of the oranges. Arrange the duck breasts in a single layer in a dish and sprinkle over the zest. Squeeze the juice from these oranges over the breasts, then turn them over several times. Cover with cling film and marinate in the fridge for at least 1 hour, or overnight.

2 When you are ready to cook, remove the duck from the fridge and allow to come to room temperature. Preheat the oven to 180°C/gas 4. Peel the remaining 2 oranges and cut each into 8 segments.

3 Heat the oil in a shallow flameproof casserole over a moderate heat. Add the onions and celery and stir for 3 minutes. Add the garlic and continue frying for about 1 minute until the onions are softened but not brown. Using a draining spoon, remove the onions and celery from the pan and set aside.

4 Lift the duck breasts out of the marinade and place in the casserole. Spoon the onions and celery over them, then pour over the marinade. Add the potatoes and half the orange segments, scattering them around the duck breasts. Pour over the stock, add the chilli, if using, and bring to the boil.

5 Cover the casserole and put it in the oven. Cook for 35–40 minutes until the duck and potatoes are tender. Season to taste.

6 Remove the duck breasts from the casserole and slice them. Spoon the onions and celery into soup plates and scatter the potatoes around the side. Top each portion with sliced duck, then spoon the juices over. Garnish with reserved orange segments and sprinkle with chopped parsley.

Roast vegetables with pears & bacon

A warming **autumnal dish** of roasted root vegetables with aubergines, pears and bacon. Roasting brings out **the sweetness** of the vegetables and, unlike boiling, **retains all the goodness.**

SERVES 4
PREPARATION TIME 20 minutes
COOKING TIME 40–50 minutes

1 aubergine, cut into 8 lengthways
3 sweet potatoes, peeled and
  cut into 8 lengthways
3 parsnips, quartered lengthways
150g baby leeks
2 tbsp olive oil
2 tbsp chopped fresh thyme,
  or 2 tsp dried
2 firm pears, cored and quartered
8 lean smoked back bacon rashers
1 tbsp balsamic vinegar

each serving provides

321kcals • 15g protein
10g fat of which 2g saturates
47g carbohydrate of which
22g sugars • 10g fibre
820mg sodium • 268 fruit
and vegetables

3 portions fruit & veg

321 kcals

comfort food

1 Preheat the oven to 200°C/gas 6. Arrange the aubergine, sweet potatoes, parsnips and leeks in a single layer in a wide roasting tin. Use a pastry brush to coat lightly with oil.

2 Sprinkle the thyme over the vegetables and season with freshly ground black pepper. Bake for 25–30 minutes until the vegetables are almost tender, then turn the vegetables and add the pear wedges, turning to coat lightly in oil. Arrange the bacon rashers over the vegetables.

3 Return the tin to the oven for 15—20 minutes until the vegetables and pears are tender and the bacon is lightly browned. Drizzle over the balsamic vinegar and serve hot.

variations

• When quinces are in season, they can be used instead of pears.
• Add garlic instead of pears – simply halve the bulbs (unpeeled) across the middle and add to the tin for the final 20 minutes of cooking. The garlic will taste mild and sweet, tender enough to squeeze out and serve with the vegetables.
• If baby leeks are not available, replace them with ordinary leeks, sliced diagonally, or alternatively use wedges of red onion instead.

cook's tip

• If you arrange all the vegetables parallel in the tin, they are easier and quicker to brush with oil.

SERVES 6
PREPARATION TIME 25 minutes
COOKING TIME 1¾ hours

- 1 boneless, unsmoked ham or gammon joint, about 1.3kg, with its skin on (soaked if necessary)
- 1 bay leaf
- 12 large parsnips, quartered lengthways
- 2 red onions, each cut into 6 wedges
- 3 tbsp vegetable oil
- 20 whole cloves
- 1 tbsp Dijon mustard
- 1 tbsp runny honey
- 1 tbsp light soft brown sugar
- 3 courgettes, trimmed and thickly sliced
- 1 tbsp sesame seeds

Mustard-roast ham with parsnips

This is an excellent way of cooking all your vegetables with a joint of meat in one roasting tin. Parsnips as well as courgettes and red onions provide a colourful and delicious mixture.

1 Place the ham or gammon joint in a large saucepan with the bay leaf and enough cold water to cover it. Slowly bring to the boil, skimming off any scum that rises to the surface. Reduce the heat, cover and gently simmer for 40 minutes. Remove the joint from the pan of water and set it aside on a board.

2 Preheat the oven to 180°C/gas 4 and put a large roasting tin in to heat. Add the parsnips and onions to the simmering water, bring back to the boil and cook for 2 minutes, then drain in a colander. Leave to cool for a few minutes, then return to the pan. Drizzle over 2½ tbsp of the oil and toss to coat. Tip the vegetables into the roasting tin and roast for 20 minutes.

3 Meanwhile, use a sharp knife to cut the rind off the ham or gammon, leaving a thin, even layer of fat. Score deep lines across the fat, cutting into the flesh slightly so the glaze can penetrate, then score the fat in the opposite direction to make neat diamond shapes.

4 Stud the surface of the joint with whole cloves, placing one in the centre of each diamond. Blend the mustard, honey and sugar together to make a smooth paste, then spread over the fat. Push the vegetables to the sides of the roasting tin and place the joint in the middle. Roast in the oven for 10 minutes.

5 Increase the oven temperature to 220°C/gas 7. Toss the courgettes in the remaining oil. Add to the tin, turning the roasted vegetables at the same time, then roast for a further 30 minutes until the joint is well glazed and golden. Check that the ham is cooked by inserting a fine skewer into the centre for a few seconds – when removed the juices should run clear.

6 Remove the ham, cover with foil and leave in a warm place. Turn the vegetables, then sprinkle the sesame seeds and a little freshly ground black pepper over them. Roast for a final 5 minutes until tender and nicely browned. Thickly slice the ham and serve hot with the vegetables.

each serving provides 464kcals • 26g protein • 17g fat of which 4g saturates • 55g carbohydrate of which 19g sugars • 10.5g fibre • 1027mg sodium • 425g vegetables

5 portions fruit & veg

464 kcals

Braised mackerel with fennel

Oily fish, such as mackerel, are a major source of heart-healthy, polyunsaturated omega-3 fatty acids. They're traditionally served with **slightly tart fruit** or **aromatic flavourings** to balance their richness, provided here by **apple juice, cider and aniseed-scented fennel.** Serve with crusty wholegrain bread to mop up the delicious juices.

SERVES 4
PREPARATION TIME about 30 minutes
COOKING TIME about 30 minutes

- 4 small mackerel, cleaned and trimmed
- 1 lemon, halved lengthways and thinly sliced
- 2 garlic cloves, thinly sliced
- 5–6 large sprigs of fresh rosemary, divided into smaller sprigs
- 1 tbsp olive oil
- 1 large fennel bulb, thinly sliced
- 1 bay leaf
- 150ml dry cider
- 300ml apple juice
- 1 tsp fennel seeds
- 200g kale, finely shredded

1 Preheat the oven to 190°C/gas 5. Season the fish inside and out, then make 4–5 diagonal slashes on each side. Tuck 3–4 halved lemon slices inside each fish together with a few slivers of garlic and rosemary sprigs. Insert the remaining garlic and rosemary into the slashes to flavour the fish as it cooks.

2 Heat the oil in a pan over a moderate heat. Add the fennel and cook, stirring frequently, for about 3 minutes until it starts to soften. Add the bay leaf, cider and about half of the apple juice. Cook for a further 4–5 minutes until the liquid has reduced by about half. Add the remaining apple juice and warm through.

3 Transfer the fennel mixture to an ovenproof dish, large enough to allow the fish to lie in a single layer. Lay the mackerel on top and sprinkle with fennel seeds. Cover with foil, then cook in the oven for 20 minutes.

4 Scatter the shredded kale over the fish, then cover again and return to the oven. Cook for a further 8–10 minutes until the kale is tender. Serve hot.

Cod boulangère

White fish, such as cod, lends itself to gentle oven-braising on a bed of vegetables. Sliced potatoes and onions provide the vegetable base with peas and cherry tomatoes scattered on top.

SERVES 4
PREPARATION TIME 25 minutes
COOKING TIME about 1 hour 10 minutes

750g waxy potatoes, peeled and thinly sliced
1 onion, thinly sliced
1 tsp fresh thyme leaves
15g fresh chives, snipped
grated zest and juice of 1 lemon
400ml fish stock, hot
4 thick cutlets or fillets of white fish, such as cod, haddock or hake, about 500g in total
300g shelled fresh or thawed frozen peas
200g cherry or baby plum tomatoes, halved

variations
• Replace the onion with a thinly sliced bulb of fennel.
• Fresh or frozen broad beans can be used instead of peas.

1 Preheat the oven to 190°C/gas 5. Layer the sliced potatoes and onions in a large, greased ovenproof dish, adding the thyme and half the chives plus a little seasoning between each layer. Mix the lemon zest and juice with the stock and pour over the vegetables. Cover the dish with foil, then bake in the heated oven for 45 minutes or until the potatoes are almost tender.

2 Meanwhile, cut the fish into large, bite-sized chunks, discarding any skin and bones. Uncover the dish and arrange the fish on top of the potatoes in a single layer. Re-cover the dish and return it to the oven. Bake for a further 15 minutes.

3 Uncover the dish and scatter the peas over the fish and potatoes. Finish with the tomatoes, cut-side uppermost, then sprinkle with coarsely ground black pepper. Cover the dish and return it to the oven for a final 10 minutes.

4 Scatter the rest of the chives over the fish and vegetables and serve.

variations
• Leave out the cider and use all apple juice, if you prefer.
• Other fish such as tilapia or red mullet can be cooked in the same way. Use a combination of dry white wine, orange juice and light fish or vegetable stock instead of the cider and apple juice.

each serving provides
479kcals • 35g protein
32g fat of which 6g saturates
11g carbohydrate of which
10g sugars • 3g fibre
143mg sodium • 190g fruit and vegetables

easy fish dish
2.5 portions fruit & veg
479 kcals

each serving provides
325kcals • 32g protein
4g fat of which 1g saturates • 43g carbohydrate of which
6g sugars • 7g fibre • 148mg sodium • 150g vegetables

1.5 portions fruit & veg
325 kcals

Sea bass with chermoula

Sea bass makes an impressive meal, and its delicious flesh is **moist, tender and sweet.** Here it's stuffed with an **exotic Moroccan-style fresh herb and spice mixture** called chermoula, then braised on a bed of vegetables.

SERVES 4

PREPARATION TIME 20 minutes, plus at least 30 minutes marinating

COOKING TIME 50–60 minutes

1 whole sea bass, about
  1kg, cleaned
4 garlic cloves
1 small red chilli, deseeded
40g fresh coriander
1 tsp paprika
½ tsp ground cumin
3 tbsp vegetable oil
juice of 1 lemon
175g fine green beans, halved
600g floury potatoes (such as
  Maris Piper), peeled
2 shallots, finely chopped
250g baby plum tomatoes
50g stoned black olives
300ml fish stock, hot

1 Cut 5–6 deep, diagonal slashes in the flesh on each side of the fish. Place it in a wide, non-metallic dish.

2 Put the garlic, chilli, coriander, paprika, cumin, oil and lemon juice in a food processor and process until blended and finely chopped. Season to taste. Spread about half of this 'chermoula' inside the fish and into the slashes. Cover the fish and the remaining chermoula, and leave in the fridge for at least 30 minutes (or overnight).

3 Preheat the oven to 200°C/gas 6. Drop the beans into a pan of boiling water and blanch for 1 minute, then drain and refresh in cold water. Thinly slice the potatoes and spread in a shallow layer with the shallots in a wide, deep ovenproof dish. Scatter over the beans, tomatoes and olives.

4 Pour the stock over the vegetables and place the fish on top. Cover with foil and cook in the oven for 40–50 minutes until the potatoes are tender and the fish flakes easily when tested with a fork.

5 Serve the fish with the vegetables, and the reserved chermoula as a sauce.

variation

• If you prefer, use 4 small sea bass, about 300g each, or 4 sea bass fillets, about 175g each (or fillets of another firm white fish). Cook the vegetables on their own for 30 minutes, then arrange the small whole fish or fillets on top and cook for a further 20 minutes or until the fish flakes easily.

each serving provides 402kcals • 38g protein • 15g fat of which 3g saturates
31g carbohydrate of which 5g sugars • 4g fibre • 422mg sodium • 128g vegetables

1.5 portions fruit & veg

402 kcals

spicy treat

4

5

Lentil & cashew nut roast

Not only are low-fat lentils richer in protein than most other pulses, but their slightly smoky flavour makes a great base for this tasty nut roast, packed with colourful vegetables and served with a quick tomato sauce.

SERVES 4 V

PREPARATION TIME 30 minutes
  plus 10 minutes standing
  before serving
COOKING TIME 1 hour

200g red split lentils
450ml vegetable stock
1 bay leaf
100g unsalted cashew nuts
1½ tbsp olive oil
1 large onion, finely chopped
1 large or 2 small leeks, trimmed
  and finely chopped
1 red pepper, deseeded and chopped
100g mushrooms, finely chopped
1 garlic clove, crushed
1 tbsp lemon juice
75g mature Cheddar cheese, grated
100g wholemeal breadcrumbs
3 tbsp chopped fresh parsley
1 egg, lightly beaten

QUICK TOMATO SAUCE
1 tbsp tomato purée
½ tsp paprika
400g can chopped tomatoes
150ml dry red wine or
  vegetable stock
¼ tsp dried mixed herbs

cook's tips
• If you don't have a loaf tin in this size, use an alternative tin with a similar capacity. The mixture should come to a depth of 4–5cm.
• The mixture should be warm, not steaming hot when adding the egg. If necessary allow it to cool for a few minutes.

1 Rinse the lentils in a sieve under cold running water. Drain, then tip into a saucepan. Add the stock and bay leaf and bring to the boil. Reduce the heat to a gentle simmer, then cover and cook for 15 minutes until the lentils are soft and pulpy and the stock has been absorbed. Stir once or twice towards the end of cooking time to prevent the lentils sticking. Discard the bay leaf.

2 While the lentils are cooking, put the cashew nuts in a non-stick frying pan and toast over a moderate heat until lightly browned, stirring frequently. Set aside to cool, then roughly chop. Preheat the oven to 190°C/ gas 5. Line the bottom of a 1.4 litre loaf tin with a piece of greaseproof paper.

3 Add the oil to the frying pan and cook the onion over a moderate heat for 5 minutes. Remove half the onion and set aside for the sauce. Add the leeks, red pepper, mushrooms and garlic to the pan and cook for a further 5 minutes, stirring occasionally, until tender. Stir in the lemon juice.

4 Tip the lentils and vegetables into a mixing bowl. Stir in the breadcrumbs, cashew nuts and 2 tbsp of the parsley, followed by the grated cheese and beaten egg. Season to taste, then spoon into the loaf tin. Level the top and cover with a piece of lightly oiled foil.

5 Bake the loaf for 30 minutes, then remove the foil and bake for a further 30 minutes or until a skewer inserted into the centre comes out clean. Remove from the oven and leave to cool and set in the tin for 10 minutes before turning out and cutting into thick slices.

6 While the loaf is baking and resting, make the tomato sauce. Put the reserved onion and remaining sauce ingredients in a small pan. Bring to the boil, then reduce the heat, and simmer for 20 minutes, until slightly reduced. Stir in the remaining chopped parsley before serving with the loaf.

3 portions fruit & veg

584 kcals

each serving provides 584kcals • 29g protein 26g fat of which 8g saturates • 55g carbohydrate of which 13g sugars • 8g fibre • 350mg sodium • 255g vegetables

SERVES 4 V
PREPARATION TIME 1 hour
COOKING TIME 25 minutes

250g long-grain brown rice
2 tbsp olive oil
2 onions, thinly sliced
4 large celery sticks, thinly sliced
1 large leek, thinly sliced
1 tbsp finely chopped fresh sage
200g vacuum-packed, peeled
   whole chestnuts, halved
75g extra-mature Cheddar
   cheese, grated
1 egg, beaten
few drops Tabasco sauce

TO GARNISH sprigs of fresh sage

each serving provides

499kcals • 14g protein
17g fat of which 6g saturates
77g carbohydrate of which
10g sugars • 6g fibre
188mg sodium • 169g vegetables

2 portions fruit & veg

499 kcals

crunchy delight

Cheesy chestnut galette
This delicious galette, made with brown rice, crunchy stir-fried vegetables, chestnuts, fresh sage and cheese, is a cross between a roasted rice cake and a risotto. Serve with a simple salad and cranberry sauce.

1 Cook the rice in a saucepan of boiling water for about 30 minutes or according to the pack instructions, until tender. Drain thoroughly and leave to cool while preparing the vegetables.

2 Preheat the oven to 180°C/gas 4. Lightly oil and line the base of a 22cm springform or deep round cake tin.

3 Heat the oil in a frying pan, add the onions, celery and leek and cook gently, stirring frequently, for about 15 minutes or until softened and lightly coloured. Stir in the sage and chestnuts and cook for another minute.

4 Tip the rice into a mixing bowl. Add the cooked vegetables and grated cheese. Mix the egg with about 5 drops of Tabasco sauce and add to the bowl with a little seasoning. Thoroughly combine all the ingredients, then spoon into the prepared cake tin and level the surface.

5 Bake for 25 minutes until lightly browned. Cool in the tin for 5 minutes, then turn out onto a large serving platter. Garnish with small sage sprigs and serve.

cook's tip
• The rice can be cooked in advance, then quickly cooled and chilled for up to 48 hours before assembling the galette. Make sure the rice is thoroughly heated before serving.

Casseroles & curries

Wholesome, warming casseroles and exotic, spicy curries are the ultimate, adaptable one-dish meals. They can be prepared ahead and doubled in quantity, then reheated or frozen for later. Long, slow cooking tenderises cuts of meat and poultry, develops a rounded flavour and maintains all the nutrients in a delicious sauce. Try Coq au vin avec légumes, a healthy take on the classic French casserole. Or there are tempting vegetarian recipes, from a Creamy vegetable fricassée to an aromatic Red lentil and vegetable dahl.

SERVES 4 ✳
PREPARATION TIME 30 minutes
COOKING TIME 2 hours

2 tbsp olive oil
500g lean boneless lamb, cubed
1 onion, chopped
¼ tsp saffron
500ml vegetable stock, hot
1 tbsp tomato purée
zest of 1 orange, cut into strips
¼ tsp ground ginger
1 tsp ground cinnamon
½ tsp ground coriander
½ tsp harissa, or to taste
1 tbsp runny honey
16 baby onions, about 275g
   in total, peeled
125g ready-to-eat stoned dates
125g ready-to-eat dried apricots
2 x 400g cans chickpeas,
   drained and rinsed
2 tbsp chopped walnuts

cook's tip
• You can prepare ahead up to the
end of step 4, then cool and chill.
Freeze if liked. Thaw and reheat
gently until piping hot throughout,
adding a little extra stock.

Lamb tagine with dried fruit An aromatic

North African-style casserole, **richly flavoured with dried fruits**
and **warmly spiced with ginger and cinnamon.** The sweetness of
the **honey tempers the fiery harissa,** and chickpeas add a high
fibre carbohydrate to the dish.

1 Heat the oil in a large, deep saucepan or flameproof casserole. Add the
cubes of lamb and fry until lightly browned. Push the meat to one side and
add the chopped onion to the pan. Fry for 5–10 minutes, stirring frequently,
until golden.

2 Stir the saffron into the hot stock, then pour into the pan. Add the tomato
purée, strips of orange zest and spices. Stir well, then bring to the boil.
Reduce the heat, cover and leave to simmer gently for 1½ hours.

3 Uncover the pan and take out about a teacup of the sauce. Stir in the
harissa and honey, then stir this back into the pan.

4 Add the baby onions, dates, apricots and chickpeas and stir to mix.
Simmer gently, uncovered, for a further 20 minutes, stirring occasionally.

5 Season to taste and scatter the chopped walnuts over the top, then serve.
Put a little extra harissa on the table for those who like more heat.

variation
• During the autumn months, you could replace the onions, dates and apricots
with 2 tbsp raisins, 1 large courgette, trimmed and diced, and 1 chopped beef
tomato, plus a slice of pumpkin or squash, peeled, cored and diced.

2 portions fruit & veg

554 kcals

prepare ahead

each serving provides 554kcals • 38g protein • 22g fat of
which 1g saturates • 54g carbohydrate of which 33g sugars • 9g fibre
287mg sodium • 169g fruit and vegetables

Lamb & aubergine dhansak

A spicy, low-fat and very **satisfying curry** that combines lots of vegetables with **lean, tender lamb chunks** and lentils. Serve with wholemeal chappatis.

SERVES 4 ✶
PREPARATION TIME 30 minutes, plus 2 hours or overnight marinating
COOKING TIME 30—35 minutes

1 tsp cumin seeds
1 tsp coriander seeds
1 tsp fennel seeds
½ tsp black mustard seeds
4 cardamom pods, seeds only
1 tsp crushed dried chillies
400g lean leg of lamb,
   cut into 2.5cm cubes
1 tbsp vegetable oil
1 onion, sliced
2 red peppers, deseeded
   and cut into 2cm chunks
1 aubergine, cut into 2cm chunks
100g red split lentils
400ml lamb or vegetable stock
1 cinnamon stick

TO GARNISH 25g toasted flaked almonds

1 Place the cumin, coriander, fennel, mustard and cardamom in a mortar and crush with a pestle. Add the chillies. Place the lamb in a bowl, add the spices and toss to coat evenly. Cover and chill for about 2 hours, or overnight.

2 Heat the oil in a large pan or flameproof casserole and fry the onion, peppers and aubergine for about 10 minutes, stirring occasionally, to soften.

3 Add the spiced lamb and lentils, then stir in the stock and cinnamon. Bring to the boil, then stir, reduce the heat and cover. Simmer gently for 30–35 minutes until the meat is tender. Serve scattered with toasted almonds.

cook's tip

• Curries improve in flavour if made ahead, allowing time for the flavours to mingle. Chill, then reheat gently until thoroughly heated through.

each serving provides 293kcals • 28g protein 11g fat of which 1g saturates • 22g carbohydrate of which 7g sugars 5g fibre • 15mg sodium • 200g vegetables

293 kcals

prepare ahead

2.5 portions fruit & veg

New century Lancashire hot-pot

Inspired by the more traditional Lancashire hot-pot, this modern version is still slow-cooked for maximum flavour, but is lighter, using **lean lamb neck fillet and more vegetables** than the old recipe. If liked, sprinkle the top with a little **tangy Lancashire cheese** at the end of cooking.

SERVES 4 ★
PREPARATION TIME 20 minutes
COOKING TIME about 2 hours

**500g lean lamb neck fillet,
    trimmed of fat and sliced**
1 garlic clove, crushed
2 tbsp Worcestershire sauce
1 onion, thinly sliced
2 leeks, thinly sliced
3 carrots, peeled and sliced
**250g closed cup chestnut
    mushrooms, halved**
1 bay leaf
small bunch of fresh thyme
1 sprig of fresh rosemary
**500g new potatoes, scrubbed
    and thickly sliced**
2 tbsp tomato purée
400ml lamb or chicken stock, hot
**50g Lancashire cheese,
    crumbled (optional)**

variation

• Instead of sliced potatoes, top the hot-pot with a layer of coarsely grated potato, or mix potato half-and-half with grated parsnips. Bake in the same way as in the main recipe, topping with either Lancashire or Parmesan cheese if you like.

1 Preheat the oven to 180°C/gas 4. Toss the lamb pieces together with the garlic and Worcestershire sauce.

2 Spread a layer of onions, leeks and carrots in the bottom of a large casserole. Top with a layer of meat and mushrooms and season lightly, then repeat the layers until the ingredients are all used up.

3 Tie together the bay leaf, thyme and rosemary with cotton string and tuck into the centre of the casserole. Top with a thick layer of overlapping potato slices.

4 Mix the tomato purée into the hot stock and pour over the potatoes. Cover tightly with a lid and bake for 1½ hours or until the meat and potatoes are tender. (Prepare ahead up to this stage and leave in the fridge for a few hours or overnight, if more convenient.)

5 Remove the lid and sprinkle the cheese over the potatoes, if using. Increase the oven temperature to 230°C/gas 8 and bake uncovered for a further 25–30 minutes until golden.

each serving provides 414kcals • 30g protein 19g fat of which 8g saturates • 33g carbohydrate of which 13g sugars • 6g fibre • 228mg sodium • 229g vegetables

414 kcals

prepare ahead

2.5 portions fruit & veg

Beef in ale with horseradish dumplings

A hearty beef and vegetable casserole that **can be left to cook** or made ahead and then reheated before serving. Cook the dumplings on top shortly before serving.

SERVES 4 ✳ (cooked casserole without dumplings)
PREPARATION TIME 35 minutes
COOKING TIME about 2½ hours

2 tbsp olive oil
500g lean braising steak, cubed
2 onions, sliced
1 tbsp plain flour
600ml good ale or stout
1 tbsp redcurrant jelly
1 tsp wholegrain mustard
1 bay leaf
6 carrots, thickly sliced diagonally
200g baby or small turnips, trimmed and quartered if necessary
4 large portabello mushrooms, thickly sliced

DUMPLINGS
175g self-raising flour
6 sprigs of fresh parsley
5 tbsp cottage cheese
2 tsp horseradish sauce
2 tbsp semi-skimmed milk, or as needed

prepare ahead

3 portions fruit & veg

580 kcals

each serving provides
580kcals • 42g protein
15g fat of which 5g saturates
65g carbohydrate of which
27g sugars • 7g fibre
514mg sodium • 263g vegetables

1 Preheat the oven to 160°C/gas 3. Heat the oil in a large, heavy flameproof casserole and quickly fry the pieces of steak until they are a good brown colour. Lift out of the casserole onto a plate using a draining spoon. Add the onions to the pan, reduce the heat to moderate and fry gently for about 10 minutes until the onions are golden brown.

2 Sprinkle the flour over the onions, stir well and cook for 1 minute. Pour in the ale and bring to the boil, stirring to dislodge any bits stuck to the casserole.

3 Add the redcurrant jelly, mustard and bay leaf, then return the meat to the casserole, followed by the carrots, turnips and mushrooms. Cover and transfer to the oven. Cook for 2 hours or until the meat is very tender. (Prepare ahead up to this point, if more convenient. Keep chilled, then reheat thoroughly before adding the dumplings.)

variations
• Use stewing venison instead of braising steak, and replace the turnips with chunks of swede or baby onions.
• Use 200g smaller chestnut mushrooms instead of portabellos.

4 Shortly before the end of the cooking time, make the dumplings. Put the flour, a little seasoning and the parsley sprigs into a food processor. Process briefly to chop the parsley. Mix the cottage cheese with the horseradish and milk and add to the processor. Mix to make a soft dough, adding a little more milk if necessary. (Alternatively, chop the parsley, then mix everything together in a mixing bowl.) Turn the dough out onto a lightly floured work surface and divide into 8 equal portions. Roll each into a ball with floured hands.

5 Increase the oven temperature to 180°C/gas 4. Uncover the casserole, stir and season to taste. Gently place the dumplings on the top of the meat and vegetables, but do not submerge them. Cover, return to the oven and cook for a further 20 minutes. Serve at once.

SERVES 4
PREPARATION TIME 20 minutes
COOKING TIME about 1½ hours

300g baby onions
1 tbsp olive oil
450g lean braising steak,
   cut into chunks
2 garlic cloves, crushed
½ tsp ground cumin
½ tsp ground cinnamon
400g can chopped tomatoes
400ml red wine
1 bay leaf
350g baby new potatoes
400g can artichoke hearts,
   drained and halved
200g frozen broad beans, thawed
50g Kalamata olives, stoned
   and roughly chopped

cook's tips

• You can make the whole stew up
to 3 days ahead, just leaving out the
artichoke hearts, beans and olives.
Allow to cool, then cover and keep in
the fridge. When ready to serve, allow
to come to room temperature, then
add the remaining ingredients and
reheat gently over a low heat until
bubbling hot.
• If more convenient, cook slowly in
a moderate oven at 180°C/gas 4.

Greek stifado

An exciting beef casserole – with artichoke hearts, broad beans, new potatoes and juicy, purple-skinned Kalamata olives – that's **ideal for a family Sunday lunch or easy entertaining,** and needs only a green salad alongside.

1 Cut the ends from the onions and place in a large bowl. Cover with boiling water and allow to stand for about 2 minutes to loosen the skins.

2 Meanwhile, heat the olive oil in a large flameproof casserole over a moderate heat. Add the beef and brown evenly, stirring occasionally, for about 8 minutes.

3 Slip the skins from the onions and add them to the casserole to brown lightly, stirring frequently, for about 5 minutes. Stir in the garlic with the ground spices.

4 Pour in the tomatoes and red wine and bring to the boil. Add the bay leaf, reduce the heat to low, cover the casserole and simmer gently for 1 hour.

5 Stir the potatoes into the casserole and continue to simmer for a further 30 minutes, covered, until the meat and potatoes are tender. Add the artichoke hearts, beans and olives and cook for a final 5 minutes to heat through. Season to taste.

variation

• If you are serving this to a family where the younger members may dislike the olives and artichoke hearts, you can easily replace them with 200g button mushrooms added with the potatoes.

each serving provides 416kcals • 32g protein • 12g fat of which 3g saturates
31g carbohydrate of which 9g sugars • 6g fibre • 412mg sodium • 285g vegetables

3.5 portions fruit & veg

416 kcals

prepare ahead

SERVES 4
PREPARATION TIME 30 minutes
COOKING TIME about 45 minutes

2 tbsp vegetable oil
4 lean pork loin steaks
800g Victoria plums, halved
  and stoned
4 spring onions, trimmed
4 sweet potatoes, peeled
220g can water chestnuts,
  drained and sliced
3cm piece fresh root ginger,
  peeled and grated
2 garlic cloves, crushed
1 red chilli, deseeded and finely
  chopped (optional)
2 tsp sugar
1 tbsp dark soy sauce
1 tbsp cider vinegar
2 tbsp Chinese Shaoxing rice
  wine or dry sherry
¼ tsp five-spice powder

TO GARNISH 2 tbsp chopped
  fresh coriander

Chinese pork with plums

All the family will love this sweet and sour casserole that makes the most of seasonal fresh plums. It's traditionally flavoured with ginger, five-spice, vinegar, soy and spring onions, and the addition of water chestnuts and cubes of sweet potato turn it into a complete, low-fat dish.

1 Preheat the oven to 180°C/gas 4. Heat the oil in a large frying pan, then quickly fry the pork steaks on both sides until lightly browned. Transfer to a large casserole with a lid.

2 Roughly chop the plums, cut the spring onions into 2cm lengths and cut the sweet potatoes into 1cm cubes. Add all of these to the casserole with the water chestnuts.

3 Put the ginger into a small bowl. Add the garlic, chilli if using, sugar, soy sauce, vinegar, wine or sherry and the five-spice powder. Mix well, then spoon over the ingredients in the casserole. Cover with the lid, then cook in the oven, stirring occasionally, for about 45 minutes until the meat is tender and the sauce is thick.

4 Taste the sauce and add more sugar or vinegar if needed, depending on the flavour of the plums, to give a good balance of sweet and sour tastes. Scatter over the chopped coriander and serve.

variation
• This recipe would work equally well with skinless, boneless chicken thighs.

cook's tip
• Chinese Shaoxing rice wine can be found in the 'special ingredient' section in larger supermarkets or can be bought from Chinese food stores.

each serving provides
448kcals • 31g protein
11g fat of which 3g saturates
57g carbohydrate of which
31g sugars • 7g fibre
365mg sodium • 219g fruit
and vegetables

2.5 portions fruit & veg

448 kcals

prepare ahead

Highland venison casserole with chestnuts

Venison is low in fat and, like all red meat, provides plenty of iron and minerals. It makes a **mouth-watering casserole** when cooked with **beer and winter vegetables.** For the best flavour choose a real ale or one of the popular 'designer' beers.

SERVES 4 ✻
PREPARATION TIME 30 minutes
COOKING TIME 1–1½ hours

500g lean boneless venison, cubed
2 tbsp fine oatmeal
2 tbsp extra virgin olive oil
2 onions, finely chopped
600ml good beer
1 tsp fresh thyme leaves
3 juniper berries, crushed
2 good pinches of allspice
150g baby shallots, peeled
250g baby carrots, scrubbed
   and trimmed
250g baby parsnips (or turnips),
   scrubbed and trimmed,
   or diced swede
1 baguette (French stick)
100g canned or vacuum-packed
   cooked chestnuts

variations

• If preferred, or if venison is unavailable, use lean stewing steak or wild boar. Spread the croûtes with mustard before adding to the casserole.

• Use 450ml beer with 150ml beef stock.

1 Preheat the oven to 160°C/gas 3. Toss the pieces of venison in the oatmeal to lightly coat, then shake to remove any excess.

2 Heat the oil in a heavy flameproof casserole and quickly cook the venison until lightly coloured. Transfer to a plate. Add the chopped onions to the casserole and cook gently over a low heat, stirring frequently, for about 10 minutes until softened and golden.

3 Add the beer, thyme, juniper and allspice plus a little seasoning to taste, and bring to the boil, stirring constantly.

4 Stir in the shallots, whole baby carrots and parsnips (or baby turnips or diced swede) plus the venison and any meat juices. When the liquid comes to the boil, cover the casserole and put into the oven. Cook, stirring occasionally, for 1¼–1½ hours until the meat is really tender.

5 Towards the end of the cooking time, cut the baguette into slices about 2.5cm thick and lay on a baking tray. Bake for about 15 minutes until they are lightly brown and crisp.

6 When the meat is cooked, stir in the chestnuts, then taste and adjust the seasoning. Arrange the toasted bread on top of meat and vegetables and cook uncovered for a further 5 minutes. Serve hot, in the casserole.

cook's tips

• Shallots and baby onions are easy to peel if you make a small cut in the skin at the top and then soak in boiling water for 2 minutes.
• To prepare ahead, cook up to the end of step 4, then cool and store in the fridge for up to 48 hours, or freeze. Thaw, if frozen, then reheat thoroughly before adding the chestnuts and bread croûtes.

prepare ahead

2.5 portions fruit & veg

547 kcals

each serving provides

547kcals • 38g protein
12g fat of which 2g saturates
70g carbohydrate of which
18g sugars • 9g fibre
509mg sodium • 213g vegetables

Rabbit with fennel & rosemary

Rabbit is an under-used meat, considering it's easily digestible and **low in fat and cholesterol**. Farmed rabbit is **tender and delicate** in flavour, but if you buy wild rabbit, the flavour is gamier and the meat will require longer cooking. Serve this delicious meal with a good, rustic-style bread.

SERVES 4 ✴
PREPARATION TIME 20 minutes
COOKING TIME 45–50 minutes

1 tbsp vegetable oil
8 rabbit joints, about 550g in total
4 shallots, quartered
1 fennel bulb, thinly sliced
300g carrots, peeled and sliced
150ml dry white wine
200ml chicken or vegetable stock, hot
1 tsp fennel seeds
3 sprigs of fresh rosemary
400g can cannellini beans, drained and rinsed

variations

• If preferred, use 400g boneless diced rabbit, and reduce the cooking time to about 30 minutes.
• If fennel is not available, celery makes a good alternative. Instead of fennel seeds, add 1 tbsp of chopped fresh sage leaves or 1 tsp dried.
• Instead of white wine, try using dry cider for a different flavour. If you prefer not to add alcohol, use a well-flavoured stock for the whole liquid quantity.
• For a chicken casserole, replace the rabbit pieces with 8 small skinless chicken joints.

1 Heat the oil in a large flameproof casserole and fry the rabbit joints on a fairly high heat for about 10 minutes, turning occasionally, until golden. Remove the joints and keep warm.

2 Add the shallots to the casserole and fry for 3–4 minutes until beginning to brown. Return the rabbit, and add the fennel (reserve the feathery fronds for garnishing), carrots, wine, stock, fennel seeds and rosemary.

3 Bring to the boil, then reduce the heat to a simmer, cover the casserole and leave to cook gently for 45–50 minutes until the rabbit and vegetables are tender. (Prepare ahead up to this stage, if more convenient. Chill for a few hours or overnight, then reheat thoroughly.)

4 Stir in the beans and heat through for about 5 minutes. Season to taste, then garnish with the reserved fennel fronds and serve.

2 portions fruit & veg

prepare ahead

250 kcals

each serving provides

250kcals • 28.5g protein
4.5g fat of which 2g saturates
18g carbohydrate of which
8g sugars • 7g fibre
82mg sodium • 171g vegetables

Coq au vin avec légumes

This lighter version of the great French classic, chicken in red wine sauce, is **lower in fat and includes more vegetables.** It just needs some crusty, rustic-style bread and perhaps a **light green salad.** The dish is better if made a full day ahead so the flavours can mature.

SERVES 4 ★
PREPARATION TIME 30 minutes
COOKING TIME 45 minutes

8 large skinless, boneless chicken
   thighs, about 700g in total
8 thin slices pancetta or lean,
   thinly cut streaky bacon
2 tbsp olive oil
3 large garlic cloves, chopped
1 large red onion, halved and sliced
2 carrots, peeled and thickly sliced
1 fennel bulb or 3 celery sticks,
   thinly sliced
1 turnip, peeled and cut into chunks
2 bay leaves
3–4 sprigs of fresh thyme
350ml red wine
1 tbsp redcurrant jelly
2 tbsp brandy (optional)
450ml chicken or vegetable stock
8 baby onions or small shallots
250g button chestnut mushrooms

TO GARNISH chopped fresh parsley

variation
• Use large chunks of pork or veal instead of the chicken and omit the pancetta or bacon.

1 Trim any excess fat from the thighs, then wrap each one in a thin rasher of pancetta or bacon. Heat 1 tbsp of the oil in a large flameproof casserole and add the chicken, join-side down, and brown for 2–3 minutes. Turn to brown the other side, then remove to a plate.

2 Add the remaining oil to the casserole and gently fry the garlic, onion, carrots, fennel or celery and turnip, stirring a couple of times, until softened. If you need to moisten, add 2–3 tbsp of water, not extra oil.

3 Add the herbs, red wine, redcurrant jelly and brandy, if using, and simmer for 5 minutes. Stir in the stock and bring to the boil.

4 Meanwhile, blanch the baby onions in boiling water for 2 minutes, then cool and peel. Add to the casserole with the chicken thighs and season to taste. Cover and cook very gently for about 30 minutes.

5 Add the mushrooms, stir well and cook for a further 15 minutes. Remove from the heat and allow to cool for about 10 minutes, then serve, sprinkled with chopped parsley.

prepare ahead

4 portions fruit & veg

474 kcals

each serving provides 474kcals • 46g protein 18g fat of which 5g saturates • 15g carbohydrate of which 13g sugars • 6g fibre • 454mg sodium • 320g vegetables

SERVES 4 ★ (without olives)
PREPARATION TIME 30 minutes
COOKING TIME 25–30 minutes

2 tbsp olive oil

2 onions, roughly chopped

2 garlic cloves, crushed

1 tbsp chopped fresh rosemary

40g chorizo sausage, skinned
and diced

2 large red peppers, deseeded
and roughly chopped

40g sun-dried tomatoes,
roughly chopped

400g can chopped tomatoes

3 tbsp white wine

4 skinless chicken breast fillets or
large thighs, about 450g in total

50g stoned olives (black, green
or a mixture)

variation

• For another Mediterranean dish in the same style, omit the chorizo, red peppers and sun-dried tomatoes and make the sauce using 3 x 400g cans of chopped tomatoes and 2 tbsp thyme or lavender honey. Simmer uncovered for 30 minutes or until the sauce reduces and thickens. Serve scattered with 50g toasted flaked almonds.

Mediterranean chicken with olives

This is a dish of bright, **vivid colour and bold flavours.** Onions, tomatoes and red peppers make a chunky vegetable sauce for chicken pieces, with spicy chorizo sausage, **sun-dried tomatoes, rosemary and olives** adding tastes of the Mediterranean. Serve with crusty bread.

1 Heat the oil in a large, heavy flameproof casserole or deep frying pan. Add the onions, garlic and rosemary and cook gently, stirring frequently, for about 15 minutes until soft and golden.

2 Add the chorizo sausage and red peppers and cook over a moderate heat, stirring frequently, for a couple of minutes or until the sausage turns slightly golden.

3 Add the sun-dried tomatoes, the canned tomatoes with their juice, and the wine. Season with freshly ground black pepper (salt should not be needed because of the salt in the sausage, canned tomatoes and olives), then stir well and bring to a simmer.

4 Add the chicken and stir to coat with the sauce. Bring to the boil, then reduce the heat so the sauce simmers. Cover and cook for 25–30 minutes until the chicken is tender and the sauce is thick. (Prepare ahead up to this stage, if more convenient. Keep chilled or freeze, then reheat thoroughly.)

5 Just before serving, stir in the olives and heat through.

each serving provides 293kcals • 32g protein 11g fat of which 2g saturates • 15g carbohydrate of which 13g sugars • 4g fibre • 452mg sodium • 280g vegetables

prepare
ahead

3.5
portions
fruit &
veg

293
kcals

Mixed bean cassoulet

A vegetarian version of the hearty **French country dish,** this uses canned beans for a **quick and easy one-pot.** It's finished in the traditional way, with a **crunchy breadcrumb and herb topping,** plus nuts for extra protein.

SERVES 4 V
PREPARATION TIME 20 minutes
COOKING TIME 45 minutes

1 tbsp olive oil
1 onion, chopped
2 garlic cloves, crushed
1 butternut squash, deseeded
  and cut into 1.5 cm cubes
300ml vegetable stock, hot
400g can chopped plum tomatoes
1 tbsp tomato purée
2 bay leaves
2 sprigs of fresh thyme
410g can butter beans,
  drained and rinsed
410g can borlotti beans,
  drained and rinsed

BREADCRUMB CRUST
100g wholemeal or Granary
  breadcrumbs
50g mixed nuts, coarsely chopped
2 tbsp chopped fresh parsley

1 Preheat the oven to 200°C/gas 6. Heat the oil in a flameproof casserole and gently fry the onion for 6–7 minutes until softened. Add the garlic and butternut squash and cook for a further minute, stirring all the time.

2 Add the stock, tomatoes with their juice, tomato purée, bay leaves, thyme and beans. Stir well (the mixture may look slightly dry at this stage, but the squash will produce extra juices as it cooks), then slowly bring to the boil. Cover the casserole with a lid and transfer to the oven to cook for 25 minutes.

3 Meanwhile, mix together the breadcrumbs, nuts and parsley. Remove the casserole from the oven and season to taste. Scatter the top with the breadcrumb mixture and return to the oven, uncovered, for a further 20 minutes or until the crust is lightly browned.

cook's tip
• Use any combination of canned beans available, such as red kidney, cannellini or mixed beans, to suit your preference.

each serving provides 359kcals • 17g protein 11g fat of which 2g saturates • 51g carbohydrate of which 16g sugars • 12g fibre • 466mg sodium • 320g vegetables

359 kcals

4 portions fruit & veg

Creamy vegetable fricassée

For this fricasée, a selection of colourful vegetables is lightly cooked in a **tarragon-flavoured** stock, which is finished with crème fraîche to make a **wonderful, creamy coating sauce.** Serve with wholegrain or seeded bread, for a delicious, satisfying meal.

SERVES 4 V
PREPARATION TIME 10 minutes
COOKING TIME 20 minutes

1 tbsp olive oil
250g carrots, peeled and cut
   into sticks
250g new potatoes, scrubbed
   and halved or quartered
   (depending on size)
150g button mushrooms, halved
400ml vegetable stock
2 tbsp white wine
2 tsp fresh tarragon leaves
   or ½ tsp dried
150g frozen broad beans
100g asparagus tips
3 tbsp crème fraîche
50g cashew nuts

TO GARNISH fresh tarragon leaves

cook's tip
• You can partly prepare this dish up to 6 hours ahead. Cook the vegetables up to the end of step 2 and allow to cool. When ready to serve, reheat gently and finish as above.

1 Heat the oil in a large flameproof casserole over a moderate heat. Add the carrots, potatoes and mushrooms, and cook, stirring frequently, for about 4 minutes.

2 Pour in the stock with the white wine and stir in the tarragon. Bring to the boil, then reduce the heat, cover and simmer gently for about 10 minutes until the vegetables are almost cooked.

3 Stir in the broad beans and lay the asparagus on top. Cover and simmer for a further 6 minutes or until the vegetables are tender.

4 Lift out the vegetables onto a plate, using a draining spoon. Stir the crème fraîche into the liquid in the casserole and heat through gently, then season to taste. Return the vegetables to the casserole, coating them with the sauce. Scatter over the nuts and tarragon leaves, then serve.

237 kcals
prepare ahead
2 portions fruit & veg

each serving provides 237kcals • 8g protein
13g fat of which 4g saturates • 22g carbohydrate of which
8g sugars • 6g fibre • 35mg sodium • 163g vegetables

Spiced potatoes & cauliflower with nuts

The warm, **golden colour** and flavour of saffron with **a mild kick of ginger** help to make this vegetable curry a real winner. **Garlic is an important ingredient** not just for flavour, but for its many health benefits. Serve with warm naan bread.

SERVES 4 Ⓥ
PREPARATION TIME 15 minutes
COOKING TIME 12 minutes

400g potatoes, peeled and cut into 2cm dice
pinch of saffron
15g fresh root ginger, peeled and finely chopped
2 garlic cloves, crushed
1 small onion, chopped
1 small cauliflower, cut into small florets
150ml vegetable stock, hot
150g low-fat natural yoghurt
3 tbsp ground almonds
2 tsp garam masala

TO GARNISH 50g cashew nuts, roughly chopped fresh coriander

variations
• If you don't have saffron, ½ tsp of turmeric will add a rich colour to the curry.
• Diced chicken can be added to the curry – just cut the amount of vegetables by about half and increase the cooking time to about 15–20 minutes, to ensure the chicken is cooked thoroughly.
• Scatter 2 roughly chopped hard-boiled eggs over the curry just before serving, for extra protein.

1 Place the potatoes in a large saucepan of boiling water and simmer for 5 minutes, then drain.

2 Dry the pan, then heat the saffron gently until lightly toasted. Add the ginger, garlic, onion, cauliflower, stock and yoghurt. Stir in the potatoes and ground almonds.

3 Bring to the boil, then reduce the heat, cover and simmer, stirring occasionally, for about 10 minutes until the vegetables are just tender. Stir in the garam masala and cook for a further 2 minutes.

4 Meanwhile, toast the cashew nuts under a hot grill. Scatter the toasted cashews and coriander over the curry and serve.

cook's tip
• Toasting saffron helps to bring out the colour and flavour, but must be done very lightly to prevent scorching. Keep shaking the pan over the heat to keep the saffron moving.

each serving provides
256kcals • 12g protein 11g fat of which 2g saturates • 28g carbohydrate of which 8g sugars • 4g fibre • 45mg sodium • 120g vegetables

winter warmer

256 kcals

1.5 portions fruit & veg

Red lentil & vegetable dahl

A dhal is a **dish of simmered lentils** flavoured with **aromatic spices** and usually served as a sauce. But add **extra vegetables** and it becomes a light and easy vegetarian meal that's **low in fat.** Serve it with Indian-style breads and natural yoghurt or raita.

SERVES 4 Ⅴ ★
PREPARATION TIME 15 minutes
COOKING TIME 20 minutes

1 onion, chopped
2 large garlic cloves, crushed
1 green chilli, deseeded and chopped
1 carrot, grated
1 aubergine, chopped
1 tbsp vegetable oil
1 tsp ground cumin
1 tsp mild curry powder
2 tsp black mustard seeds
150g split red lentils
800ml vegetable stock, hot
1 courgette, halved and sliced
1 large tomato, chopped

TO GARNISH chopped
  fresh coriander

1 Put the onion, garlic, chilli, carrot and aubergine into a flameproof casserole or large saucepan and stir in the oil plus 2 tbsp of water. Heat until it starts to sizzle, then cover and cook gently for about 5 minutes until softened.

2 Uncover and stir in the spices. Cook for 1 minute, then stir in the lentils and stock. Bring to the boil, then add the courgette and tomato.

3 Cover and simmer gently for 15 minutes, then uncover for a further 5 minutes, by which time the lentils should have burst open and thickened the liquid. Serve garnished with roughly chopped fresh coriander.

variations

• For a more authentic dhal, use yellow split peas instead of the lentils. These will need to be soaked in cold water for about 2 hours first.
• Instead of a courgette, add 225g baby leaf spinach at the end of step 3 and cook for 1–2 minutes, until just wilted, before seasoning.

each serving provides 192kcals • 11g protein • 4g fat of which 1g saturates
30g carbohydrate of which 8g sugars • 5g fibre • 26mg salt • 200g vegetables

192 kcals **2.5** portions fruit & veg **prepare ahead**

SERVES 6 V
PREPARATION TIME 20 minutes
COOKING TIME 40 minutes

3 tbsp vegetable oil
1 onion, thinly sliced
50g raisins
1 cinnamon stick, broken in half
8 black peppercorns
6 cloves
6 green cardamoms, crushed
    and shells discarded
1 tbsp coriander seeds,
    lightly crushed
2 tsp ground cumin
½ tsp cayenne pepper
4 garlic cloves, crushed
200g new potatoes, scrubbed
    and cubed
1 carrot, peeled and sliced
150g fine green beans,
    trimmed and chopped
1 courgette, sliced
150g frozen peas
200g Greek yoghurt
300g basmati rice, rinsed
pinch of saffron

TO GARNISH   1 tbsp toasted flaked
    almonds, fresh coriander sprigs,
    3 hard-boiled eggs, quartered

Mixed vegetable biryani

Here is a vegetarian one-pot feast of **golden saffron-scented basmati rice** combined with spiced vegetables. **Serve with mint raita** (see page 27), or a simple cucumber and mint salad.

1 Heat 1 tbsp of the oil in a large flameproof casserole or deep frying pan. Add the onion and fry on a moderate heat, stirring occasionally, for 12–15 minutes until golden. Remove from the pan and set aside. Add the raisins to the pan and stir around for 30 seconds, then remove and set aside with the onion.

2 Add the remaining oil to the pan and heat, then add the cinnamon, peppercorns, cloves, cardamom and coriander seeds and stir around for 1 minute. Reduce the heat to low. Add the ground cumin, cayenne and garlic and stir for a further 30–60 seconds until you can smell the aroma of the spices.

3 Stir in all the vegetables, then gradually add the yoghurt, still on a low heat. Add 4 tbsp of water, cover the pan tightly and leave to simmer gently for 12 minutes.

4 Meanwhile, put the rice in another pan with the saffron, 550ml water and a pinch of salt, stir and bring to the boil. Reduce the heat to low, cover the pan tightly and leave to simmer for about 10 minutes until the liquid is absorbed and the rice is just starting to become tender.

5 Spoon the rice on top of the vegetables. Re-cover the pan tightly and cook gently for a further 10–15 minutes until both the rice and vegetables are tender. Alternatively, layer the vegetable curry and rice in a casserole, cover and bake at 180°C/gas 4 for 20–30 minutes.

6 Scatter the reserved onions and raisins over the top together with the almonds, coriander and wedges of egg. Serve immediately.

1.5 portions fruit & veg
413 kcals

each serving provides
413kcals • 13g protein
13g fat of which 3g saturates
63g carbohydrate of which
14g sugars • 4g fibre
105mg sodium • 140g vegetables

Steamed & simmered dishes

These gentle, moist, low-fat cooking methods are excellent for tenderising lean cuts of meat such as gammon, and cooking delicately flavoured foods like fish, chicken breasts, vegetables and dumplings. Steaming locks in flavour and preserves vitamins, so is a particularly healthy way to cook. Make dinner a special occasion with paper parcels of Aromatic steamed Asian swordfish, or go for one of the wonderfully quick and easy pasta dishes that combine delicious, healthy ingredients with a minimum of fuss.

SERVES 2
PREPARATION TIME 20 minutes
COOKING TIME 15–20 minutes

280g even-sized new potatoes, scrubbed
175g pork tenderloin
1 tbsp light soy sauce
1 tbsp dry sherry
1 tsp vegetable oil
25g fresh root ginger, peeled and finely chopped
½ tsp ground allspice
1 courgette, cut into fine julienne sticks
1 red pepper, deseeded and thinly sliced
150g mange-tout

each serving provides

294kcals • 26g protein
6g fat of which 0.5g saturates
34g carbohydrate of which
11g sugars • 5g fibre
554mg sodium • 205g vegetables

2.5 portions fruit & veg

294 kcals

Quick steamed pork supper

Pork fillet (tenderloin) is an **excellent cut of meat for steaming** as it's so lean and tender. These **aromatic parcels** contain slices of pork with new potatoes, courgettes and red pepper, steamed with **Oriental flavourings** for an easy, light meal.

1 Put the potatoes in a steamer basket over a pan of boiling water and steam for 10 minutes. Remove and leave until cool enough to handle.

2 Meanwhile, trim any fat from the pork fillet. Cut it across into an even number of slices, each about 1cm thick. Mix together the soy sauce, sherry, oil, ginger, allspice and a little pepper for seasoning, in a bowl. Add the pork slices and toss to coat with the mixture.

3 Place 2 pieces of foil, each about 30 x 20cm (about the size of a sheet of A4 paper) on the work surface. Thinly slice the steamed potatoes (you can remove the skins first, if you prefer) and spread out on one half of each piece of foil, leaving a border of at least 2.5cm around the edge. Arrange the pork slices on top and pour over the juices. Scatter the courgettes and peppers on top.

4 Fold the other half of each foil rectangle over the top and make small overlapping folds along the edges to seal. Place the foil parcels in the steamer basket and steam for 15–20 minutes, until the meat and vegetables are cooked. About 4 minutes before the end of the cooking time, add the mange-tout to the water in the pan under the steamer.

5 Transfer the cooked parcels to warmed plates, open to reveal the contents and serve with the drained mange-tout.

variation

• For steamed turkey parcels, replace the pork with turkey breast fillet, cut into thin slices or strips. Omit the potatoes and instead cook Chinese noodles in the boiling water under the steamer, following the pack instructions. Serve with a salad in place of the mange-tout.

Somerset gammon

A spicy mixture of ginger, cardamom and cinnamon livens up a gammon joint cooked in cider. Poached apples and pears and whole baby vegetables cooked in the same pot add texture and vital nutrition.

SERVES 6

PREPARATION TIME 20 minutes

COOKING TIME about 1½ hours

1 boneless, smoked gammon joint, about 1.2kg, soaked if necessary

40g fresh root ginger, peeled and thickly sliced

1 cinnamon stick

6 green cardamom pods

2 litres medium cider

2 large dessert apples (such as Braeburn or Cox's)

4 firm pears

2 tbsp orange marmalade

12 baby turnips, peeled

12 baby carrots, peeled

250g baby corn

each serving provides

347kcals • 29.5g protein

15g fat of which 5g saturates

25g carbohydrate of which

24g sugars • 5.5g fibre

1430mg sodium

254g fruit and vegetables

sweet & savoury

3 portions fruit & veg

347 kcals

1 Check the weight of the gammon and calculate the cooking time, allowing 40 minutes per kg, plus 40 minutes. Place in a stockpot or large saucepan big enough to hold the joint and whole vegetables.

2 Add the ginger, cinnamon, cardamom and cider. Bring to the boil, skimming off any scum from the surface. Reduce the heat, cover and simmer gently for the calculated time: 1½ hours for a 1.2kg joint.

3 After about 40 minutes of cooking, prepare the fruit. Cut each apple into 8 wedges and core them. Quarter and core the pears. Add the fruit to the simmering cider and poach for 5–10 minutes or until just tender. Use a draining spoon to transfer the fruit to a dish. Mix the marmalade with 1 tbsp of the cooking liquid, add to the fruit and toss to glaze. Set aside.

4 About 20 minutes before the gammon has finished cooking, add the whole turnips and carrots to the pan. When the gammon is ready, use a meat fork and spatula to lift it from the pan. Set aside, loosely covered with foil, to rest. Add the corn to the vegetables in the pan and cook for a final 5 minutes. Drain the vegetables.

5 Serve the gammon thickly sliced on a platter with the vegetables and cooled glazed fruit arranged around it.

Chinese slow-cooked pork

Star anise, soy and ginger add wonderful flavours to this **deliciously tender pork joint casserole,** simmered with shallots, carrots and mushrooms. Vegetables and rice noodles cooked in **exotic, rich juices** make this into a complete meal.

SERVES 4
PREPARATION TIME 15 minutes
COOKING TIME 1–1¼ hours

500g lean, boneless loin of pork with skin, tied firmly
400ml chicken stock, hot
2 tbsp dark soy sauce
2 tbsp Chinese rice wine or dry sherry
2 tbsp runny honey
2 garlic cloves, crushed
15g fresh root ginger, peeled and finely chopped
3 star anise
4 shallots, halved
2 large carrots, peeled and diagonally sliced
6 spring onions
25g dried Chinese (shiitake) mushrooms, soaked to rehydrate
125g oyster mushrooms, sliced or halved
225g dried flat rice noodles

variation

• Omit the spring onions and instead stir 75g bean sprouts into the hot juices just before adding the rice noodles. Garnish with chopped coriander instead of spring onion curls.

1 Place the pork in a large flameproof casserole and pour over boiling water to cover. Bring back to the boil on the hob, then pour off the water. Add the stock, soy sauce, rice wine or sherry, honey, garlic, ginger, star anise, shallots and carrots to the casserole and bring to the boil. Thickly slice 4 of the spring onions, roughly chop the drained shiitake mushrooms and add both to the casserole. Reserve the strained mushroom soaking liquid.

2 Cover and simmer gently on a very low heat for 1–1¼ hours, stirring the vegetables and basting the meat occasionally until everything is tender. Add the oyster mushrooms for the last 20 minutes of the cooking time. If necessary, top up using the reserved mushroom soaking liquid or more stock or water.

3 Meanwhile, cut the remaining spring onions into 6cm lengths, then cut lengthways into fine shreds. Place in a bowl of iced water and leave to curl. Soak the rice noodles in a bowl of boiling water for 4 minutes or until softened, then drain.

4 Carefully lift the meat out of the casserole with a draining spoon and keep hot. Bring the juices to the boil on the hob, then add the rice noodles and remove from the heat. Turn and stir the noodles to coat with the juices. Slice the pork thinly.

5 Spread the noodles on a large shallow serving platter, using a draining spoon to lift them from the casserole. Arrange the sliced meat and vegetables on top, then spoon over the casserole juices. Scatter over the spring onion curls to garnish.

Far East feast

2 portions fruit & veg

461 kcals

each serving provides 461kcals • 34g protein
5g fat of which 0.2g saturates • 69g carbohydrate of which 17g sugars
3g fibre • 464mg sodium • 160g vegetables

2

3

4

5

cook's tip

• Soak dried mushrooms in boiling water for 20 minutes to rehydrate, then drain. The soaking liquid makes a tasty stock but needs to be strained through a fine sieve to remove any gritty bits.

Poached chicken with chilli & coriander dressing

In this light, very low-fat dish, chicken is poached in an aromatic stock with new potatoes, asparagus and green beans steamed over the top. A zingy Oriental-style dressing is a great finishing touch.

SERVES 4
PREPARATION TIME 15 minutes
COOKING TIME 20–25 minutes

400ml chicken stock
4 slices fresh root ginger
4 spring onions, sliced
2 large sprigs of fresh coriander
4 skinless chicken breast fillets,
   about 150g each
500g small new potatoes, scrubbed
   and halved if large
150g thin asparagus spears
150g fine green beans
1 Little Gem lettuce, divided
   into leaves

DRESSING
4 tbsp lime juice
2 tbsp light muscovado sugar
1 tsp Thai fish sauce
1 red chilli, deseeded and
   finely chopped
2 tbsp chopped fresh coriander

cook's tip
• The leftover flavoured stock can be used to make a simple Thai-style soup. Simply strain it, then simmer briefly with egg noodles and a handful of finely shredded vegetables or chicken.

each serving provides
296kcals • 41g protein
3g fat of which 1g saturates
29g carbohydrate of which
10g sugars • 3g fibre
161mg sodium
130g vegetables

296 kcals

1.5 portions fruit & veg

low-fat treat

1 Place the chicken stock in a large saucepan and add the ginger, spring onions and coriander. Arrange the chicken fillets on the bottom of the pan and place the potatoes over them in a single layer. Reduce the heat, cover and simmer for 15 minutes.

2 Place a steamer basket on top of the pan and lay the asparagus and beans in it. Cover and simmer for a further 5–8 minutes until the vegetables are tender and the chicken is thoroughly cooked.

3 Meanwhile, make the dressing by whisking together all the ingredients in a jug. Arrange the lettuce leaves on a serving plate.

4 Lift out the chicken and vegetables with a draining spoon and slice the chicken. Arrange the chicken and vegetables over the lettuce leaves, then drizzle with the dressing. Serve immediately.

Japanese shabu shabu

Japanese-style fondue includes **thin strips of lean steak,** baby vegetables and udon noodles, all **cooked at the table** in simmering stock. Enjoy with Japanese dips and pickles for a **fun, one-pot meal.**

SERVES 4

PREPARATION TIME
20 minutes

COOKING TIME
(at table) 1 minute each forkful

400g lean rump or sirloin steak,
  thinly sliced
100g baby leeks, trimmed
100g baby carrots, scrubbed
100g shiitake mushrooms
125g baby pak choi, trimmed
250g udon or soup noodles
2 tsp toasted sesame oil
500ml beef stock
1 tsp soy sauce
1 tsp freshly grated root ginger

TO SERVE wasabi (Japanese horseradish), soy sauce, pickled ginger or sushi ginger, pickled vegetables

1 Wrap the steak in cling film and chill in the freezer for about 20 minutes until firm but not solid. This makes it easier to slice thinly.

2 Meanwhile cut the leeks into short pieces. Cut the carrots lengthways into thin strips. Wipe the mushrooms with damp kitchen paper, then halve each one. Cut each pak choi into quarters lengthways. Arrange all the vegetables on a large serving platter.

3 Cook the noodles in boiling water for about 2 minutes, or according to the pack instructions, until tender. Drain in a colander and rinse briefly under cold running water, then drain again. Put into a serving bowl, sprinkle with the sesame oil and toss gently.

4 With a very sharp, large knife, cut the slices of beef into thin strips about 1cm wide. Arrange on a serving platter.

5 Heat the stock with the soy sauce and grated ginger in a fondue pot. Set the pot over a fondue burner in the centre of the table, surrounded with the platters of vegetables and steak and bowl of noodles. Put the wasabi, soy sauce, pickled ginger and pickled vegetables in separate, small side dishes.

6 To serve, let each person dip pieces of meat and vegetables into the simmering stock, using fondue forks, swishing the food around briefly until lightly cooked. Eat with the wasabi (mix a tiny amount with soy sauce to make a 'hot' dip), ginger and pickles to taste.

7 When all the meat and vegetables have been cooked, add the noodles to the stock, then divide among serving bowls. Season to taste with any remaining sauces and pickles and enjoy as a soup.

1 portion fruit & veg

420 kcals

each serving provides 420kcals • 30g protein
11g fat of which 2g saturates • 54g carbohydrate of which 4g sugars
3g fibre • 104mg sodium • 106g vegetables

Steak & kidney pudding

This is a lighter version of the delicious traditional pudding. The richly flavoured meat filling is mixed with sweet root vegetables and the herbed pastry is made with light vegetable suet.

SERVES 4

PREPARATION TIME 30–35 minutes

COOKING TIME 3 hours

FILLING

250g lean beef stewing steak, cut into small pieces
100g beef kidney, cut into small pieces
2 tsp vegetable oil
2 leeks, trimmed and sliced
200g swede, peeled and cubed
175g carrots, peeled and thickly sliced
2 tsp plain flour
300ml beef stock

PASTRY

2 small slices wholemeal bread, about 50g
150g self-raising flour
½ tsp dried thyme
100g 'light' shredded vegetable suet

cook's tip

• The filling mixture can be made up to 1 day ahead, then covered and kept in the fridge. Allow to come to room temperature before using to fill the pastry-lined basin.

486 kcals

2 portions fruit & veg

prepare ahead

each serving provides

486kcals • 28g protein
23g fat of which 8.5g saturates
45g carbohydrate of which 8g sugars
8g fibre • 170mg sodium
162g vegetables

1 Heat a non-stick frying pan over a high heat. Add the beef and fry, stirring occasionally, for 4 minutes until browned on all sides. Transfer to a bowl, add the kidney and set aside.

2 Heat the oil in the pan, then add the leeks. Stir, then cover and cook gently for 4 minutes until starting to soften. Stir in the swede and carrots, cover and cook for a further 4 minutes until lightly browned. Add the beef and kidney and season to taste, then add the flour and toss well to coat. Pour in the stock and bring to the boil, stirring. Simmer for 2 minutes. Remove from the heat and set aside.

3 Tear the bread into pieces and put into a food processor. Pulse, to turn into fine crumbs. Add the flour, thyme and suet and season with a little salt and pepper. Pulse again to combine, then, with the motor running, pour in 4–6 tbsp cold water to form a soft dough.

4 On a lightly floured surface, roll out three quarters of the dough, to a circle large enough to line a 1 litre pudding basin. Line the basin carefully, and fill with the steak and kidney mixture. Trim excess pastry. Roll out the remaining pastry to form a lid, wet the edges of the dough and place on top of the filling, sealing the edges well with your fingers.

5 Cover the basin with a double thickness of foil, pleated in the middle and secured with string. Steam the pudding over simmering water for 3 hours. Serve hot.

variation

• For vegetarians, you could replace the steak and kidney with 250g button mushrooms, browning them lightly first. The steaming time could then be reduced to 2 hours.

5

4

8 spring onions, trimmed
200g pak choi, finely shredded
100g mange-tout, cut lengthways
    into fine strips
2 tbsp lime juice
1 tbsp Thai fish sauce (nam pla)
2 tsp toasted sesame oil
4 swordfish steaks, about 1cm thick
    and 140g each
1 lemongrass stalk, finely chopped
1 red chilli, deseeded and
    finely chopped
1 garlic clove, finely chopped
2cm piece of fresh root ginger,
    peeled and finely chopped
1 kaffir lime leaf, shredded
600ml vegetable stock, hot
225g mixed basmati and wild rice

Aromatic steamed Asian swordfish

Swordfish has a **distinctive, firm, meaty texture,** but can become dry if grilled. Here it is steamed with vegetables and spicy Thai flavourings in paper parcels to ensure the flesh stays **tender and succulent.**

1 Cut the spring onions across in half, then finely shred lengthways. Put into a bowl with the pak choi and mange-tout. Whisk together 1 tbsp of the lime juice with the fish sauce and sesame oil. Sprinkle 1 tbsp of this mixture over the greens and toss to lightly coat.

2 Cut out 4 x 30cm squares of baking parchment. Arrange one quarter of the shredded greens in the middle of each paper square. Top each with a swordfish steak.

3 Reserve 1 tsp of the chopped lemongrass. Put the rest in a mortar with the chilli, garlic and ginger and lightly crush with a pestle to release the flavouring oils. Stir in the remaining lime juice mixture, then spread this evenly over the fish. Scatter over the shredded lime leaf, then loosely fold over each paper to form a parcel. Twist the edges of the paper together to seal. Arrange the parcels in a steamer basket.

4 Pour the stock into a saucepan. Add the reserved lemongrass, remaining lime juice and the rice. Bring to the boil, then cover with a tight-fitting lid. Cook for 5 minutes. Place the steamer basket with the fish parcels on top, cover again and cook for a further 15 minutes. Remove from the heat and leave to stand for a further 2–3 minutes until the fish and rice are tender and the stock has been absorbed.

5 Carefully open the parcels, tip the juices into the rice and gently stir to mix. Spoon the rice onto warmed plates. Carefully transfer the fish and greens to the plates using a fish slice. Serve straight away.

393 kcals

each serving provides

393kcals • 31g protein • 8g fat of which 1.5g saturates • 52g carbohydrate of which 2g sugars 3g fibre • 347mg sodium • 98g vegetables

1 port fruit ve

25g unsalted butter
2 leeks, trimmed and thinly sliced
1 fennel bulb, trimmed and
    thinly sliced
1 garlic clove, crushed
125ml vegetable stock
4 tbsp Pernod
2kg fresh mussels in shell, cleaned
4 tbsp extra-thick single cream
2 tbsp chopped fresh parsley

cook's tip
• To clean mussels, scrub them well using a small, stiff brush under cold running water, to remove any grit, sand and barnacles. Pull off and discard the hairy 'beard' protruding from the side of the shells. Sharply tap any open mussels with the back of a knife, and discard any that don't close. Rinse and drain the mussels once again before use.

variation
• Instead of Pernod, use Greek ouzo or dry white wine.

each serving provides
284kcals • 25g protein
12g fat of which 6g saturates
11g carbohydrate of which
6g sugars • 3g fibre
493mg sodium
120g vegetables

1.5 portions fruit & veg

284 kcals

seafood special

Mussels with Pernod

The combination of Pernod and fennel adds a **wonderful aniseed flavour** to this **popular seafood dish,** which just needs some crusty wholemeal bread to mop up the tasty juices. Mussels are low in fat and rich in many minerals, **including iron and zinc.**

1 Melt the butter in a saucepan large enough to hold the mussels. Add the leeks, fennel and garlic and fry gently for 5 minutes.

2 Add the stock and bring to the boil, then cover and cook gently for 8–10 minutes until the vegetables are softened. Stir in the Pernod and bring back to the boil.

3 Add the mussels to the pan, cover tightly again and cook over a moderate heat for 4–5 minutes until the shells open, shaking the pan occasionally. Discard any unopened mussels.

4 Carefully pour the cooking liquid into a small pan and set the covered pan of mussels aside. Stir the cream and chopped parsley into the cooking liquid and heat gently, without boiling. Season to taste with freshly ground black pepper. Tip the mussels and vegetables into a large, warmed dish or tureen and pour over the sauce. Serve at once.

Sole and prawn parcels with couscous

For this elegant dish, fillets of sole are wrapped around a filling of prawns, asparagus and spring onions, subtly flavoured with lemon and ginger, then steamed over couscous with courgettes and peas.

SERVES 4
PREPARATION TIME 20 minutes, plus 3 minutes standing time before serving
COOKING TIME 5 minutes

15g unsalted butter
6 spring onions, trimmed and very finely sliced
15g fresh root ginger, peeled and grated
2 tbsp lemon juice
4 large lemon sole fillets, skinned
500ml vegetable stock, hot
1 strip lemon zest
3 sprigs of fresh thyme
2 courgettes, halved lengthways and sliced across
12 thin asparagus spears, trimmed
100g cooked peeled prawns
375g couscous
100g frozen petits pois, thawed

TO GARNISH lemon wedges

1 Melt the butter in a saucepan and gently cook the spring onions for 2–3 minutes until tender. Remove from the heat, stir in the ginger and cook for a few seconds in the residual heat, then stir in 1 tbsp of the lemon juice. Lay the sole fillets on a board, skinned-side up. Lightly season, then spoon the spring onion mixture down the middle of each fillet and pat down gently.

2 Pour the stock into the pan and add the lemon zest, thyme and courgettes. Bring back to the boil, then place the asparagus in a steamer basket over the stock. Cover and gently steam for 2 minutes, then remove from the heat. Remove the basket with the asparagus, then cover the pan with the lid, so that the stock doesn't evaporate.

3 Scatter the prawns over the sole fillets. Top each with 3 asparagus spears, placed at right angles to the fillets, then roll up from the tail end to enclose the filling. Place the stuffed sole in the steamer basket, with the ends tucked underneath.

4 Return the pan of stock to the heat and bring back to the boil. Tip the couscous and petits pois into the stock and stir, then place the steamer basket, holding the fish, back on top. Cover and steam on a very low heat for 3 minutes or until the fish is just cooked through. Remove from the heat and leave to stand for another 3 minutes.

5 Remove the lemon zest and thyme sprigs from the couscous and sprinkle with the remaining lemon juice, then spoon onto serving plates. Carefully lift the sole parcels onto the couscous and serve, garnished with lemon wedges.

each serving provides 429kcals • 41g protein 7g fat of which 2.5g saturates • 53g carbohydrate of which 3g sugars • 3g fibre • 543mg sodium • 121g vegetables

1.5 portions fruit & veg

429 kcals

Ricotta & spinach dumplings

Creamy little ricotta dumplings are **quite delicious** cooked with smoked tofu and vegetables in this **fragrant vegetarian dish** that's a cross between a soup and a stew.

SERVES 4 V ✱ (uncooked dumplings only)
PREPARATION TIME 35 minutes
COOKING TIME 25—30 minutes

225g baby spinach leaves, cooked, drained and finely chopped
grated zest of 1 lemon
4 spring onions, finely chopped
250g ricotta cheese
freshly grated nutmeg
1 egg
175g plain flour
220g firm smoked tofu
2 garlic cloves, crushed
1½ tbsp olive oil
1 leek, trimmed and thinly sliced
4 carrots, peeled and thinly sliced
1 litre vegetable stock
250g frozen baby broad beans
1 tbsp chopped fresh tarragon (optional)

cook's tip

• The shaped dumplings can be prepared ahead and chilled or frozen. Open-freeze until firm before packing, to prevent them from sticking. Cook from frozen in boiling stock, allowing an extra minute or so.

1 Mix the spinach, lemon zest, spring onions and ricotta cheese. Add nutmeg and seasoning to taste. Mix in the egg and then the flour to make a stiff mixture. Shape heaped teaspoons of the mixture into small round dumplings, wetting your hands under cold running water to prevent sticking. This will make 30–35 dumplings. Place on a baking tray and chill until ready to cook.

2 Preheat the grill to high. Place the tofu on a sheet of foil in the grill pan. Mix the garlic and oil in a large saucepan. Brush the tofu with some of this garlic oil, then turn it and brush the second side. Grill for 2–3 minutes on each side until browned. Remove and set aside.

3 Heat the garlic oil in the pan. Add the leek and carrots and cook, stirring often, for 5 minutes. Use a draining spoon to transfer the vegetables to a bowl.

4 Pour the stock into the pan and bring just to the boil. Cook the dumplings in batches, allowing 3–4 minutes each, until they are firm and float. They are best cooked a few at a time so that the water simmers constantly and they cook quickly without sticking. Use the draining spoon to remove them as they are cooked.

5 Add the broad beans and tarragon, if using, to the stock and replace the vegetables with all their juices. Bring to the boil and simmer for 5 minutes. Cut the tofu in half and then into slices. Put the dumplings into the soup and add the tofu. Heat gently for 1 minute. Ladle into large bowls to serve.

each serving provides 453kcals • 23g protein 20g fat of which 6g saturates • 48g carbohydrate of which 10g sugars • 9g fibre • 184mg sodium • 254g vegetables

3 portions fruit & veg

prepare ahead

453 kcals

Gnocchi with blue cheese, artichokes & walnuts

SERVES 4 V
PREPARATION TIME 10 minutes
COOKING TIME 5 minutes

2 tsp olive oil
500g pack of potato gnocchi
280g jar mixed or red
   pepper antipasto
400g can artichokes,
   drained and rinsed
75g walnut pieces
225g baby spinach leaves
100g Gorgonzola or Stilton
   cheese, crumbled

each serving provides

485kcals • 16g protein
25g fat of which 7g saturates
48g carbohydrate of which
1.5g sugars • 3.5g fibre
605mg sodium • 165g vegetables

485 kcals

2 portions fruit & veg

quick & easy

Gnocchi are Italian-style dumplings and they can be found alongside fresh pasta in supermarket chiller cabinets and delis. Combined with colourful and tasty ingredients, they make a sophisticated yet incredibly simple supper. Serve with crusty wholemeal bread.

1 Bring a large saucepan of lightly salted water to the boil. Add 1 tsp of the oil, then reduce the heat to a fast simmer. Tip in the gnocchi, bring back to the boil and simmer for 2–3 minutes, or according to the pack instructions, until tender. Gently stir halfway through cooking to ensure the gnocchi remain separate.

2 Meanwhile, drain the antipasto, cutting the pieces of pepper in half if large, and reserving 1 tbsp of the oil. Cut the artichokes into quarters.

3 Tip the gnocchi into a colander and leave to drain, covered with a lid to keep warm. Add the remaining olive oil to the pan and place over a moderate heat. Tip in the walnuts and lightly fry, stirring, for 1 minute. Stir in the antipasto with the reserved oil and the artichokes. Gently heat for 30 seconds, stirring, then mix in the gnocchi. Remove from the heat.

4 Put the spinach leaves in a bowl or on individual plates. Add the cheese to the gnocchi, quickly toss together, then spoon on top of the salad leaves. Serve straight away.

Penne with summer pesto

Wholewheat pasta is a good source of complex carbohydrate and has **a low GI value.** Tossed with **steamed summer vegetables** and a **fresh herb pesto,** perhaps made ahead, this makes a tempting and satisfying meal.

SERVES 4 Ⓥ
PREPARATION TIME 15–20 minutes
COOKING TIME 11–13 minutes

15g fresh flat-leaf parsley
15g fresh coriander
15g fresh mint
40g pine nuts
1 large garlic clove
85ml extra virgin olive oil
50g Parmesan or Italian-style hard cheese, freshly grated
3 courgettes, sliced
8 spring onions (white part only), sliced
200g shelled fresh peas
200g shelled fresh baby broad beans, or fine green beans, halved
350g wholewheat penne or fusilli (quills or spirals)

1 Remove large stalks from the herbs, then put the leaves in a small blender or food processor with the pine nuts, peeled garlic and a little of the oil. Blend until well mixed. Gradually add the remaining oil to form a fairly smooth paste. Add the Parmesan and freshly ground black pepper to taste and process briefly to mix. Set the pesto aside.

2 Bring a large pan of lightly salted water to the boil. Put the courgettes, spring onions, peas and broad beans or green beans in a steamer basket that will sit over the saucepan.

3 Add the pasta to the boiling water and bring back to the boil, then reduce the heat and set the steamer basket on top. Boil the pasta and steam the vegetables for 11–13 minutes until both are just tender.

4 Drain the pasta and turn it into a large serving bowl. Stir the pesto sauce through the pasta, then add the vegetables and toss gently to mix. Serve immediately.

Pasta carbonara with leeks

A fabulously quick egg and bacon pasta favourite with added vegetables to make it super healthy. It's surprising how little pancetta and Parmesan cheese you need to achieve a really deep, rich flavour.

SERVES 4
PREPARATION TIME 10 minutes
COOKING TIME 10–15 minutes

2 leeks, trimmed and sliced
85g smoked pancetta
300g fettuccine (flat ribbons)
175g frozen petits pois
4 eggs, lightly beaten
3 tbsp half-fat crème fraîche
50g Parmesan, freshly grated
2 tbsp chopped fresh parsley

variation
• Replace the pancetta with 85g smoked salmon or smoked lean ham, cut into strips. Neither needs cooking. Just toss into the cooked pasta at step 4.

1 Put a large pan of lightly salted water on to boil. Add the leeks and cook gently for 3 minutes until just tender. Remove the leeks to a plate using a draining spoon. Preheat the grill to medium.

2 Place the pancetta on the rack of the grill pan and grill for 2 minutes until beginning to crisp. Remove and break into rough pieces.

3 Bring the water back to the boil and if necessary, top up with a little more boiling water from the kettle. Drop the pasta into the water and cook for 6 minutes, or according to the pack instructions, until 'al dente'. Add the peas to the water for the last 3 minutes of the cooking time and bring back to the boil. Stir occasionally to make sure that no pasta is sticking to the base of the pan.

4 Lightly whisk the eggs with the crème fraîche and freshly ground black pepper to season. Drain the pasta and peas and immediately return them to the hot pan. Stir in the egg mixture, which will cook in the heat of the pasta. Then quickly add the pancetta, leeks and parsley and lightly toss everything together.

5 Sprinkle over the Parmesan and season to taste with more pepper. Serve immediately.

variation
• For a more traditional pesto, use fresh basil leaves rather than coriander and mint. Flaked almonds work well as an alternative to pine nuts.

each serving provides
636kcals • 26g protein
30g fat of which 6g saturates
71g carbohydrate of which
8.5g sugars • 14g fibre
215mg sodium • 200g vegetables

636 kcals

2.5 portions fruit & veg

each serving provides 574kcals • 30g protein
24g fat of which 8g saturates • 64g carbohydrate of which
5g sugars • 6g fibre • 188mg sodium • 124g vegetables

574 kcals

Italian style

1.5 portions fruit & veg

Tomato & prawn pasta with char-grilled peppers

Rice and corn pasta is great for those with a **wheat intolerance.** It cooks and tastes just like wheat pasta and comes in a variety of shapes. This is a **flavour-packed dish** and simply needs a **crunchy green salad** to complete the meal.

SERVES 4
PREPARATION TIME 10 minutes
COOKING TIME 10 minutes

250g rice and corn pasta spirals
2 large red peppers, deseeded
   and cut into wide strips
1 tbsp olive oil
16 raw tiger prawns, about
   225g in total
125ml tomato passata
2 tbsp vermouth or dry sherry
2 tbsp chopped fresh coriander

variations
• You could use scallops or sliced
squid in place of the prawns, cooking
them in the same way until just
cooked through.
• Use wheat pasta if preferred
and cook according to the pack
instructions.

1 Bring a large pan of lightly salted water to the boil. Add the pasta and cook
for 8–10 minutes, or according to the pack instructions, until tender.

2 Meanwhile, preheat a cast-iron, ridged griddle. Add the pepper strips and
cook for about 3 minutes on each side until lightly charred. Remove from
the heat and transfer to a bowl. Pour over the oil and toss to coat. Cover
and reserve.

3 Reheat the griddle and cook the prawns quickly for about 1 minute on each
side until pink and cooked through. Add to the peppers.

4 Drain the pasta in a colander. Pour the passata and the vermouth or sherry
into the pan and place over a low heat for 1 minute to warm through.

5 Return the pasta to the pan with the peppers, prawns and the chopped
coriander. Season to taste. Toss well to combine and serve at once.

each serving provides 328kcals • 16g protein
4g fat of which 0.5g saturates • 58g carbohydrate of which
10g sugars • 4g fibre • 213mg sodium • 125g vegetables

328 kcals

1.5 portions fruit & veg

super quick

Sardine, tomato & olive pasta
Brilliant for a mid-week meal,
this **punchy pasta dish** uses heart-healthy oily fish with a mixture of popular deli foods
– **salami, olives and sun-blush tomatoes** – for speed and convenience.

SERVES 4
PREPARATION TIME 20 minutes
COOKING TIME about 15 minutes

300g wholewheat conchiglie
   (pasta shells)
2 x 120g cans sardines
   in oil, drained
1 tsp extra virgin olive oil or oil
   from the tomatoes
8 thin slices Milano salami, about
   50g, cut into thin strips
400g can artichoke hearts, drained
   and quartered
8 sun-blush or mi-cuit tomatoes,
   drained and chopped
1 tbsp bottled capers, rinsed
12 stoned black olives, rinsed
1 tsp red wine or sherry vinegar
12 large fresh basil leaves,
   roughly torn

1 Cook the pasta in a large pan of boiling water for 10–12 minutes, or
according to the pack instructions, until al dente.

2 Meanwhile, split each sardine in half lengthways and remove the skins, if
preferred. A few minutes before the pasta is cooked, heat the oil in a large,
non-stick frying pan, add the salami strips and cook over a moderate heat
for a minute, until the fat from the salami starts to run. Stir in the
artichokes, tomatoes, capers and olives, then sprinkle over the vinegar.

3 Carefully place the sardine halves on top, then cover with a lid. Turn the
heat to the lowest possible setting, so that they warm through in the steam.

4 Drain the pasta, reserving a few spoons of the cooking water, then add
to the sardine mixture. Carefully toss together for 1–2 minutes until
everything is piping hot. If the mixture seems dry, add a little of the pasta
cooking water. Gently stir in the basil leaves, then serve straight away.

571 kcals

1 portion fruit & veg

deli dish

each serving provides 571kcals • 29g protein
28g fat of which 5g saturates • 55g carbohydrate of which
4g sugars • 7g fibre • 892mg sodium • 81g vegetables

Linguine with crab

This dish bursts with the colour and flavour of fresh herbs, zesty lemon and piquant chilli that enhance the sweet crab meat and pasta. It's an all-round star – easy to make in the time that it takes to cook some noodles.

SERVES 4
PREPARATION TIME 15 minutes
COOKING TIME 10 minutes

250g cherry tomatoes, halved
1 tbsp olive oil
350g linguine (flat ribbon noodles)
1 red chilli, deseeded and
    finely chopped
½ cucumber, finely diced
grated zest of 1 lemon
25g fresh herb fennel, chopped
20g fresh chives, snipped
200g fresh crab meat
100g wild rocket

TO SERVE lemon wedges

variations
• Add flaked smoked mackerel fillets, smoked salmon pieces or cooked, peeled prawns instead of the crab meat.
• If fresh crab is unavailable, substitute 2 x 150g cans of crab meat, drained.
• Add another red chilli for an extra kick.

1 Preheat the grill to high. Place the tomatoes, cut-sides up, on a heatproof dish. Sprinkle generously with freshly ground black pepper and trickle over the oil. Grill for 4–5 minutes or until browned on top but still firm. Turn off the heat and leave under the grill to keep warm.

2 Meanwhile, cook the linguine in a large pan of lightly salted boiling water for 10 minutes, or according to the pack instructions, until tender but still firm.

3 Combine the chilli, cucumber, lemon zest, fennel and chives in a large serving bowl. Add the crab meat and mix lightly.

4 Drain the cooked pasta, add to the crab mixture and toss together. Add the tomatoes and their juices together with the rocket and mix lightly, taking care not to break up the tomatoes. Serve at once, with lemon wedges to squeeze over the top.

each serving provides
412kcals • 22g protein • 8g fat of which 1g saturates • 68g carbohydrate of which 6g sugars • 4g fibre 224mg sodium • 160g vegetables

2 portions fruit & veg

412 kcals

special supper

SERVES 4
PREPARATION TIME 10 minutes
COOKING TIME 9 minutes

250g tagliatelle
250g thin asparagus, trimmed and cut into 3cm lengths
125g frozen baby broad beans
100g half-fat crème fraîche
grated zest of ½ lemon
2 tsp snipped fresh chives
2 tsp chopped fresh dill or fennel fronds
250g Arbroath hot-smoked trout fillets, flaked into pieces

variation

- For a vegetarian dish, replace the smoked trout with slices of bottled pimiento peppers.

Tagliatelle with asparagus & smoked trout

A perfect **last-minute pasta supper,** this is ideal for using **fresh asparagus** when in season. Half-fat crème fraîche provides **a creamy sauce,** but with less fat and fewer calories than the full-fat version.

1 Cook the tagliatelle in a large pan of boiling water for just 5 minutes.

2 Add the asparagus and broad beans to the pan with the pasta, bring back to the boil and cook for a further 4 minutes or until the pasta and vegetables are all just tender.

3 Meanwhile, combine the crème fraîche with the lemon zest and chopped herbs in a large serving bowl. Place the smoked trout pieces on top.

4 Drain the pasta and vegetables well and add to the bowl. Gently toss together until evenly mixed. Serve at once.

each serving provides 393kcals • 26g protein • 10g fat of which 4g saturates • 52g carbohydrate of which 4g sugars • 5g fibre • 758mg sodium • 94g vegetables

1 portion fruit & veg

393 kcals

seasonal treat

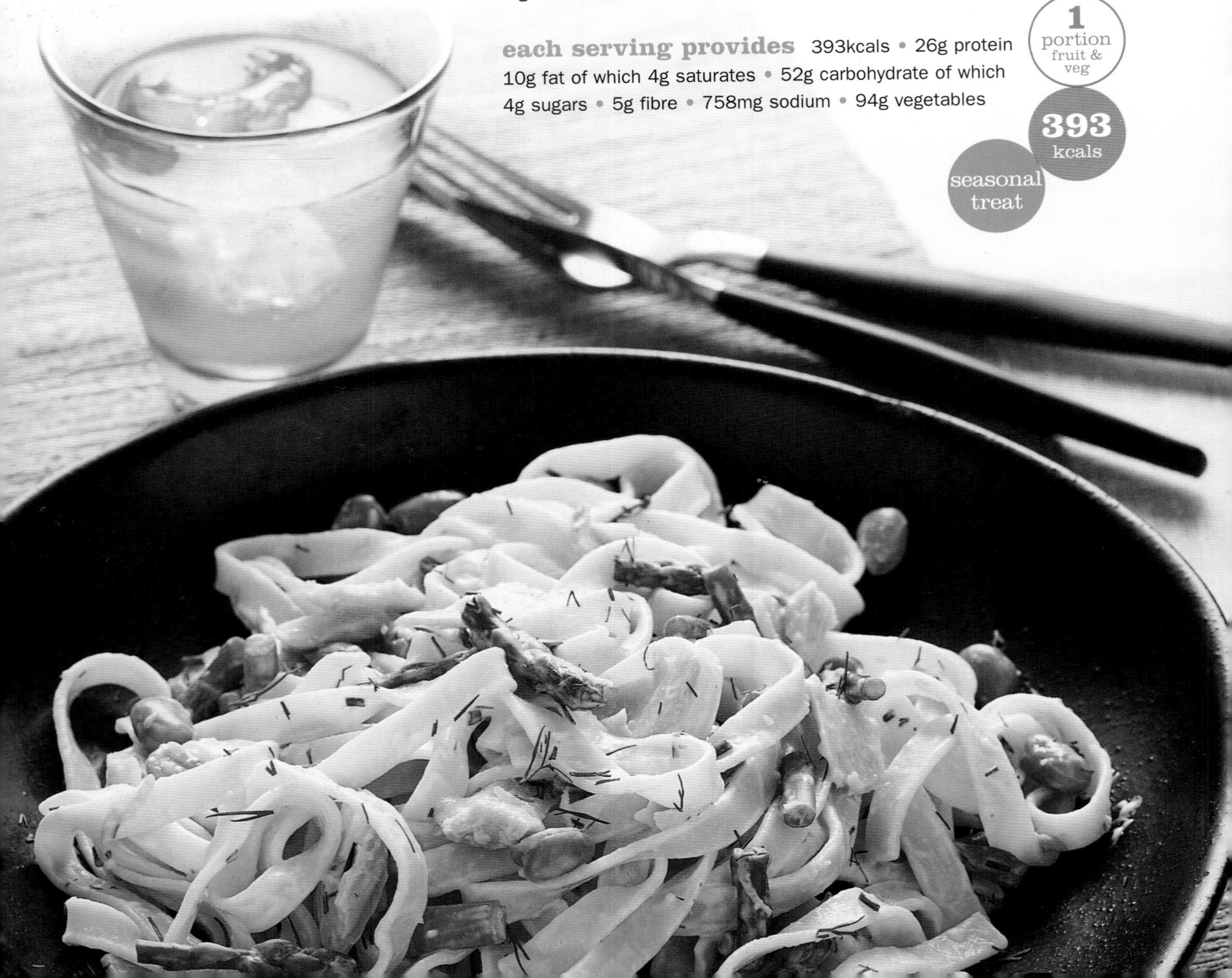

Chicken
tikka pasta
This simple pasta dish is sure to be a winner with all the family. It uses ready-cooked pieces of chicken tikka added to a tomato and yoghurt sauce that is tossed with fresh, chilled spinach and ricotta stuffed pasta.

SERVES 4
PREPARATION TIME 10 minutes
COOKING TIME 15 minutes

1 tbsp olive oil
1 red onion, finely chopped
450ml passata with garlic and herbs
300g ready-cooked chicken tikka
  pieces, roughly sliced
2 x 250g packs fresh spinach and
  ricotta tortelloni or capelletti
200g natural Greek yoghurt
2 tbsp chopped fresh coriander

TO GARNISH sprigs of fresh
  coriander (optional)

variation
• Use half-fat crème fraîche in place
of Greek yoghurt.

1 Heat the oil in a small saucepan, add the onion and cook gently for 8–10 minutes until softened. Add the passata and chicken pieces and bring gently to the boil, stirring. Reduce the heat, cover and simmer for 2–3 minutes, stirring occasionally.

2 Meanwhile, cook the pasta in a large saucepan of lightly salted, boiling water for 1–2 minutes, or according to the pack instructions, until tender. Drain thoroughly, then return the pasta to the pan.

3 Stir the yoghurt and chopped coriander into the passata mixture and heat through gently, stirring constantly.

4 Pour the passata sauce over the cooked pasta and toss gently to mix, then tip into a serving dish and serve immediately, garnished with sprigs of coriander, if liked.

each serving provides 424kcals • 31g protein 14g fat of which 4g saturates • 46g carbohydrate of which 12g sugars • 3g fibre • 742mg sodium • 150g vegetables

1.5 portions fruit & veg

424 kcals

easy family meal

Oven bakes

Healthy bakes can often be prepared ahead and then just popped in the oven and left to cook – making them ideal for easy family meals or informal entertaining. Give your traditional favourites a vegetable boost with the Healthiest ever lasagne, or New toad in the hole. A range of pasta bakes, stuffed vegetables and fish cakes provide comfort food that will go down a treat at any time of year, while making your five-a-day target easily achievable.

variation

- Large beef tomatoes can be filled with the same mixture. Slice a lid off each tomato (allow 2 per serving) and scoop out the seeds and core. The tomatoes do not need to be cooked in boiling water. Chop the cores and add to the stir-fry lamb mixture with 1 finely chopped onion.

Spicy lamb & sultana stuffed onions

Stuffing vegetables is a great way of using them to make a **healthy one-dish meal.** This stuffing, of spiced lean lamb and bulghur wheat, has a distinct **Middle Eastern flavour.**

SERVES 4 (makes 8)
PREPARATION TIME 1 hour
COOKING TIME 30 minutes

8 large Spanish onions,
  about 2kg in total
4 tbsp sultanas
4 tbsp bulghur wheat
3 garlic cloves
1 tbsp olive oil
400g lean minced lamb
2 tsp ground cumin
½ tsp ground cinnamon
1 tsp ground coriander
¼ tsp cayenne pepper

each serving provides

461kcals • 28g protein
12g fat of which 0.5g saturates
65g carbohydrate of which
41g sugars • 7.5g fibre
20mg sodium • 518g fruit
and vegetables

461 kcals

5+ portions fruit & veg

1 Preheat the oven to 190°C/gas 5. Carefully peel the onions and trim off the hairy root end so that the onions stand upright. Bring a large pan of water to the boil, add the onions, bring the water back to the boil and cook for 10 minutes. Drain well, reserving 300ml of the water, then leave the onions to cool.

2 Put the sultanas and bulghur wheat into a heatproof bowl. Pour over the hot, reserved onion water, so the wheat is well covered. Leave to soak for 20 minutes until the water has been absorbed. Drain if necessary.

3 Meanwhile, slice off the top 1cm of each onion. Scoop out the centre of each onion with a grapefruit spoon or pointed teaspoon. Finely chop the onion lids, centres and the garlic. (This can be done in a food processor.)

4 Heat the oil in a non-stick frying pan over a medium heat. Add the minced lamb and fry for about 5 minutes, stirring frequently with a wooden spoon, until the meat is lightly coloured.

5 Push the cooked meat to one side of the pan, then lower the heat and add the cumin, cinnamon, coriander and cayenne to the pan. Stir-fry for 20 seconds, then add the chopped onion mixture and stir-fry for 1 minute. Stir in the meat mixture and cook over a medium heat for 10 minutes, stirring occasionally. Stir in the soaked bulghur mixture and season to taste.

6 Sit the onions in a large, lightly greased roasting tin and fill with the lamb mixture. Cover with foil and bake for 20 minutes, then uncover and bake for a further 10 minutes. Serve immediately.

Peppers stuffed with beef & tomatoes

Choose large, firm peppers – they make the perfect container for a herby beef, tomato and fresh breadcrumb mixture, topped with cheese.

SERVES 2 as a main meal, or 4 as a light meal with bread and a simple side salad.

PREPARATION TIME 25–30 minutes

COOKING TIME 40 minutes

- 50g fresh wholemeal breadcrumbs
- 4 large yellow peppers
- 1 tbsp olive oil
- 1 onion, finely chopped
- 350g lean minced beef
- 1 garlic clove, crushed
- 200g can chopped tomatoes
- 1 tbsp chopped fresh sage or 1 tsp dried
- 1 tsp chopped fresh rosemary or ½ tsp dried
- 300ml vegetable stock, hot
- 40g mature Cheddar cheese, grated
- 2 fennel bulbs, cut into 5mm slices lengthways

variation

• Use the beef mixture to fill courgettes. Cut 4 large courgettes, about 200g each, in half lengthways. Scoop out the centres with a teaspoon. Fill with the beef mixture. Arrange the courgettes in a baking dish, sprinkle with the cheese, then cover with foil and bake for 40 minutes. Remove the foil for the last 10 minutes to brown the cheese.

1 Preheat the oven to 190°C/gas 5. Spread the breadcrumbs on a plate and leave them to dry a little while preparing the rest of the ingredients.

2 Cut the tops off the peppers and scoop out the seeds and membranes. Blanch the peppers and their tops in a saucepan of boiling water for 1 minute. Remove from the heat. Lift out the peppers with a draining spoon, then let them drain, cut-side down, on kitchen paper.

3 Heat the oil in a large frying pan over a medium heat. Add the onion and cook for 10 minutes, stirring frequently, until softened. Turn up the heat a little, then add the beef and garlic and fry, stirring and breaking up the meat with a wooden spoon, until browned and crumbly. Add the tomatoes, herbs and 3 tbsp of the stock. Cook for a further minute, then remove from the heat and stir in the breadcrumbs. Season to taste.

4 Stand the peppers upright in a lightly oiled, large ovenproof dish or roasting tin, spoon in the beef mixture and press it down gently. Sprinkle with the grated cheese and replace the tops on the peppers. Scatter the sliced fennel in a single layer around the peppers and pour the rest of the stock into the dish or tin.

5 Cover the dish with foil and bake for 40 minutes or until the peppers and fennel are tender, basting halfway through cooking with the stock in the dish. Serve hot or warm.

each serving (for 4) provides 300kcals
27g protein • 12g fat of which 5g saturates • 21g carbohydrate
of which 15g sugars • 8g fibre • 228mg sodium • 400g vegetables

5 portions fruit & veg

easily doubled

300 kcals

Scottish stovies with lamb

This hearty dish of **lean lamb** layered with **delicious root vegetables** and baked in a covered casserole is perfect for busy lives. Once assembled, **it can simply be left to cook** and won't be spoilt if left in the oven a little longer.

SERVES 4 *
PREPARATION TIME 20 minutes
COOKING TIME 2 hours

450g lean boneless lamb (such as leg), trimmed of excess fat
1 tbsp vegetable oil
750g floury potatoes (such as King Edwards), peeled
350g turnips, peeled
2 large leeks, trimmed
2 tsp chopped fresh thyme or ½ tsp dried
2 tbsp chopped fresh parsley
1 bay leaf
900ml lamb or vegetable stock, hot

variation
• Use sliced carrots or swede instead of the turnip, if preferred.

1 Preheat the oven to 150°C/gas 2. Cut the lamb into 3cm chunks. Heat the oil in a large flameproof casserole, with a capacity of at least 2 litres, over a moderate heat. Fry the lamb in batches until it is browned on all sides. Remove using a draining spoon and set aside.

2 Cut the potatoes, turnips and leeks into slices about 4mm thick. Place a generous layer of potato slices over the base of the casserole, then top with a layer of turnip slices, followed by half the leeks. Lightly season between the layers with a little salt and freshly ground black pepper and scatter with the thyme and half the parsley.

3 Place the lamb on top of the leeks, tucking in the bay leaf. Top with the remaining leeks, followed by the rest of the turnip slices. Finish with the remaining potato slices, arranging them so that they overlap slightly.

4 Pour over the stock – don't worry if it doesn't completely cover the vegetables as they will cook in the steam. Cover with a tight-fitting lid and bake for 2 hours or until the meat and vegetables are tender and cooked. Just before serving, sprinkle the top with the remaining chopped parsley.

each serving provides
372kcals • 29g protein • 12g fat of which 0.5g saturates
39g carbohydrate of which 7g sugars • 7g fibre
29mg sodium • 188g vegetables

2 portions fruit & veg

372 kcals

prepare ahead

variation
• For a vegetarian dish, use 350g mushrooms and 1 finely chopped fennel bulb and cook them with the rest of the vegetables for about 15 minutes. Omit the meat and use vegetable stock. Add 2 tbsp tomato purée, simmer for 30 minutes, then add 200g shredded spinach and 2 x 400g cans of chickpeas. Stir for 1–2 minutes until the spinach has wilted, then layer with the pasta and bake.

each serving provides
619kcals • 36g protein
18g fat of which 6.5g saturates
77g carbohydrate of which
22g sugars • 6g fibre
230mg sodium
293g vegetables

3.5 portions fruit & veg

619 kcals

prepar ahead

Healthiest-ever lasagne

Lasagne is everybody's favourite but it can be very high in fat, especially if shop-bought. This version includes **plenty of fresh vegetables** and **lean minced steak** in its scrumptious filling. Serve with a crisp green salad.

SERVES 4 *
PREPARATION TIME about 1 hour, plus 10 minutes standing before serving
COOKING TIME 40–45 minutes

2 tbsp olive oil
1 large onion, finely chopped
4 carrots, peeled and finely chopped
2 celery sticks, finely chopped
2 garlic cloves, crushed
350g lean minced steak
150g button mushrooms, chopped
300ml beef stock
150ml dry red wine or extra
   beef stock
400g can chopped tomatoes
2 tsp tomato purée
1 tsp dried oregano or mixed herbs
3 tbsp chopped fresh parsley
10 sheets dried no-pre-cook lasagne
40g mature Cheddar cheese, grated

SAUCE
3 tbsp cornflour
600ml semi-skimmed milk
pinch of freshly grated nutmeg

1 Heat the oil in a large saucepan over a low heat. Add the onion and fry gently for 5 minutes. Add the carrots, celery and garlic and cook for a further 5 minutes until the onion is soft and just beginning to colour.

2 Turn up the heat a little, then add the beef and cook, stirring and breaking up the meat with a wooden spoon until browned and crumbly. Add the mushrooms and cook for 1 more minute. Stir in the stock, wine or extra stock, tomatoes, tomato purée and dried herbs. Bring to the boil, then cover and gently simmer over a low heat for 45 minutes, stirring occasionally. Stir in the parsley and season to taste.

3 Preheat the oven to 180°C/gas 4. To make the sauce, mix the cornflour to a smooth paste with a little of the milk. Heat the remaining milk to boiling point, then pour some of it onto the cornflour mixture, stirring. Return this to the milk in the saucepan. Bring to the boil, stirring until the sauce thickens, then simmer for 2 minutes. Stir in the nutmeg and season to taste.

4 Spoon half the meat sauce over the base of a 3 litre ovenproof dish or roasting tin. Cover with a layer of lasagne, then spoon over the remaining meat sauce and cover with another layer of pasta. Pour over the white sauce to cover the lasagne completely. Scatter over the grated cheese.

5 Place the dish on a baking sheet and bake for 40–45 minutes until the lasagne is bubbling and the top is lightly browned. Remove from the oven and leave to settle for 10 minutes before serving.

Sausage, pasta & bean bake

This **hearty, colourful** and **very nutritious** main dish is perfect for an easy mid-week meal, and can be **rustled up quickly** from store-cupboard ingredients. Serve with a green salad.

SERVES 4
PREPARATION TIME 30 minutes
COOKING TIME 25–30 minutes

400g good quality pork sausages
1 large onion, diced
2 large celery sticks, sliced
250g quick-cook penne pasta (pasta quills)
400g can mixed beans, drained and rinsed
200g can sweetcorn, drained
500g jar or carton passata
1 tbsp Worcestershire sauce

variations

• For a vegetarian version of this dish, you can replace the sausages with chunks of Quorn or vegetarian sausages.
• Alternatively, omit the sausages and replace with cheese, adding diced mozzarella to the mixture, and sprinkle the top with a little mature Cheddar cheese.
• Instead of the canned mixed beans use a can of baked beans in chilli sauce, and omit the Worcestershire sauce.

1 Preheat the oven to 200°C/gas 6. Fry the sausages in a non-stick frying pan on a moderate heat, turning occasionally, for 12–15 minutes, until golden brown. Remove and cool slightly, then slice thickly.

2 Add the onions to the pan and fry, stirring often, for 4–5 minutes, until softened. Add the celery and fry for a further 2 minutes.

3 Combine the onions and celery, sausages, penne, beans and sweetcorn in a large ovenproof dish, about 33 x 25cm in size. In a large jug, mix together the passata, Worcestershire sauce and 250ml water. Pour over the ingredients in the dish.

4 Cover the dish closely with a lid or foil, then bake for 25–30 minutes until the pasta is tender and most of the liquid absorbed. Serve immediately as the pasta will go soggy if left to stand.

611 kcals

3 portions fruit & veg

easy supper

each serving provides
611kcals • 29g protein
21g fat of which 7g saturates
79g carbohydrate of which
15g sugars • 7g fibre
1190mg sodium • 259g vegetables

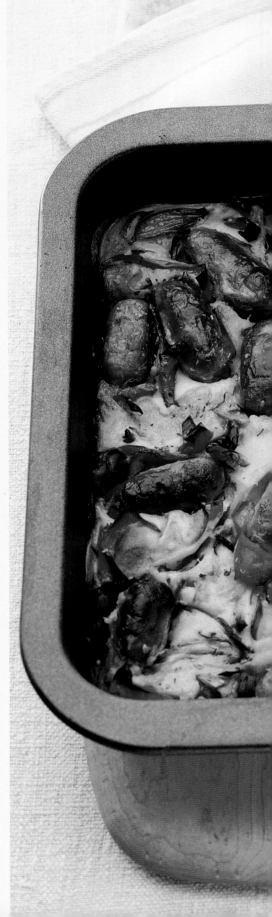

New toad in the hole

Red onions, sweet red peppers and aromatic herbs bring extra flavour and higher nutrient value to this popular family favourite, as well as turning it into an easy, all-in-one dish. Serve puffed and golden, straight from the oven, with a mixed side salad.

SERVES 4
PREPARATION TIME 20 minutes
COOKING TIME 50–55 minutes

2 large red peppers, deseeded
   and thickly sliced
2 red onions, halved and
   finely sliced
2 tsp dried herbes de Provence
25g stoned black olives,
   sliced (optional)
2 tsp olive oil
8 good-quality Cumberland
   sausages
125g plain flour
1 egg
300ml semi-skimmed milk

variations

If you have some fresh thyme or sage, use 1 tbsp chopped in place of the dried herbs.

For a vegetarian version, replace the sausages with 2 x 400g cans soya beans, drained and rinsed. Scatter the beans over the roasted vegetables at the beginning of step 4, then pour over the batter.

1 Preheat the oven to 200°C/gas 6. Mix the peppers, onions, herbs, olives, if using, and olive oil in a deep roasting tin that measures about 30 x 23cm. Spread out the mixture evenly.

2 Gently squeeze and twist each sausage in the middle, then snip through to make 16 short, plump sausages. Arrange these on top of the vegetables in the tin. Bake for 15 minutes or until the sausages are beginning to brown.

3 Meanwhile, sift the flour into a bowl and make a well in the middle. Add the egg and a little of the milk. Whisk, gradually incorporating the flour to make a thick, lump-free batter. Slowly whisk in the remaining milk to make a smooth batter.

4 Turn the sausages and the vegetables. Pour in the batter and bake for a further 35–40 minutes until the batter is risen and golden brown and the sausages are nicely browned. Serve at once.

each serving provides

465kcals • 24g protein • 23g fat of which 8g saturates 43g carbohydrate of which 13g sugars • 3g fibre
876mg sodium • 121g vegetables

465 kcals

healthy twist

1.5 portions fruit & veg

SERVES 4
PREPARATION TIME 20 minutes
COOKING TIME 40 minutes

**750g potatoes, peeled and
thinly sliced**
**300g celeriac, peeled and
thinly sliced**
350g leeks, trimmed and sliced
**250g turkey breast steak, cut
widthways into thin strips**
**1 tbsp chopped fresh thyme
or ½ tsp dried**
250ml chicken stock, hot
**75g Stilton or other firm blue
cheese, crumbled**
25g butter, cut into small pieces

TO GARNISH fresh thyme leaves

each serving provides

354kcals • 25g protein
13g fat of which 8g saturates
35.5g carbohydrate of which
3.5g sugars • 6g fibre
299g sodium
120g vegetables

354 kcals

1.5 portions fruit & veg

Turkey & blue cheese gratin
A layered bake of **sliced potatoes, celeriac and leeks** with turkey, topped with cheese, makes a **perfect dish for an autumn day.** Serve with a tomato and green bean salad and some crusty bread.

1 Preheat the oven to 200°C/gas 6. Place the potatoes and celeriac in a pan of lightly salted water, cover and bring to the boil over a moderate heat. Remove the lid and simmer for 3 minutes or until starting to soften. Remove from the heat and drain well.

2 Spread about a third of the potatoes and celeriac over the bottom of a 2 litre baking dish. Scatter over about half the leeks, turkey strips and thyme. Season with freshly ground black pepper.

3 Continue layering the potatoes and celeriac with the remaining leeks, turkey and thyme. Finish with a layer of the remaining potatoes and celeriac.

4 Pour over the stock, then scatter the crumbled cheese and butter over the top. Cover with foil and bake for 20 minutes.

5 Remove the foil from the dish and continue to bake for a further 20 minutes or until the cheese has melted and the top is golden and bubbling.

variation
• In place of the turkey you could use the same amount of shredded sliced ham, or a mixture of ham and turkey.

Chicken parmigiana

An **easy, Italian-style dish** of chicken breasts, oven-baked with a **low-fat, chunky vegetable sauce,** with a Parmesan topping. Serve with warm ciabatta or baguette to mop up the delicious sauce.

SERVES 4
PREPARATION TIME 30 minutes
COOKING TIME 25 minutes

2 tbsp olive oil
1 small onion, finely chopped
2 garlic cloves, crushed
200g small mushrooms, quartered
1 large aubergine, diced
450g plum tomatoes,
   roughly chopped
15g fresh basil, roughly torn
4 skinless, chicken breast fillets,
   about 500g in total
2 tbsp freshly grated
   Parmesan cheese

variations

• Replace the mushrooms with a 400g can of artichoke hearts, drained and quartered, or with 4 courgettes, diced.
• This dish would also work well using pheasant breasts or turkey escalopes.

1 Preheat the oven to 190°C/ gas 5. Heat the oil in a deep frying pan or flameproof casserole, add the onion and garlic and stir for 2 minutes over a medium heat. Add the mushrooms and cook for 3–4 minutes until lightly coloured, stirring frequently.

2 Stir in the diced aubergine, cook for 2 minutes, then add the chopped tomatoes and stir over a medium-high heat for 2 minutes to combine. Reduce the heat and leave the sauce to simmer for 15 minutes until thick. Stir in the basil and season to taste.

3 If using a flameproof casserole, lay the chicken in the sauce. Alternatively, arrange the chicken in a single layer in a deep ovenproof baking dish or casserole and spoon the sauce over. Cover and bake for 25 minutes or until the chicken is thoroughly cooked.

4 Towards the end of the cooking time, preheat the grill. Uncover the chicken and sprinkle over the cheese. Put the dish under the grill for 1–2 minutes until the cheese is melted and bubbling.

each serving provides 253kcals • 35g protein • 9g fat of which 2g saturates • 8g carbohydrate of which 7g sugars 4g fibre • 128mg sodium • 285g vegetables

253 kcals

3.5 portions fruit & veg

Chicken & broccoli pasta bake

A healthy, **quick and easy family meal,** this combines **ready-cooked chicken and wholewheat pasta** in a cheesy sauce. Including little broccoli florets is a great way to encourage children to enjoy this **super-nourishing vegetable** as part of a five-a-day target.

SERVES 4
PREPARATION TIME 20 minutes
COOKING TIME 20 minutes

**250g wholewheat penne
   (or other pasta shapes)**
250g broccoli
2 leeks, sliced
**4 cooked chicken breasts,
   about 350g in total**
500ml semi-skimmed milk
30g cornflour
**85g mature cheese, such as
   Gouda, smoked Cheddar or
   vintage Cheddar, grated**
12 cherry tomatoes, halved
**20g Parmesan or Pecorino cheese,
   freshly grated**
1 tsp dried oregano
**3 tbsp dried wholemeal
   breadcrumbs**

variations

• Cubes of cooked ham could
be used instead of the chicken
and any other of your family's
favourite vegetables substituted
for the broccoli.
• For a vegetarian meal, replace the
chicken with 2 cans of mixed pulses,
drained and rinsed.

each serving provides

594kcals • 51g protein
16g fat of which 8g saturates
65.5g carbohydrate of which
11.5g sugars • 8.5g fibre
512mg sodium • 144g vegetables

comfort food · **594** kcals · **1.5** portions fruit & veg

1 Preheat the oven to 190°C/
gas 5. Cook the pasta in a
large pan of boiling water for
10–12 minutes or according to
the pack instructions, until al
dente. Trim the broccoli into
small florets and slice the stalks.
Add all the broccoli and the
leeks to the pasta for the last
5 minutes or so of cooking.

2 When just tender, drain well,
reserving about 250ml of the
cooking water. Tip the pasta and
vegetables into a large ovenproof
dish. Skin the chicken and cut
into small chunks and add to
the dish.

3 Blend a little of the milk with the
cornflour to a paste in a jug. Heat
the remaining milk and reserved
cooking water in the same pan
until on the point of boiling. Pour
about a cupful onto the cornflour
paste and stir well, then pour this
into the simmering milky water
and stir briskly with a wooden
spoon until it thickens. Remove
from the heat and mix in the
mature cheese. Season to taste.

4 Pour the sauce over the pasta,
stirring gently with a fork.
Nestle the tomato halves into
the mixture, then sprinkle
with the Parmesan, oregano
and breadcrumbs. Bake for
20 minutes until bubbling and
crispy on top. Serve hot.

West Indian pepperpot with rice

Pepperpots are slowly cooked, spicy one-pot meals prepared on all the Caribbean islands. This version, using chicken rather than the more traditional fatty pieces of pork, also includes rice for an easy, oven-baked meal.

SERVES 4

PREPARATION TIME 30 minutes, plus 5 minutes standing before serving

COOKING TIME 30 minutes

100g spicy sausage (such as chorizo or salami), diced and casing removed, if necessary
2 tbsp vegetable oil
4 skinless chicken thighs, about 500g in total
1 large onion, chopped
1 red pepper, deseeded and chopped
1 green pepper, deseeded and chopped
2 garlic cloves, crushed
1 green chilli, deseeded and finely chopped
½ tsp cayenne pepper, or to taste
200g long-grain rice
400g can kidney beans, drained and rinsed
500ml chicken or vegetable stock, hot

TO GARNISH chopped fresh parsley

TO SERVE hot pepper sauce

each serving provides

556kcals • 32g protein
21g fat of which 5g saturates
64g carbohydrate of which
10g sugars • 6.5g fibre
461mg sodium • 163g vegetables

2 portions fruit & veg

556 kcals

hot & spicy

1 Preheat the oven to 200°C/ gas 6. Fry the sausage in a flameproof casserole over a moderately high heat for 5 minutes, stirring frequently. Remove, using a draining spoon and set aside on kitchen paper to drain.

2 Add 1 tbsp of the oil to the sausage fat remaining in the casserole. Add the chicken pieces and fry for about 3 minutes to colour, moving them around occasionally so they don't stick to the pan. Remove with tongs or a draining spoon and drain on kitchen paper with the sausage.

3 Add the onion, peppers, garlic and chilli to the casserole and stir for about 5 minutes, until the onions are tender, but not brown. Stir in the cayenne pepper, then add the rice and stir until the grains are lightly coated in oil. Stir in the kidney beans, then return the sausage and chicken to the casserole and give all the ingredients a good stir.

4 Add the stock and bring to the boil, then cover the casserole and transfer to the oven. Cook for 20 minutes. Turn the chicken pieces over and stir, then cover again and return to the oven to cook for a further 10 minutes until the chicken is cooked through, the stock is absorbed and the rice is tender.

5 Remove from the oven and leave to stand, covered, for 5 minutes, then fluff up the rice with a fork. Sprinkle with parsley and serve with hot pepper sauce, to be sprinkled over each individual serving.

variation
• For a vegetarian option, omit the chicken and increase the total number of peppers to 4. Callaloo greens are often included in traditional Jamaican recipes, but finely chopped spinach makes a good substitute.

cook's tip
• If you don't have a flameproof casserole that can be used on the hob as well as in the oven, start the cooking in a large saucepan, then transfer the contents to an ovenproof casserole or covered baking dish.

SERVES 4
PREPARATION TIME 20 minutes,
plus 30 minutes chilling
COOKING TIME 20 minutes

500g potatoes (such as Desirée
   or Maris Piper) peeled and
   cut into chunks
2 tbsp low-fat soft cheese or ricotta
125g peeled prawns, thawed if
   frozen, and roughly chopped
170g can white crab meat,
   well drained
2 spring onions, chopped
few dashes Tabasco sauce,
   or to taste
125g fresh leaf spinach
4 large tomatoes

BREADCRUMB COATING
30g wholemeal flour
1 egg, beaten
75g dried wholemeal breadcrumbs
1 tsp dried thyme or oregano
2 tbsp olive oil, warmed

Crab & prawn cakes

Homemade fishcakes are always a special treat.
They are the **ultimate all-in-one dish,** as they contain **fish, potato and vegetables.**
These can be made ahead and chilled, ready to bake when you need them.

1 Cook the potatoes in a pan of boiling water for 12–15 minutes until tender.
Drain and return to the pan over the heat to dry out a little, then mash until
smooth. Beat in the soft cheese or ricotta. Season and set aside to cool.

2 Pat the prawns dry with kitchen paper, then chop roughly. Mix with the crab,
chopped onions and Tabasco sauce.

3 Cook the spinach in the microwave in a covered bowl until just wilted.
Cool, then squeeze dry and chop roughly. When the potato mixture is cold,
mix with the seafood and spinach. Chill for about 30 minutes.

4 Preheat the oven to 190°C/gas 5. Shape the seafood mixture into 4 large
cakes, dipping your hands in a little flour if necessary.

5 Put the flour in a shallow bowl, the beaten egg in another shallow bowl and
the breadcrumbs mixed with the dried herbs in a third. Coat the fishcakes
evenly first in flour, then in beaten egg and, finally, in the crumbs.

6 Halve the tomatoes and place around the fishcakes on the baking tray.
Season and sprinkle with any leftover crumbs. Brush the fishcakes with the
warmed oil, then bake for 20 minutes until they are crisp and the tomatoes
softened. Allow to stand for 3–4 minutes before serving.

variation
• Use flaked cooked cod, haddock
or salmon instead of the crab
and prawns.

each serving provides
383kcals • 25g protein
13g fat of which 3g saturates
45g carbohydrate of which 6g sugars
4.5g fibre • 508mg sodium
139g vegetables

1.5 portions fruit & veg

383 kcals

prepare ahead

Salmon & asparagus lasagne

It's always interesting to ring the changes with a familiar dish. This is an attractive and healthy variation on lasagne, with flakes of salmon and chopped asparagus in a light lemon and herb sauce layered with the pasta. It's perfect for when asparagus is in season.

SERVES 4
PREPARATION TIME 40 minutes
COOKING TIME 30–35 minutes

400g skinless salmon fillet
450ml fish stock
small bunch of fresh dill
6 black peppercorns
grated zest and juice of 1 lemon
750g fresh asparagus, trimmed
25g butter
3 tbsp flour
300ml semi-skimmed milk
3 tbsp half-fat crème fraîche
300g fresh lasagne, about 12 sheets
2 tbsp freshly grated
   Parmesan cheese

666 kcals

1.5 portions fruit & veg

each serving provides
666kcals • 40g protein
25g fat of which 9g saturates
75g carbohydrate of which
10g sugars • 5g fibre
170mg sodium • 150g vegetables

1 Preheat the oven to 200°C/gas 6. Put the salmon fillet in a shallow pan in which it fits snugly and add the stock, the stems from the dill (reserve the fronds for the sauce), the peppercorns and lemon juice. Bring to the boil, then simmer gently for 8–10 minutes until barely cooked. Remove the fish from the stock and, when cool enough to handle, break up into coarse flakes. Strain the stock and discard the flavourings. Set aside.

2 Steam the trimmed asparagus for about 3 minutes until barely tender. Cut off and reserve the tips, then chop the stalks into short pieces.

3 To make the sauce, melt the butter in a medium saucepan and stir in the flour, then gradually stir in the reserved stock and the milk. Bring the mixture to the boil, stirring constantly, to make a smooth light sauce. Simmer for 1 minute, then remove from the heat. Add the lemon zest, the chopped dill, crème fraîche and seasoning to taste. Stir in the salmon and chopped asparagus stalks.

4 Arrange 3 sheets of lasagne over the bottom of a greased lasagne dish or large shallow ovenproof dish, of about 1.5 litre capacity. Spoon over a third of the salmon mixture. Repeat the layers twice more, then cover with the remaining lasagne sheets. Top with the reserved asparagus tips and press down gently all over, so the sauce comes up to moisten the top layer of lasagne.

5 Cover the dish with greased foil or a lid, then bake for 30–35 minutes until bubbling. Uncover the dish, sprinkle with the Parmesan cheese and serve immediately.

variation
• Use undyed smoked haddock instead of salmon and replace the asparagus with tiny broccoli florets (there is no need to cook them before layering up).

Cheesy haddock & potato bake

Here's a really simple supper dish of smoked haddock with a **crispy topping of sliced potatoes finished with cheese.** Preferably, choose undyed smoked fish fillets – **a pale gold colour** rather than the tan-coloured dyed fish. Peas and leeks add vitamins, minerals and fibre.

SERVES 4
PREPARATION TIME 20 minutes
COOKING TIME 35–40 minutes

600g small new potatoes, scrubbed
500g skinless, smoked
haddock fillets
1 tbsp snipped fresh chives
150ml fish stock, hot
200g fresh shelled or frozen peas
4 small leeks, about 200g in total,
trimmed and thinly sliced
50g extra mature Cheddar
cheese, grated

cook's tip
• To prepare ahead, use chilled rather than hot stock to assemble the dish, then cover tightly and chill for up to 12 hours before cooking. Add an extra 5 minutes to the cooking time.

1 Preheat the oven to 190°C/gas 5. Put the potatoes in a saucepan, cover with boiling water and bring back to the boil. Reduce the heat and simmer for 10 minutes until just tender. Drain.

2 Using kitchen scissors, cut the fish into large chunks and arrange in the base of greased, shallow ovenproof dish. Season with freshly ground black pepper and sprinkle over the chives. Pour in the hot stock, and scatter with the peas and leeks.

3 Thinly slice the par-boiled potatoes and arrange in an even layer over the fish and vegetables. Season again with freshly ground black pepper. (There's no need to season with salt as the fish is quite salty.) Cover with a lid or greased kitchen foil and bake for 30 minutes.

4 Remove the dish from the oven and increase the oven temperature to 230°C/gas 8. Sprinkle the cheese over the potatoes, then return the dish to the oven and bake for a further 5–10 minutes until crisp and golden. Serve immediately.

variation
• The smoked haddock can be replaced with fresh haddock fillets (or use half fresh and half smoked haddock) or fresh salmon.

each serving provides 318kcals • 34g protein • 6g fat of which 3g saturates
33g carbohydrate of which 3g sugars • 5g fibre • 180mg sodium • 100g vegetables

1 portion fruit & veg

prepare ahead

318 kcals

Tray-baked salmon

Succulent salmon steaks are rich in **heart-healthy fats.** Here they are oven-baked on a **luscious bed of sliced tomatoes,** aubergines and potatoes and served with a **light lemon mayonnaise.** If liked, put some garlic bread in the oven as a tasty accompaniment.

SERVES 4
PREPARATION TIME 20 minutes
COOKING TIME 40 minutes

500g potatoes, peeled and sliced
1 aubergine, thickly sliced
4 large ripe tomatoes, sliced
**4 anchovies, drained, rinsed
   and finely chopped**
2 tbsp olive oil
**1 tbsp bottled capers, rinsed
   and chopped**
4 salmon steaks, about 150g each
5 tbsp reduced-fat mayonnaise
grated zest and juice of ½ lemon

1 Preheat the oven to 200°C/gas 6. Cook the potatoes in boiling water for about 8 minutes until they are just tender, then drain.

2 Arrange the potato, aubergine and tomato slices in overlapping rings in a large, lightly oiled roasting tin.

3 In a small bowl, combine the anchovies with the oil and capers, season well with pepper (no salt needed). Pour the mixture over the vegetables. Cover the dish with foil and bake in the oven for 20 minutes.

4 Arrange the salmon steaks on top of the vegetables, re-cover with the foil and cook for 10 minutes. Remove the foil and cook for a further 10 minutes until the salmon and vegetables are cooked through.

5 Meanwhile, in a small bowl, mix the mayonnaise with the lemon zest and juice. Serve the mayonnaise with the cooked salmon and vegetables.

cook's tip
• Cook the vegetables up to the end of step 3. Allow to cool then cover and chill for up to 6 hours. Finish as above but cooking the vegetables and salmon, covered, for 12 minutes.

variations
• If preferred, replace the anchovies and capers with finely chopped lemon zest and 2 crushed garlic cloves.
• Prepare fresh tuna or swordfish steaks in the same way.

prepare ahead

2 portions fruit & veg

502 kcals

each serving provides
502kcals • 35g protein
28g fat of which 5g saturates
28g carbohydrate of which 6g sugars
4g fibre • 444mg sodium
175g vegetables

Goat's cheese, spinach & pesto lasagne

Fresh pasta needs only brief oven-baking. Used in a vegetarian lasagne it is layered with **wilted fresh spinach** and **juicy cherry tomatoes,** then baked with a creamy goat's cheese topping.

SERVES 4 Ⅴ
PREPARATION TIME 30 minutes
COOKING TIME 25 minutes

450g baby spinach leaves
250g mild creamy goat's cheese
200g Quark (skimmed milk
    soft cheese)
1 tbsp pesto sauce
pinch of freshly grated nutmeg
225g fresh lasagne, about 9 sheets
350g cherry tomatoes, halved
2 eggs, lightly beaten
125ml semi-skimmed milk
50g fresh white breadcrumbs
15g Parmesan or Italian-style hard
    cheese, freshly grated

variation

• Use sun-dried tomato pesto sauce in place of the basil variety. (See cook's tip on page 116.)

cook's tip

• Use chèvre frais, a mild, soft young goat's cheese, sold in tubs, for this recipe. Alternatively, use all Quark cheese rather than a mixture.

each serving provides

572kcals • 39g protein
27g fat of which 11g saturates
46g carbohydrate of which
10g sugars • 3.5g fibre
764mg sodium • 200g vegetables

572 kcals • **2.5** portions fruit & veg

1 Preheat the oven to 190°C/ gas 5. Put the spinach in a large saucepan, with just the rinsing water clinging to the leaves. Cover and wilt it over a low heat for about 5 minutes, turning it occasionally. Tip the spinach into a colander and allow to drain, but do not squeeze dry. Reserve 2 tbsp of the juices.

2 Put the goat's cheese and Quark in a large bowl and mix together, then take out half the mixture and set aside. Add the pesto and reserved spinach juice to the cheese in the bowl and blend until smooth. Stir in the spinach and nutmeg and seasoning to taste.

3 Lay the lasagne sheets in a roasting tin and pour over enough boiling water to cover. Leave for 5 minutes until softened, then carefully drain.

4 Spread a third of the spinach mixture in a 25 x 18 x 8cm dish. Scatter a third of the cherry tomatoes in an even layer, then cover with a layer of pasta, trimming to fit the dish. Add half of the remaining spinach mixture in a thin layer, top with half the remaining tomatoes and cover with pasta as before. Cover with the last of the filling and arrange the remaining pasta sheets over the top.

5 Whisk the reserved cheese mixture with the eggs, milk and seasoning. Pour over the lasagne, then sprinkle with a mixture of the breadcrumbs and Parmesan. Bake for 25 minutes until the topping is lightly set and browned. Serve hot.

each serving provides

322kcals • 18g protein
18g fat of which 8g saturates
22g carbohydrate of which
5g sugars • 4g fibre
521mg sodium • 113g vegetables

1 portion fruit & veg

322 kcals

treat yourself

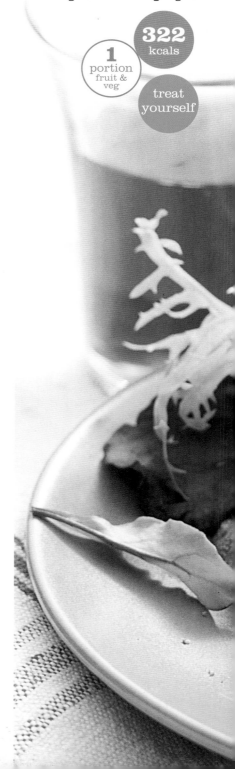

Jumbo mushrooms with Camembert & pine nuts

Large flat mushrooms are ideal for stuffing. These are topped with creamy cheese, sprinkled with nuts and served on toast for a smart, no-fuss light lunch or supper.

SERVES 2 V
PREPARATION TIME 15 minutes
COOKING TIME 15 minutes

4 large flat or portabello mushrooms
a little olive oil
100g Camembert or Brie cheese
15g dried wholemeal crumbs
15g pine nuts
4 slices wholemeal or
    multigrain bread
1 ripe beef tomato

1 Preheat the oven to 190°C/gas 5. Pull out the mushroom stalks and discard, then wipe the tops with kitchen paper (don't wash or peel). Rub the tops lightly with a little olive oil, then place them upside down on a non-stick, shallow roasting dish. Season with freshly ground black pepper and bake for 10 minutes.

2 Slice the cheese thinly and place in the mushroom cups. Mix together the crumbs and nuts and sprinkle over the cheese. Return to the oven and bake for 5 minutes until the cheese just melts.

3 Meanwhile toast the bread. There's no need to butter the toast, but you can brush it with a little olive oil, if liked.

4 Trim the ends from the tomato, then cut it into 4 even slices. Lay a slice of tomato on each slice of toast, then top with a hot baked mushroom and serve at once.

cook's tip
• Choose either large, white, flat mushrooms or the firmer textured brown or chestnut flat type, called portabello, which has a stronger, nuttier flavour.

Vegetable moussaka

This is a **clever variation** on the traditional, meat-based Greek dish that is usually quite high in fat. The meat has been replaced with a selection of **vibrantly coloured vegetables** and the protein is supplied by **borlotti beans.** The dish is topped in the traditional way but with a yoghurt-based sauce.

SERVES 4 Ⓥ
PREPARATION TIME 20 minutes
COOKING TIME 40 minutes

2 courgettes, sliced
1 aubergine, sliced
300g new potatoes, scrubbed
    and sliced
2 red peppers, deseeded and
    cut into thick strips
400g can borlotti beans,
    drained and rinsed
4 ripe tomatoes, about
    450g in total, chopped
3 tbsp chopped fresh basil
2 tbsp olive oil
150g plain low-fat natural yoghurt
1 egg, lightly beaten
30g Parmesan or Italian-style hard
    cheese, freshly grated

variations

• For non-vegetarians, add 200g chopped cooked chicken to the vegetables in step 3 and omit the beans.
• To save time, instead of grilling peppers, you can use bottled grilled pimiento peppers, cut into strips.

cook's tip

• You can prepare all the vegetables a day ahead, up to the end of step 3. Cover and refrigerate. When ready to use, allow to come to room temperature, then cover with the yoghurt mixture and bake as described.

1 Preheat the oven to 180°C/ gas 4. Bring a large pan of salted water to the boil. Add the courgettes and cook for 2 minutes. Remove from the water with a draining spoon and drain well on kitchen paper. Add the aubergine slices to the water and cook for 2 minutes, then remove and drain. Add the potato slices to the water and cook for about 8 minutes until just tender. Drain and set aside with the other blanched vegetables.

2 Meanwhile, heat a cast-iron, ridged griddle over a high heat. Cook the pepper slices for about 5 minutes, turning occasionally, until slightly charred all over and starting to soften. Remove from the pan and roughly chop.

3 Combine all the vegetables with the beans, chopped tomatoes and basil in a large baking dish. Drizzle over the olive oil, season to taste and stir well.

4 In a mixing bowl, stir together the yoghurt, egg and Parmesan cheese until blended. Spread this mixture over the top of the vegetables in an even layer (it may not cover the vegetables completely, depending on the shape of the dish).

5 Bake for 40 minutes or until the vegetables are tender and the topping is golden brown.

each serving provides

310kcals • 16g protein
12g fat of which 3g saturates
37g carbohydrate of which 16g sugars
8g fibre • 126mg sodium
353g vegetables

310 kcals   4 portions fruit & veg   prepare ahead

3

4

5

Mushroom pasta bake

Using a variety of **fresh and dried mushrooms** combined with **tasty artichoke hearts** gives an **exotic flavour** to this tempting dish. A great addition to your repertoire.

SERVES 4 Ⅴ
PREPARATION TIME 40 minutes
COOKING TIME 20 minutes

20g dried porcini mushrooms
250ml boiling water
2 tbsp olive oil
2 onions, chopped
2 garlic cloves, crushed
4 tbsp red wine
1 tsp dried sage
450g mixed fresh mushrooms
  (such as shiitake, chestnut and
  oyster), trimmed and sliced
2 x 400g cans chopped tomatoes
½ tsp sugar
400g conchiglie (pasta shells)
390g jar or can artichoke hearts,
  drained and quartered

variations
• Boost the fibre content by using wholewheat pasta shells.
• If liked, sprinkle the baked pasta with freshly grated Parmesan cheese.

each serving provides
506kcals • 19g protein
9g fat of which 1g saturates
91g carbohydrate of which
14g sugars • 7g fibre
93mg sodium • 453g vegetables

5+ portions fruit & veg

prepare ahead

506 kcals

1 Put the dried mushrooms in a heatproof bowl, pour over the boiling water to cover and set aside to soak for 15 minutes.

2 Meanwhile, heat the oil in a large flameproof casserole. Add the onions and garlic and cook, stirring, for 5–7 minutes, until the onions are soft and just starting to brown.

3 Drain the soaked mushrooms in a sieve set over a jug to catch the soaking liquid. Line the sieve with kitchen paper and strain the liquid to remove any grit. Add the liquid to the onions, along with the red wine and sage. Bring to the boil, then reduce the heat. Add the fresh and soaked mushrooms and stir for 3–4 minutes until the mushrooms start to give off their juice.

4 Stir in the tomatoes, the sugar and seasoning to taste. Cover and simmer for 12–15 minutes until the sauce thickens and the tomatoes start breaking down. Meanwhile, preheat the oven to 190°C/gas 5.

5 While the sauce is simmering, add the pasta to a large pan of boiling water and cook for just 5 minutes until the pasta is just beginning to become tender (do not cook until tender).

6 Drain the pasta well, then stir it into the sauce along with the artichokes. Taste and adjust the seasoning, if necessary. Place the casserole in the oven, uncovered, and bake for 20 minutes until the pasta is al dente. Serve straight from the dish.

cook's tips
• The pasta and artichokes can be tossed in the sauce up to a day in advance and then left, covered, in the fridge overnight. Leave the ingredients to return to room temperature before sprinkling with cheese, if using, and putting in the oven.
• It's worth making double quantities of the mushroom and artichoke sauce as it can be chilled for up to 3 days before re-heating and spooning over freshly boiled spaghetti.

Cauliflower & broccoli gratin

A favourite vegetarian dish gets a new twist here, with **super-healthy broccoli** added to cauliflower, in a cheese sauce thickened with breadcrumbs. Crunchy walnuts on top make this **mouth-wateringly good.**

SERVES 4 V
PREPARATION TIME 25 minutes
COOKING TIME 20 minutes

1 large cauliflower
500g broccoli
3 spring onions, trimmed and sliced
25g cornflour
550ml semi-skimmed milk
75g mature Cheddar or Gruyère cheese, grated
1 egg, beaten
100g fresh breadcrumbs
25g walnut pieces

variations

• Pine nuts are a good alternative to walnuts.
• You could also arrange 100g halved baby plum tomatoes, cut-side up, on top of the vegetables in the sauce, before adding the breadcrumbs and nuts.

1 Preheat the oven to 190°C/gas 5. Trim away the leaves from the cauliflower, then cut off the florets from the main stem. Cut the broccoli florets away from the stem. Blanch both the cauliflower and broccoli florets in a large saucepan of boiling water for 1 minute, then drain thoroughly.

2 Put the spring onions into the saucepan. Mix the cornflour with a little of the milk in a heatproof bowl to make a smooth paste. Add the rest of the milk to the onions and bring to the boil. Stir half of the hot milk into the cornflour paste, then return the mixture to the pan. Bring to the boil, stirring frequently, to make a smooth sauce.

3 Remove the sauce from the heat and stir in the grated cheese, beaten egg and half the breadcrumbs. Stir in the blanched vegetables and season to taste.

4 Transfer the mixture to a greased, ovenproof baking dish or gratin dish. Scatter the rest of the breadcrumbs and the walnuts over the top, then bake for 20 minutes until golden. Serve immediately.

each serving provides 373kcals • 25g protein • 18g fat of which 7g saturates • 31g carbohydrate of which 13g sugars • 6g fibre 361mg sodium • 263g vegetables

373 kcals

3 portions fruit & veg

Mexican vegetable bake

Turn a tray of roasted vegetables into a spicy meal by adding **kidney beans, a tomato sauce and a cheesy topping.** This should prove a popular dish for teenaged vegetarians and is great served with warmed soft tortillas.

SERVES 4 Ⓥ
PREPARATION TIME 15 minutes
COOKING TIME 35–40 minutes

1 red onion
2 large garlic cloves, chopped
1 large red or yellow pepper, deseeded and cut into chunks
1 small fennel bulb or 2 celery sticks, thinly sliced
1 large courgette, thickly sliced
2 tbsp olive oil
280g jar artichoke hearts in oil, drained
1 tsp dried oregano
1 tsp paprika or mild chilli powder
½ tsp ground cumin
400g can chopped tomatoes
400g can red kidney or pinto beans, drained and rinsed
200g Quark (skimmed milk soft cheese)
120ml semi-skimmed milk
85g mature Cheddar cheese, grated
2 tbsp dried wholemeal breadcrumbs

variations
• For meat eaters, add some stir-fried minced turkey instead of the beans.
• Try grated Spanish Manchego cheese instead of Cheddar and ricotta (11% fat) instead of the Quark.

1 Preheat the oven to 200°C/ gas 6. Halve the onion lengthways, then cut into thin wedges. Place in a big food bag with the garlic, pepper chunks, fennel or celery, courgette slices and oil. Toss together well, then tip out into a shallow ovenproof dish.

2 Mix in the artichoke hearts and season, then sprinkle over the oregano, paprika or chilli and cumin. Roast for 15 minutes.

3 Stir in the tomatoes and the drained beans. Return to the oven for a further 10 minutes.

4 Meanwhile, stir the Quark with the milk, to thin it to a thick cream. Drizzle over the vegetables. Mix the grated cheese and crumbs together and scatter on top. Return to the oven to bake for a further 10–15 minutes until golden and bubbling.

366 kcals

4 portions fruit & veg

each serving provides 366kcals • 23g protein 16g fat of which 6g saturates • 34g carbohydrate of which 16g sugars • 8g fibre • 803mg sodium • 337g vegetables

Polenta & corn pudding

This is a satisfying, **sunny yellow dish** made with instant polenta and canned sweetcorn kernels baked in a cheesy batter. Serve with a **chunky homemade tomato sauce** (see page 238).

SERVES 4 Ⓥ
PREPARATION TIME 20–25 minutes
COOKING TIME 40–45 minutes

2 tbsp fresh or dried wholemeal
  breadcrumbs
350g instant polenta
1 tsp mustard powder
400ml boiling water
2 large eggs, separated
2 x 198g cans sweetcorn with
  peppers, drained
8 spring onions, chopped
2 tbsp snipped fresh chives
75g mature Cheddar cheese,
  coarsely grated
150ml buttermilk

cook's tip

• Buttermilk, a tangy cultured milk product, contains slightly less fat than semi-skimmed milk. It is stocked next to cream in the chiller cabinet at supermarkets. If you can't find any, you can substitute semi-skimmed milk mixed with 1 tsp lemon juice and left to stand for 5 minutes before using.

561 kcals

1 portion fruit & veg

each serving provides

561kcals • 20g protein
13g fat of which 5g saturates
93g carbohydrate of which
10g sugars • 3g fibre
430mg sodium • 101g vegetables

1 Preheat the oven to 220°C/ gas 7. Lightly oil a large ovenproof baking dish of about 2.4 litre capacity, then sprinkle the breadcrumbs around the inside of the dish.

2 Put the polenta in a large heatproof bowl and stir in the mustard, then pour in the boiling water and stir until smooth. Cool slightly, then stir in the egg yolks, sweetcorn, spring onions, chives and about 40g of the cheese. Add the buttermilk and stir to form a thick batter.

3 Whisk the egg whites in a separate bowl until stiff peaks form. Beat 1 large spoonful of the egg whites into the batter to lighten it, then fold in the remaining whites.

4 Spoon the mixture into the prepared dish and sprinkle the remaining cheese over the top. Bake for 40–45 minutes until the top is set and golden brown. Serve at once, straight from the dish.

variation

• Boost the vegetable content by adding diced steamed carrots, sliced leeks or frozen peas (no need to thaw).

Cheesy bread & butter pudding

A popular, farmhouse-style recipe, but with the addition of juicy leeks and sun-blush tomatoes for a healthier result. Excellent for brunch or for an easy lunch or supper, served with a simple salad.

SERVES 4
PREPARATION TIME 25 minutes, plus 20 minutes soaking
COOKING TIME 25–30 minutes

1 medium oatmeal loaf
25g unsalted butter, softened
1 tbsp Dijon mustard
300g small leeks, trimmed and very thinly sliced
75g sun-blush tomatoes, drained and roughly chopped
500ml semi-skimmed milk
4 eggs
2 lean unsmoked back bacon rashers
85g Gruyère cheese, grated

variation

• For a fishy bake, replace the bacon with 200g smoked haddock fillets, poached in milk, then skinned and flaked. For extra flavour use the poaching milk to mix with the eggs. Scatter the fish over the leeks before soaking with the milk and egg mixture.

1 Trim the crusts off the loaf, then cut the bread into slices about 1cm thick. Mix the softened butter with the mustard and spread thinly over half the slices. Make sandwiches by putting the unbuttered slices on top of the buttered ones, then cut each sandwich in half. Place in a lightly greased, 2 litre shallow, ovenproof dish, arranged like a jigsaw so that they fit snugly.

2 Scatter the leeks and tomatoes over the bread. Whisk the milk with the eggs and season with freshly ground black pepper. Pour over the bread and vegetables, then leave to soak for 20 minutes.

3 Meanwhile, preheat the oven to 190°C/gas 5. Heat the grill and lightly grill the bacon rashers until just cooked – they will crisp up in the oven. (Alternatively, the bacon can be cooked in the microwave.) Drain on kitchen paper and leave to cool.

4 When ready to bake, chop the bacon into small pieces and scatter over the bread and vegetables. Sprinkle the grated cheese on top, then bake for 25–30 minutes until puffed and golden. Serve immediately.

country fare

503 kcals

1 portion fruit & veg

each serving provides 503kcals • 28g protein • 25g fat of which 12g saturates • 42g carbohydrate of which 12g sugars • 5g fibre 1003mg sodium • 100g vegetables

Stuffed courgettes

In this delicious vegetarian dish, **thick slices of large courgettes** are hollowed out and filled with a **tasty stuffing** based on **creamy cannellini beans** and fennel. A crispy topping of **breadcrumbs and walnuts** makes the perfect finishing touch. Serve with extra bread and a seasonal salad.

SERVES 4 V
PREPARATION TIME 25 minutes
COOKING TIME 45–50 minutes

6 large courgettes, about 250g each
1½ tbsp walnut or vegetable oil
2 shallots or ½ small onion,
   finely chopped
1 garlic clove, crushed
1 fennel bulb, finely chopped
400g can chopped tomatoes
410g can cannellini beans, drained
   and rinsed
3 tbsp chopped fresh coriander
½ tsp crushed chilli flakes (optional)
4 tbsp vegetable stock

BREADCRUMB TOPPING
50g wholemeal breadcrumbs
50g walnuts, roughly chopped
50g Parmesan or Italian-style hard
   cheese, freshly grated

variation

• When marrows are in season, use
them in place of courgettes. Peel and
cut a 1.5kg marrow into 9 rings, then
scoop out and discard the seeds.
Finely chop the flesh of 1 slice to add
to the stuffing mixture, made with
butter beans instead of cannellini.
Stuff the remaining rings and bake
as in the recipe.

1 Preheat the oven to 190°C/gas 5. Trim the
ends from the courgettes, then take off thin
strips of skin, lengthways, to achieve a striped
effect. Cut across into pieces 4cm long and
remove the soft centre flesh with a 3cm round
cutter or by hollowing out with an apple corer
or small sharp knife. Finely dice the removed
courgette flesh and set aside.

2 Put the courgette rings in a bowl and pour
over enough boiling water to cover. Leave for
2 minutes, then drain in a colander and arrange
them, upright, in a single layer in a large
ovenproof dish.

3 Heat the oil in a frying pan and gently cook the
shallots or onions and garlic for 3–4 minutes,
until beginning to soften. Add the garlic, fennel
and diced courgette flesh and continue cooking
over a low heat for a further 5 minutes until
they are almost tender. Remove from the heat.
Stir in the chopped tomatoes, the cannellini
beans, the coriander and the chilli flakes, if
using, then season to taste.

4 Spoon the bean mixture into the courgette rings,
piling it up on top. Pour the stock into the dish
around them. Cover with a 'tent' of foil, tightly
sealing around the edge, but allowing space for
the courgettes to steam. Bake the courgettes
for 30 minutes.

5 Remove the foil and sprinkle the tops with a
mixture of the breadcrumbs, walnuts, cheese
and a little freshly ground black pepper, if liked.
Return to the oven and bake, uncovered, for a
further 15–20 minutes until the courgettes are
very tender and the tops are crisp and brown.

5+ portions fruit & veg

312 kcals

veg boost

each serving provides
363kcals • 21g protein • 19g fat of which
4g saturates • 28g carbohydrate of which
12g sugars • 10g fibre • 209mg sodium
565g vegetables

Goat's cheese & cherry tomato clafouti

Traditionally a sweet pudding, this savoury version of the French clafouti is made with small cherry tomatoes taking the place of the usual cherries, and soft goat's cheese. Serve with a rustic, wholegrain bread and a mixed leaf salad with sliced mushrooms and hazelnuts.

SERVES 4 V
PREPARATION TIME 10 minutes
COOKING TIME 35–40 minutes

350g cherry tomatoes
6 eggs, lightly beaten
225ml semi-skimmed milk
3 tbsp plain flour
3 tbsp snipped fresh chives
100g soft goat's cheese

each serving provides

305kcals • 21g protein
18g fat of which 8g saturates
17g carbohydrate of which
6g sugars • 2g fibre
315mg sodium • 88g vegetables

special supper | 1 portion fruit & veg | 305 kcals

1 Preheat the oven to 180°C/gas 4. Spread the tomatoes in an even layer in the bottom of a lightly oiled, 23cm round ovenproof dish, that is about 5cm deep.

2 Place the eggs in a mixing bowl and whisk in the milk. Add the flour and whisk to combine thoroughly. Add the chives and season to taste. Pour this batter over the tomatoes. Crumble the cheese over the top.

3 Bake for 35–40 minutes until the top is golden and the pudding is almost set (it will carry on cooking once removed from the oven). Leave to cool for a few minutes before serving as the tomatoes will be very hot inside.

variations

• Vary the cheese to your own taste – grated Gruyère, Cheddar, Parmesan and crumbled Stilton would all make good choices.
• Instead of cherry tomatoes, try chopped grilled peppers or sautéed button mushrooms.

SERVES 4 ⓥ
PREPARATION TIME 35 minutes,
  plus 5 minutes standing time
COOKING TIME 15 minutes

**8 large beef tomatoes,
  about 200g each**
**75g ready-to-eat dried
  apricots, chopped**
**75g dates (preferably
  medjool), chopped**
50g sultanas
**300ml hot vegetable stock,
  or as needed**
1 tbsp olive oil
100g pine nuts
**4 spring onions, trimmed
  and finely sliced**
½ tsp ground cumin
½ tsp ground coriander
175g couscous
2 tbsp chopped fresh parsley

TO SERVE 250ml Greek yoghurt
  or tzatziki

variation
• Dried peaches can be used instead
of dried apricots, and almond or
hazelnuts instead of pine nuts.

each serving provides
537kcals • 14g protein
28g fat of which 6g saturates
61g carbohydrate of which
38g sugars • 6.5g fibre
85mg sodium
460g fruit and vegetables

5+ portions fruit & veg

537 kcals

Baked couscous tomatoes
Large beef tomatoes make juicy containers for a **spicy dried fruit and nut couscous** mixture, served with **creamy yoghurt**. All that's needed is some warm crusty bread to complete the meal.

1 Preheat the oven to 200°C/gas 6. Cut the tops off the tomatoes and scoop out the insides using a teaspoon. Place in a single layer in a baking dish (if necessary, cut a very thin sliver from the base of each tomato so that it will sit flat). Put the seeds and scooped-out flesh in sieve set over a jug, and press with the back of the spoon to squeeze out the juices. Discard the seeds and flesh.

2 Put the apricots, dates and sultanas in a small bowl and spoon over 4 tbsp of the tomato juice. Stir to coat with the juice, then leave to soak. Make up the remaining tomato juice in the jug to 350ml with vegetable stock.

3 Heat ½ tbsp of the oil in a non-stick saucepan. Add the pine nuts and cook over a low heat, stirring all the time, for 2 minutes, until golden. Remove from the pan with a draining spoon and set aside.

4 Add the remaining ½ tbsp oil to the pan and gently cook the spring onions for 2 minutes, until soft. Stir in the ground cumin and coriander and cook for a few more seconds. Pour in the stock and bring to a rapid boil. Remove from the heat, then add the couscous in a steady stream, stirring constantly. Cover and leave to stand for 3 minutes.

5 Stir the dried fruit, pine nuts and parsley into the couscous, then season to taste. Spoon the couscous mixture into the hollowed-out tomatoes and replace the tops. Bake for 15 minutes or until tender. Leave to stand for 5 minutes before serving with Greek yoghurt or tzatziki.

Pies

A traditional British favourite, pies are full of flavour, and these ones are healthy too. Prepared with a wide range of lower-fat toppings and nutritious fillings, many of these are just as good served cold as warm. Filo pastry needs only a little oil between the layers, and always looks impressive. Why not pack some Tunisian briks in a picnic basket? Or satisfy your hungry family on the coldest of days with a warming Liver, bacon and mushroom pie.

SERVES 4
PREPARATION TIME 40 minutes
COOKING TIME 30–35 minutes

FILLING
400g lamb's liver
2 tbsp plain flour
100g unsmoked back bacon
2 tbsp olive oil
150g shallots, peeled and
  cut into wedges
200g carrots, peeled and diced
150g button chestnut mushrooms
1 garlic clove, crushed
1 tsp finely chopped fresh rosemary
300ml lamb or vegetable stock, hot
2 tbsp dry sherry

SUET PASTRY
100g self-raising flour
75g fresh white breadcrumbs
1 tsp finely chopped fresh rosemary
50g 'light' shredded vegetable suet

each serving provides
506kcals • 32g protein
23g fat of which 3g saturates
43g carbohydrate of which 6g sugars
4g fibre • 612mg sodium
125g vegetables

1.5 portions fruit & veg   **prepare ahead**   **506** kcals

Liver, bacon & mushroom pie
Nothing beats a traditional pie, and this one with a **healthy touch** uses 'light' shredded vegetable suet for the fresh **rosemary-flavoured crust.**

1 Preheat the oven to 180°C/gas 4. Cut the liver into strips about 1cm thick. Toss in the flour and a little seasoning to lightly coat. Cut the bacon into strips the same size as the liver. Heat the oil in a heavy, deep frying pan, then quickly stir-fry the liver and bacon until lightly browned. Remove from the pan to a plate and set aside.

2 Add the shallots and carrots to the pan and cook, stirring frequently, until lightly coloured. Add the mushrooms and cook, stirring frequently, for a couple of minutes, then add the garlic, herbs, stock and sherry. Bring to the boil, stirring.

3 Return the liver and bacon to the pan and stir together. Transfer to a 1 litre pie dish, mounding the filling in the centre, and leave to cool while making the pastry.

4 Combine the flour, breadcrumbs, rosemary, suet and a little seasoning in a mixing bowl. Stir in enough cold water, about 5 tbsp, to make a soft but not sticky dough. Turn out onto a lightly floured work surface and gently roll out to an oval slightly larger than the pie dish.

5 Dampen the rim of the dish, then gently lift the pastry over the filling and press the pastry to the rim to seal. Trim off any excess pastry with a sharp knife, make a steam hole in the middle and press the back of a fork onto the pastry rim to decorate. Bake for 30–35 minutes until golden brown, then serve hot.

cook's tip
• This recipe can be made ahead then cooled, covered and chilled for up to 48 hours. Reheat in a preheated 180°C/gas 4 oven for 20 minutes before serving. Make sure the filling is piping hot.

Filo shepherd's pie

An updated version of an old favourite. This pretty pie combines lean meat with lots of fresh vegetables, all topped with crisp and light filo pastry.

SERVES 4
PREPARATION TIME 45 minutes
COOKING TIME 25–30 minutes

500g lean boneless lamb (such as leg), trimmed of excess fat and cut into 2cm cubes
2½ tbsp flour
2½ tbsp vegetable oil
250g shallots, peeled and left whole
2 garlic cloves, crushed
4 carrots, peeled and thickly sliced
1 celery stick, sliced
125ml red wine
350ml lamb or vegetable stock
1 tbsp Worcestershire sauce
1 tbsp wholegrain mustard
1 bouquet garni
2 leeks, halved lengthways and thickly sliced
2 tbsp chopped fresh parsley
3 sheets filo pastry, about 135g in total

1 Toss the meat with the flour to coat lightly. Heat 1½ tbsp of the oil in a large flameproof casserole or a deep frying pan over a moderate heat. Fry the lamb in batches until browned on all sides. Remove using a draining spoon and set aside.

2 Add the shallots to the fat left in the pan and fry, stirring frequently, for 5–8 minutes until lightly browned. Add the garlic, carrots and celery.

3 Stir in the red wine, turn up the heat and cook until the wine has almost evaporated. Then add the stock, Worcestershire sauce, mustard and bouquet garni. Return the lamb to the pan with any juices. Bring to the boil, then reduce the heat, cover and simmer for 20 minutes.

4 Stir in the leeks, cover and simmer for 10 more minutes. Season to taste. Preheat the oven to 190°C/gas 5.

5 Remove and discard the bouquet garni, then spoon the mixture into a 1.75 litre ovenproof dish and stir in the parsley.

6 Cut the filo pastry into squares between 9 and 12cm, depending on the size of your filo sheets. Lightly brush each square on one side with a little of the remaining oil, then crumple them up loosely and place them, oiled-side up, over the filling. Bake for 25–30 minutes until the pastry is crisp and golden.

variation
• Instead of pastry, top the pie with 750g potato, mashed (see cover picture).

each serving provides
482kcals • 33g protein • 19g fat of which 1g saturates • 41g carbohydrate of which 13g sugars • 6g fibre
313mg sodium • 230g vegetables

482 kcals

2.5 portions fruit & veg

Fruity Wiltshire lattice

A healthy twist on a sausage roll makes a supper dish all the family will enjoy. Lean sausagemeat is combined with apple and dried apricots to make a tangy filling for a reduced-fat pastry wrapping. Serve with a tomato and watercress salad.

SERVES 4

PREPARATION TIME 35 minutes, plus 20 minutes chilling

COOKING TIME 25–30 minutes

PASTRY

225g plain flour

140g reduced-fat sunflower spread, suitable for baking, chilled

1 tsp poppy seeds

SAUSAGEMEAT FILLING

450g lean pork and herb sausages or sausagemeat

1 large cooking apple

75g ready-to-eat dried apricots

1½ tsp chopped fresh sage

variation

• Look out for lean sausages made from venison, wild boar or beef – remove the casings, then use as in the recipe. Other flavourings could be grated red onion and sliced sun-blush tomatoes, or chopped cooked spinach with grated fresh root ginger and a pinch of chilli pepper.

each serving provides

519kcals • 27g protein
21g fat of which 7g saturates
60g carbohydrate of which
16g sugars • 6g fibre
731mg sodium • 84g fruit

1 portion fruit & veg

519 kcals

1. To make the pastry, put the flour in a large bowl, add the spread and rub in using your fingertips. Add 2 tbsp iced water and mix well with a fork until thoroughly combined and a soft dough is formed. (If preferred, use a food processor to make the pastry.) Wrap in cling film and chill for 20 minutes.

2. Meanwhile, prepare the filling. If using sausages, remove the casings, then put the sausagemeat into a large bowl. Peel and core the apple, then cut into small 1cm pieces. Cut the apricots into thin slivers. Put the fruit into the bowl with the sausagemeat and add the sage and plenty of freshly ground black pepper. Mix well with your hands until thoroughly combined.

3. Preheat the oven to 220°C/gas 7. Unwrap the chilled pastry and roll out on a lightly floured work surface to a rectangle measuring about 28 x 30cm. Trim the edges to neaten, if necessary.

4. Lightly dust your hands with flour, then shape the sausagemeat filling into a roll the same length as the pastry. Lay the roll down one side of the pastry. Brush the long edges with cold water, then fold the pastry over so the filling is covered and the 2 long edges meet. Press the edges firmly together to seal.

5. Lift the roll onto a lightly greased baking sheet. Score the top of the pastry with the point of a knife to make a lattice pattern. Lightly brush the pastry with water, then sprinkle with the poppy seeds. Bake for 25–30 minutes until the pastry is golden. Serve warm.

SERVES 4
PREPARATION TIME 50 minutes
COOKING TIME 20 minutes

PASTRY
225g plain flour
5 tbsp vegetable oil

FILLING
4 lean unsmoked back bacon rashers, diced
1 tbsp vegetable oil
325g baby leeks, thinly sliced
1 tsp chopped fresh rosemary
150ml semi-skimmed milk
1 tbsp cornflour
2 egg whites

TO GARNISH small sprigs of fresh rosemary

Souffléed leek & bacon tartlets

A combination of leeks and bacon in a light sauce with whisked egg whites makes a fluffy filling for these shortcrust tartlets. Fresh rosemary lifts the flavour. Serve with a mixed salad.

1 Preheat the oven to 200°C/gas 6. Sift the flour with a pinch of salt into a large bowl. Add 5 tbsp cold water to the oil, then stir into the flour using a fork to mix together and form a dough. Sprinkle with a little more water if necessary. Knead the dough briefly on a lightly floured work surface.

2 Roll out the dough to about 3mm thickness. Using a round metal cutter (or cutting around a saucer), cut out 4 circles, each about 15cm in diameter. Re-roll the trimmings as necessary. Carefully fit the pastry circles into 4 individual, 12cm diameter tartlet cases.

3 Put the bacon and oil into a non-stick frying pan and set over a moderate heat. Cook for 2–3 minutes, then add the sliced leeks and rosemary. Reduce the heat and cook gently for about 5 minutes, stirring frequently, until the leeks are tender. Remove from the heat and leave the mixture to cool in a bowl while making the sauce.

4 Mix 2 tbsp of the milk with the cornflour in a heatproof bowl. Heat the rest of the milk in a medium pan. As soon as it comes to the boil, pour it onto the cornflour mixture, whisking constantly. Tip this mixture into the pan, return to the heat and stir constantly until the sauce boils and thickens. Add the sauce to the leek and bacon mixture and season to taste (you may not need to add salt as the bacon is salty).

5 Whisk the egg whites in a clean bowl until they stand in soft peaks. Using a large metal spoon, gently fold the egg whites into the leek and bacon mixture. Carefully spoon into the pastry cases.

6 Bake for about 20 minutes until the filling is golden and set and the pastry is crisp. Serve immediately, garnished with little sprigs of rosemary.

448
kcals

1
portion
fruit &
veg

each serving provides 448kcals • 16g protein • 21.5g fat of which 3g saturates
54g carbohydrate of which 4g sugars • 3.5g fibre • 637mg sodium • 81g vegetables

SERVES 4 *
PREPARATION TIME 1 hour
10 minutes
COOKING TIME 45–50 minutes

PASTRY

125g plain wholemeal flour
125g plain white flour
6 tbsp vegetable oil
1 beaten egg, to glaze

FILLING

175g lean braising steak, diced
1 large carrot, peeled and diced
125g swede, peeled and diced
2 tbsp frozen peas
1 small onion, finely chopped
1 tbsp chopped fresh parsley
1 tsp dried mixed herbs

cook's tip

• You can prepare the filling and pastry ahead. Wrap the pastry in cling film and keep both in the fridge. Remove pastry from the fridge about 20 minutes before using. Freeze pasties baked or unbaked. Thaw in the fridge before reheating and/or cooking thoroughly.

each serving provides

469kcals • 20g protein
22g fat of which 4g saturates
51g carbohydrate of which
6.5g sugars • 6g fibre
65mg sodium • 96g vegetables

1 portion fruit & veg

469 kcals

prepare ahead

Wholemeal Cornish pasties

This traditional lunch-on-the-go, made with a quick-mix pastry, is always a great favourite and perfect for busy weekends. The filling is a tasty combination of lean beef and vegetables.

1 Preheat the oven to 200°C/gas 6. First make the pastry. Sift both the flours with a pinch of salt into a large bowl. Tip the bran left in the sieve back into the flour. Add 5 tbsp cold water to the oil, then stir into the flour using a fork to mix together and form a dough. Sprinkle with a little more water if needed. Knead the dough lightly, then wrap in cling film and put aside while preparing the filling.

2 Combine the steak, vegetables and herbs in a large bowl and season with salt and pepper. Make sure all the ingredients are diced into small pieces, so that they will cook thoroughly in the pasties.

3 Divide the pastry into 4 and roll out each piece on a lightly floured surface to a circle 20cm in diameter, using a plate to draw round. Each time, add the pastry trimmings to the remaining pastry before rolling so as to use it all.

4 Put a quarter of the filling onto each pastry circle, spooning it down the centre and making sure the meat is spread evenly. Brush a little of the beaten egg around the edges, then bring up the edges and pinch together to seal. Crimp to give the traditional pasty shape.

5 Place on a non-stick baking sheet and lightly brush the pasties with egg. Prick with a fork a couple of times to make sure they don't burst while cooking. Bake for 10 minutes, then reduce the oven temperature to 180°C/gas 4 and cook for a further 35–40 minutes until golden.

Spicy samosas

Samosas are traditionally deep-fried, but in this delicious version they are made with **crunchy filo pastry,** brushed with a little oil and baked. Serve with **fruit chutney or yoghurt raita** and **a mixed salad** for a casual, light lunch.

SERVES 4 (makes 12 samosas)
PREPARATION TIME 35 minutes
COOKING TIME 12–15 minutes

250g lean minced beef
1 onion, finely chopped
1 tbsp curry powder
½ tsp ground cumin
198g can chickpeas,
    drained and rinsed
200g frozen peas, thawed
20g fresh coriander,
    coarsely chopped
6 sheets filo pastry,
    about 270g in total
3 tbsp olive oil
1 tbsp mustard seeds

1 Preheat the oven to 190°C/gas 5. Heat a large frying pan over a moderate heat. Add the minced beef and cook for about 5 minutes, stirring frequently, until evenly browned. Add the onion, curry powder and cumin, stir then reduce the heat to low, cover and cook for about 10 minutes, stirring occasionally until the onions are softened. Stir in the chickpeas, peas and coriander, heat through and season to taste.

2 Using a sharp knife, cut the filo pastry lengthways into 12 strips, each measuring about 12 x 36cm. Make a neat pile of the strips, and loosely cover with cling film.

3 Taking one strip of pastry at a time, lay it out lengthways on the work surface and brush it lightly with oil. Place about 1 heaped tbsp of the beef filling at the end nearest you. Lift up the bottom left-hand corner of the strip and fold it diagonally over the filling. Continue folding diagonally to the end of the strip, ending with a triangular parcel.

4 Place the parcel on a baking sheet, brush lightly with a little of the remaining oil and sprinkle with a few mustard seeds. Repeat with the remaining pastry and filling to make 12 samosas.

5 Bake for 12–15 minutes until golden and crisp on top. Transfer to a wire rack and allow to cool.

cook's tip

• Filo pastry is sold in different sized packs, and the weight and size of the sheets vary considerably. You can use any type, adapting it by cutting to size or making larger pieces by joining sheets, overlapping edges that have been lightly oiled (see step 3 on page 332). If the pastry sheets are very thin, double them up with a light layer of oil between, so that the pastry is strong enough to hold the filling.

variation

• For vegetarian samosas, use the same weight of Quorn mince in place of the minced beef or a 400g drained and rinsed can of chickpeas with 250g mixed peas or diced vegetables.

each serving provides 396kcals • 25g protein • 15.5g fat of which 3g saturates • 39g carbohydrate of which 7g sugars • 5.5g fibre 339mg sodium • 88g vegetables

396 kcals • **1** portion fruit & veg • spicy treat

3

4

5

Chinese spring rolls

These popular Chinese light bites, filled with chicken and crisp vegetables, are given a new twist, wrapped with filo pastry rather than the usual wonton wrappers, then baked, not deep-fried. Enjoy with a fruity chutney and an Oriental-style salad, or serve as party nibbles.

SERVES 6 (makes 18 rolls)
PREPARATION TIME about 1 hour
COOKING TIME 12–15 minutes

3 tbsp vegetable oil
1 tbsp toasted sesame oil
2 skinless chicken breast
   fillets, about 300g in total,
   finely chopped
4 spring onions, trimmed
   and thinly sliced
2 carrots, peeled and
   coarsely grated
1 large courgette, coarsely grated
150g bean sprouts
220g can water chestnuts,
   drained and coarsely chopped
220g can bamboo shoots,
   drained and coarsely chopped
2 tbsp soy sauce
1 tbsp dry sherry
6 sheets filo pastry, about
   270g in total

1 portion fruit & veg
310 kcals
prepare ahead

each serving provides
310kcals • 20g protein
10g fat of which 2g saturates
32g carbohydrate of which
9g sugars • 3g fibre
568mg sodium • 80g vegetables

1 Heat 1 tbsp of the vegetable oil with the sesame oil in a large frying pan over a moderate heat. Add the chicken and fry, stirring constantly, for about 5 minutes until almost cooked through.

2 Add the spring onions with the grated carrots and courgette. Stir well to mix. Cover the pan, reduce the heat to low and cook, stirring occasionally, for 4 minutes.

3 Stir in the bean sprouts with the water chestnuts and bamboo shoots and cook, uncovered, for a further 5 minutes, stirring occasionally. Stir in the soy sauce and sherry and season to taste. Remove from the heat.

4 Preheat the oven to 190°C/gas 5. Unroll the filo, keeping the sheets in a stack. (See cook's tip on filo on page 324.) Then, using a sharp knife, cut the pastry widthways into 3 strips, each measuring about 16 x 24cm. Lay these 18 strips in a stack.

5 Lay the top strip lengthways on the work surface and place 1 heaped tbsp of the chicken filling along the end of the strip closest to you, but not quite up to the edge. Fold the long edges of the filo over the filling, then roll up. Lightly oil the end to seal. Place the roll seam-side down on a baking sheet and brush lightly all over with oil. Repeat with the remaining filo strips and filling.

6 Bake the rolls for 12–15 minutes until golden and crisp. Transfer to a wire rack and allow the rolls to cool slightly before serving.

variation
• To give these rolls a Thai flavour, add 1 finely chopped stalk of lemon grass with the spring onions, then stir in juice of 1 lime and 3 tbsp chopped fresh coriander at the end of step 3. Omit the soy sauce and sherry.

cook's tip
• To prepare in advance, make and bake the rolls up to a day ahead, then keep chilled. To serve, reheat them at 190°C/gas 5 for about 5 minutes.

Turkey cobbler

A richly flavoured combination of lean turkey and vegetables, cooked in cider, with a topping of light, herby scones, makes a great winter supper.

SERVES 4
PREPARATION TIME 40 minutes
COOKING TIME 20 minutes

500g diced turkey
2 tbsp plain flour
1½ tbsp olive oil
2 onions, finely chopped
450ml dry cider
1 bay leaf
4 carrots, peeled
150g button mushrooms, wiped
   and halved if large
3 courgettes, trimmed
100g sweetcorn (canned or frozen)

COBBLER TOPPING
175g self-raising flour
1 tbsp chopped fresh parsley
1 tbsp snipped fresh chives
1 tbsp chopped fresh oregano,
   or 1 tsp dried
30g unsalted butter,
   chilled and diced
100ml semi-skimmed milk

cook's tip
• To prepare ahead, cook the turkey and vegetables, then cool and chill. Reheat gently, then bake with the cobbler topping.

1 Preheat the oven to 200°C/gas 6. Toss the turkey in the flour mixed with a little seasoning to coat. Heat 1 tbsp of the oil in a deep frying pan. Add the turkey and fry over a moderate heat, stirring frequently, for about 3 minutes. Stir in the remaining oil and the onions, lower the heat and cook for a further 5 minutes until the onions are golden.

2 Stir in the cider and bay leaf and bring to the boil. Quarter the carrots lengthways, then chop into 2cm chunks and add to the pan with the mushrooms. Reduce the heat and simmer gently for 20 minutes.

3 Meanwhile, cut the courgettes into quarters lengthways, then cut across into chunks, about the size of the carrots. Mix with the sweetcorn and set aside.

4 To make the cobbler topping, combine the flour, herbs and a little seasoning in a bowl. Using your fingertips, rub in the butter until the mixture looks like fine crumbs, then stir in the milk until the ingredients come together to make a soft dough. (This can be done in a food processor.) Turn the dough out onto a floured work surface and press out with floured fingers until about 1cm thick. Using a floured 6cm round biscuit or scone cutter, cut out 8 rounds, re-using the trimmings.

5 Stir the courgettes and sweetcorn into the turkey mixture and season to taste. Transfer to an ovenproof dish and arrange the 'cobblers' on top. Cook, uncovered, for 20 minutes until the topping is golden. Serve hot.

2.5 portions fruit & veg

533 kcals

prepare ahead

each serving provides 533kcals • 38g protein 15g fat of which 6g saturates • 59g carbohydrate of which 14g sugars • 5g fibre • 282mg sodium • 231g vegetables

Mediterranean chicken with oaty crumble

This **colourful dish** contains chunks of tender chicken breast, first roasted with **aubergine, courgettes and red pepper,** then baked in a herby tomato and olive sauce with a **crumbly oat crust.**

SERVES 4
PREPARATION TIME 20 minutes
COOKING TIME 1 hour

3 chicken breast portions (skin on)
3 small sprigs of fresh rosemary
1 aubergine, cut into 2cm cubes
2 courgettes, cut into 2cm
   thick slices
1 red pepper, deseeded and
   cut into 2cm pieces
1 tbsp olive oil (or oil from the
   jar of sun-dried tomatoes)
400g can chopped tomatoes
   with herbs
12 stoned black olives

OATMEAL CRUMBLE
125g rolled oats
40g butter, chilled and diced
50g sun-dried tomatoes
   in oil, drained
2 tsp chopped fresh oregano

1 Preheat the oven to 190°C/ gas 5. Loosen the skin on each chicken breast and tuck a sprig of rosemary underneath, between the skin and the flesh. Place the chicken in a large roasting tin and roast for 5 minutes.

2 Combine the aubergine, courgettes and red pepper in a bowl. Drizzle over the oil, then toss to coat. Push the chicken portions to one side in the roasting tin, then add the vegetables. Roast the vegetables and chicken for 20 minutes, then turn the vegetables. Roast for a further 5–10 minutes until the vegetables are well browned and tender and the chicken is cooked through.

3 Meanwhile, make the crumble topping. Put the oats in a food processor and pulse briefly to make a fairly fine 'flour'. Add the butter, then pulse again until the mixture comes together in small lumps. Pat the sun-dried tomatoes on kitchen paper to blot up excess oil, then snip into small pieces with kitchen scissors. Stir into the crumble mixture with the oregano.

4 Transfer the roasted vegetables to a baking dish, and stir in the chopped tomatoes and black olives. Season to taste. Cover and cook in the oven for 10 minutes. Meanwhile, discard the chicken skin and rosemary sprigs, then remove the chicken meat from the bone and cut into large bite-sized pieces.

5 Stir the chicken into the vegetable mixture, then scatter the crumble topping over the top, making sure to cover any vegetables that are already browned. Bake, uncovered, for 20 minutes until the topping is crisp and golden, then serve.

each serving provides

405kcals • 28g protein
19.5g fat of which 7g saturates
31g carbohydrate of which
10g sugars • 7g fibre
500mg sodium • 328g vegetables

405 kcals

4 portions fruit & veg

veg boost

Seafood pie with potato pastry

A very special fish pie that is sure to please everyone. The recipe uses a mixture of white fish, seafood and vegetables in a quick white sauce, topped with a golden tumeric potato pastry crust.

SERVES 4

PREPARATION TIME 20 minutes, plus 15 minutes cooling

COOKING TIME 25 minutes

POTATO PASTRY

150g plain flour
½ tsp ground turmeric
100g mashed potato
100g sunflower margarine, chilled and diced
1 tbsp semi-skimmed milk, to glaze
1 tbsp dried breadcrumbs

FILLING

400g skinless white fish fillets (such as cod, haddock, coley or hoki)
200g peeled prawns or seafood mix (including mussels and squid)
2 leeks, trimmed and thinly sliced
125g frozen peas, thawed
2 tbsp chopped fresh parsley
leaves from 2 sprigs of fresh thyme
grated zest of 1 lemon
30g cornflour
500ml semi-skimmed milk

1 First make the pastry. Sift the flour and turmeric into a bowl and, using a fork, mix with the potato until blended. Rub in the margarine, then draw together into a dough, adding trickles of cold water if necessary to bind together. Wrap in cling film and chill in the fridge for about 20 minutes.

2 Meanwhile, prepare the filling. Cut the fish into small chunks and put into a medium pie dish of about 1.25 litre capacity. Mix in the prawns or seafood, leeks, peas, parsley, thyme and lemon zest.

3 Blend the cornflour with a little of the milk in a basin. Heat the rest of the milk until almost boiling, then stir into the cornflour paste. Return to the pan and cook, stirring, until the sauce thickens. Season to taste and pour over the fish filling. Set aside to cool for 15 minutes. Preheat the oven to 200°C/gas 6.

4 Roll out the pastry between 2 large sheets of cling film to approximately the size and shape of the top of the pie dish. Remove the top sheet of film and lay the pastry on top of the filling. Remove the other sheet of film.

5 Press and trim the pastry edges to neaten, and make a small slash in the centre of the lid. Brush with the milk, then sprinkle with the crumbs. Place the pie dish on a baking sheet and bake for 10 minutes, then reduce the heat to 180°C/gas 4 and bake for a further 15 minutes.

variation

• Alternatively, top the pie with mashed potatoes flavoured with chopped fresh parsley or chives. Bake for 20 minutes at 200°C/gas 6.

each serving provides

603kcals • 39g protein
26g fat of which 7g saturates
56g carbohydrate of which 9g sugars
4g fibre • 456mg sodium
81g vegetables

1 portion fruit & veg

603 kcals

SERVES 4 (makes 12)
PREPARATION TIME 25 minutes
COOKING TIME 15–18 minutes

200g can tuna in spring water,
  well drained
100g frozen chopped spinach,
  thawed and well drained
5 spring onions, thinly sliced
3 tbsp chopped fresh parsley
3 tbsp chopped fresh mint
2 medium carrots, peeled and grated
115g cooked wild rice (40g raw rice)
1 egg, beaten
zest of 1 lemon
12 sheets filo pastry, about
  150g in total
3 tbsp olive oil
2 tsp sesame seeds

variation

• To make vegetarian Cheese and
Spinach Briks, omit the tuna and add
100g crumbled feta cheese to the
filling mixture.

each serving provides

369kcals • 19g protein
13g fat of which 2g saturates
42g carbohydrate of which 10g sugars
4g fibre • 460mg sodium
136g vegetables

1.5
portions
fruit &
veg

369
kcals

Tunisian briks These little savoury
pasties are traditionally deep-fried, but this healthier version is
baked to keep the fat content low. They make a great lunch or
picnic dish, served with a tomato salsa or minty yoghurt and a
crisp vegetable salad.

1 Preheat the oven to 190°C/gas 5. Mix together the tuna, spinach, spring
onions, parsley, mint, carrots, rice, egg and lemon zest. Season to taste
with plenty of freshly ground black pepper.

2 Take 2 sheets of filo (keep the rest covered). Lay one flat and brush with a
little of the oil, then cover with the second sheet. Cut in half lengthways to
make 2 strips, each measuring about 9 x 30cm. (Alternatively, use 6 thicker
filo sheets and cut into similar sized strips. Thicker filo doesn't need
layering for these briks; see cook's tip on page 324.)

3 Place a well-heaped tablespoon of the tuna filling on the end of one strip.
Fold a bottom corner of pastry over the filling to the opposite side, then
turn over the opposite way. Continue to fold over down the length of the
strip to make a triangular pasty. Seal the end with a little oil. Repeat with
the second strip. Continue making pasties in this way, using all the filo
and filling mixture.

4 Place the pasties on 2 non-stick baking sheets. Brush with the remaining
oil and sprinkle with sesame seeds. Bake for 15–18 minutes or until
golden brown and crisp. Serve the briks warm or cold.

SERVES 4
PREPARATION TIME 20 minutes
COOKING TIME 20 minutes

2 tbsp soy sauce
3 spring onions, trimmed
   and chopped
juice of 1 lime
1 garlic clove, chopped
2 tsp sesame seeds
400g skinned fresh salmon
   fillet, cut into small cubes
225g pack baby leaf spinach
100g frozen minted peas, thawed
4 sheets filo pastry,
   about 180g in total
1 tbsp vegetable oil
2 tsp sesame seed oil
100g reduced-fat soft cheese

Salmon & spinach filo pouches

These attractive filo parcels open to reveal a delicious mixture of cubed salmon and soft cheese, with flavoursome spinach, minted peas and spring onions. Serve with a light green salad.

1 Preheat the oven to 190°C/ gas 5. Lay a sheet of non-stick baking paper on a baking tray.

2 Mix together the soy sauce, spring onions, lime juice, garlic and 1 tsp of the sesame seeds. Season with freshly ground black pepper. Add the salmon and turn it over a few times to coat, then set aside to marinate.

3 Meanwhile, lightly cook the spinach in the microwave, according to the pack instructions. Drain the spinach in a sieve, pressing down to extract the liquid. Cool, then chop roughly and mix with the salmon and the peas.

4 Cut the filo pastry in half widthways and trim the edges to make 8 x 24cm squares. (See cook's tip on filo on page 324.) Lay out one square on a board. Mix together the 2 oils in a cup and brush the pastry lightly with some of the mixture. Top with another square of pastry. Spoon a quarter of the salmon mix into the centre, then spoon a quarter of the cheese on top. Draw up the pastry edges, then squeeze together and twist slightly into a pouch. Brush the outside of the pouch lightly with a little more oil and sprinkle with a pinch or two of the remaining seeds. Place on the baking tray.

5 Repeat with the remaining ingredients to make 3 more pouches. Bake for about 20 minutes until golden brown. Cool on a wire tray for 10 minutes, then serve.

each serving provides
456kcals • 32g protein
23g fat of which 6g saturates
28g carbohydrate of which 5g sugars
4g fibre • 875mg sodium
91g vegetables

stylish parcels
456 kcals
1 portion fruit & veg

Double mushroom & spinach strudel

Filo pastry makes a perfect **light, crispy casing** for a **delicious creamy mushroom mixture,** combining chestnut and shiitake mushrooms. Spinach and char-grilled peppers add colour, further flavour and **vitamin value.**

SERVES 4 V
PREPARATION TIME 35 minutes
COOKING TIME 25 minutes

**1 large red pepper, deseeded
  and cut into strips
3 tbsp olive oil
2 garlic cloves, crushed
250g chestnut mushrooms, sliced
125g shiitake mushrooms, sliced
¼ tsp dried thyme
150g frozen spinach
100g reduced-fat soft cheese
9 sheets filo pastry, about
  125g in total
2 tbsp sesame seeds**

1 Preheat the oven to 200°C/ gas 6. Heat a cast-iron, ridged griddle over a high heat. Add the red pepper strips and cook for about 6 minutes until lightly charred all over. Remove from the heat and allow to cool, then roughly chop them and set aside.

2 Heat 1 tbsp of the oil in a large frying pan over a moderate heat. Add the garlic, mushrooms and thyme and cook, stirring frequently, for about 8 minutes, until the mushrooms have softened. Add the spinach, cover the pan, reduce the heat to low and cook, stirring occasionally, for about 3 minutes, until the spinach has thawed and blended with the mushroom mixture. Stir in the red pepper and soft cheese and cook for a further 2 minutes. Season to taste. Remove from the heat.

3 Place 1 sheet of filo on the work surface with a short side towards you and brush very lightly with oil all the way to the edges. Place a second sheet next to it so the sides overlap by about 2cm. Brush again with oil. Add a third sheet in the same way, to now make a large rectangle measuring about 30 x 50cm. Brush with oil. Add another layer, with 3 more overlapped filo sheets lightly brushed with oil.

4 Spread half the filling over the pastry layer almost all the way to the edges. Cover with 3 more sheets of filo, overlapping them as before. Finish with the remaining filling. Fold the side edges over the filling and roll up into a neat strudel shape.

5 Carefully lift the strudel onto a baking sheet, placing it seam side down. Brush lightly all over with the remaining oil and sprinkle with the sesame seeds. Bake for 25 minutes or until golden. Serve hot.

variation

• If using a different size of filo pastry, simply position the sheets to make a rectangle about 30 x 50cm, layering them as here (see cook's tip on filo, page 324).

each serving provides

305kcals • 10g protein
18g fat of which 5g saturates
25g carbohydrate of which 5g sugars
3g fibre • 309mg sodium
174g vegetables

2 portions fruit & veg   **305** kcals   **roll up for flavour**

Butternut squash tart with Parmesan

Club-shaped butternut squash are widely available and make any dish look attractive and taste superb. Their glorious, sweet, orange flesh is rich in beta-carotene, as well as containing vitamins C and E.

SERVES 4 Ⓥ

PREPARATION TIME 55 minutes, plus 5 minutes standing before serving

COOKING TIME 25 minutes

PASTRY
175g plain wholemeal flour
1 tbsp sesame seeds
85g sunflower or soya spread, suitable for baking, chilled and diced

FILLING
1 butternut squash
1 large red pepper, halved and deseeded
1 tbsp olive oil
2 eggs
150ml semi-skimmed milk
3 tbsp Parmesan or Italian-style hard cheese, freshly grated
2–3 pinches crushed dried chillies or freshly ground black pepper

cook's tip
• The tart can be made ahead, then gently warmed before serving.

each serving provides
509kcals • 16g protein
29g fat of which 7g saturates
48g carbohydrate of which
14g sugars • 8g fibre
271mg sodium • 230g vegetables

prepare ahead

509 kcals

2.5 portions fruit & veg

1 Preheat the oven to 230°C/gas 8. To make the pastry, combine the flour, sesame seeds and a pinch of salt in a bowl, then rub in the spread with your fingertips. When the mixture resembles breadcrumbs, stir in 4–5 tbsp iced water, or as much as is needed, with a round-bladed knife, to form the mixture into a soft dough. (If preferred, use a food processor to make the pastry.) Wrap with cling film or greaseproof paper and chill for 15–20 minutes.

2 Meanwhile, cut the squash lengthways into wedges and discard the seeds and stringy fibres. Peel away the skin and cut the flesh into 3cm dice. Cut the pepper into squares, slightly smaller than the squash. Put the vegetables into a roasting tin, drizzle over the olive oil, sprinkle with freshly ground black pepper and toss together.

3 Roast the vegetables for 30 minutes until browned. Remove and leave to cool. Reduce the oven temperature to 180°C/gas 4. Put a baking tray into the oven to heat.

4 Unwrap the pastry and roll out on a floured work surface to a circle about 25cm round. Lift it over a 21cm flan tin and gently press the pastry onto the base and sides. Trim off the excess.

5 In a wide jug or mixing bowl, combine the eggs with the milk and cheese. Season with the chillies or pepper. Spoon the roasted vegetables into the pastry case, mounding them in the centre, then pour over the cheesy egg custard.

6 Set the tin on the heated baking tray and bake for 25 minutes until just set, puffed and golden. Remove from the oven and leave to stand for 5 minutes before serving. Eat warm from the oven or at room temperature.

variations
• Use a pumpkin instead of butternut squash. You'll need about 700g prepared flesh.
• Replace half the butternut squash with diced courgettes and green peppers.

300g quick-cook polenta
40g sweetcorn, (frozen or canned)
2 spring onions, trimmed and
  finely chopped
2 good pinches dried oregano
85g sun-dried tomato pesto
175g reduced-fat mozzarella cheese
400g baby plum tomatoes, halved
40g pine nuts

TO GARNISH few sprigs of
  fresh basil, 7–8 black olives

variation

• Replace the sun-dried tomato pesto
with roasted red pepper pesto, and
top with thin rings of red pepper and
halved plum tomatoes.

each serving provides

595kcals • 19g protein
28.5g fat of which 7g saturates
65g carbohydrate of which
4.5g sugars • 3g fibre
499mg sodium • 120g vegetables

1.5 portions fruit & veg

595 kcals

Tomato & mozzarella polenta

Why not try something different?
Here, ready-made pesto is spread on a savoury polenta base,
then topped with melt-in-the-mouth mozzarella, juicy plum
tomatoes and crunchy pine nuts.

1 Bring 1 litre of water to the boil in a large saucepan. Remove from the heat,
then add the polenta in a slow, steady stream, stirring constantly with a
wooden spoon. Put the pan back onto the heat and cook gently, still stirring,
for 5 minutes, until very thick.

2 Remove from the heat and stir in the sweetcorn, spring onions, oregano and
freshly ground black pepper to taste. Transfer to an oiled Swiss roll tin or
rectangular baking tin measuring about 20 x 30cm, and spread out evenly.
Leave for about 20 minutes until cool and firm.

3 Preheat the oven to 220°C/gas 7. Spread the pesto evenly over the polenta
base. Thinly slice the mozzarella, then cut into strips and scatter over the
polenta base.

4 Arrange the tomato halves on top, cut-side uppermost. Sprinkle with freshly
ground black pepper, then scatter over the pine nuts.

5 Bake for 15–20 minutes until golden and bubbling. Serve hot or at room
temperature garnished with fresh basil leaves and some olives.

Elizabethan carrot tart

Carrot tarts, both sweet and savoury, were popular during Elizabethan times because they were naturally sweet and colourful. Here the smooth and creamy filling is made with low-fat soft cheese, plus cashew nuts for extra protein. The oats in the pastry provide a lovely nutty flavour.

SERVES 4 V
PREPARATION TIME 40 minutes, plus 20 minutes chilling
COOKING TIME about 18 minutes

PASTRY
125g plain flour
50g porridge oats
75g sunflower or soya spread, suitable for baking, chilled and diced

FILLING
450g carrots, peeled and sliced
75g reduced-fat soft cheese
1 egg
grated zest of 1 orange
50g cashew nuts, chopped

cook's tip

• The pastry case can be made up to 1 week in advance. Once cool, double-wrap in cling film, then keep chilled. Allow the pastry to come to room temperature, before baking blind.

1 Mix together the flour, oats and a pinch of salt, then rub in the spread with your fingertips. Add 2–3 tbsp iced water to bind to a soft dough. Wrap with cling film and chill for 20 minutes.

2 Preheat the oven to 180°C/gas 4, with a baking sheet inside. Roll out the pastry on a lightly floured work surface to a round large enough to line a 23cm flan tin. Gently push down into the corners of the tin and trim the edge. Prick the base with a fork, then line the pastry case with baking paper and fill with baking beans.

3 Place the pastry case on the hot baking sheet and bake for 20 minutes, then remove the paper and beans and bake for a further 3 minutes.

4 Meanwhile, put the carrots into a saucepan of water, bring to the boil and simmer for about 8 minutes until very soft. Drain well and transfer to a food processor or blender. Purée the carrots until smooth, then add the cheese and pulse to combine, scraping down the sides occasionally. Add the egg and orange zest and pulse a few times to mix. Season to taste.

5 Pour the mixture into the pastry case and sprinkle the top with the cashew nuts. Bake for about 18 minutes until the nuts look golden. Serve warm.

1 portion fruit & veg

463 kcals

prepare ahead

each serving provides 463kcals • 11g protein • 28g fat of which 7g saturates • 44g carbohydrate of which 9.5g sugars • 5g fibre 246mg sodium • 113g vegetables

Goat's cheese & red pepper quiche

A colourful vegetarian quiche with a filling of juicy roasted peppers and ruby red onions in a tangy goat's cheese filling. The pastry includes oats, adding a lovely nutty flavour and valuable fibre. Enjoy with a mixed salad.

SERVES 4 V
PREPARATION TIME 35 minutes, plus 30 minutes cooling before serving
COOKING TIME 25–30 minutes

PASTRY
150g plain flour
50g porridge oats
½ tsp dried thyme
100g sunflower or soya spread, suitable for baking, chilled and diced

FILLING
280g jar roasted antipasto peppers
1 red onion, halved and thinly sliced
leaves of 1 small sprig fresh rosemary, finely chopped
1 tsp balsamic vinegar
100g soft goat's cheese
2 tbsp snipped fresh chives
2 eggs
50g Quark (skimmed milk soft cheese)
150ml skimmed milk

variation
• If you have some, spread onion 'marmalade' on the pastry base instead of the red onions. And try sliced roasted artichokes in oil instead of the peppers, plus a few snipped sun-dried tomatoes.

1 Mix together the flour, oats, thyme and a pinch of salt, then rub in the spread with your fingertips. Add 2–3 tbsp iced water, as necessary, to bind to a soft dough. Wrap with cling film and chill for 15 minutes.

2 Meanwhile, drain the oil and juices from the jar of peppers into a small saucepan. Add the onion, rosemary and balsamic vinegar and cook gently for about 10 minutes until softened. Remove from the heat.

3 Place a baking sheet inside the oven and preheat to 200°C/gas 6. Roll out the pastry on a lightly floured work surface to a round large enough to line a 21cm flan tin, 3cm deep. Prick the pastry base with a fork, then line the flan case with baking paper and fill with baking beans.

4 Place the pastry case on the hot baking sheet and bake for 15 minutes, then remove the paper and beans and bake for a further 3 minutes. Reduce the oven temperature to 170°C/gas 3.

5 Chop the peppers into smaller pieces and spoon into the flan case along with the cooked onions. Crumble over the goat's cheese in small chunks and scatter over the chives.

6 Beat together the eggs, Quark, milk and seasoning. Pour most of the mixture into the flan case. Return the flan to the oven with the shelf pulled out and pour in the remaining custard, filling it right to the top. Push in the oven shelf gently and bake for 25–30 minutes until the filling is just firm. Remove and allow to cool for 30 minutes before serving.

1 portion fruit & veg   515 kcals   veggie delight

each serving provides 515kcals • 15g protein • 32g fat of which 8g saturates 45g carbohydrate of which 8g sugars • 4g fibre • 596mg sodium • 80g vegetables

SERVES 4 Ⅴ
PREPARATION TIME 25 minutes
COOKING TIME 20 minutes

1 butternut squash, peeled,
  deseeded and cut into 1cm dice
400g carrots, peeled and
  thickly sliced
300g trimmed leeks, halved
  lengthways and sliced
2 garlic cloves, finely chopped
500ml bottled chunky passata
300ml vegetable stock
½ tsp sugar
6 sprigs fresh thyme, tied
  together, or ½ tbsp dried

GRATIN TOPPING
40g butter
85g fresh wholemeal breadcrumbs
2 tbsp snipped fresh chives
50g mature Cheddar cheese, grated

Cheesy vegetable gratin

A comforting, chunky vegetable stew is topped with a cheesy breadcrumb crust to evoke the flavours of traditional farmhouse cooking.

1 Put the butternut squash, carrots, leeks and garlic in a large pan or flameproof casserole. Pour over the passata and stock and add the sugar. Bring to the boil, stirring, then reduce the heat. Add the thyme and cook for 12–15 minutes until the vegetables are almost tender when pierced with the tip of a knife. Season to taste.

2 Meanwhile, preheat the oven to 200°C/gas 6. For the gratin topping, melt the butter in a saucepan and stir in the breadcrumbs and chives. Remove from the heat.

3 If you are not using a flameproof casserole, transfer the vegetables to an ovenproof dish. Spread the breadcrumb mixture over the vegetables and sprinkle over the cheese. Bake for 20 minutes or until the gratin topping is crisp and golden.

each serving provides 327kcals • 11g protein • 14g fat of which 8g saturates
42g carbohydrate of which 25g sugars • 8.5g fibre • 657mg sodium • 494g vegetables

327 kcals · 5+ portions fruit & veg · country fare

SERVES 4 V
PREPARATION TIME 20 minutes
COOKING TIME about 1¼ hours

6 small red onions, quartered
400g sweet potatoes, cut
    into 3cm chunks
2 tbsp olive oil
1 garlic clove, crushed
2 tsp fresh thyme leaves
2 large courgettes, cut
    into 3cm slices
100g baby button mushrooms
350g plum tomatoes,
    quartered lengthways

CRUMBLE TOPPING
75g wholemeal flour
25g butter, cooled and diced
40g fresh wholemeal breadcrumbs
40g Parmesan cheese, freshly grated
25g mixed chopped nuts
25g sunflower seeds
25g pumpkin seeds

each serving provides

480kcals • 16g protein
25g fat of which 8g saturates
52g carbohydrate of which 16g sugars
9g fibre • 236mg sodium
275g vegetables

3 portions fruit & veg

480 kcals

Roasted vegetable crumble

Sweetly flavoured, roasted vegetables topped with a savoury crumble that includes Parmesan, nuts, pumpkin and sunflower seeds for added texture and protein value, make an irresistible vegetarian meal.

1 Preheat the oven to 190°C/gas 5. Put an ovenproof dish, preferably metal and measuring about 30 x 20 x 4cm, in the oven and allow it to heat for 10 minutes. Combine the onions and sweet potatoes in a bowl, drizzle over 1 tbsp of the oil and gently toss to coat. Tip into the heated dish and roast for 30 minutes, turning the vegetables after 15 minutes.

2 Blend the remaining oil with the garlic and 1 tsp of the thyme in the bowl. Add the courgettes, mushrooms and tomatoes, and gently toss to coat. Tip into the dish and roast for a further 20 minutes.

3 Meanwhile, put the flour in a bowl and rub in the butter using your fingertips. Sprinkle over 1 tbsp cold water and mix together with a fork to make large crumbs. Stir in the breadcrumbs, Parmesan cheese, nuts, seeds and remaining thyme.

4 Sprinkle the crumble mixture over the vegetables. Bake for 15–20 minutes until the topping is golden brown and all the vegetables are tender. Remove from the oven and leave to stand for 3–4 minutes before serving.

variation

• Other root vegetables, such as parsnips, carrots and beetroot, cut into 3cm chunks, are also good cooked in this dish.

Spiced vegetable dhal pasties

A vegetarian version of Cornish pasties made with a spiced, wholemeal pastry crust, gets an extra exotic touch from a filling of lightly curried red lentils, potatoes and peas. Serve warm with mango chutney and a crisp, green salad.

MAKES 4 V

PREPARATION TIME 50 minutes, plus 15 minutes standing before serving

COOKING TIME 45–50 minutes

SPICED PASTRY

150g plain wholemeal flour
150g plain white flour
½ tsp ground coriander
½ tsp ground cumin
100g white vegetable fat, chilled and diced
1 tbsp semi-skimmed milk, to glaze

FILLING

125g red split lentils
1 onion, finely chopped
1 garlic clove, crushed
3 cardamom pods, seeds only
1 tsp garam masala
200g potatoes, peeled and cut into small dice
175g shelled or frozen peas
½ tsp ground cinnamon

each serving provides

663kcals • 21g protein
28g fat of which 5.5g saturates
88g carbohydrate of which 6g sugars
9.5g fibre • 265mg sodium
90g vegetables

663 kcals

1 portion fruit & veg

1 First, make the spiced pastry. Combine both the flours, the coriander, cumin and a pinch of salt in a large bowl. Rub in the fat, using your fingertips, until the mixture resembles breadcrumbs. Slowly stir in 4–6 tbsp cold water to form a soft dough. (If preferred, the pastry can be made in a food processor.) Shape the dough into a ball, wrap in cling film and chill for about 20 minutes.

2 Meanwhile, put the lentils in a saucepan with half the onion, the garlic, cardamom seeds and garam masala. Add 800ml boiling water. Bring back to the boil, stirring, then reduce the heat and simmer, uncovered, for 15 minutes or until the lentils are very soft and most of the liquid is absorbed.

3 Preheat the oven to 200°C/ gas 6. Drain the lentils and return them to the pan. Stir in the potatoes, peas, remaining onion and cinnamon. Simmer over a low heat for 2–3 minutes to 'dry' the mixture and thaw the peas, if frozen. Season to taste and set aside.

4 Cut the pastry into quarters. Roll out each piece on a lightly floured surface to a circle that is about 20cm in diameter, using a plate as a guide. Each time add the trimmings to the next piece of pastry before rolling out, in order to use it all.

5 Divide the the filling evenly among the pastry rounds, spreading it down the centre. Brush a little water round the edges, then bring up the edges over the top and pinch together to seal. Crimp to give the traditional pasty shape. Continue until each pasty is shaped.

6 Place the pasties on a baking sheet and lightly brush with milk. Bake for 10 minutes, then reduce the temperature to 180°C/gas 4 and continue baking for a further 35–40 minutes until the pastry is lightly browned. Leave to stand for about 15 minutes before serving warm.

variation

• Lentils have an advantage over other pulses in that they do not require soaking before cooking. Red lentils are used in Indian dahl recipes because they reduce to a mush during cooking, but green Puy lentils, from France, which hold their shape, are also suitable for this recipe.

SERVES 6 Ⓥ
PREPARATION TIME 30 minutes
COOKING TIME 25 minutes

50g pine nuts
2 tbsp olive oil
1 large onion, roughy chopped
2 garlic cloves, crushed
200g frozen spinach
3 ripe tomatoes, finely chopped
   and drained
100g ricotta cheese
100g feta cheese
pinch of grated nutmeg
6 sheets filo pastry,
   about 270g in total

Savoury baklava

A **deliciously light, crunchy,** layered filo pastry bake, with a filling of **spinach, feta cheese, tomatoes and pine nuts** – a classic Greek combination.

1 Preheat the oven to 190°C/gas 5. Place the pine nuts in a dry frying pan and cook over a moderate heat, stirring constantly, until they start to brown and give off their aroma. Set aside.

2 Add 1 tbsp of the oil, the onion and garlic to the pan. Cook gently on a low heat, stirring occasionally, for about 8 minutes, until softened. Add the spinach and chopped tomatoes and continue cooking for about 6 minutes. Tip into a large bowl and allow to cool slightly.

3 Stir the ricotta and feta cheeses into the spinach mixture together with the pine nuts and season to taste with a little salt and pepper and the nutmeg.

4 Lightly oil a shallow baking dish measuring about 20 x 28cm. Line the bottom and sides of the dish with 2 of the filo sheets, one on top of the other. (See cook's tip on filo on page 324.) Leave the excess pastry to hang over the edges of the dish. Cover with half of the spinach mixture, spreading it out to the edges in an even layer. Cover with 2 more sheets of filo, then another layer of the spinach.

5 Fold the excess filo in over the top, then place the remaining 2 filo sheets on top, folding the edges under neatly. Brush the top lightly with the remaining oil and bake for 25 minutes or until crisp and golden.

variation
• For a non-vegetarian baklava, add 150g chopped, smoked streaky bacon with the onions in step 2 and cook for 10 minutes. Continue with the recipe, omitting the feta cheese and adding 30g grated Parmesan cheese instead.

cooks' tip
• The filling can be made up to 2 days ahead and kept chilled. When ready to serve, bring the mixture to room temperature, then complete the recipe.

prepare ahead | 2 portions fruit & veg | 321 kcals

each serving provides
321kcals • 12g protein
17g fat of which 5g saturates
28g carbohydrate of which 7g sugars
3g fibre • 542mg sodium
160g vegetables

Goat's cheese & cranberry strudel

An impressive centrepiece for a **festive vegetarian meal,** this crisp filo pastry ring is filled with mushrooms, chestnuts, **vivid, tart cranberries** and cubes of **tangy goat's cheese.** Serve with cranberry sauce and a mixed leaf salad.

SERVES 4 Ⓥ
PREPARATION TIME 45 minutes
COOKING TIME 25–30 minutes

100g bulghur wheat
2 tbsp olive oil
2 red onions, finely chopped
200g button chestnut mushrooms,
    quartered if large
200g vacuum-packed,
    peeled, cooked chestnuts,
    roughly chopped
150g fresh or frozen cranberries,
    thawed if necessary
1 tbsp fresh thyme leaves
200g firm, medium-fat goat's cheese
6 sheets filo pastry, about
    270g in total

1 Put the bulghur wheat into a pan with 750ml cold water. Bring to the boil, then reduce the heat and simmer gently for about 10 minutes until just tender. Drain thoroughly.

2 Meanwhile, heat 1 tbsp of the oil in a medium frying pan. Add the onions and stir well. Cover the pan with a lid or press a circle of greaseproof paper on top of the onions, and cook very gently for 10–15 minutes until the onions are very soft. Uncover the onions and add the mushrooms. Cook, stirring frequently, for 5 minutes.

3 Tip the bulghur wheat into a bowl, and stir in the onions and mushrooms. Add the chestnuts, cranberries and thyme, plus seasoning to taste and mix well. Cut the cheese into small dice and set aside.

4 Preheat the oven to 190°C/gas 5. Unwrap the filo pastry and arrange 4 of the sheets, slightly overlapping, to make a rectangle about 50 x 30cm, using a little of the oil to lightly brush between the filo sheets. (See cook's tip on filo on page 324.)

5 Spoon the filling along one long end of the pastry, 6cm from the edge. Scatter the cheese over the mound of filling. Fold the border over the filling, then carefully roll up the strudel, like a Swiss roll. Seal the ends together to enclose the filling, then carefully transfer to a large greased baking tray and shape into a horseshoe. Lightly brush with olive oil.

6 Cut the reserved filo sheets into wide strips using kitchen scissors, then scrunch up and drape over the strudel (this will also cover up any cracks). Brush with the remaining oil. Bake for 25–30 minutes until the pastry is golden and crisp. Serve warm.

variation

• When cranberries are not in season, replace with roughly chopped, ready-to-eat dried apricots. You could also replace the chestnuts with 100g toasted whole hazelnuts.

each serving provides

606kcals • 17g protein
23g fat of which 7g saturates
81g carbohydrate of which
15g sugars • 6g fibre
638mg sodium • 163g fruit
and vegetables

606 kcals

festive food

2 portions fruit & veg

Vegetable pies with cheese & herb pastry

There is always something appealing about individual pies. These are filled with vegetables in a parsley sauce and topped with a light shortcrust pastry flavoured with tasty Cheddar and fresh chives.

SERVES 4 V ✻
PREPARATION TIME 40 minutes
COOKING TIME 20–25 minutes

PASTRY
175g plain flour
85g sunflower or soya spread suitable for baking, chilled and diced
25g mature Cheddar cheese, finely grated
2 tbsp snipped fresh chives

FILLING
600ml vegetable stock
200g broccoli florets
1 leek, sliced
200g shelled broad beans (fresh or frozen)
125g shelled peas (fresh or frozen)
8 cherry tomatoes, halved
2 tsp cornflour
2 tbsp chopped fresh parsley

variations
• Use any selection of fresh, seasonal vegetables. Tomatoes add a splash of colour, but you could use sweetcorn or diced red pepper instead.
• For meat-eaters, add 4–6 diced rashers of lean bacon to the filling.

1 Preheat the oven to 200°C/gas 6. To make the pastry, place the flour in a bowl and rub in the spread with your fingertips until the mixture resembles fine breadcrumbs. Stir in the cheese and chives, then add 2–3 tbsp cold water to bind the mixture to a soft, not sticky, dough. Wrap in cling film and chill, while you make the filling.

2 Heat the stock in a large pan until boiling, then add the broccoli, leek, beans and peas. Bring back to the boil, cover and simmer for 5 minutes. Drain the vegetables, reserving 300ml of the stock.

3 Place the vegetables with the tomatoes in 4 x 350ml individual ovenproof pie dishes. Mix the cornflour with 1 tbsp cold water and stir in the reserved stock. Pour into the pan and stir over a moderate heat until thickened and smooth. Add the parsley and season to taste. Pour over the vegetables.

4 Roll out the pastry and use to cover the pie dishes, sealing with a little water on the rims. Cut a small steam vent in each pastry lid with the point of a knife. Place on a baking sheet and bake in the oven for 20–25 minutes until the pastry is firm and golden brown. Serve hot.

each serving provides 432kcals • 14g protein 22g fat of which 5g saturates • 47g carbohydrate of which 4g sugars • 8g fibre • 199mg sodium • 190g vegetables

432 kcals

2 portions fruit & veg

Index

Conversion chart

All food in the UK is now sold in metric units so it makes sense to cook using these measurements. However, if you feel happier or more confident using imperial measurements, you can use the conversion chart below. Remember though, use either metric or imperial and don't mix the two.

Weight		Volume	
Metric	**Imperial (approx)**	**Metric**	**Imperial (approx)**
5g	⅛oz	30ml	1fl oz
10g	¼oz	50ml	2fl oz
15g	½oz	75ml	2½ fl oz
20g	¾oz	85ml	3fl oz
25g	1oz	90ml	3¼ fl oz
35g	1¼oz	100ml	3½ fl oz
40g	1½oz	1 litre	1¾ pints
50g	1¾oz		
55g	2oz		
60g	2¼oz		
70g	2½oz		
75g	2¾oz		
85g	3oz		
90g	3¼oz		
100g	3½oz		
1kg	2lb 4oz		

PHOTOGRAPHERS CREDITS Abbreviations are used as follows:
MB Martin Brigdale, **TF** Tara Fisher, **HJ** Hugh Johnson, **WL** William Lingwood, **DM** David Munns, **EN** Emma Neish, **WR** William Reavell, **KT** Karen Thomas, **t** top, **b** bottom, **l** left, **r** right.

8-9 WL, 10 HJ, 11 tl DM, br WL, 12 WL, 13 bl WR, tr HJ, 14-15 WL, 16 br WR, 17 WR, 18 WR, 19 WR, 20 l WL, r WR, 21 l WL, r WL, 22 WL, 23 WL, 24 WR, 25 WR, 26 WR, 27 WR, 28-29 WR, 30-31 HJ, 32 DM, 34 WR, 35 KT, 36 TF, 39 HJ, 40 DM, 41 WR, 42 WL, 43 WL, 44 EN, 45 KT, 46-47 WL, 48 MB, 49 WR, 50-51 EN, 52-53 HJ, 54 KT, 55 WR, 56-57 WR, 58-59 KT, 60 HJ, 63 TF, 65 WR, 66-67 DM, 69 HJ, 70 MB, 71 KT, 72 EN, 73 KT, 75 TF, 77 WR, 79 WL, 80 HJ, 82-83 WL, 84 DM, 87 WL, 88-89 WR, 90 WL, 91 WL, 92 KT, 95 WL, 96-97 HJ, 99 HJ, 100-101 EN, 102-103 WL, 104 KT, 106 MB, 107 DM, 108 TF, 110 HJ, 111 KT, 112-113 HJ, 114-115 HJ, 116 WR, 119 WR, 121 HJ, 122 EN, 123 KT, 124-125 HJ, 126 TF, 127 MB, 128 HJ, 129 DM, 130 WR, 132-133 WL, 134 HJ, 136-137 WL, 138 KT, 140 MB, 142-143 DM, 144 WL, 147 HJ, 148 KT, 151 WR, 153 WR, 154 KT, 155 DM, 156-157 HJ, 158 WL, 161 KT, 162-163 WL, 164-165 WR, 166 WL, 168 WR, 170-171 HJ, 172 MB, 173 WL, 174 HJ, 175 DM, 177 WL, 178-179 WR, 181 WL, 183 HJ, 184-185 HJ, 187 HJ, 188-189 HJ, 190-191 HJ, 192 DM, 193 DM, 194 KT, 195 HJ, 196 KT, 198-199 DM, 200 KT, 201 WL, 202-203 HJ, 204-205 WL, 207 WL, 208-209 DM, 211 WL, 212-213 MB, 215 MB, 217 WR, 218-219 DM, 220 KT, 222 WR, 223 DM, 224 WL, 226 MB, 227 DM, 228 DM, 231 MB, 232 HJ, 233 MB, 234 KT, 236-237 WL, 239 WL, 240-241 HJ, 242 KT, 243 HJ, 245 HJ, 246-247 HJ, 248 DM, 249 WL, 250 DM, 252-253 DM, 254 KT, 255 DM, 256-257 DM, 258 HJ, 259 WL, 260-261 KT, 262 MB, 263 DM, 264-265 HJ, 266-267 KT, 268-269 DM, 270 KT, 271 HJ, 273 KT, 274 DM, 275 KT, 276 WL, 278 KT, 281 WL, 282 KT, 283 WL, 284-285 WL, 286 WL, 287 WL, 289 MB, 290-291 WL, 292 HJ, 293 KT, 294 DM, 297 DM, 298-299 WL, 300 KT, 301 WL, 303 HJ, 304-305 WL, 307 DM, 309 WL, 310-311 HJ, 312 HJ, 314 HJ, 315 HJ, 316-317 WL, 318 HJ, 319 MB, 320-321 EN, 322 WL, 323 WL, 324-325 WL, 327 WL, 328-329 WL, 330 HJ, 331 WL, 332-333 WL, 335 WL, 336 WL, 338 HJ, 339 WL, 341 WL, 342-343 HJ

Acknowledgments

Healthy One-Dish Cooking was published by
The Reader's Digest Association Limited, London

First edition copyright © 2006
The Reader's Digest Association Limited
11 Westferry Circus, Canary Wharf
London E14 4HE
www.readersdigest.co.uk

Paperback edition copyright © 2008

We are committed both to the quality of
our products and the service we provide to our
customers. We value your comments so please
do contact us on 08705 113366 or via our
website at **www.readersdigest.co.uk**

If you have any comments or suggestions about
the content of our books you can contact us at
gbeditorial@readersdigest.co.uk

For cover recipe, see the variation to
Spring vegetable risotto on p.116.

Concept Code: UK1874/G
Book Code: 400-388 UP0000-1
ISBN: 978 0 276 44406 7
Oracle code: 250010146S.00.24

Created by Amazon Publishing Limited
7 Old Lodge Place, Twickenham TW1 1RQ

Editor Maggie Pannell
Editorial assistant Ella Fern
Copy editor Jill Steed
Recipe writers Catherine Atkinson, Anna Brandenburger,
Linda Collister, Roz Denny, Christine France, Bridget
Jones, Beverly LeBlanc, Maggie Pannell, Anne Sheasby
Recipe testers Catherine Atkinson, Anna Brandenburger,
Linda Collister, Christine France, Emma-Lee Gow,
Bridget Jones, Emma Patmore, Anne Sheasby,
Gina Steer, Susanna Tee
Nutritionists Jane Griffin, Fiona Hunter
Designers Maggie Aldred, Vivienne Brar, Colin Goody
Indexer Hilary Bird

Photography
All images RD copyright © 2006
Art director Luis Peral
Photographers Martin Brigdale, Tara Fisher,
Hugh Johnson, William Lingwood, David Munns,
Emma Neish, William Reavell, Karen Thomas
Cover photograph Gareth Morgans
Food stylists Valerie Berry, Silvana Franco, Jane Lawrie,
Jaqui Malouf, Lucy McKelvie, Tracey Meharg,
Annie Nichols, Jane Oddie, Bridget Sargeson,
Penny Stephens, Sunil Vijayakar, Jenny White
Props stylists Helen Trent, Rachel Jukes,
Penny Markham, Roisin Nield

For Reader's Digest General Books, UK
Editor Lisa Thomas
Editorial director Julian Browne
Art director Anne-Marie Bulat
Head of book development Sarah Bloxham
Managing editor Nina Hathway
Picture resource manager Sarah Stewart-Richardson
Pre-press account manager Dean Russell
Product production manager Claudette Bramble
Production controller Katherine Bunn

Origination Colour Systems Ltd
Printed and bound in China